Ms. Gail Branum
431 Hoffman Rd.
Washougal, WA 98671

To my darling daughter Gail,
hoping that on reading this you
will have a better understanding
of your fathers' early life

All my love
Dad.

Joining The Grey Funnel Line

*The story of a Canadian boy who entered the
Royal Navy in World War II at the age of fifteen*

Frank Saies-Jones

Order this book online at www.trafford.com
or email orders@trafford.com

Most Trafford titles are also available at major online book retailers.

Note for Librarians: A cataloguing record for this book is available from Library
and Archives Canada at www.collectionscanada.ca/amicus/index-e.html

Printed in Victoria, BC, Canada.

ISBN: 978-1-4269-0255-0 (sc)

*Our mission is to efficiently provide the world's finest, most comprehensive book publishing
service, enabling every author to experience success. To find out how to publish your book, your
way, and have it available worldwide, visit us online at www.trafford.com*

Trafford rev. 01/05/2010

 www.trafford.com

North America & international
toll-free: 1 888 232 4444 (USA & Canada)
phone: 250 383 6864 ♦ fax: 812 355 4082

DEDICATION

To my boyhood friends
who went to war; some of whom
did not return:

Peter Brassington, Royal Navy.

Jim Farquharson, Royal Air Force

Phillip Harris, Royal Navy

Phillip Hollingshead, Royal Air Force

Michael Hollingshead, Royal Air Force.

Keith Martin, Royal Air Force.

John Melville, Merchant Marine.

Edgar Munn, Royal Canadian Signal Corps

Keebel Munn, Canadian Guards Regt.

Robert Munn, United States Navy.

Roy Watson, Royal Artillary.

And

My wife and best friend Barbara,
without whose help, encouragement,
patience, and understanding, this
story would never have been written.

CONTENTS

FOREWORD

Eighty-three years have passed since the events described at the beginning of this story occurred. Many who will read this book may wonder how, over such a long period in time, the author can still recall in detail the events related. Some readers may doubt my ability to remember the names of ships, individuals, and minute details of daily events recounted. While many of the events are still fresh in my memory, I must confess that I relied heavily on the diary I kept (contrary to the rules and regulations prevailing at that time) throughout the war years.

In addition to referring to my diary, I have made use of information gleaned from a myriad of sources; not only on individuals I encountered during my term in the service, but those events mentioned throughout this narrative in which I personally played no part (as in the case of how my shipmate, Leading Seaman 'Mick' Magennis, earned his Victoria Cross). I wish, however, to emphasize that this is a true story, not only of my formative years, but also of events leading to my joining the Royal Navy, and the eight or more years that followed. Whenever possible, I have used the real names of people. Only when my memory failed did I substitute a fictitious name, which I trust will not detract from the authenticity of this narrative.

It now remains for me to explain why, after all the years, I decided to put pen to paper. For many years I was encouraged by both friends and family to describe my early days on the island of Jamaica, and what some people consider the somewhat unorthodox manner in which I entered the Royal Navy. It has been suggested that my story might make interesting reading. This may be so, but I leave you, the reader, to be the judge of that. The truth of the matter probably lies in the old adage: *"there is a book in all of us waiting to be written"*. If that is the case, I have now done so. Many people have stated envy of my having been born and raised in what they consider a 'tropical paradise'. There are also some who think my family was fortunate to have escaped the economic hardships encountered by so many others throughout the world during the depression years. Both these ideas are misconceptions. While it is true that my father had a job and that as a family we were able to make ends meet, the great depression affected everyone, and our family was no exception.

Jamaica is truly a beautiful island, but living there today, as an independent member of the British Commonwealth, is nothing like it was in the past. During my childhood, the majority of its inhabitants made up of many races, lived in peace and harmony alongside a minority of Caucasians who were responsible for good government and the maintenance of British law and order. As a teenager in Jamaica, I considered my horizons to be limited in what I thought was a backward and insignificant part of our planet, far removed from the more advanced countries of Europe and North America. Following my visit to Port Arthur, Texas, with my father in 1936, I developed resentment toward my parents for having brought me into what, I then considered, a backwater of civilization. As this resentment grew, my frustration with everything and everyone on the island intensified, to the point that I wished for nothing better than to leave home.

The Great War in which my father and grandfather played a part, had been over for seven years when I was born, but was still fresh in the memory of many people. I was brought up believing in the greatness of the British Empire, and in a society that looked upon the English-speaking people as the 'salt of the earth'. To my way of thinking, my father was Canadian and my mother English, so why then were we not living in Canada or England.

In 1914, an earlier generation had fought "the war to end all wars". When in 1939, the people of my generation were faced with having to do it all over again there was little hesitation on their part to become involved. The outbreak of hostilities was regarded by many as an opportunity to end a monotonous existence and avoid a doubtful future brought about by world-wide depression. In my case, however, I had expressed a desire to go to sea at an early age, and now viewed the outbreak of war with mixed feelings. On one hand it upset plans that had been made for me to enter HMS *Conway* as a naval cadet, but on the other I experienced a sense of excitement at the possibility of joining the navy as a boy seaman and by-passing *Conway* entirely. Not being prepared to accept that fact, I explored all avenues available that would lead to my fulfilling my ambition.

Reluctant at first to allow me to leave home, my parents finally relented on my returning to Jamaica from Vancouver where they had hoped I would continue my education before joining the navy. However, I think they realized how important it was that I be given the chance to fulfill my life long dream as I had shown no interest in continuing my education on the island, and any further delay in joining *Conway* would only be detrimental to my future career. It is also possible that my mother considered that, by joining as a cadet, the war would be over before I was old enough to be sent to sea.

The events that followed after my leaving home are the subject of this book. The story ends on my release from the navy in 1949, when I was only twenty-four years of age. I had been forced to face the fact that in my haste to leave home and enlist, I had ruined my chance to make a successful career at sea due to having left school at the age of fifteen.

At the outbreak of hostilities in Korea, there was a distinct possibility that I could be recalled to the navy as a member of the Royal Fleet Reserve. In anticipation of this, I volunteered for service in the Canadian Army, and although I did not serve in Korea, this move led to my being involved in the military in one capacity or another for the next thirty-six years. In recounting my early years, I hope that I am able to convey to young people who might read this book, an insight into what it was like to be a teenager in the thirties and forties compared to that of today's generation.

CHAPTER I
Family Roots

I first saw the light of day on either August 21 or 22, 1925, depending on whether you are willing to accept August 22, as shown on my birth certificate, or August 21, which I have always considered to be correct. This confusion stems from the fact that my birth was not officially recorded by my father until September 26, at which time he mistakenly used the date of August 22 when, according to my mother, it was actually August 21. I have always been inclined to take the word of my mother, due to the fact that she was actually there for the momentous occasion, and not my father who, I was led to believe, was not even at home! In any event, for the past 83 years I have regarded August 21 as my date of birth.

My father had to take the blame for getting things muddled on more than one occasion. An example of this occurred on the day of my christening. The ceremony took place in the home of my grandfather and both of my parents had agreed that my Christian name was to be Frank. This was my mother's choice in memory of her younger brother who had lost his life in the Great War. My father's choice, however, was Harold in honour of his father. Having lost the argument, it came as a shock to my mother, when my father, in response to the question by the minister as to what my Christian names should be, in a loud voice replied "Harold Frank". Hence, for the next fifteen years I was known in the family as Harold. I too preferred the name Frank in association with a photograph of a handsome young lieutenant in his uniform of the Royal Flying Corps which adorned a wall in the drawing room of my grandparents' home. On leaving home to joint the navy at the age of fifteen years I used the name of Frank and have done so ever since; however, there are still members of the family who persist in calling me Harold. To the best of my knowledge, my paternal grandfather was never told this story, but I am sure he would have been quite happy knowing that one of my names was given in his honour.

Both of my parents were children of families whose roots lay in the United Kingdom. Originally from London, my paternal grandfather, Harold, had been raised in Tanbey, Wales by his grandfather, Ebenezer Saies, as a result of the early death of his own father and re-marriage of his mother. As a young lawyer in later years, he moved to London and began his practice under the name of Saies-Jones. It was there that he met his future bride, Violet Wilson, the youngest daughter of a regular army officer, Major General Charles Watson Wilson, CBE, of the Royal Artillery. Violet Wilson was born in India, together with seven brothers and three sisters. The Wilson family was commonly referred to in those days as a "service family", meaning that most members of the family by tradition had served in the British Army or the Royal Navy for generations past. In the case of the Wilson family, service in the military dated back to 1777 when my great-great-great-grandfather, Vice-Admiral Sir William Charles Fahie, KCB, RN, had joined the Royal Navy at the age of fourteen years. Shortly after they were married, my paternal grandparents and their three children immigrated to Canada and settled in Toronto, Ontario.

My maternal grandparents were descended from both Scottish and English families. Grandfather, William Baillie, was the son of Andrew Baillie, a Scot and joiner by trade who had early in life settled in Barrow-in-Furness, England. My grandfather had entered the ministry as a member of the Wesleyan Church and as a young man went to the West Indies as a missionary in 1887. After settling in Jamaica he was found to be suffering from diabetes and was forced into early retirement. Having met and married my grandmother, Jenny Watson, the daughter of the Mayor of Kingston, Jamaica, they purchased a home in the country where he established a small printing and stationery store which sold books and school supplies to the various protestant denominations on the island. They raised two boys and two girls and, in keeping with the local custom, the children were sent to England to be educated. Due to the outbreak of the Great War, my mother and her sister, my Aunt Cynthia, had to wait for hostilities to end before they were able to continue their education overseas. The eldest son, Fred, graduated as a surgeon from Edinburgh University in Scotland and returned to Jamaica to practice medicine. His younger brother, Frank, joined the Royal Flying Corps in 1918 and lost his life in a flying accident shortly after enlisting. In 1919, my mother, Edith, enrolled as a student nurse at Kings County Hospital in Brooklyn, New York, while her younger sister, Cynthia, studied music in England and returned to Jamaica to teach music at St. Andrew's Girls School in Kingston.

I firmly believe that the two most important factors in life during one's formative years are hereditary and environment. The dictionary describes hereditary as "the passing on of physical or mental characteristics genetically from one generation to another"; while environment relates to "the physical surroundings, conditions, and circumstances in which a person lives, works, etc." Generally the combination of a sound and healthy environment, together with the inherited characteristics of honesty, integrity, intelligence, and morals, leads to a successful, happy, and productive life. It is possible for a person who has inherited all the good qualities of human behaviour to overcome the drawbacks of a poor environment. It is also true that a good environment does not necessarily lead to a successful and productive life if one has not inherited the previously-mentioned good qualities of human behaviour. The ideal situation; therefore, is to be blessed with both, and I would like to think that this was the case in my early upbringing.

My parents were by no means wealthy. As noted earlier, my mother had trained as a nurse in New York and upon graduation was employed by Kings County Hospital in that city. My father was a radio operator in the Merchant Marine and employed by the United Fruit Company, an American shipping company whose ships were involved in the banana trade between the West Indies and United States. These ships also carried a number of passengers on each voyage and it was on one of those vessels that my mother booked a passage to Jamaica to spend Christmas with her parents in 1921. Whether by accident or design, on her return to New York, she travelled in the same ship that had carried her to Jamaica and she was able to renew a friendship with the ship's radio officer. In any event, my parents continued to meet whenever the ship was in New York and on December 19, 1922, they married in the Harvard Street Congregational Church in Brookline, Massachusetts, my father being twenty-two years of age at the time.

As the wife of a sailor, my mother no doubt hoped that my father would leave the sea and settle down to raise a family. With this thought in mind she persuaded a family friend to offer him a job of over-seeing a banana plantation located close to Montego Bay on the north coast of Jamaica. Needless to say, dad did not know the first thing about cultivating bananas, much less the operation of a tropical plantation of over two hundred acres. As far as he was concerned, however, that was a minor detail and he gladly accepted the position. In very short order he and my mother moved to their new home, a large stone mansion bearing the name of *Virgin Valley*.

In the spring of 1925 my mother, who was approximately five months pregnant, went to stay with her parents who were living in the rectory of a church located a few miles from the small town of Mandeville, Jamaica. The rectory was situated on a hill behind the church and provided a panoramic view of the surrounding country. Both the hill and church were known locally as *Wesley Mount*.

During the summer months, considered in the West Indies to be the hurricane season, the air is hot and humid and many Europeans and North Americans sought refuge in the mountains where the climate was more suitable for their well-being. Furthermore, there were those who considered the climate of the coastal plains to be downright unhealthy at that time of the year. It was therefore understandable that as her confinement drew close my mother chose to give birth in the comfortable and pleasant surrounding of her parents' home in the hills. It therefore came about that I was born in the guest bedroom of the rectory on *Wesley Mount*, in the County of Manchester, District of Mandeville, Jamaica, British West Indies.

For the next six years our family lived in *Virgin Valley*, and three years after my arrival my mother gave birth to my brother, Dennis. Only three years of age at the time of his birth, I recall going to visit my mother in the Mandeville Hospital, that being perhaps my earliest recollection. Although my memory of our six years spent in *Virgin Valley* is somewhat vague, apart from this event there were four other events during the years that followed which remain as vague memories today. I shall briefly describe these as: the snake, the raft, the pony incident, and my meeting with the Royal Navy in Montego Bay.

The story of the snake began one morning when the supervisor of our field hands arrived at our house in an agitated state to inform my father that some of his men had encountered and killed a large snake. In those days snakes were not commonly found in Jamaica and, although it was known they existed, few people had ever seen one. The non-venomous yellow snake had been introduced to the island by the early sugar planters as a means of ridding the cane fields of the numerous rats that were blamed for damaging the crops. It was thought that by importing this harmless reptile from India, the rat population could be brought under control, and over many decades this experiment had proven successful. This had resulted in a sharp reduction in the rat population but led to an abundance of snakes on the island. The snakes were harmless and flourished and multiplied in their new environment where the climate was similar to their native habitat. Humans; however, thought otherwise and decided to get rid of them by introducing the mongoose, also a native of India, and noted for their ability to kill snakes, venomous or otherwise.

After the introduction of the mongoose, the snake population declined until they were almost extinct. It was, therefore, understandable that, when our field hands found an eight-foot Yellow Snake, they reacted violently, killing it instantly by decapitation. The body of the reptile now lay on our front lawn where a small crowd of natives gathered in awe. Word of what had happened spread to the local hamlet of Summerton, and as the day wore on more and more people arrived to view the carcass. Much to the relief of my father, a

Chinese shopkeeper from Summerton made him an offer of twenty shillings for the reptile, which he gladly accepted. No questions were asked as to what he planned to do with it, but I was told later that it had provided a meal for his family, and my father evenly divided the twenty shillings among our men who had slain the reptile.

The second event that stands out in my memory is my early experiment in naval architecture. After my mother read to me the book, *Swiss Family Robinson*, I decided that in order to travel the high seas I would require a raft and set about designing and constructing one that was capable of accommodating me and my dog, Ginger, on a trip around the world. The spot chosen for the construction was the very spot on the lawn where the body of the snake had previously been put on display. With the assistance of our gardener I was able to obtain a quantity of bamboo poles which he cut into eight-foot lengths. These were then laid out on the lawn to form a square. A second deck was added at right angles to the first, and where the poles met, they were securely lashed in place with twine. A mast was erected complete with a yard arm from which a square sail (one of my mother's sheets) was suspended. An old packing crate provided a cabin and, together with Ginger, I was ready to leave home. Many hours of work went into the construction of this raft, and the fact that there was no water for miles around was of no concern to me. Wearing a pair of my father's old Wellington boots, Ginger and I sailed the seven seas with a well-stocked larder of chocolate chip cookies and lemonade. Many an adventurous hour was spent fighting off sharks and pirates but unfortunately our ship came to an end the day my father accidentally ran over it with his truck.

The pony incident happened when I was approximately six years of age and apparently had decided to take up chariot racing. Our family owned a pony and trap and on occasion my father would harness up the pony and take my brother and I for a ride around the estate. On one such occasion we were about to leave home when dad remembered he had left his pipe and tobacco in the house. Leaving us sitting in the trap he went indoors to find the missing items. I picked up the reins and with a flick of the whip we were on our way.

The pony started off at a gentle trot while my brother began to cry. As we went down the hill and gathered speed my brother's crying became louder. Hanging onto the reins, while shouting at Dennis, the pony became excited and broke into a gallop. Emerging from the house, my father caught a glimpse of us just before we disappeared round a bend in the road, leaving behind a cloud of dust. As we came to the closed gate at the end of our driveway, the pony decided to put on the brakes. Coming to a sudden stop, we were both thrown off the trap and landed in the ditch. By the time dad arrived we had picked ourselves up, somewhat battered and bruised, but with no bones broken. Dennis suffered a bleeding nose and continued to cry at the top of his lungs, which annoyed me intensely as dad thought he was badly hurt and completely ignored me. While dad carried him in his arms all the way back to the house, I was left to recover the pony grazing by the side of the road. Needless to say I went to bed that night with a very warm rear end and to this day I have maintained a healthy respect for all forms of horseflesh.

The final event I recall, and which probably made a lasting impression on me, was my first encounter with sailors of the Royal Navy. On Saturdays my mother would drive to Montego Bay to do her shopping, following which we would go for a swim and a picnic lunch on the beach. On one such outing a large warship was anchored in the bay and from which a number of boats filled with men were heading inshore. On reaching the beach it became evident that these were sailors of the Royal Navy coming ashore to have a picnic of their own, and in short order a football game was underway. Those not involved in the game enjoyed a swim, while others went for a walk to town. I do not know the name of their ship but suspect she was the Battle Cruiser *Hood,* who was on a cruise of the West Indies and on her way to Barbados at that time from the islands of Trinidad and St. Vincent. Her brief call at Jamaica was to give the ship's company some well-earned recreation. As I watched these sailors having fun, I thought to myself that if this was what life in the navy was like, I certainly wanted to be a part of it. I can not honestly say that this event led to my joining the navy, but I do know that the memory of that day stayed with me for a very long time. Later, when I was actually in the service, that memory served to remind me that a sailor's life could be fun, even when all was not going well.

The years our family spent at *Virgin Valley* were happy ones, but would soon come to an end. When my brother was approximately three years of age, he became seriously ill with a high fever. For many weeks doctors thought he was suffering from malaria and subjected him to massive doses of quinine, without results. My mother, on the other hand, was of the opinion that he was suffering from typhoid. Against the advice of our family physician, mother decided to move him to my grandparents' home in the hills where the air was cooler and cleaner. Warned that he would probably die on the journey, mother decided to make the trip anyway saying, "I'll take my chance on that happening as I know that if he stays here he will certainly die". Travelling by train, they arrived safely in Mandeville and within a matter of days Dennis' condition improved. It later transpired that the Montego Bay area was subject to a major typhoid epidemic which had spread from the near-by town of Savanna-la-Mar.

CHAPTER II
Preschool

In 1932, the effects of the great depression (which had begun in 1929) had spread to many countries, including Jamaica. High unemployment, coupled with inflation and the spread of the Panama Disease in the banana plantations, was taking its toll and many landowners faced financial ruin. When it became apparent that the *Virgin Valley* property might be forced to close, dad successfully sought employment as a Radio Officer with Canadian National Steamships. Mother, who was a registered nurse, accepted a position as private nurse to an elderly gentleman living in Kingston and moved to the city. Arrangements were made for Dennis and me to live with our grandparents in Manchester. Our new home was a lovely old plantation house named *Tan-y-Bryn*, which I have been told is from the Welsh meaning nestled among the hills. The house was located at the head of a long valley which extended to the southern coast of the island and on a clear day it was possible to see the ocean. At night the flashing beam of a distant lighthouse could be seen as well as lights of passing ships. Looking south from the front of the house one could see Wesley Mount Church and the rectory where I was born, and to the west a low mountain, devoid of any form of habitation, sloped gently down to the sea. To the east the land was lower and the main highway leading to Mandeville passed through the village of Walderston about a mile or two from our home. This somewhat isolated place was to be out home for the next two years and, while we did not see our parents that often, Dennis and I held fond memories of that time. The house was still standing when I visited the island fifty years later and found that little had changed.

Tan-y-Bryn was a wooden building consisting of two floors with a veranda on both floors running around the south, east, and north sides. The lower floor consisted of a kitchen, pantry, dining room, and drawing room. A wide mahogany staircase located in the centre of the house led to the upper floor which had originally been built with three very large bedrooms. My grandparents later divided one of these rooms and added three smaller rooms by enclosing the veranda on the north side, making it a seven-bedroom home. The floors throughout the house were highly polished native ligum viate wood. Furniture in the dining room was mahogany and in the drawing room stood a stone fireplace complete with mantle (the only house on the island seemingly to have one) which I recall was never used. We did not have the luxury of electricity or running water and depended on Coleman lanterns for light and each bedroom was furnished with a wash stand, water pitcher, and wash basin. The outside toilets were located at the back of the house and for night use a chamber pot was located under each bed. A single bathroom was in a room attached to the house with water being drawn by pump from a large catchment tank adjacent to the property. Each night the ritual of filling the lanterns with naphtha gas, cleaning the lenses, and replacing the burnt out mantles, was carried out by my grandfather as he would not trust the servants to do the job properly.

Like the Europeans and North Americans who lived on the island, my grandparents employed native servants. At *Tan-y-Bryn* we had a cook named Mary and a maid named Gwendolyn (Gwen). These two ladies were of extremely different personalities, but despite this worked well together and served my grandparents faithfully for many years.

Mary, whose domain was the kitchen, was a tall, slim, elderly woman. She would not tolerate any interference in the performance of her duties and as children, my brother and I were probably a little afraid of her. Despite her stern appearance, I am sure she was quite fond of us as she would invite us to sample her freshly baked pies and cookies. Gwen, who was about the same age as Mary, had a friendly, outgoing personality. She was short in stature and somewhat on the stout side but her cheerful disposition was contagious and there was a perpetual smile on her face. Gwen's duties were many. She was chambermaid, kitchen maid, children's nurse, and did the weekly washing on a Monday. Together both women made a great team and my grandmother was fortunate to have such loyal and devoted servants. Our only male servant was a young man named Selvyn. He had come to work for the family as a fifteen year-old orphan and, despite the fact that he had received little schooling, was quick to learn and my grandfather had taught him to drive the car. Selvyn's duties were varied. He looked after the garden, fed and watered the livestock, served as a general handyman, and became the family chauffeur whenever the car was required. All three servants had their own quarters, were fed the same food as us, and given a substantial weekly salary. In a sense they were part of our family and served us faithfully.

Like many native Jamaicans, Gwen and Mary were deeply religious and would walk four or five miles to church each Sunday. The Anglican Church was the original established church on the island but in latter years other denominations such as the Methodists, Baptists, Wesleyans and Moravians, played an important factor in the development of the island. As I recall Catholicism was not widespread but 1 must admit that I was in no position to judge. My grandfather was a Wesleyan, and our family would often attend services in other protestant churches as he was frequently invited by other ministers to give the sermon. We never attended a Catholic church, nor do I recall knowing any friends of the family who were of that faith. I have heard it said that the island of Jamaica probably has more churches per capita than any other country, and I am inclined to believe it.

Every morning after breakfast my grandfather would read a passage from the bible followed by a daily prayer and all three of the servants would join with the family in the dining room for this devout ceremony. The property on which *Tan-y-Bryn* was located was quite large. To the north of the house was a steep hill, the lower half of which had been cleared of trees and on which the six or so cattle we owned grazed. The top of the hill was heavily wooded and a stone dyke surrounded the entire area. Immediately behind the house was a concrete tennis court on which my brother and I learned to ride a bicycle. Approximately one hundred yards to the east of the house stood a small bungalow, which was used by my grandfather as his office, book store, and printing shop. Looking back on those early days I can honestly say it was the book shop that left the greatest impression on me. A large section of the shop contained books for sale, but there was also a library containing my grandfather's private collection which he encouraged me to use whenever I wished. It was here that I developed my love of books which I retain to this day.

Before learning to read, I recall my grandfather reading to my brother and me each evening before bedtime books such as *Treasure Island*, *Robinson Crusoe*, *Alice in Wonderland*, *Black Beauty*, *Swiss Family Robinson*, *Peter Pan*, and *Gulliver's Travels*. As we grew older we were introduced to *Pilgrims Progress*, *Masterman Ready*, *Lawrence of Arabia*, *Voyage of Discovery*, and many others. Without modern forms of home entertainment, we provided our own. Some evenings we would gather around the piano to sing, while at other times we played cards or had a game of snakes and ladders. While we did not have electricity we did possess a radio, which drew its power from a wet battery. My father had erected a thirty-foot mast to which the radio antenna was connected resulting in us being able to listen to the BBC news broadcast from London each evening. How well I remember the chimes of Big Ben as we tuned in and sat quietly listening to the announcer's voice over the ever-present static, followed by the playing of God Save the King at the conclusion of the program.

The time was fast approaching when my parents and grandparents had to make a decision with respect to my education. Traditionally, most European or North American families sent their children off to Britain, Canada, or the United States of America for their education, but in the early thirties, few families could afford to do so, and our family was no different. By Canadian standards we were relatively well off financially. My parents had jobs, there was plenty to eat, we could afford to own and operate an automobile, and we maintained a home that did not require heating in the winter. Despite these benefits, the great depression had touched everyone and even our family had trouble making ends meet.

One of the drawbacks of the British colonial administration in those days was failure of the government to provide children with an adequate educational system. While there were many elementary schools on the island, the standard of education offered was not considered good enough for the children of European or North American parents. I should explain that this point of view was not the result of racial or social prejudice for, on reaching the age of entry to one of the many good public schools available, where white and black races were mixed, white families had no reservations when it came to enrolling their children. Elementary schooling at home was therefore the answer and a young lady with a teaching degree, Miss Sheldon, was employed by my grandparents to provide Dennis and I with the necessary knowledge to pass the entrance exam required before being accepted into a public school. In order to pay her salary, other families faced with the same problem were approached, and when our little school started there were eight children in attendance. In addition to my brother and me, our two female cousins, Joy and Fay, came to live with us. At a later date two brothers, Philip and Michael Hollingshead, sons of a friend of the family, also joined the group. Two other un-related girls, Eva and Mamie, whose parents lived nearby, were driven to school each day and returned home in the evening. We started our lessons right after breakfast at eight. At noon we had a one-hour lunch break, and in the afternoon we worked until three. There were no classes on Saturday or Sunday. Because of the difference in our ages and our various levels of achievement, it was necessary for Miss. Sheldon to teach each of us individually. She managed to do so quite successfully, instructing one pupil at a time and giving them an assignment before moving on to the next. Under Miss. Sheldon's supervision I learned to read and write very quickly, but had difficulty with math. In future years, as a result of not having mastered the basics of math, I did very poorly in calculus and trigonometry, both of which I was required to use in the military service at a later date. Other subjects taught were geography, history, and art, all of which I enjoyed and which proved most helpful when it came time to enter public school.

When not in class, we made our own entertainment. We spent a great deal of time making and flying kites constructed out of bamboo frames to which we glued coloured tissue paper. By attaching a razor blade to the tip of the kite's tail we would try to maneuver it in such a manner that when the blade came in contact with the string of another kite it would cut it loose.

One of our favourite sports was 'rounders', but most of our exercise came from bicycle-riding, tennis, or badminton. On one occasion we planned an all-day hike to the summit of the mountain that lay to the west of the property. We had learned that in years past the original owner of the adjoining property had requested that on his death his body be laid to rest at the highest point of the mountain, and that a beacon be lit each night, which would serve as a navigation aid to passing ships. In order to comply with his wish it was necessary to employ a large number of his slaves, not only to carry his coffin to the chosen site, but to make a road through the heavy undergrowth in order that the materials required to construct his crypt could be drawn by oxen to the summit. The nightly lighting of the beacon had long since been discontinued and the lonely grave was seldom visited, but the challenge of ascending the mountain and finding it was our intention. All of us, including Miss Sheldon, set out on our 'safari' early one morning and reached the site of the grave late in the afternoon. We found the monument to be in good condition and at its base was inscribed the following: "As a tree falls, so shall it lie. As a man lives, so shall he die"; hardly what one would consider a very profound sentiment! After retracing our steps, a very tired group arrived back home late that evening suffering from sunburn, blistered feet, and our bodies infested with cattle ticks picked up by fighting our way through the underbrush. We spent hours that night getting rid of these bloodsucking parasites before taking a hot bath and being marched off to bed.

It was around this time that I expressed a wish to join the scouting movement. There were no scout troops close by, but my grandmother found a Cub Pack that met on Saturdays in the nearby town of Mandeville and I was duly enrolled. Every Saturday I would go to their meetings when I accompanied my grandmother to town on her weekly shopping trips. Initially I was very proud of my new uniform but soon lost interest in Cubs and the games they played. I considered the other boys in the pack to be somewhat juvenile (although they were all about my age) and I found Kipling's jungle stories just short of being boorish. I can recall being given a book as a prize, which I considered an insult to my intelligence. It was an illustrated copy of *Black Beauty* printed in large block letters and far more suitable for a child in kindergarten than someone who had just finished reading *Moby Dick*. You will have gathered that I was not impressed with Cub Scouts and my time with them was short-lived. A few years later I joined a Sea Scout troop, which was more to my liking. As a Sea Scout I learned boat work, rope work, and many other aspects of seamanship, all of which I found useful in later years. It was now 1933, and in August of that year I would be eight years of age. The time had come for me to leave my grandparents home in the country and move to the big city of Kingston.

CHAPTER III
Public School

My mother accepted a job as the housekeeper for an American gentleman who maintained a dental practice in Kingston. Dr. Stoddart had lived in Jamaica for over forty years, having left his home in Vermont as a young man to live on the island. Regarded by many as somewhat eccentric he nevertheless maintained a successful practice and was considered by his many patients to be good at his chosen profession. In his early years he had been married, but I do not recall him ever mentioning his wife. I believe he also had a son named Lee who resided in the United States, but to the best of my knowledge the good doctor lived a lonely life in Jamaica, maintaining no contact with his family.

The house that Dr. Stoddart lived in had been purchased when he arrived in Jamaica. In 1907 the building was severely damaged by an earth quake which had virtually destroyed the city of Kingston. Most people would have rebuilt their home but Dr. Stoddart levelled the damaged portion of the house and continued to live in the undamaged section. The building had originally been built with three floors but the earthquake destroyed half of the upper floor. What was left of the upper floor was a single bedroom which I occupied, and which I was to discover swayed a good twelve inches in even a mild breeze. How this room survived the strong hurricane winds that swept the island in following years is a mystery to me. One of the advantages of having this room was a wonderful view of the city. From my window I could see most of the docks on the waterfront and across the harbour to the palasadoes (a thin strip of sand forming the southern arm of Kingston Harbour) at the western end of which was the old town of Port Royal, or what was left of it following the 1692 earth quake when it had almost been entirely swallowed up by the sea.

From my window in the attic I was able to keep track of visiting ships, both merchant and warships, and soon learned to recognize the funnel markings and house flags of the various shipping companies that serviced the island. For the most part, these consisted of the Elders and Fyffes Line (British), Canadian National Steamships (Canadian), Jamaica Banana Producers Ltd. (British), United Fruit Company (US), Grace Line (US), and last but not least, Webster Steamship Lines (Jamaica) with whom my father was employed. During the tourist season, the island was visited by numerous cruise ships, many so large that they had to anchor in the stream. Then there were the ships of the Royal Navy and visiting warships of other countries, all of whom aroused my interest. Most of the Royal Navy ships belonged to the British North American Squadron, which had its base in Bermuda, but occasionally a major warship would pay the island a visit. On one occasion the Royal Navy battleship HMS *Nelson* arrived to show the flag. The general public were invited aboard, and along with thousands of others, my mother and I made a trip out to see her in one of her picket boats.

Two things stand out in my memory of that day. First was the size of the links in her anchor cable; I found them to be unbelievably large and can still picture in my mind a bluejacket sitting on the fo'c'sle reading the local newspaper and using one of those links as a backrest. The second was a display of items that had belonged to Admiral Nelson. On leaving England the *Nelson* had been loaned a number of artifacts from HMS *Victory* which were exhibited in a glass case located in the wardroom flats. The case was guarded by two members of the Royal Marines and contained the frock coat that the great man had worn at Trafalgar on the day of his death. I recall being intrigued when shown the torn fabric where the ball had entered his shoulder and to see the dark blood stain. *Nelson* was the first ship that I had ever been aboard and my visit that day made quite an impression on me. If there had been any doubt as to what I wanted to do as an adult, no such doubt remained after that day. As far as I was concerned, I intended to join the navy when I grew up and nothing from that day forward caused me to change my mind.

In the years that followed I was able to convince my parents of this ambition and they in turn raised no objections to my choice of career. The only advice my father gave to me was that I should obtain a good education before entering the service. I regret to state that I did not heed his advice in later years as impatience got the better of me after the outbreak of war, and the thought of having to spend three or four more years in school with the possibility of missing the show was unthinkable.

Having moved to the city for the purpose of starting my formal education, my parents then had to decide which school I should attend. Although there were a number of very good public schools in Kingston at the time, they selected Woolmer's School which also happened to be the oldest public school on the island, having been founded in 1736 by John Woolmer, a goldsmith from Kingston who had left in his will the princely sum of two thousand, three hundred and sixty pounds for the founding of a 'free' school. A 'free' school it might have been in 1736, but in 1933 it certainly was not, and the annual fee required put quite a strain on the family's finances. Woolmer's School was a day school and did not accept boarders, as some of the other public schools did. It was within a few miles of our home on Duke Street and served by public transportation. For the first year I travelled to-and-from school by public transportation but the following year rode my bicycle. The school buildings were situated on a large parcel of land with ample room for playing fields. Track and field events, soccer, and cricket were the main sports for boys, while the adjoining girls' school competed in field hockey and tennis. A high fence separated the boys from the girls, and between the two main buildings stood a third building which served as a chemistry and biology laboratory for boys and girls. Directly in front of this building stood the school cenotaph engraved on which were the names of scholars who had lost their lives in the Great War.

As with the other public schools on the island, Woolmer's School was patterned after the British public school system. Upon entry a boy was placed in Form 1 and moved up through the system each year one Form at a time. Forms 2 and 3 were sub-divided; i.e., 2A, 2B, 3A and 3B, followed by Form 4. After passing the exam for Junior

Matriculation in Form 4, one moved up to Forms 5 and finally 6, when Senior Matriculation was required in order to enter university or college. As a boys' school, the faculty was comprised entirely of males, the majority of whom were graduates of English or American universities. Many of them were English or American nationals, but quite a few were island-born and had returned to the country after graduating abroad. Teaching standards were generally high, many having attended either Oxford or Cambridge, and over the years Woolmer's School produced a number of Rhodes scholars.

Like most schoolboys I had my favourite teachers, one of whom was Mr. Cover who taught Geography and English Grammar. 'Old Man' Cover, as he was affectionately referred to, was an American gentleman who bore a striking resemblance to the well-known actor Edward Everett Horton. His suits were cut from Harris Tweed and always worn with a waistcoat. In his vest pocket was a large gold watch which he had a habit of removing and studying when angry. Considered by most as somewhat eccentric, I liked him and considered him an excellent teacher. On one occasion he asked me if I knew how to patch a bicycle tire. When I assured him that I did, he told me that his tire had been punctured and offered me the sum of two shillings if I repaired it. After the job was completed I declined the offer of the two shillings and in return he immediately asked me to be his full-time bicycle mechanic. I was promised one shilling per week if I would maintain his bike in top-notch condition. With a shilling a week being more than I was getting for pocket money at home, I accepted the job without hesitation resulting in Mr. Cover and I having an excellent relationship from that day forth. My other teachers were equally interesting. Those we thought highly of were given nicknames. Mr. Thomas, a Welshman, taught chemistry and biology and, because he was blessed with a turned up nose, was commonly known as 'Puggy' Thomas. Mr. Cunningham, nick-named 'Bunny', was famous for his method of dealing with those of us who did not measure up to his standards. Rather than sending us to the headmaster for a caning, he would meter out his own punishment in the classroom. He would first ask the culprit to come to the front of the class and have the student bend over his knee while he administered a spanking with the palm of his hand on the buttocks.

Caning, either on the palm of the hand or across the buttocks, was the practiced form of corporal punishment and the prerogative of the headmaster. When a teacher wished to have one of his pupils disciplined, the boy was given a note describing the offence and instructed to report to the headmaster. He in turn would decide on the seriousness of the crime and degree of the punishment. The caning was normally carried out in the privacy of his study and ranged from a minimum of one, two, or three strokes of the cane across the palm of the hand, to a maximum of three, four, or five strokes across the buttocks. Serious crimes such as stealing, called for the punishment to be witnessed by the entire student body in the main assembly hall. In all my years at Woolmer's School I can only recall one occasion where a boy was caned in front of his peers, and in that instance the caning was followed by expulsion. In retrospect I do not consider that the caning of delinquent boys was in any way harmful, either mentally or physically. I know there are those today who consider the practice barbaric, but when I was caned, the only thing hurt was my pride. I had only been in school one week before I was given my first caning. My crime was that I had failed to complete an assignment. We had been told to copy a weekly time-table, which had been posted in the classroom for our guidance, and to have it pasted in our journal within seven days. On the seventh day, when asked to produce the finished product, I was unable to do so and consequently was given a note to take to the headmaster's study where I received three sharp cuts of the cane to the palm of my hand. This must have had the required effect as I was never again late handing in an assignment.

Over fifty years later, as a guest in the home of my former headmaster, Sir Phillip Sherlock, I recalled this incident and was surprised to have him tell me that, in his old age, he regretted having resorted to corporal punishment as a means of maintaining discipline. I was able to convince him that it had done me no harm and that the experience served me well in later years in the navy. I also recounted for him two lines of a poem I had learned in his school:

"The men who tanned the hides of us, our daily foes and friends.
They shall not loose their pride in us, howe'er the journey ends".

On entering Woolmer's School I experienced somewhat of a cultural shock. Apart from having to meet a large number of strangers and getting to know the teachers, I discovered that I was going to have to learn such subjects as Latin, Algebra, Geometry, French, Chemistry, and Biology. Initially I had difficulty understanding why I had to learn Latin, but as the months went by I began to see the reasons for it being taught. Math was my poorest subject, followed by French, and to this day I am not good with numbers. Subjects I enjoyed were History, Geography (both political and physical), and English. When I began French lessons it was a toss up as to which I disliked the most, Math or French.

Participation in sports was not mandatory but gymnastics was. I tried soccer but realized I probably would not be good at it due to my relatively small stature. As I considered cricket and track akin to watching grass grow, I opted to take up small bore rifle-shooting, at which I became fairly proficient. While I was not involved in any team sports I enjoyed other physical activities such as swimming and small boat sailing. In Kingston there was a wonderful Olympic-sized outdoor swimming pool known as Bournemouth Baths where I would swim most weekends. Our family did not own a boat but a girl by the name of Marjorie Campbell, daughter of the Postmaster General, did, and she was only too pleased to teach me how to sail. Together we spent many hours on the water in Kingston harbour, and the fact that my instructor was a girl did not bother me a bit. Marjorie was somewhat of a tomboy, and I was not interested in the opposite sex at that time. That came a few years later!

As a British colony, Jamaica was garrisoned by the British Army. Every three years an infantry battalion would arrive from England to relieve the troops on the station. On arrival, the incoming battalion would disembark at the Kingston waterfront and march to their quarters at Up-Park-Camp, located on the outskirts of the city. The following day the departing troops would reverse the procedure by marching from the camp to the docks. This changing of the guard every three years drew a large crowd of spectators as the troops marched through the city on their way to board the troopship that would carry them home. From 1931 to 1933, the garrison was occupied by the Argyll and Sutherland Highlanders, followed by the Manchester Regiment from 1933 to 1935, the Sherwood Foresters 1935 to 1937, and the King's Own Shropshire Light Infantry (KOSLI) from 1937 to 1939. Shortly after the outbreak of war in 1939, the KOSLI was relieved by the Winnipeg Grenadiers of Canada, the advanced party arriving from Montreal in the Canadian National Steamship's liner *Lady Rodney*. During June, July, and August, the troops at Up-Park-Camp would occupy a hill station in the Blue Mountains known as Newcastle Camp. Newcastle was built by the Royal Engineers three thousand feet above sea level and situated on the side of a steep mountain on which giant steps had been cut in order to erect the buildings. The largest of these served as the parade ground and doubled as a football field. Above the parade ground were the officers' quarters, officers' mess, NCO's mess, Anglican Church, post office, and general store. The buildings below the parade ground were used for the men's barracks, stores, canteen, mess halls, kitchens, and hospital.

Over the years many British soldiers on the island died of yellow fever and malaria during their tour of duty and a large military cemetery, located on the lower side of parade ground, marked their final resting place. When Newcastle was built all construction material was carried up the mountain by mules and men. In later years the Royal Engineers constructed a road to the station, which was truly an engineering feat, and no longer were the PBI (poor bloody infantry) required to march to their summer quarters each year and descend the mountain in the winter months on foot. The camp Post Office was managed by a friend of our family, a middle-aged lady by the name of Miss Doyen. Although her post office home was government-owned and came with her job as postmistress, she was allowed to take in paying guests. Members of our family, my mother included, would often spend a short holiday at Newcastle in Ms. Doyen's home. My brother and I were often there during the summer holidays and I learned a great deal about life in the British Army during peacetime and what it took to be a soldier in those days. Unlike many other British posts around the world, such as Hong Kong and Singapore, military personnel serving in Jamaica did not dominate the social life of the locals or British expatriates. This was particularly true of the Army. However, officers and men of visiting naval vessels were frequently invited to social functions and as guests to people's homes when their ships were in harbour. On one such occasion, when two field hockey teams from the cruiser HMS *Ajax* played an exhibition game on the grounds of St. Andrews Girls' School, I was introduced to an officer from this ship and proceeded to engage him in a lengthy conversation with respect to making a career in the navy. At his suggestion I prevailed on my father to contact the training ship HMS *Conway* in Liverpool with a view to future enrollment as an officer cadet. To my surprise my father thought this was a good idea and was only too willing to write a letter on my behalf.

In 1934, my parents purchased a home on approximately one hundred acres about twelve miles from Kingston. The property had previously been owned by an American engineer named Steed who decided to retire after many years in Jamaica and return to the United States. Mr. Steed had developed a successful coffee plantation and also grew bananas, cocoa, citrus fruit, and pineapples. While my mother and I continued to live in Kingston (and were later joined by my brother) my father remained with the Webster Steamship Company in order to pay down the mortgage and hired a supervisor to maintain the newly-acquired plantation. While living at Dr. Stoddart's house on Duke Street, each weekend mother and I would commute to our new home in the country which we named *Belcour*. The house was situated in a deep valley in the foothills of the Blue Mountains near the road to Newcastle Military Camp. In the valley the Mammee River marked the western boundary of the property and further south joined the Hope River to provide water for the city of Kingston. As a major source of the city's water supply, swimming in the river was prohibited by law. However, my brother and I located a deep pool that suited our purpose and we spent many pleasant hours bathing in the Mammee's cool waters. On one occasion we were caught by the police and escorted home. Faced with the prospect of a large fine, mother was able to mollify the arresting officer and we were let off with a warning, promising never to swim in the river again. Within one or two days we were back at the old swimming hole, but from that day on made certain that when one of us was in the water, the other would act as a look-out. This system worked well for, although we were visited by the authorities on a number of occasions, we were never actually caught in the water, innocently claiming to be merely sunbathing when confronted.

By purchasing *Belcour* my parents had hoped that the plantation would provide us with a steady income and that in due course my father would be able to leave the sea and settle down. However, it soon became apparent that this was not to be. The property was unable to produce a coffee crop of sufficient yield to make it profitable, and even with the sale of the other crops, the total income was barely sufficient to pay the mortgage. The previous owner of *Belcour*, Mr. Stead, had developed an ingenious number of machines to process his coffee crop which were housed in a long building at one end of which was the pulping mill. The mill consisted of two very large copper drums which rotated in opposite directions and through which the ripe coffee beans were fed. Lubricated with a steady stream of water, the soft skin and flesh of the bean was washed away leaving the core which was then spread out on a giant concrete barbecue to dry in the sun. Each evening, or if it rained, the drying beans would have to be gathered up and put under cover. When properly dried they were considered ready for husking. When the round beans were passed through the husker the hard outer membrane was removed allowing the two oval-shaped coffee beans to separate. These oval-shaped beans were then ready to be roasted and ground for packaging. Being an engineer, Mr. Stead had devised an elaborate system of drive belts, drive shafts, conveyor belts, and clutches, all of which were powered by a steam boiler fired by wood chips. The entire contraption had the appearance of a Heath Robinson design and required hours of preparation to set it in motion. Each machine could be operated separately by simply connecting its drive belt to the main drive shaft but the danger of fire was ever present whenever the boiler was in use, as sparks flew in all directions from its smokestack.

As previously mentioned, the plantation was not able to produce marketable coffee in sufficient quantity to provide a profitable return due in part to the fact that there was no one my parents knew that they could trust to operate the machinery when my father was at sea. Dad tried to solve the problem by coming up with the great idea of using the family car to provide a power plant for the machinery. A large hole was cut in the wall of the shed and our old Austin was placed in position with the rear of the car directly in front of the opening. The car was then raised off its rear axle and one tire removed. A belt drive made from one inch manila rope was then looped around the rim of the wheel and led to a pulley inside the building. The pulley was in turn connected by a second belt to the main drive shaft, and all that was required was to start the car and put it in gear. While this was a vast improvement over the old steam boiler, it did not result in an increase in production, and other means had to be found to supplement the family income. It was then that my mother came up with the idea of taking in a paying guest. Advertising in the local newspaper, she offered accommodation in the form of room and board, and was contacted by an English gentleman who had recently arrived on the island with the intention of spending at least six months. Our new boarder was a retired British Army Officer, John Winter. He had served as a Major in France with the Royal Artillery during the Great War and his army service had resulted in a medical condition which required that he live in a tropical climate during the English winter months. He had spent the past two winters in Jamaica in a hotel and was hoping to find more congenial accommodation, preferably with a family in the country.

Major John Winter was truly charming and, what started as a business relationship with my parents, ended by his being regarded as a member of our family and my mother maintained a friendship with he and his wife for the rest of her life. Typically British in appearance, he looked, dressed, and acted exactly as one would expect of an English army officer. He got along extremely well with my father, and the two of them would converse for hours, smoking their pipes and enjoying numerous after-dinner glasses of port. When Major Winter learned of my desire to enter the navy he fully supported my decision, and to this day I believe he played an important role in convincing my parents to allow me to leave home in 1941. Having a paying guest in our home meant that my mother was able to spend more time at *Belcour*, but because of school, I continued to live in town and spend my weekends in the country.

Early in 1942, while on sick leave in England, I visited the major and his wife at their home in Dorset. Their house was a small thatched cottage located in the little village of Blandford, surrounded by a beautiful English garden. It was there that I was first introduced to West Country cider for the Major had a large hogshead of this powerful liquid in his cellar and he and I had many a pint as we warmed ourselves in front of an open hearth in his cozy cottage.

Another big event which took place at this time was the installation of an electric generator at our house. My father had purchased a small gas-powered generator on one of his trips to Texas and between voyages, had wired the house. There were not many homes in the rural areas of the island with electric lighting, and ours was one of the first. We had running water which was gravity fed from a large catchment tank on the hill behind the house. There were no telephones or electrical appliances, and practically everything, other than vegetables and some fresh meats, had to be purchased in the city. Despite the drawbacks of rural living I enjoyed our days at *Belcour*, and was pleased to find the house still standing and little changed when I visited the island some fifty years later.

When I was old enough to be accepted as a Boy Scout I joined our school's Sea Scout Troop and found it more to my liking than Cubs. Our troop owned a 27-foot clinker-built whaler which had been given to us by one of the locally-based shipping companies. This boat was used by our troop on a regular basis both for pulling and sailing. Under the leadership of our scoutmaster, Mr. Levy, we spent many hours sailing in the harbour. Occasionally we would leave the calm waters and venture out to sea, camping overnight in one of the small cays situated a mile or two south of Port Royal. Of the four small cays (Lime Cay, South East Cay, Drunkenman's Cay, and South Cay) our favourite was Lime Cay, and it was off the beach of Lime Cay one night that I almost lost my life.

It was our custom to tow a small skiff wherever we went which was used to ferry our gear ashore when forced to anchor some distance from the beach due to coral reefs. One night, having anchored about fifty yards from the beach, we were transferring our camping equipment in the skiff when I decided not to wait for the small boat to return but to swim ashore instead. Diving off the whaler I struck out for the beach but soon found out that I had underestimated the distance. There was a light chop on the surface of the water which gave me some trouble, but it was the unexpected undertow I encountered which really frightened me. After swimming for fifteen or twenty minutes I was no closer to the beach and was actually being swept out to sea. Fortunately, one of our group in the skiff while returning to the whaler caught sight of me and I was pulled from the water completely exhausted, and having swallowed a great quantity of salt water. It was a close call and had it not been a moonlight night, I would not have been seen.

Shortly after my eleventh birthday I asked my father if he would consider taking me on one of his voyages. His ship, SS *Magister*, was due to sail in ballast to Port Arthur, Texas in December, 1936. As her sailing date coincided with the Christmas break from school, he agreed to seek permission from her owners to have me signed on as a cabin boy for the trip. Permission having been granted, we sailed from Kingston early in December and, while I do not recall the exact date, I do remember the abdication crisis in Britain was reaching a climax and the controversy raging throughout the British Empire was making history. On one-hand there were those who supported the king and thought he should be allowed to marry Mrs. Simpson, while others felt their beloved Prince of Wales had let them down and should abdicate. In order to fully appreciate the situation it should be remembered that in those days the monarchy was held in high esteem and Edward, Prince of Wales, was the darling of the fair sex and thought highly of.

SS *Magister*, the former *Canadian Volunteer*, in which
I sailed to Port Arthur, Texas in 1936, and to
Vancouver, British Columbia, in 1940   *The Macpherson collection*

Soon after joining the *Magister* it became apparent that the captain and chief engineer viewed the crisis differently. Captain Arkle, a man in his late forties and who hailed from Newcastle-on-Tyne, was a staunch supporter of the King. He was of the opinion that the Prime Minister, Mr. Stanley Baldwin, and his ministers in Whitehall, along with the Archbishop of Canterbury, were involved in a conspiracy to get rid of the king. It was his opinion that the king should be allowed to marry Wallis Simpson and retain his right to the throne. Chief Engineer Higginbotham, a man somewhat older than the captain, who came from Wigan, Greater Manchester, contended that Edward had disgraced himself by cavorting around with a divorced woman, and having done so, was not fit to sit on the throne of England. As is often the case in the Merchant Navy, there was no love lost between the captain and his chief engineer and much to the amusement of the other officers, including my father, these two senior officers acted like spoiled children. During meals when the captain sat at the head of the table and the chief at the foot, they would eat in silence and only communicate through our steward. For example, if the captain required the potatoes to be passed he would not speak directly to the chief but would say to the steward: "Have the chief engineer pass the potatoes please." The steward would then address the chief, saying: "The captain would like you to pass the potatoes"; whereupon the chief would glare at the captain, making no move to comply with the request. The steward would then pick up the dish of potatoes and carry it to the head of the table. Initially this strange behaviour put a damper on conversation during meals but in time the officers came to ignore both of them, acting as though they did not exist. As a youngster of eleven I found the situation somewhat odd and said nothing at meals. The situation between the captain and the chief lasted the entire trip and continued long after our return to Jamaica. Despite their dislike for each other they continued to sail together for many years until Captain Arkle left the company and returned to England.

On our third day at sea my father picked up the king's broadcast to the Empire in which he stated: "I give up the throne for the help and support of the woman I love". This message was posted on the ship's bulletin board, as was the custom each day after receiving the United Press reports. Needless to say the chief was delighted. On learning of the abdication of Edward VIII, I recalled an incident involving my Aunt Cynthia, which had occurred in 1931, when I was only six years of age.

In February, 1931, Edward VIII, who was then the Prince of Wales, travelled in the Pacific Steam Navigation liner, *Oropesa*, from the United Kingdom to a number of South American countries on an unofficial trip. On her way to Buenos Aires the ship called in at Kingston and on the day of her arrival a reception was held for the prince, to which my aunt was invited. During the course of the evening she was introduced to one of the ship's officers who was obviously smitten (my aunt being quite an attractive flapper in those days) and before the evening was over he invited her to a cocktail party to be held in the ship the following afternoon. For some obscure reason (probably because she thought that I would like to go aboard a large ship) she got permission from my mother for me to accompany her. On our arrival we were met by our host at the gangway and joined the party being held in the main dining room of the ship. While the adults enjoyed their cocktails I did my best to consume as much cake and ice cream as my stomach would hold. At some point in the afternoon Aunt Cynthia must have expressed a desire to be shown the stateroom occupied by the prince who was not aboard at the time. Her host (no doubt in an effort to impress her) agreed to give us a tour of the royal suite and, having made sure that none of the royal party were aboard, we were let into the prince's cabin. It was while my aunt was checking on the colour of the prince's pyjamas and admiring the photographs of King George and Queen Mary on the desk, that the cabin door suddenly opened and we were confronted by the prince's equerry who had returned to the ship unexpectedly on an errand for him. I can still recall the embarrassment of both our host and my aunt at being caught snooping, and I suspect the young officer would have a lot of explaining to do after we went ashore.

Returning to my voyage in *Magister*, most days Chief Higginbotham could be found sun-bathing on the weather deck which had been built over the stern of the ship. One day in a calm sea when we well out into the Gulf of Mexico, he came up with the idea of using the ship's log line to catch sharks. Having removed the vane on the end of the line, he spliced on a three to four inch long barbed hook and baited it with a strip of pork rind provided by the cook. Paying out the line (which was about one-quarter inch in diameter) to a distance of about seventy-five yards, he positioned his chair so that he could keep an eye on the baited hook as it broke the surface of the sea from time to time in the wake of the ship. Word soon spread throughout the ship of what the chief was doing and a small audience of off-duty seamen and firemen gathered on the poop deck to watch. Much to the surprise of everyone the line suddenly became taut and it became apparent that a fish of some size had taken the bait. Calling for assistance from those watching, six or seven strong men began to retrieve the line and succeeded in bringing the fish (which was a large white shark) to within a few yards of our stern where it now threatened to get tangled in the rudder or screw. Aware of the danger of having the line foul the screw the chief, acting on his own initiative and using the after steering position telegraph, rang down to the engine room to stop engines. On hearing the telegraph bells and feeling the normal vibration of the ship cease as the engines came to a stop, the captain came racing up to the bridge from his cabin seeking an explanation from the mate on watch. On looking aft he could not bring himself to believe what he saw. Pandemonium seemed to reign as a dozen or more men appeared to be about to throw themselves over the side. The chief stood in the centre of the mob of off-duty firemen, apparently trying to restore order.

Having brought the shark up to the ship it became apparent it was going to be impossible to pull it out of the water from the stern. As the ship was in ballast she was riding high in the water and the distance from the poop to the waterline was twelve feet or more. In order to land the shark the men had worked the line around the hull to a point abreast the after hatch and were now down on the well deck trying to pass a running bowline around its tail. In due course they were able to do so and the shark was heaved inboard. The captain appeared to be having an epileptic seizure and it was some time before he was able to regain his power of speech. The chief, having been ordered to report to the bridge, claimed to be the hero of the moment as he explained his reason for stopping the engines. According to his version of the story he had saved the captain from the embarrassment of having the log line wrap around the screw and there was no mention of the fact that it had been he who had thought of using the line for catching fish.

The 'old man' appeared to accept the explanation undoubtedly thinking one of the deckhands was responsible. The following day; however, while at breakfast the chief, who was about to lift a fried egg off his plate onto a slice of toast, found a cockroach under the egg. Without a word he rose from his chair, glared at the captain, and departed to his cabin. It was quite obvious that he suspected the captain of having bribed the steward to put the 'roach under the egg. It is far more likely to have been an accident, however, as *Magister* was home to thousands of roaches.

On our arrival at Port Arthur we berthed alongside one of the docks owned by Texaco Petroleum Incorporated and quickly learned that the company was in the midst of a labour dispute. The situation appeared to be quite serious as militant union members had picketed the property and roughed up a number of company officials who attempted to cross the picket lines. A few days before our arrival shots had been fired and the Governor of Texas had been forced to call out the National Guard. The guardsmen had set up machine gun posts at strategic points around the dock area and at night, with the aid of searchlights, maintained a constant watch on the cyclone fence which surrounded the property in order to guard against possible sabotage. The Texaco Company was using non-union employees to load the freighters and tankers, and these people required protection as they reported for work each morning and left the docks to return home at the end of the day. Those of us in the ship who wished to visit the city of Port Arthur (located a number of miles from the docks) were given identification cards enabling us to pass in and out of the main gates but we had to be back at the dock by midnight when the gates were closed. People trespassing after dark took the risk of being shot on sight. On our second night in port my father and I, along with his friend Jim Hunter, the second engineer, decided to go into town to see the sights. On boarding the city bus at the main gate I experienced an embarrassing situation when, on taking a seat, the driver refused to move because I was sitting in the section of the vehicle reserved for black people. This was my first encounter with racial discrimination, as practiced in the southern states, and having been born and raised in a British colony where this type of prejudice was almost non-existent, it came as quite a shock.

In 1936, Port Arthur was a typical American city on the Gulf of Mexico. As it was only a few weeks before Christmas the streets were crowded with shoppers and I suspect my presence put a cramp in my father's style. With his eleven year-old son tagging along, he and Jim Hunter could not visit any of the many taverns. The three of us did some Christmas shopping and I got an early present in the form of a .22 bolt action rifle which dad purchased for me. (On our return trip to Jamaica we set up a rifle range on the shelter deck over the poop and spent many hours at target practice.) On one of our trips to town we came across an amusement arcade with a shooting gallery and an ongoing contest, requiring great skill, caught our eye. For one dollar the contestant was given twelve rounds of .22 ammunition. The object of the contest was to fire three rounds at a card on which was printed in red the number 5 in each corner. Three perfectly placed shots on the target would completely obliterate the printed number and win the marksman one hundred dollars. The target was posted at a distance of approximately twenty five yards from the firing point and cutting the printed numerals out of the card was far more difficult to do than one would think. The prize of one hundred dollars offered to a successful contestant was never won while we were on the premises, although hundreds of Nimrods must have tried to beat the odds each night, including all three of us. Having spent a small fortune on this entertainment without success, we came to the conclusion that one of the reasons no one ever won was that the owner of the gallery always had a large Havana cigar clamped in one side of his jaw. Whenever a contestant was about to squeeze the trigger, he exhaled tobacco smoke across the line of sight, having the effect of completely throwing them off their aim.

Early one morning after having embarked our cargo of forty-five gallon drums and five gallon cans of kerosene oil, we were preparing to sail when a car drew up alongside our gangway and the driver, an elderly, portly gentleman, enquired of our quartermaster as to whether we had a doctor on board. When informed that we did not but that our captain could render first aid in an emergency, he ascended the gangway and was escorted to the captain's cabin. It transpired that the driver of the car was a high-ranking member of the Longshoreman's Union and someone had fired at him as he drove through the dockyard gates. Fortunately the assailant's aim had been poor and the bullet had only creased the fleshy part of his upper arm. After the captain bandaged the wound, he provided the patient with a glass of brandy. Later, as he left the ship, he was heard to mutter: "Some son of a b.....'s going to have to pay for ruining my three hundred dollar suit." Those of us who witnessed the event could only surmise that this was an everyday occurrence in this part of the world as the police were not called nor did anyone on the dock seem too concerned.

Magister arrived back in Kingston in time for me to start school in January. Four years later I was to join her again to travel to Vancouver at which time Captain Arkle was still the master but both the first and second mates had been replaced. The chief was still aboard but minus the thumb on his left hand, which he had lost as the result of an incident in Kingston harbour. From what I was told he had locked himself in his cabin in a fit of despondency after engaging in harsh words with the captain. For two or three days he had not come out for meals and refused entry to all, including the steward who had knocked on his door repeatedly. It was known that he had a good stock of rum on hand, and having acted in this manner on previous occasions, everyone expected him to eventually emerge when the rum was consumed. On this occasion the steward observed that the chief seemed to be sulking in the dark as no light could be seen in the transom over the door. On the third day of his self-imposed exile the sound of a gunshot was heard. Fearing the worst an attempt was about to be made to break down the door when he emerged with his left hand wrapped in a bloody towel, wearing only his underwear and a foolish grin on his face. When the facts became known, it appeared he had been shooting at a rat in his cabin in the dark with the aid of a torch and had accidentally blown away his left thumb. The rat, with which he shared his cabin, had been reluctant to come out in daylight and the lights had therefore been turned off. Unable to take aim in the dark, a flashlight had been held in his left hand at arms length while the right hand held the hand gun aimed between a pair of shining eyes, the net result being that the rat escaped and the chief was minus his thumb!

In the years to follow leading up to the outbreak of war in 1939, I regret to state that I made a dismal showing at school. The trip to

Texas with my father had left me with a burning desire to leave the island, and I found school dull and un-interesting. In the summer of 1937, my parents became quite concerned and employed a tutor. I regret that this experiment ended with my parents spending a great deal of money to no avail. It was at about this time I became friendly with a boy my own age. Roy Watson was the son of the officer commanding the Royal Artillery Battery stationed in Port Royal and was a typical English schoolboy. With his uncombed blonde hair, freckled face, and a noticeable gap between his front teeth, he reminded me of the boys described in the great English classic *Tom Brown's School Days*. The Watson family had recently arrived from England and both Roy and his sister had been enrolled in Wolmer's School. Roy and I quickly became friends and together we managed to add a number of years to our respective parents' lives. Despite our frequent escapades, Major and Mrs. Watson often invited me to spend weekends at their home; an invitation that I was only too willing to accept as Port Royal proved to be a wonderful place for eleven year-old boys to have fun.

Along the beach the British army had built observation bunkers connected to modern gun emplacements by a network of deep trenches, all of which provided a great location to play war games with the other boys of the garrison. There was also Fort Charles which had been commanded by Captain Horatio Nelson in 1779, when it was expected that a Spanish fleet was about to attack the island. A marble tablet was set in the wall engraved with the following words: "In this place dwelt Horatio Nelson. You who tread his footprints remember his glory." There were old buildings to explore such as the Royal Artillery store built in 1888 and the Military Hospital Laboratory constructed in 1800. The store was quite interesting as it had been tipped on its side by the earthquake of 1907, and to this day sits at about a forty-five degree angle giving one a sense of dizziness when standing inside. Another interesting building was the Anglican Church which served communion wine in a silver chalice presented to the Garrison by Sir Henry Morgan when he was Governor of the island. In the churchyard were graves of officers and men of the navy and army who died on the station.

One grave of particular interest was that of Lewis Galdy Esquire who, as it states on his tombstone, was: "Swallowed up in the great earthquake and, by the Providence of God was, by another shock, thrown into the sea and miraculously saved by swimming until a boat picked him up."

Roy and I managed to get into our share of trouble. One morning we decided to go hunting for lizards that lived in the sandy soil of the palisadoes. We were using BB air rifles but soon got tired of shooting lizards that sat in the sun and presented no challenge to our marksmanship. Looking around, we sighted a flock of pigeons circling around and coming to roost on the roof of the officers' mess. For the next hour or so we concentrated on trying to bring down one of these birds, but an air rifle was not a very accurate weapon. Unknown to us, our shots were hitting the metal roof of the building and we had managed to crack a few panes of glass on the upper floor of the mess. This resulted in a visit from the Military Police who confiscated our rifles and, on learning that Roy was the son of the commanding officer, marched us off to meet the major. Needless to say it was some time before we were allowed to use our rifles again!

Today, the little village of Port Royal is all that is left of what was considered to be the "wickedest city on earth" during the seventeenth century. At one time the buccaneer capital of the Caribbean, it had been the haunt of such pirates as Henry Morgan, Edward Teach (Blackbeard), John Rackman (Calico Jack), Mary Read, and Anne Bonny. Port Royal was well situated to command the narrow entrance to the harbour from the east while across Green Bay stood Fort Clarence guarding the harbour entrance to the west. On June 7, 1692, a violent earthquake tore away the greater part of Old Port Royal sinking it into the sea in a matter of minutes. As stated earlier, Port Royal was a great place for an eleven year-old boy with a sense of history and a vivid imagination.

In 1937, many great events were taking place throughout the world. In May 1937, Mr. Neville Chamberlain became Prime Minister of Britain, and between August and November a series of events occurred leading to China and Japan going to war. In October 1935, Italy made her move against Abyssinia, and in July 1936, the Spanish civil war started. Early in 1936, Germany occupied the Rhineland, a move that many considered an evil omen of things to come. The dark clouds of war were starting to gather across Europe. With my heart set on joining the navy, I followed these world events with somewhat more than an average interest for someone my age. I also took every opportunity to meet and talk to anyone remotely connected with the sea resulting in making friends with a number of seamen serving in ships that visited the island.

One such encounter led me to form a friendship with a seaman named Bert Rollinson from the British cruiser *Ajax*, and he arranged for me to visit his ship on a number of occasions. I also made friends with a steward, Tim Hancock, serving in the merchant ship SS *Camito* out of Liverpool, and whenever *Camito* was in harbour, I could count on being invited aboard by him. As a steward, he was able to offer me wonderful meals from the galley and I spent many an enjoyable afternoon in his ship meeting members of the crew and learning what life was like in the Merchant Navy.

In 1938, the American and West Indies squadron of the Royal Navy consisted of the cruisers *Orion*, *Ajax*, and *Exeter*, who were frequent visitors to the island. From time-to-time warships from other countries would arrive to show the flag and I can recall visits by the French cruiser *Jean 'd Arc*, the German cruiser *Emden*, and the American cruiser USS *Tuscaloosa*. I did not know it at the time, but the *Emden*, which was on a world cruise when she came to call, was commanded by Captain Karl Donetz, but I do remember that her ship's company were not given the warm welcome generally accorded a visiting warship in those days. The highlight of her visit was a concert presented by the ship's band and held in the central park of the city where the native population was treated to classical German music. If this concert was intended to impress the locals by exposing them to the music of Mendelssohn, Schubert, Straus, and Bach, in the name of 'German Kultur', I regret that it did not go over too well with the audience, most of whom would much rather have listened to good old West Indian calypso. Together with the language barrier and the memory of the Great War, which was still fresh in the minds of many people, I doubt that the German sailors considered their visit a great success.

My dismal performance at school continued to alarm my parents as I entered my teen years. Surprisingly I managed to make it into Third Form at the start of 1938, but it was evident that I was not working to my full potential. The end-of-year report I brought home noted that: "He shows little interest in Latin, French, or Math, while on the other hand he works well in the subjects which interest him most; i.e., Geography, History, and English." Actually, my French improved slightly that year as a result of a new teacher being hired and whom I grew to like. He was Eric Stivens who had recently arrived from England where he graduated from Cambridge University with an LLB degree. While at Cambridge he had joined the university squadron of the Royal Air Force Reserve in which he had flown Hurricane fighters. These qualifications, together with him being a personable young man much younger than any of my other teachers, was the reason for the improvement in my attempt to learn French. Mr. Stivens may have made a good air force officer, and might have become a good lawyer, but he was certainly not cut out to be a school teacher. He was liked by almost everyone in our school and maintained strict discipline in the classroom, but out of school he acted like one of our peers.

Mr. Stivens established a friendship with a select number of boys, including myself, that the rest of the faculty would have frowned on. Admittedly this familiarity was mainly with the older boys in the fourth and fifth forms, but as many of my friends were in this age group, I came to be accepted as one of the gang. An example of this occurred when four of our group decided to purchase an automobile with the intention of using it to transport us to and from social events in the country. We found a 1925 Buick that was somewhat roadworthy, and for the amount of five pounds, became the proud owners. After making a few improvements, such as putting a small couch in the back to replace the seat that was missing, and mounting two battery-operated torches on the front as headlights, we left town one night to attend a dance being held at a friend's home in the country. Before reaching the city limits someone suggested that Mr. Stivens might like to join us so we called at his home where he gladly accepted our invitation.

The party was somewhat wild and there were a number of girls our age in attendance. Needless to say there was a large supply of rum and coke despite the fact that most of us were under the legal drinking age. On our way back to town around 03:00, and descending a rather steep hill at a fairly good speed, we rounded a curve and found a large cow standing in the middle of the road. Our driver, Keith Martin, applied the brakes to no avail and we struck the poor animal broadside, sending it over the embankment and into the ravine below. The cow's horns had punctured our car radiator and the electric torch headlamps were shattered. We therefore limped home in the dark with steam rising from the radiator like a circus calliope about to explode. Fortunately we did not encounter the police, but by the time we got back to town the Buick had given up the ghost and Eric, who was in no condition to drive, had to get his car out of the garage and drop us off at our respective homes. My mother was sleeping when I entered the house and never knew what happened that night, and at school the next day it was business as usual in the classroom.

Early in 1938, political unrest finally came to a head on the island. A trade union, formed by Alexander Bustamente, called for longshoremen, sugar estate labourers, and civil servants to go on strike. These strikes were accompanied by violence at many locations resulting in martial law being declared by the governor. Police were armed, special constables enlisted, the British army garrison put on alert and, at the request of the Foreign Office in London, the Admiralty dispatched the cruiser *Ajax* to the island from her base in Bermuda where she had been on an exercise with HMS *Exeter*. I will not dwell on events leading to these disturbances or the final outcome, which eventually led to full self-government for the island in 1944. Suffice to say that civil unrest continued for a number of months. During those months I witnessed how Great Britain reacted to insurrection within the empire with the use of gunboat diplomacy. Also, as a result of my friendship with Eric Stivens, I managed to be present at a confrontation between the long arm of the law and the rioters. When the governor appealed to law-abiding citizens to enroll as special constables to assist the regular police, Mr. Stivens was one of the first to volunteer. The minimum age for those who wished to serve was seventeen, and three of my schoolmates immediately followed his example and were sworn in. However, at thirteen I was not old enough to participate.

At the time Eric was the proud owner of a 1938 Ford Mercury and, on being enlisted as a special constable, he had converted his car into something resembling a cross between a police cruiser and an armed personnel carrier. The headlights were protected by a steel grill bolted to the front bumper which extended the width of the car. The windshield was removed and replaced with a heavy wire screen. A two-way radio was installed, a battery operated spotlight mounted on the hood, and in the trunk he installed a first-aid box, road flares, fire department axe, and six steel helmets. On the day that the conversion was completed he arrived at school in his "tank" and the entire student body turned out to inspect it.

Despite the fact that martial law had been declared shortly after the outbreak of violence, the citizens of Kingston returned to their normal activities a day or two later. During the day the streets were patrolled by armed soldiers and police, and at night most people stayed home. The Royal Navy arrived and *Ajax* lay at anchor in the harbour having landed a party of Royal Marines who spent their days exercising drills for riot control in a large warehouse on the waterfront. A few days after her arrival, *Ajax* went to sea and carried out a shoot close enough to the coast so that the natives could hear the bark of her six-inch guns. When violence again erupted in Kingston, the Marines and a platoon of seamen led by a lieutenant armed only with a revolver, succeeded in controlling and dispersing a mob of rioters.

Those who had signed on as special police were normally required to patrol the suburban streets at night and, when things quieted down, I was able to persuade Eric and the others into taking me along with them on one of their patrols. Shortly after starting out on patrol we received a radio call to proceed to a sugar plantation situated a few miles west of the city where it had been reported that a dozen regular police had been confronted by a hostile crowd of labourers intent on setting fire to the estate owner's home. Upon arrival at the scene, Eric parked the car to the rear of the police line, which was formed up in line abreast, at about five yard intervals and facing the mob. To the rear of the line stood a youthful, somewhat nervous, white police inspector with a loud-speaker in his hand addressing the crowd. Occasionally someone in the mob would hurl a rock at the young officer who stood his ground, but was obviously quickly loosing patience. As the mob grew bolder and pressed forward, he produced a card from his pocket and began to read the riot act in a clipped English accent, only to be showered with a barrage of rocks, empty bottles, and rotten fruit, soiling his immaculately ironed khaki uniform. In accordance with the law, which required that the riot act be read three times before giving the order to fire on the crowd, he repeated the performance, this time reading the required words much faster. Again he was subjected to a barrage of garbage. For the third reading his words tumbled out in a torrent followed by his orders to "load, present, and fire". A dozen rifles fired as one and the crowd surged forward to be met with a second volley, this time aimed at shoulder level instead of over their heads. It was all over in a minute or so, with the disorderly crowd disbursing and leaving behind a number of wounded and dying. During the riots ten strikers were killed, a very large number wounded, and scores arrested, and we drove away in a somber mood shortly after the crowd dispersed ending my involvement with the special police patrol.

In August of that year there was a disastrous train wreck that took the lives of hundreds of people and which was regarded by many natives as a sign that God was displeased with what was happening on the island. Before the year was out the island Governor, Sir Edward Denham became ill and died in Kingston General Hospital, leading the superstitious to regard his death as a further sign that God was not pleased with his people in Jamaica. By a strange turn of fate, the ship that had been sent to the island by the Admiralty to quell disturbances was the one tasked to ceremoniously carry Governor Denham's body for burial at sea. The body lay in state in the parish church for a number of days and, on the day of the funeral, the ship's Royal Marine band, followed by two platoons of seamen drawing the gun carriage bearing Governor Denham's casket, slowly marched to Victoria Pier at the foot of King Street where a motor cutter carried it out to *Ajax* at anchor in the harbour. Hoisted inboard, the casket was then placed on the quarterdeck. The ship weighed anchor and proceeded to a position three miles off the coast where the late governor's remains were committed to the sea. Once again, the superstitious natives claimed that God had indicated his displeasure with the inhabitants of Jamaica when it was later reported by media who had witnessed the ceremony, that the bottom of the casket had dropped out when it hit the sea and the body sank, leaving the casket floating on the surface.

In due course life returned to normal and the events of the summer were soon overshadowed by events in Europe leading to the Munich crisis. Almost everyone following the daily newspaper reports were of the opinion that, upon his return from Germany, Prime Minister Chamberlain had only postponed the inevitable and that it would only be a matter of time before we would be at war with Germany once gain. I began taking a great deal of interest in what was going on in Europe as I was concerned that if war were to be declared it might very well put an end to my plans for entering *Conway*.

Early in 1939, Eric Stivens was offered a job as Deputy Administrator General on the island of Zanzibar and left Jamaica for East Africa. Other than one letter that he wrote to me after taking up his new post, I never heard from him again and have often wondered if he rejoined the RAF following the outbreak of war.

During the Munich crisis few Jamaicans understood how close

we had come to the onset of the Second World War. As photographs, news reels, and stories reached the island showing how the British had reacted during the crisis, for example, digging trenches in London, trying on gas masks, and making plans to evacuate children from the cities, they began to realize just how serious the situation had been. Some wanted to believe Prime Minister Chamberlain when he told the Empire: "I believe that it is peace for our time", but I believed that most were apt to agree with Churchill when he told the House of Commons: "England has been offered a choice between war and shame and she has chosen shame and will get war."

Our family spent Christmas 1938 at *Tan-y-Bryn*. There was a large gathering of both friends and relatives and was particularly memorable for me as my father's ship was in port and our family was all together. Early in the New Year my father informed us that Captain Arkle was relinquishing command of *Magister* and the company had appointed a new master by the name of Wood who had been serving as a first mate for a number of years, although qualified as a Master Mariner. The post war slump in British mercantile trade had forced many qualified merchant navy captains to accept berths as first, second, and in some cases, even third mates.

The Wood family lived in Liverpool, and the captain intended to have his wife and daughter join him in Jamaica after taking up his new command. Prior to the arrival of his family from England, Captain Wood was a frequent guest in our home, and when Mrs. Wood and their daughter Judy arrived my mother invited the family to live with us until they were able to find a home of their own. This arrangement was very much to my liking as Judy was a good looking girl, close to my own age, and possessing, what I considered, a wonderful figure. She and I became very good friends during the time she lived in our home and having discovered the attractions of the opposite sex, it was not surprising that Mrs. Wood was more than a little suspicious of my motives with regard to her daughter. To the best of my knowledge, at no time did she confront my mother with her suspicions, but over time I began to sense her hostility towards me and noticed that she took great care to ensure that Judy and I were seldom left alone. My mother appeared somewhat amused by this situation, but said nothing. In all fairness to Mrs. Wood, she had every right to feel the way she did as I probably would have seduced her daughter were it not for the fact that some unknown lad in Liverpool had already beaten me to it. In any event, temptation was removed when the family eventually found a house for rent.

As the summer of 1939 drew to a close, the clouds of war were beginning to build again in Europe. On my way home from school each day I would stop at the local cable and wireless office to read the latest United Press bulletins posted on a public notice board. On August 23, 1939, two days after my fourteenth birthday, the German and Russian non-aggression pact was signed and everyone could read the writing on the wall. On Friday, September 1, 1939, my parents decided to spend Labour Day weekend at *Belcour* and the entire family left for the country early that afternoon. The party consisted of my parents, Dennis, Captain and Mrs. Wood, and their daughter, Judy. I did not go as I had pleaded with my mother to allow me to stay in Kingston until the Sunday when *Camito* was due to dock on her return trip from England and I could once again visit my friend, Tim. On Saturday I spent a number of hours on board *Camito* in Tim's company, and it was the general opinion of the crew that war was inevitable. I think most people believed that a declaration of war would lead immediately to air raids and the mass slaughter of innocent civilians. That evening Tim and I went to see a movie and I listened to the latest news before going to bed. The next morning I slept late and awoke to the sound of the parish church bell and on turning on the radio learned that Britain was at war with Germany as of 11:00 London time.

Following a hasty breakfast, I rode my bike to the local newspaper office where I found that the Daily Gleaner had issued a special bulletin which vendors were selling on the street at six pence per copy. Ever mindful of making a quick buck, I purchased thirty copies at two pence per copy and quickly sold them all at six pence each, making myself a handsome profit of ten shillings. Within the hour I was back at the newspaper office for another thirty copies and by noon had made myself a net profit of one pound. Realising I had promised my mother that I would be home around noon on Sunday, I reluctantly gave up on further sales and boarded a street car to the outskirts of the city, then a one-hour walk to the house, eventually arriving around 15:00. On walking up the path to the house, I saw my father and Captain Wood enjoying rum punch on the veranda, my mother and the rest of the family being nowhere in sight. Sensing my father's displeasure at my late arrival, I took the bull by the horns and spoke first saying: "Have you heard the news?" They both replied "no", so I told them everything that had happened that day and informed them that the Prime Minister's speech was to be broadcast later that night on the BBC's overseas program.

As we had no radio at *Belcour*, it was decided that after dinner we would all walk to the hotel, *Mount Mansfield*, two miles down the road leading to Kingston. There we would be able to hear Mr. Chamberlain's speech while enjoying a night-cap on the hotel patio under the stars. Having walked all the way from town that day, I was not keen on the idea; however, when I learned that Judy intended to go for the walk, it did not take me long to change my mind. It was a somber group who listened to the broadcast that night with lengthy discussions among the adults as to what a new war with Germany would mean. Would the United States join in? What would Italy do? Was England prepared for a lengthy war? How long would it last? And so it went while Judy and I sipped soda pops and held hands under the table with thoughts racing through my head far removed from war. I was glad Mrs. Wood was unable to read my mind as no doubt I might have been the first 'casualty'.

CHAPTER IV
1940 The Restless Year

On the Monday following the declaration of war, the Jamaica Militia was mobilised and a great deal of activity in and around the local armoury ensued. It was later announced that these troops were to be used for local defence duties and would supplement the regular British troops stationed on the island. Towards the end of September, a prominent local lawyer by the name of Cargill, who had served in the British Army during the first war with the rank of Major, advised the government that he was willing to raise an infantry battalion of five hundred men at his own expense providing that the local garrison would accept responsibility for training and equipping the recruits. The regiment was to be known as The Jamaica Reserve Regiment (JRR) and Major Cargill would be the commanding officer with the rank of Colonel. Major Cargill's offer was accepted with some reservations, and a recruiting campaign started. The British regiment on the island, the Kings Shropshire Light Infantry (KSLI), agreed to provide NCOs as drill instructors and the government provided rifles and bayonets. Recruits retained their civilian jobs, were given a uniform at Major Cargill's expense, and drilled three evenings a week on the polo field at Up-Park-Camp in Kingston.

On learning of the proposed formation of the JRR, I applied at their headquarters for enlistment and was very disappointed when rejected due to my age. Undeterred, I made an appointment to meet Major Cargill (the fact that he knew my parents helped) and was able to convince him that his regiment needed the services of a bugler. Much to my delight I was enrolled as the regimental bugler (the youngest member of the battalion) and introduced to a Corporal Nightingale of the KSLI whose duty it was to teach me to play the bugle. Corporal Nightingale was a man of infinite patience and a military musician of great talent so it did not take him long to discover that I had a mental block when it came to learning how to read music. As there are only five notes on a bugle, it did not take long before I was able to master this instrument. I was not tone deaf but I was unable to convert the printed notes into sound. However, once I memorized a tune, I was able to play it by ear. Therefore, I had to learn all the bugle calls by ear, and if I did not know the call by ear, someone had to teach me. Despite this handicap I became the regimental bugler and, other than the Corporal, no one else knew I could not read a note of music.

The loss of the liner *Athenia* on the day war was declared was an indication of what could be expected in the months to follow as the war at sea heated up. However, it came as a shock when news came of the loss of HMS *Courageous* seventeen days later, and all wondered what was happening to the Royal Navy when, on October 14, 1939, U-47 crept into Scappa Flow and sank the *Royal Oak*. Our faith in the Royal Navy was restored later when, on December 13, 1939, we learned of the Battle of the River Plate in which *Ajax* was involved. Day-by-day I followed the events leading up to the destruction of the *Graf Spee* and wondered if my friend, Able Seaman Bert Rollinson had survived. War came even closer to home early in December when the Canadian destroyer HMCS *Assiniboine* arrived in Kingston harbour with the German ship *Hannover* in tow. *Hannover* was still on fire when she arrived, her crew having tried to scuttle her when she was intercepted in the Mona Passage between Haiti and Puerto Rico. *Assiniboine* was the first Canadian warship I had seen, although others had visited Jamaica from time-to-time when they were in the West Indies on pre-war exercises with the Royal Navy. Fifteen days following the declaration of war, nine merchant ships formed the first small convoy to leave Kingston, Jamaica, for the United Kingdom designated as KJF-1 under the protection of HMS *Orion*, all arriving safely at their destination. A total of nine convoys sailed from Kingston, Jamaica, between September 15 and October 10, 1939, the largest and last consisting of thirty-three ships, after which the Port of Kingston ceased to be a convoy assembly point.

One noticeable result of the war was that most merchant ships entering Kingston Harbour had been painted grey and gone were the peace time funnel markings I had learned to recognise. I have previously mentioned that many of the Jamaica militia were employed in local defence duties, a number of them being stationed at forts guarding the entrance to Kingston Harbour. At the eastern entrance to the harbour were a number of coastal defence guns around Port Royal. Across the harbour mouth on the western shore was another battery of guns at Fort Clarence (previously mentioned). There were no anti-submarine nets in place and all shipping was restricted to entering the harbour during daylight hours only. At night searchlights located in Port Royal and Fort Clarence illuminated the harbour entrance and any vessel attempting to enter the harbour was challenged. This defence of the port was the subject of heated arguments by members of the military and many were of the opinion that a determined U-boat captain would have no trouble sailing past both forts undetected and sinking ships at anchor in the harbour. The army; however, insisted that defences were more than adequate, and nothing could enter the harbour after sunset while they were on the job.

As a result of these discussions, I was fortunate to be invited to take part in an experiment intended to prove the army wrong. This came about when my Uncle Fred invited me to go deep-sea fishing. He was an avid deep-sea fisherman and loved the sport so much that over the years owned a number of boats each larger than its predecessor. In 1940, his pride and joy was the *Southern Cross*, a thirty-foot sloop fitted with an auxilliary Chrysler marine engine. Before the war he had moored his boats at Black River on the south-west coast of the island and employed a Cayman islander named 'Butch' as his caretaker. *Southern Cross* was now moored alongside the dock of the Royal Jamaican Yacht Club in Kingston, my Uncle having offered to lease her to the navy for the duration of the war. In his dealings with the navy he had met Commander Scaife, RN, an officer with Naval Intelligence on the island. Aware of my desire to enter the Royal Navy he invited me to join him on a three-day, deep sea fishing expedition with the intention of introducing me to Commander Scaife who was to be his guest. At the conclusion of our trip the three of us were sitting in the lounge of the yacht club enjoying a drink (coke for me, and whisky and soda for the adults) when we were joined by a group of army officers who had obviously been holding up the bar all afternoon. Later that evening the argument as to how effective our harbour defences were was again raised. The commander stated he would have no trouble sailing past the forts after nightfall which resulted in a challenge by the Army to do just that, and in a matter of minutes a bet had been made as follows:

"The Artillery Coastal Defence Force challenges Dr. Baillie, Commander Scaife, and whoever they may wish to join them in an attempt to enter Kingston harbour by sea after sunset on any night of their choice during the next fourteen days. In the event of a successful penetration of the harbour defence, Dr. Baillie's boat is to proceed to the Royal Artillery dock located in Port Royal where a report is to be made to the officer on duty. If, on the other hand, penetration of the harbour mouth is detected, a challenge will be made by light from the fort in Morse code using the letter 'A', to which the correct reply will be the letters 'SC', also signalled by light. Members of the respective teams agree that the loser will provide a round of drinks for all members of the winning team, either in the officers' mess at Fort Clarence or at the Royal Jamaican Yacht Club at a date and time acceptable to both parties."

I was therefore delighted when Commander Scaife suggested to my uncle that I be allowed to accompany them.

As school was closed for Easter holidays my mother had no objection to my going with her brother on what was described as a fishing trip. Within twenty-four hours a plan of action had been decided on, the *Southern Cross* had been provisioned, our personal gear stowed away, and we had set sail for Drunkenman's Cay approximately two and one-half miles due south of Port Royal. Our crew of four consisted of my uncle, Commander Scaife, 'Butch', and me.

The first night out we anchored in a small cove in the lee of the

Cay. The following day we passed the time fishing, going ashore and exploring the island, and swimming over the side. That evening we laid our plans for entering the harbour. Commander Scaife had excellent qualifications for what we were about to undertake. That afternoon, under an awning spread over our after-deck and, while enjoying a long cool drink, he entertained my uncle and me by relating to us some of his exploits in the Gallipoli Campaign of 1915. He was a man who I judged to be in his early forties, although his bushy hair was completely white. After telling us of his early life as a midshipman in the Royal Navy, he went on to relate how, in 1915, as a young lieutenant he had been serving in submarines in the eastern Mediterranean. His boat, the E-7 commanded by thirty-three year-old Lieutenant Commander Cochrane, had been ordered to patrol the Sea of Marmara and, on September 4, 1915, set out to pass through the straits into that sea. Off Nagara Point, E-7 became entangled in a Turkish anti-submarine net at a depth of 100 feet and a torn piece of net snarled the starboard propeller, winding itself around the shaft before the starboard motor could be shut down. Assisted by the net's surface marker buoys indicating E-7's every move, the enemy exploded a mine a few hundred feet from the boat without causing damage. Two hours later, following repeated attempts to get clear of the net without success, a second mine was exploded close to the boat, again causing little or no damage to the submarine. In the hope that further attempts to destroy his boat might result in completely destroying the net, Lieutenant Commander Cochrane decided to remain submerged at a good depth until dark when it might be possible to surface and escape.

After burning all confidential papers, a third mine exploded a few feet from the hull. The resulting explosion was extremely violent with electric circuits and many other fittings being put out of action. A decision was therefore made to surface at once in order to save the lives of the crew before blowing up the boat. The electric motors were therefore started despite the fact that battery power was much reduced and, on surfacing without any further difficulty, Lieutenant Scaife went on deck to surrender the crew. Subsequently he came under fire from three motor boats in the vicinity and one shell went through the conning tower, while another pierced the tanks. When the initial reaction of the enemy quietened down, two Turkish motor boats came alongside and the officers and men were taken off as prisoners of war. E-7 sank a few seconds after the last man had left her, and a time fuse, having been previously set, she subsequently blew up. Commander Scaife went on to tell of his experiences as a prisoner of war in Turkey, claiming that, as a result of that eventful day, his hair had turned snow white.

Our plan for entering the harbour called for a very dark night and preferably a moderate sea. It was thought that native fishermen were often able to sneak by the two forts unseen when returning to harbour or that the soldiers would turn a blind eye to such vessels, if indeed they were spotted. It was also thought that the best time to run the gauntlet would be during the early hours of the morning when watchful eyes were less alert. With these thoughts in mind, two nights later, under a cloudy sky and with a force five wind blowing, we furled our mainsail, and using only our jib and auxiliary engine, set a course for the harbour mouth. It was decided that we would attempt to pass ourselves off as a native fishing boat and that by only using our jib it might be mistaken for the mainsail of a native canoe. We also decided to run in as close to the west shoreline as possible in order to pass under the bluff on which Fort Clarence stood, hoping that we would reduce the chances of being spotted by the battery at Port Royal. The searchlight beams swung very slowly across the harbour entrance at regular intervals, and it took four minutes for a beam to travel through its arc. Therefore, with the aid of a stopwatch we could put the tiller up and bring our bow round so that it was head on to the beam of light each time it crossed our course. In this manner we hoped to avoid presenting ourselves beam on. As we were only doing two to three knots, this game of hide-and-seek went on for well over an hour, but getting closer to the land we began to feel naked in the glare of the light as it swept by us.

Around 03:00 the light from Fort Clarence passed over us, hesitated for a moment, stopped moving, then swung back and settled on the *Southern Cross*; we had been spotted. Within seconds we were challenged by a signal lamp flashing the letter 'A'. Commander Scaife reached for a torch (flashlight) to reply to the challenge but being unable to find it in the cockpit; I was sent below to look for it. Due to the fact that we had been sailing blacked out, the cabin was in complete darkness, making it impossible to see anything. Eventually my uncle switched on our navigation lights and threw the master switch to illuminate the cabin. Locating the missing torch I quickly passed it up the hatch to the commander who then made his reply to Fort Clarence, but it was too late. Having repeated the challenge a number of times without receiving a reply, the fort sent up a flare followed by a flash from one of the guns as they fired a round across our bows. It was all very exciting as searchlights from the Port Royal side of the harbour joined in and flares lit up the sky. A boat from Fort Clarence came to meet us and took us in tow. Upon our arrival at the jetty we were met by the officer on duty and his commanding officer (wearing bedroom slippers and pyjamas). Before long, these two gentlemen were joined by other members of the officers mess and the commanding officer agreed to the bar being opened. Due to my age, I was left in the boat with 'Butch', while Uncle Fred and Commander Scaife departed for the officer's mess where a party began which lasted until the early hours of the morning. At around 06:30 a messenger came down to the dock to tell 'Butch' and I that breakfast was being served, and after eating we said goodbye to our hosts and set sail for the yacht club arriving around noon. The Army having won the wager fair and square, Commander Scaife admitted they were correct in claiming they could easily detect a vessel on the surface, but he continued to maintain that a submerged submarine could creep by Port Royal and Port Clarence unseen.

Before the year ended the British garrison at Up-Park-Camp had been relieved by a Canadian regiment, the Winnipeg Grenadiers, the advance party having arrived on the island in the Canadian liner, *Lady Rodney*, which had sailed from Montreal. Consisting of newly-recruited, and for the most part untrained Canadian farm boys with a sprinkling of World War I veterans, the Canadians made quite a contrast to the seasoned British regulars who had garrisoned the island for so many years. Despite this, the troops were well-behaved, settling into their new home quickly and making friends with the local people. It was obvious they were poorly equipped in comparison to the British troops who had recently departed but this was no drawback when it came to being accepted into the social life of the islanders. Little did them, or any of us, realise what the future held, for within a few months they were to return to Canada and be transferred to Hong Kong, where the regiment was to be all but wiped out by the Japanese when that island fell.

The first anniversary of the outbreak of war fell twelve days after my fifteenth birthday. During the early months of 1940, the British and French armies were enjoying what was to become known as the 'phoney war', but by the end of January events in Europe started to heat up. The Russian Army which attacked Finland in December 1939 found the Fins to be a formidable foe and in April Germany invaded Norway and Denmark. In May Prime Minister Chamberlain was replaced by Winston Churchill and before the month was out the Germans had attacked the allies in the West. Holland and Belgium quickly fell, and on May 29, 1940, Germans had reached the channel and the evacuation of Dunkirk began. On June 4, 1940, Prime Minister Churchill made his famous speech in which he told the world: "We will never surrender". On June 10, 1940, Italy declared war on the allies and four days later Paris fell.

As the days went by I was convinced that if I did not get into the navy in a hurry the war would be over before my parents would allow me to travel to England. As my fifteenth birthday drew near I began to press my parents into making some definite plans for my future and was encouraged when they agreed to do so. In October 1940, my father wrote to *Conway* to confirm that I would still be accepted as a cadet. The following month a letter of acceptance was received subject to my passing the entrance exam. As I would have had to sit the exam in England, and because my mother was reluctant to allow me to make, what she considered far too dangerous a journey in those days, this option was shelved. A letter was then sent to my Aunt Betty, my father's sister who lived in Toronto, asking if she would be willing to have me live with her while I continued my education in Canada. As a single mother with two children and an elderly father living in the same home, she replied that, as much as she would like to help, she had to refuse.

My grandfather in Toronto, who was on the Ontario Board of the Navy League of Canada, then suggested to my father that he should consider contacting the two aunts on his side of the family (my great-aunts) living in Vancouver in the event that either one of them might be willing to take me in. He went on to say that if either of them were willing to do so, I could continue to go to school until I was seventeen, and at that time I might consider joining the Canadian Navy. Also, while waiting for my seventeenth birthday, I could consider joining the Royal Canadian Sea Cadet Corps, which would help dampen my burning desire to get into a naval uniform. My mother agreed with this as I would be living with relatives, would not have to leave school at such an early age, and Vancouver was thousands of miles from where the war was being fought.

Shortly after my grandfather's letter arrived, my father learned that his ship was to sail to Vancouver. The timing was perfect as he would be able to have the owners agree to have me sign on as one of the crew, thus saving the cost of my passage to Vancouver. The only drawback was there being little time before sailing to allow us to contact my great-aunts in Vancouver to find out if they were willing to accept a fourteen year-old boy as a boarder. Bearing in mind that both ladies were quite elderly and living in very small homes with husbands who were long retired, it is not surprising that when they were eventually contacted, neither was willing to take on the responsibility. This we were to discover in due course.

It was in the first week of December that the decision was made by Webster's Shipping Company that I could be signed on as a cabin boy with the crew of *Magister*. I applied for, and was issued, a passport followed by rounds of visits to friends to say good-bye. On December 24, 1940, *Magister* slipped her lines and sailed for the west coast of Canada by way of the Panama Canal. I had some misgivings regarding having to spend two more years in school and was not too thrilled at the prospect of joining the Royal Canadian Navy, which I understood to be quite small. However, I was glad to eventually be leaving Jamaica and setting out on what might prove be a great adventure.

CHAPTER V

A West Coast Visit

Christmas 1940 was the first I had spent away from home and little did I know that it would be six long years before I would be able to spend another Christmas with any of my family. On our passage to the Canal Zone we experienced calm seas and sunny skies and I spent the first day or two getting to know my fellow shipmates. There were a few members of the crew who I had already met on my previous trip to Port Arthur four years earlier. Captain Arkle was still in command as Captain Wood, who had been hired to replace him, had been given command of another ship in the company's fleet. Chief Engineer Higginbotham was still on board, minus his thumb, as was our steward and a number of the firemen and seamen. Mr. Larsen was still the First Mate, but we had a new second engineer, an elderly Scot, by the name of McGregor who hailed from Nova Scotia. The second and third mates were both from the Cayman Islands and my father was the only radio officer.

Although I had signed the ship's articles as a cabin boy, I was not considered part of the crew and was treated more or less as a passenger. We did, however, carry a real passenger by the name of Earl Latibeaudiere who had purchased a passage to Vancouver with the intention of joining the Canadian Army. Prior to sailing I had not known Earl. He was eighteen years of age and Jamaican by birth, and I recall him telling me that his parents had originally lived in Haiti. Being a tramp steamer, *Magister* did not have any passenger accommodation and Earl was given a berth in the fo'c'sle with the seamen. On our first day at sea (December 25, 1940) a message was received addressed to all British merchant ships at sea in the Western Atlantic. Captain Arkle read us the following signal when we sat down for Christmas dinner later that day. It was then posted on the ship's notice board for all to see and read as follows:

Admiralty Message
From: Captain in Charge Bermuda

To: All British Merchant and Fishing Vessels:

"This second wartime Christmas finds the members of the British Merchant Navy and Fishing Fleet pursuing their calling throughout the seven seas, and I wish to send them a personal greeting. You were the first of our civil population to suffer the merciless attacks of the enemy. You have carried on undaunted, maintaining the vital supplies of the Empire. Your courage and daring have been an inspiration to your fellow countrymen who are now facing the same brutal assault. In their name, I thank you, and send you all best wishes for Christmas and a good landfall."
Signed: George R.I. ends. 0001/25.

We arrived off the coast of Panama early one morning and an hour or so later made our way through the anchorage in Colon to the entrance to the canal. Before entering the first lock on the Atlantic side we were boarded by the canal pilot and an armed party of American soldiers who promptly took up positions at strategic points throughout the ship. These soldiers stayed aboard all day as we passed through the canal, leaving us at Balboa when we reached the Pacific. I spent most of the day on deck as we were pulled by the electric mules through the series of locks we had to transit on our passage through the isthmus. I was later told, but was never able to learn if it were true, that in order to prevent a ship from releasing a delayed action bomb in one of the locks the Americans had constructed a device in the form of a net which lay at the bottom of the lock and which was raised and examined after the lock gates had closed.

Our passage through the fifty-mile long canal came to an end that evening and we anchored off Balboa that night resuming our passage up the west coast of Central America the following morning. On our passage north we stood well out to sea but caught an occasional glimpse of a distant mountain peak as we passed Mexico and the coast of California. The Pacific Ocean lived up to its name and remained quite calm although we encountered a heavy westerly swell which created an uncomfortable corkscrew motion in the vessel. Off the Oregon coast the days grew cooler and by the time we were off the coast of Washington the cockroaches in the ship had come out of hiding to look for some warmth. I recall the battery-charging panel in the wireless cabin being completely covered with hundreds of them as they swarmed on and around the charging lamps. The steam radiators in the cabin were also a favourite spot, as was the galley and pantry. As we came closer to the state of Washington and rounded Cape Flattery to enter the Strait of Juan de Fuca, the Olympic Mountains presented a magnificent sight with Mount Baker in the distance capped with a mantle of snow. We picked up our pilot off the entrance to Victoria harbour and continued our passage north through the Strait of Georgia to Comox on the east coast of Vancouver Island where we docked to take on coal for our bunkers. I was fascinated to discover that the labourers who were coaling the ship all appeared to be Asian. It was raining steadily as an endless line of these workers filed up the brow, each carrying a sack of coal on his back, which they emptied down a chute to the bunkers below. The following morning after the deck had been hosed down we left Comox and, passing through Burrard Inlet, we eventually secured alongside a dock in North Vancouver adjacent to the Wallace Shipyards where the *Magister* had been built in 1919 and launched as SS *Canadian Volunteer*.

During wartime the radio transmitters of all ships in harbour were sealed for security reasons and, as my father was not required to be aboard, he arranged for us to spend the next five days ashore. It was expected that we would be in Vancouver for at least a week taking on cargo. On leaving the ship dad placed a call to his Aunt Rennie who, on learning that he was in Vancouver and that I was with him, invited us to stay with her and her husband. My Great Aunt Rennie was my grandmother Violet Saies-Jones' sister. She had married a former British Army colonel by the name of Pringle who had served in the Royal Artillery with the British Army in India. Following his retirement they had immigrated to British Columbia and now lived in North Vancouver. Colonel Pringle turned out to be a somewhat eccentric gentleman. Not only was he a staunch monarchist but also a devout member of a sect known as the British Israelites whose members believed that England was the original site of the Garden of Eden and that the Anglo Saxons were the chosen people of God. He was so convinced of this that he held forth on the subject for a full half-hour once every week on a local radio station. On our first night in their home we had all retired to the living room after dinner to listen to the CBC newscast, at the conclusion of which the National Anthem was played. As the first bars of the anthem came over the air waves Uncle Val sprang from his seat and stood rigidly at attention, catching my father and I quite unprepared and somewhat uncertain as to what was required of us. Self-consciously we slowly rose from our chairs and stood silently as God was asked to save the King and send him victorious.

The events of that evening no doubt prevented my father from discussing with the Pringles the prospect of my living with them. The following morning at breakfast he thanked them for their hospitality and explained that, because we were going to be in Canada for such a very short while, we would have to take our leave if we hoped to be able to spend some time visiting Aunt Rennie's sister, Aunt Fanny. Great Aunt Fanny had married a man by the name of Glencross who, for many years, had been employed by the British Columbia Electric Company. On his retirement they had purchased a small cottage to the north of Vancouver located on the shore of a small inlet known as Horseshoe Bay. Horseshoe Bay was the terminal for the Nanaimo-Vancouver ferry, as it still is today. The difference was however, that in 1940 it was just a collection of small cottages occupied mainly by retired couples. There was a small general store which also served as the post office, the ferry terminal, and the bus station. After leaving Aunt Rennie and Uncle Val's home, my father and I crossed the harbour by ferry to Vancouver to board a bus for Horseshoe Bay where we planned to spend a few days with the Glencross family. They were a delightful couple and I found Horseshoe Bay to be a beautiful spot. The house was surrounded by a grove of tall cedar trees and the community was situated so close to the surrounding forest that various forms of wildlife frequently visited, including the occasional black bear. Each morning we would awaken to the sound of outboard motors being started as sports fishermen set out fishing for salmon in the bay.

The prospect of my living with Aunt Fanny and her husband was out of the question for a number of reasons. Not only was their cottage too small, but transportation between Vancouver and Horseshoe Bay posed a problem. The closest high school was in North Vancouver and a return trip each day by bus was not an option. Reluctantly, we said goodbye to the Glencrosses and returned to rejoin *Magister*, which was still berthed in North Vancouver. That evening dad and I visited the home of Aunt Fanny's daughter, Rita, and her husband who lived in West Point Grey, a suburb of Vancouver. On the way back to the ship late that night, following dinner with Rita and her family, dad realized that any plans for me to live with relatives in Vancouver could not be possible. I therefore persuaded him to let me try on my own to enlist in the navy. Reluctantly he agreed, probably knowing that the chances of me being accepted were highly improbable. To be on the safe side, however, I had to promise him that I would not lie to the military about my age as I think he was afraid that the navy possibly might accept me as a boy seaman.

Magister shifted her berth the following morning and entered the Fraser River to tie up in New Westminster. That afternoon I visited the naval recruiting office and was interviewed by a fairly sympathetic naval officer who told me that under no circumstances could I join the RCN until I was seventeen.

On returning to the ship I met up with Earl Latibeaudiere who had come on board to say good bye. Earl had enlisted in the army and was now wearing the uniform of a bombardier in the Fifth Canadian Coast Artillery. When I told him of my being turned down by the navy, he suggested that perhaps I should consider joining the army. According to him, the army was desperate for recruits and having been a member of the Jamaica Reserve Regiment, my chances of being accepted were quite good, even if only as a band member. With this in mind I left for the city early the next morning telling my father that I was going back to the naval recruiting office to get more information regarding rates of pay, physical and educational requirements, etc. Once in the city I asked for directions to the Seaforth Armouries and by 10:00 had joined a long line of prospective recruits waiting to be interviewed by a recruiting sergeant of the Seaforth Highlanders at their Burrard Street Armoury.

On reaching the recruiting table, I was confronted by an elderly man with a trim moustache tapering on each side of his upper lip to a sharp point which was heavily waxed. He was a large man and on his battle dress jacket I recognized the ribbons of the 1914 to 1918 Star, and the Victory Medal of the first war. Wearing a Seaforth Highlander kilt and a wide red sash over his right shoulder he made an imposing figure. In a friendly manner he motioned me to take a seat. and, producing a blank form, commenced the interview by asking for my date of birth. The expression on his face changed when I provided the information and, with a somewhat pained look on his face, was about to speak, when I interrupted him by saying¨ "I realize I'm below the minimum age but I hope that when you hear my story that an exception might be made in my case. I have travelled quite a few thousand miles in order to enlist and I would like you to hear what I have to say." I then went on to relate how I had tried to join the navy but been rejected the day before. I explained how I had travelled to Canada from Jamaica, emphasised the fact that I had been accepted in the Jamaica Reserve Regiment as a bugler, and concluded by assuring him that my parents were aware of what I was doing and were willing to allow me to enlist, providing the authorities would accept me. Pausing for breath, I then suggested that perhaps I might be enlisted as a bandsman. For a moment he remained silent then, ordering a messenger to locate an officer, we waited.

Shortly thereafter we were joined by a young lieutenant and I was asked to repeat my story. When I had finished this officer told me that he wanted me to repeat my story to the adjutant and, leading me to an office off the parade square, I was introduced to a gentleman who wore three pips on his shoulder, indicating the rank of captain. Once again I was asked to repeat my story, and when I had done so, was taken to see a fourth person who I was to learn later, was the regimental major and the second in command of the regiment. For the third time that morning I repeated my story, which led to my eventually meeting with the colonel himself. At this point, having been through the chain of command all the way to the colonel of the regiment, I began to hope that there was a slim chance of my being accepted. It was now close to the lunch hour and the colonel invited me to lunch in the officer's mess. It was an interesting luncheon and I felt somewhat intimidated by the company, most of whom questioned me as to why the colonel had invited me to lunch. I was glad when it concluded and they all returned to their respective jobs.

On leaving the mess and returning to the parade, I was met by a group of people, some of whom were in civilian clothes while others were in uniform, including the regimental sergeant major. It later transpired that after my meeting with the colonel he had sent for the adjutant and instructed him to place a call to the news office of the Vancouver Sun. The news desk had been requested to send a reporter and photographer to the armoury as they might be interested in my story. The colonel of course had realized that this was a golden opportunity to obtain some free publicity for the current recruiting campaign. He had managed to locate Earl Latibeaudiere who had been sent for and was now present and resplendent in his new uniform. After being interviewed by the reporter we both had our picture taken and were informed that it would appear in the evening copy of the Sun.

Before returning to the ship, I was told that the regiment had requested permission to enrol me in the pipe band and that if I returned the following day they might have an answer for me. It was quite late when I returned to New Westminster and on leaving the street car I purchased an evening copy of the Sun. There on the back page was my photograph. The caption read: 'One Proud, One Disappointed' and Earl looked like a clown in his battle dress, standing rigidly at attention while I gazed at him with what was supposed to be a look of envy. The story that went along with the picture was even more embarrassing. Firstly, I had never stated that I had a powerful yen to fight in the Canadian Army, as the report claimed; secondly, I was fifteen years of age and not sixteen; thirdly, Earl Latibeaudiere was not a pal of mine as I met him for the first time when we sailed from Kingston; and finally, I had not applied three times for enlistment at the Seaforth Armouries, having applied only once that morning. My father found the whole thing quite amusing and I suspect he was relieved that he would not have to return home to tell my mother that I had joined the army.

One Proud, One Disappointed

Earl Latibeaudiere, 18 (left), native of Kingston, Jamaica, stands proudly at attention in his three-day-old uniform, as Frank Jones, 16, who made the trip to Vancouver from the West Indies with him to enlist in the Canadian Army, surveys him enviously. Young Jones was rejected because of his age.

Photograph published in the Vancouver Sun
the day Earl Latibeaudiere and I were interviewed

Vancouver Sun

That night dad and I went into town and after a meal in a

local restaurant, ended up at a dance in the basement of a church organized by a group of women for the benefit of merchant seamen in port. During the course of the evening I danced with a young lady of about sixteen who had seen my picture in the Sun. When I admitted to being the person in the picture she would not leave me alone and clung to me like a leech, pulling me on to the dance floor each time the orchestra struck up a new tune. Although I was a lousy dancer she did not seem to care, and at the close of the evening, agreed to me walking her home. On learning that she did not live a great distance from the dock dad gave me the go ahead and returned to the ship on his own. I got back to the ship around four in the morning and slept in till around ten. Dad wanted to know why it had taken me so long to get back to the ship, and I told him that I had lost my way after taking the young lady home. He probably did not believe me but asked no more questions. I had decided that Canadian girls were okay in my books. Later that day dad and I went ashore to watch a junior league hockey game in the local arena, which was a first for me and which I enjoyed thoroughly.

Magister had taken on a cargo of newsprint in Vancouver, together with a miscellaneous load of canned goods. In New Westminster we embarked a deck load of timber which now covered both well decks to a height of about eight to ten feet and extending from the fo'c'sle to the bridge and from the bridge to the poop deck. Fully loaded to the winter saltwater mark of her plimsol line we sailed the next day on our return journey to Jamaica. Having been in Canada for a total of ten days, I was now on my way home having accomplished nothing with respect to my future. Determined to convince my parents to allow me to travel to England, I discussed the subject at length with dad using every argument I could think of to persuade him to allow me to leave home. In the end I suspect I wore him down as he promised to speak to my mother about it when we got home.

Our return journey was uneventful except for one night off the coast of California. As on our trip north, Captain Arkle maintained a course on our southward voyage some seventy or more nautical miles off the coastline. As U-boats had not been reported in the eastern Pacific in 1940, and threat of attack from surface raiders was considered unlikely, ships of all nations continued to sail those waters fully illuminated. One night during the middle watch a message was passed through a voice pipe to the wireless cabin ordering my father to report to the bridge immediately. On his leaving the cabin I followed and went out on to the upper deck to find our vessel lit up from stem to stern by a brilliant light directed on us by what was apparently another ship on our port side. A signal lamp was flashing from this unidentified vessel, which I learned later requested us to state our name, nationality, port of registry, and destination. My father passed this information by lamp and a few minutes later we received a signal wishing us good luck, belated happy New Year and safe passage, at which time the searchlight was extinguished and our unexpected visitor vanished in the dark. We never did discover who had challenged us, but it was later suspected that it was the Canadian armed merchant cruiser, HMCS *Prince Robert*, who was on patrol off the west coast of north and Central America on the look-out for German merchantmen trying to break out of neutral ports to return to Germany.

When we got home I learned that my cousin had become engaged to a member of the Winnipeg Grenadiers. I was also told that one of my friends, John Melville, who had recently left Jamaica for the United Kingdom to enlist, had been lost at sea when the ship that he had been working his passage to England in had been torpedoed. On our return, as promised, my parents gave serious thought to the idea of my leaving for England. Today I can only imagine what prompted them to make the decision they did. As a typical teenager I thought only of my own gratification and was quite oblivious of the momentous sacrifice I was asking them to make.

Years later many friends have questioned me as to why my parents would have allowed their fifteen year-old son to leave both school and home to travel thousands of miles to a foreign country with the intention of joining the armed forces of a nation at war. In retrospect one should remember that I had expressed a desire to join the Royal Navy at a very early age, long before war was declared in 1939. My parents had previously indicated that they would not object to me doing so and in fact had encouraged me to the point that they had taken steps to have me enter the training ship *Conway* as a cadet. One thing that both my mother and father had impressed upon me was the necessity to obtain a good education before leaving home if it was my intention to follow the sea. The fact that I had not proven myself to be anything but an average student was definitely a mark against me, but the knowledge that long after joining as a cadet my education would be continued for a number of years before actually going to sea in either the Merchant Navy or the Royal Navy weighed in my favour. It was hoped that my lack of interest in the mundane subjects I had been taking might disappear if I were to continue my schooling in the nautical classroom of a training ship. Whether they were right in this assumption will never be known for with the outbreak of war everything had changed.

I have already described my mother's fear of me crossing the Atlantic and my parents plan to have me live with family members in Canada, an idea that was hastily conceived and poorly planned. No doubt my mother was also remembering the loss of her brother during World War I at the age of eighteen. For my part I considered the outbreak of war to be most fortunate, for the excitement that I would have experienced by merely leaving home to follow my chosen career, would be heightened by the great events that were taking place at sea. There were many others my own age who felt the same way but I doubt any of us would have admitted to being motivated by patriotism. Patriotism was not an emotion to which I had given much thought, as it was hard for me to understand how someone could betray ones country. I recalled the first mate of *Magister* telling me that I was a fool to think of joining the navy while there was a war on as I would only end up being killed.

On our passage home from Vancouver he and I held lengthy conversations in which he related to me the story of his life after leaving home as a young boy to go to sea. During the course of one of these discussions I had questioned him as to how he felt about the invasion of Norway by Germany and was surprised when he told me that it meant little to him. He went on to say that Germany had only invaded Norway because if they had not, the British would have. It was later proven that this was in a sense true, but at the time I told him that I thought it shameful that he should call his countrymen fools for resisting the Germans. He responded by stating: "Germany will eventually win the war and that when they have done so, Norway will become part of the Third Reich. Norwegians are all of true Aryan stock and are really blood brothers of the Germans". When I told my father of our conversation he replied that he had known all along that the first mate was a German sympathizer and that most of the other officers also considered him to be a shameless coward as well.

After much discussion, my parents came to the conclusion that they would reluctantly allow me to travel to England, and my father wrote to his cousin advising her that they intended to book a passage for me as soon as possible. His cousin Lorna, whom I later came to refer to as Aunt Lorna, was asked to look out for me when I landed in England and ensure that I was accepted by *Conway* upon my arrival in Liverpool.

The weeks that followed were busy ones for me. I went to see Commander Scaife who was kind enough to give me a letter of introduction, as did my former headmaster, Philip Sherlock. My parents provided me with the addresses of friends and family members living in England, and a steamship ticket was purchased. I was to travel on the Canadian National Steamship liner *Lady Rodney* from Kingston to Hamilton, Bermuda. Onward passage to the United Kingdom was to be provided by the Pacific Steam Navigation Company following my arrival in Bermuda. The one-way passage, Kingston to Liverpool, cost my parents forty pounds and I was given five pounds sterling as pocket money; all that I was allowed to leave the island with, due to wartime regulations. Forty pounds was a large sum of money in 1941; money that my parents could ill-afford. My luggage consisted of one large suitcase which contained everything I owned; shirts, socks, underwear, toilet articles, personal papers and documents, and four suits, one of which was an olive green gabardine given to me by my uncle and tailored to my size, but more about that later!

For the second time in four months I called on a number of my friends to bid them farewell and a week or two before leaving attended a gala dance held to raise money for the Red Cross. My partner on the night of the dance was a young lady of dubious virtue who, I had learned from my friends at school, was only too willing to bestow her favours on any boy she had taken a liking to. She was the daughter of a prominent civic official, and while I had heard of her escapades from others, we had never met. She called me one night to say she had heard that I was leaving to join the navy and suggested that we should get to know each other before I sailed away. We had made a date that night and gone to see a movie a few nights later, at which time I discovered that everything that I had been told about her was true. On the night of the dance we both managed to sneak two or three drinks from the bar by bribing one of the waiters, she then suggested that we go for a breath of fresh air in the garden. The band was playing Glen Millar's *In the Mood*, which set the stage for what was to follow. Taking me by the hand she led me to a secluded spot in the garden where she lived up to her reputation, which far exceeded anything I had expected.

Lady Rodney was scheduled to sail on March 3, 1941, and that afternoon I went aboard accompanied by my mother and father who had driven me to the pier. The three of us went below to inspect my cabin and stow away my gear. Afterwards we went on deck to say our goodbyes - the moment I had been dreading. My mother was very brave and made me promise to write regularly, to take care of myself, and not to do anything that she would be ashamed of. She said she was very proud of me and ended by reminding me that on arrival in England I was to contact Aunt Lorna as soon as possible. As time went on our conversation became stilted and it was obvious that my mother was making a great effort to hold back her emotions. My father came to the rescue suggesting that it might be best if they left before we actually sailed. I went with them to the gangway and watched as they walked to the car parked at the end of the dock.

Before driving away my mother, standing by the open door of the car, waved to me as I stood at the rail of the ship and I blew her a kiss in return. Little did I know that I was never again to see her. At around 17:00 we slipped our lines and set a course for Port Antonio on the north coast of the island where we were to load bananas for Halifax.

CHAPTER VI
Off To Sea

As we headed east along the south coast of the island I went below to my cabin and made the first entry in the dairy I intended to keep. I then lay in my bunk and read for a while before dozing off to be awakened by the sound of chimes being played by a steward calling the passengers to dinner. During dinner I examined my fellow passengers with some interest and was surprised to find how few there were. In normal times the *Lady Rodney* could accommodate 130 first class passengers but on this trip there seemed to be less than half that number. There were very few couples and no children in the dining room. Most of the passengers appeared to be middle-aged or elderly males. Among those present were three people in uniform: an elderly gentleman in the uniform of the Royal Air Force and wearing the insignia of a wing commander, and two very elderly sergeants in the uniform of the Winnipeg Grenadiers, both of whom wore the medal ribbons of the first war. After dinner I decided to go for a walk around the promenade deck for a breath of fresh air during which I became engaged in conversation with the two Canadian sergeants on deck for the same reason. As we stood at the rail enjoying the cool off-shore breeze on our port side, one of them lit a cigarette and was immediately pounced on by a passing member of the crew who ordered him to put it out as no smoking was allowed on the upper deck after dark, a sober reminder that there was a war on and that the ship was entirely blacked out. My new-found companions then decided to go below to the lounge where they could enjoy a smoke and a beer and invited me to join them. As the evening wore on I learned that both were being returned to Canada to be discharged from the army due to their age. They had both served in France in the first war and were now past the maximum age for service in the Canadian Army. I was soon to discover that their longevity had in no way affected their capacity to consume strong liquor. As no one questioned me as to my age, I sat with them in the lounge and consumed many glasses of rum and coke which left me with a colossal hangover the following day. At around three in the morning we entered Port Antonio harbour and secured alongside to load bananas. The bar in the lounge having closed, the three of us went on deck to watch as native workers in single file, each one carrying a bunch of fruit on his or her head, filed up the brow and into the ship to stow our cargo.

Later that day I went to visit the sergeants in their cabin which was on the starboard side of the ship directly across from mine and found them engaged in a game of poker. That evening I joined them for dinner and afterwards we headed again for the lounge to repeat the previous night's performance, only this time I was determined to stay sober. As I sat at the bar listening to their tales of army life we were joined by the RAF wing commander who was on his way back to England, having been in Jamaica to set up an office to screen prospective recruits for the Air Force. The two Canadians were not in the slightest bit intimidated in the presence of a senior officer, and I got the feeling that the Englishman rather enjoyed their complete disregard for his rank, something that he was probably not accustomed to, but willing to excuse in view of the fact that they were 'colonials'. As on the previous night my two friends were inebriated when the bar closed in the early hours of the morning, but both insisted on having one more for the road, purchasing a bottle of rum before leaving to go below. Having been invited to join them for a night cap, I followed them to their quarters and shortly afterwards, unable to stay awake, I fell asleep on the lower bunk in their cabin. At 08:00 all three of us awoke to a mighty explosion which shook the ship from stem to stern. This was followed by the sound of loud voices outside the cabin door, and my two bleary-eyed companions, whose minds were still somewhat foggy from the night before, immediately came to the conclusion that the ship had been torpedoed. They made a dash for their rifles, webbing, steel helmets, and gas masks, which were hanging on coat hooks on the inside of the cabin door. Donning their equipment and with their rifles at the high port, they attempted to leave the cabin, forgetting that their bayonets were attached to the muzzles of their rifles, making it impossible to get through the doorway. This was probably for the best as the passageway was filled with members of the ship's crew running to their emergency stations. When things had quietened down and order restored, we were told that earlier in the morning it had been announced over the ship's intercom system that an exercise drill would be conducted, at which time the four-inch gun on the stern would be fired. All passengers had been made aware of the impending exercise, but we had slept through the broadcast and knew nothing of what had been planned.

On the day following our emergency exercise the ship docked at Nassau in the Bahamas almost directly across from the *British Colonial Hotel* which was situated on the main street running parallel to the waterfront. As we were in Nassau for a full day I went ashore to do some shopping and went swimming in the afternoon from Black Diamond beach. We sailed very early the next morning for Bermuda, arriving on March 11, and docked alongside Front Street in Hamilton. My two inebriated friends insisted on sending me on my way by throwing a party in the lounge the night before we docked. I suspect this friendly gesture provided them with yet another excuse to get sloshed. I have often wondered what happened to those two reprobates when they eventually arrived in Winnipeg. I suspect they were as pleased to leave the army as the army was to see them go. Despite their outrageous behaviour I enjoyed their company during the voyage and was sorry to leave. I am sure other passengers in the ship thought it odd that a young boy of my age would spend so much time in their company. In the months to follow, when I read in the paper of the fall of Hong Kong, it was good to know that they had not been forced to endure the hell that so many of their former comrades had suffered as prisoners of the Japanese.

On leaving the ship I hailed a horse-drawn carriage (there were no automobiles on the island at the time) and directed the driver to take me to the office of the Pacific Steam Navigation Company. He was kind enough to point out that I could see their office from where I was standing less than half-a-block away. Thanking him for the information I set out on foot to make enquiries as to the name and departure date of the ship that was to carry me on the final stage of my journey. On meeting the shipping agent of the PSN Company, someone whose name I have long since forgotten, I showed him the steamship ticket which had been purchased in Kingston and was about to continue when he interrupted me in mid-sentence by holding up his hand and saying: "PSN ships are no longer calling at Bermuda. Convoys are now routed out of Halifax, and anyone having booked a passage to the UK with PSN now has to leave from that port." It took a few minutes for this information to sink in and I questioned him as what else the PSN might do to honour my ticket. He replied: "There is a remote possibility that one of our ships may be directed to Bermuda in the weeks to come," and suggested that I find accommodation on the island and contact his office on a daily basis in the event that this might happen. My problem now was being able to afford to stay in Bermuda for any length of time.

As previously noted, I left Jamaica with only five pounds, which had decreased to two pounds and five shillings as a result of my shopping expedition in Nassau and my contribution to the rum consumed in the lounge of the *Lady Rodney*. I decided to locate a friend of the family who lived in Bermuda and whose address I had been given before leaving home. Her name was Mrs. Elizabeth Fry and she was somehow connected with the Methodist church. She and her late husband had met my grandfather when they lived in Jamaica. The address given to me was the *Everest Hotel* in Hamilton, and on leaving the PSN office I set out to find her. Locating the hotel reduced my fast dwindling bankroll by three more shillings; however, it was money well spent as Mrs. Fry was very helpful and placed a call to a Mr. Tucker, superintendent of the Royal Sailors' Rest in Hamilton.

Royal Sailors' Rest hostels were the legacy of the late Dame Agnes Weston who, in 1872, raised funds to establish hostels for the benefit of British sailors in need of rest and accommodation in the three major naval ports in England: Portsmouth, Devonport, and Chatham. Since that time Sailors' Rest hostels had been established, and could be found in most of the principal naval ports in the Empire. These hostels were run on club-like lines and sleeping accommodation was available at reasonable prices for the sailor who wanted a bed ashore, or for Merchant Navy seaman who might be stranded in a foreign port for a variety of reasons. On hearing my dilemma, Mr. Tucker was only too willing to provide me room and board at an affordable price so, thanking Mrs. Fry for her assistance, I made my way along Front Street to locate my new residence and meet Mr. Tucker. To the best of my recollection, bed and breakfast cost two shillings and sixpence per night, and for an additional three shillings, I could obtain a substantial meal in the evening. However, even at these low prices, it was evident I could only afford to stay for about eight days. With the aid of Mr. Tucker, I was able to obtain employment as an assistant to the gardener on the grounds of the *Bermudiana Hotel*, a job which paid me five shillings a day. Five days later, still having had no assurance from the PSN agent that they would be able to provide me with a berth, I once again asked Mr. Tucker for his assistance. It occurred to me that there was a possibility the Royal Navy might consider providing me with a passage to Halifax if they were made aware of my intention to enlist. I therefore asked him if he knew of anyone at Admiralty House that I might speak to, and the following day, he provided me with a letter of introduction to an officer on the admiral's staff and gave me instructions as to how to find Admiralty House. Having loaned me his bicycle, off I went.

On arrival at Admiralty House I was directed by the Royal Marine sentry on the gate to a small building on the grounds which served as the administrative office of the commander-in-chief. Admiralty House was a large, white, colonial style mansion, similar in construction to plantation homes in the Southern United States. A curved concrete driveway led up to the entrance of the main building and a second building was located on the right behind a well-tended and colourful flower garden. Leaving the bicycle in a rack by the front door I entered the small building and was met by a young man in the uniform of a chief petty officer. On stating my business and producing the letter given to me by Mr. Tucker, he asked me to take a seat, and then left the room, returning a few minutes later accompanied by an officer who I recognized as being a paymaster lieutenant commander. Introducing himself, he informed me that he was the admiral's secretary and invited me into his office, enquiring as to how he could be of service. Relating to him the circumstances leading to my being there, he sat for a moment in silence before saying: "Interesting, most interesting", then walking with me to the outer office, he suddenly turned and said: "Do you smoke?" Having replied in the affirmative, he suggested that I might like to go and have a cigarette outside while my request was being considered. He pointed to a bench by the tennis court indicating that it might be a good spot for me to have a smoke while waiting and assuring me that he would return very shortly. Twenty or thirty minutes later I heard my name being called, and on my return to the office he met me at the door saying: "How long will it take you to get your gear together and return? Can you be here by 16:30?" Having assured him that I could. He then told me that he had spoken to the admiral who had agreed to me being given passage to Halifax in one of "his majesty's ships" scheduled to leave Bermuda for Canada that evening.

Returning to Hamilton as fast as I could on Mr. Tucker's bicycle, I informed him of my good news and thanked him for everything he had done to help since my arrival in Bermuda. It took me only minutes to pack my few belongings and settle up my bill before going over to the *Bermudiana Hotel* to collect the few shillings they owed me. Returning to the Sailors' Rest I had lunch in the cafeteria for the last time, said goodbye to staff who were present, and not wanting to be a minute late, called a carriage and instructed the driver to take me to Admiralty House. I was greeted by the same chief who had met me that morning, and was then conducted to the back of the building and down a pathway which ended at the waterfront and where the admiral's barge was secured to a small dock. The barge was painted dark green and gleamed in the bright sunlight, reflecting the rippled waters of the small cove where she lay. Two highly polished brass dolphins stood on their tails and supported the cabin canopy, and her teak deck had been honed to a snowy white. The crew, all dressed in tropical whites, consisted of a petty officer coxswain, a bowman, and a stern sheet-man, all of whom were wearing white tennis shoes. My guide spoke briefly to the coxswain, who saluted me as I stepped over the side, while the bowman came ashore and brought my suitcase aboard. I suspect that none of them had been told who I was and were following the old naval adage that: 'when in doubt, if it moves, to be on the safe side, salute it'. Casting off we were soon clear of the small cove and skimming across the water towards the naval dockyard at Malabar. As the barge neared the dockyard I could see a nest of destroyers moored alongside the sea-wall, one of which had four funnels. The coxswain informed me that this ship was the one that he had been ordered to deliver me to and that she was one of the fifty destroyers traded for bases by President Roosevelt in September of 1940.

She was HMS *Buxton*, formerly USS *Edwards*, and had been commissioned into the Royal Navy at Halifax on October 8, 1940. However, due to serious defects preventing her from crossing the Atlantic, she had been assigned to local duties prior to being returned to Boston for a major refit. Making a sweeping arc, the barge came alongside a small accommodation ladder on her starboard side and the coxswain, having helped to hoist my suitcase inboard, returned to the wheel while I went up the ladder onto her quarterdeck. On reaching the deck I was met by a chief petty officer who informed me that he was the coxswain of the ship. He went on to say: "The ship is singled up and ready to sail sir, the captain is on the bridge and has asked me to welcome you aboard and escort you to the wardroom where he will join you later once the ship had cleared harbour."

I could sense that curiosity was getting the better of the chief as he said: "We didn't quite know who would be joining us sir. We only got a signal from the dockyard about an hour ago telling us to expect one civilian for passage to Halifax." I replied that I too had only known I would be sailing with them at some time around noon that day. To make him feel more at ease I stated it was my intention to join the Royal Navy and that the commander-in-chief had kindly allowed me to take passage in *Buxton* in order to join a ship bound for the UK. He then said: "So you've been to sea before. What size of ship have you served in?" When I told him I had sailed on a 3,000 ton freighter, he remarked that I would find it a little bit different in *Buxton,* whose displacement was slightly over 1,000 tons; according to him: "she would roll on wet grass." By the time we reached the wardroom he had wormed a great deal of information out of me and I could tell that he felt that he could let his guard down knowing that I was just a fifteen year old boy, wet behind the ears, and anxious to go to sea. After informing me that his special sea duty station required him to be on the wheel, his parting words were: "Well lad, all the best of luck when you join the Grey Funnel Line. You'll find it quite a change from what you're used to, but you'll get used to it." Not wishing to get in any ones way by going on deck, I stayed where I was and soon realized that we had slipped our lines and were underway as the deck began to vibrate when our screws started to turn.

An hour or so later one or two officers drifted in to the wardroom, but I buried myself in a magazine, too shy to start a conversation with them before being introduced properly. Eventually the captain arrived and those present rose as a handsome man in a lieutenant commander's uniform entered the room. Glancing around he spotted me and, crossing the room to where I was standing, extended his hand saying: "Welcome aboard. I am Lieutenant Commander Beatty and may I ask your name?" As he spoke I studied his vaguely familiar face sensing that we had met before. For a moment, I recalled the picture of a dashing British admiral with his cap worn at an angle, hands in his pockets with the thumbs out, which had hung on the wall in my bedroom at home; my boyhood hero, Admiral Earl Beatty. It then became clear that I was talking to his son, Lieutenant Commander Earl David Beatty, Royal Navy. I introduce myself and he drew up a chair, insisting that I tell him everything about myself; where was I born, who were my parents, where did they come from, where had I gone to school, why was I going to England, and why did I want to join the navy. When I had answered all his questions he introduced me to a young man, whom I discovered later to be the junior officer on board, and he instructed this individual to escort me to the ship's office in order to have the coxswain find me a berth. Before leaving, he apologised for not being able to offer me anything better than the lower mess deck for accommodation as there were no cabins available and the ship was carrying a full complement of ratings. He concluded by saying: "If you intend to enter *Conway* as a cadet, you might find it interesting if you were to stand a watch with one of my officers", an offer I was quick to accept.

The coxswain was able to find me an empty bunk, and having issued me with a blanket, led me to the forward mess deck where I met the senior rating, a leading seaman from St John's, Newfoundland by the name of Hudson. I soon learned that a large number of the ship's company were from Newfoundland which, at that time, was not a Canadian province and many of the island's fishermen were members of the RNVR. Most of these men had been taken into the navy as able seamen due to their previous occupation and had been sent to Halifax to join with other Royal Navy ratings from England to man the American 'four stackers'. My newfound messmates were very friendly and made me feel at home in their company. Having been an American ship, *Buxton* was not provided with hammock bars so everyone slept in a bunk. Both upper and lower bunks were suspended from the deck-head by chains and hung over the foot lockers running along the ship's hull. These lockers were fitted with leather cushions on which we sat to eat our meals at a table bolted to the deck amidships. Having previously visited British warships, I was aware of the sparse conditions under which the ratings lived, but I had only been aboard cruisers and battleships whose broadside messes were spacious and airy by comparison.

Built in 1918, *Buxton* was three hundred and four feet in length and only nine feet three inches in the beam, causing her to roll in the mildest of weather. With a wartime compliment of ten officers and one hundred and thirty-four men, the two seamen's mess decks with close to thirty men in each might be described as somewhat cramped. Situated only a few feet below the weather deck, the messes were subject to a torrent of cold salt water cascading down the hatch each time we shipped a green one. The result was that having been at sea no more than twelve hours, we had about four inches of dirty salt water sloshing around on the deck which became contaminated with dirty socks, slices of bread and other scraps of food, plus anything else that might have dropped off the mess table or a bunk. Making matters worse all dead lights and scuttles were securely shut at sea and the ventilation system was not up to modern standards. The further north we sailed, the colder it became, and before long the steam heat from the radiators, combined with damp clothing and stale air resulted in condensation forming on the deck head which dripped continuously.

On our first night at sea I learned that I would have to stand the middle watch on the bridge. When my messmates learned that I would have to spend four hours on the bridge, many of them opened their lockers and offered to lend or give me clothing to keep me warm. On closing up on the wing of the bridge after the watch was called, I was well bundled up wearing a borrowed toque, woollen jersey, and woollen mittens. I also had a towel wrapped around my neck and tucked in to my watch coat to prevent water trickling down my collar. There was little for me to do that first night, other than observe the routine procedure. First there was the report of the helmsman to the officer of the watch, stating his rank, name, and course being steered. Next followed reports of the look-outs as they were relieved, together with those of the signalman and the bridge messenger. In my case I was given a pair of binoculars and instructed to keep a sharp lookout from dead ahead to ninety degrees port. No one told me what I was to look out for, but I presumed it was either an enemy submarine, a periscope, or a torpedo (the fact that we might run into another vessel did not occur to me) so, to be on the safe side I questioned the petty officer of the watch who said: "Report anything unusual that you might see". In any event the night was so dark that I had trouble seeing even the eye of the ship as it rose and fell in the north Atlantic swell. Halfway through the watch the bridge messenger was dispatched to the galley to fetch a 'fanny of kye'. This was my introduction to 'pussers' kye', which is the lower deck slang name for hot cocoa. Believe me, there is nothing in the entire world more welcome than a hot cup of 'kye' during the middle watch on a cold night. Shortly before 04:00, the morning watch was called and I was able to go below and crawl into my bunk, only to be awakened after two hours of sleep when the hands were called. After a breakfast of scrambled eggs, sausages, cold toast and strawberry jam, washed down with lashings of sweet hot tea, we scrubbed out the mess deck before being detailed off for a variety of jobs such as cleaning the heads, polishing brass, and other mundane chores.

Because we were in three watches I was free until 12:00 when the afternoon watch was called. Although the sun was shining and the sky was clear, I found the north-west wind bitterly cold on the open bridge. Fortunately, the officer of the watch suggested that I go to the wheelhouse and take a lesson from the helmsman on how to steer. This I found very much to my liking for not only was I out of the wind, but for about an hour or two I was allowed to take the wheel under his watchful eye until 16:00 when his relief arrived to stand the first dog watch. As we sat around the mess table that evening I engaged in a long conversation with one of the crew who hailed from Newfoundland. He was eighteen years of age and showed great interest when I produced my prized Horner harmonica purchased a year or two earlier. After I played a couple of tunes he asked if he could play, and demonstrated his expertise. As he played a number of seamen in the mess began to sing the bawdy lyrics to mess deck songs containing words not normally heard around a Boy Scouts' camp fire. My young friend told me that my harmonica was the best he had ever seen and asked if I would consider selling it. I was reluctant to do so until he offered me ten dollars for both the harmonica and the olive-green gabardine suite given to me by my uncle. I could not wear the suite on the ship and was not anxious to keep it. What I needed was warm clothing to make me less conspicuous on watch. To clinch the deal he offered to throw in an old uniform jumper and a pair of bell bottoms. As I already had been given a blue jersey by a member of the crew, all that I now required was a seaman's cap, blue jean collar, and black silk. Having managed to acquire these articles over a few days and having been assured that I would not be breaking the law by being dressed as a sailor, this is what I wore from that day forward.

Being dressed as a seaman was to create a number of problems when I eventually left the *Buxton*. Few merchant seamen wore a uniform but those employed by the larger shipping companies such as Cunard and P&O did so, and it was identical to that worn in the Royal Navy. The majority of merchant seamen wore civilian clothing and those officers who wore a uniform were normally required by their employers to do so.

Twenty-four hours before arriving in Halifax we experienced a severe winter storm which produced high seas, gale force winds, and blowing snow. The temperature fell to below freezing and the sea breaking over the fo'c'sle coated the ship with ice. Living conditions on the mess deck, which were not ideal at the best of times, became intolerable. The mess deck was awash with six inches of dirty water, the air was foul, and it was impossible to stand upright without support. For a number of reasons the galley was unable to provide a hot meal so all we had to eat was cheese, corned beef, or sardine sandwiches. As the British sailor finds it difficult to survive without tea, somehow we always managed to have a large fanny of this strong, sickly sweet liquid available. Due to the roll of the ship we were unable to place the fanny on the deck or the mess table so it was suspended from an eyebolt in the deck head by a length of rope which caused it to swing through a 30 to 40 degree arc as we rolled. On passing through the mess one had to avoid being hit by it.

On the day of the storm I had the first watch and while conditions on the bridge were both cold and wet, it was nonetheless good to get away from the foul air on the mess deck. Four hours of hanging onto a stanchion while water trickles down your neck can be enough for anyone however, and by midnight I was looking forward to the watch changing. When my relief failed to show up by ten to fifteen minutes after midnight I was about to speak to the petty officer of the watch when a hooded figure climbed onto the bridge and stood beside me. Thinking that this was my relief, I turned and cursed him for being late, only to find that I was speaking to the captain. More than a little embarrassed, I blurted out: "Sorry sir, I thought you were my relief", to which he replied: "Is that you Jones? Haven't you been relieved yet?" Calling the bridge messenger, he ordered him to go below to find the absent seaman. Fifteen minutes later a sleepy individual arrived on deck and I was able to leave the bridge to the sound of the duty petty officer raking the poor matelot over the coals.

Early on the morning of March 20, 1941, we entered Halifax harbour and immediately set about clearing the ice from the superstructure. The entire ship was encased in about an inch of it, and we had to break it loose using chipping hammers. The two bulkhead doors leading to the fo'c'sle were frozen solid and in order to berth the ship the mooring party had to use the forward magazine hatch to access the fo'c'sle. Leave was granted to the port watch that night from 16:30 to 24:00 and, on checking with the coxswain, I was told that I would be allowed to go ashore but had to be back aboard by 22:00. The young seaman who had purchased my harmonica offered to accompany me and together we walked all the way into town. With only a few dollars in my pocket I thought that we might see a movie and later find a restaurant to have a decent meal. Expecting Halifax to be similar to Vancouver was a big mistake. The movie *Gone with the Wind* was showing at the Capitol Theatre, but on locating the cinema, we soon changed our mind as there was a very long queue of people waiting to buy tickets.

The streets of Halifax were crowded with servicemen, all wandering around aimlessly looking for some place to go or something to do. We then decided to visit the Salvation Army and learned that there was a dance that night at the Masonic Hall on Salter Street. However, on arrival it was already filled to capacity. My companion, claiming to know Halifax very well, suggested that we visit a small Chinese cafe on Lower Water Street where he was certain we could purchase a bottle of bootleg whisky. On our way we happened to pass a tattoo parlour on Hollis Street and I decided to get my first tattoo. On leaving the shop thirty minutes later I proudly displayed on my left forearm, a naval white ensign, the emblem under which I was to sail for the next nine years. On entering the Chinese cafe we ordered coffee and when the waiter brought our drinks my 'newfie' friend asked if we could get something a little stronger to go with it. Our waiter informed us that it would cost ten dollars, and that we would not be allowed to stay and consume it on the premises. We paid in advance and he disappeared behind a curtain, returning a few minutes later with a 'mickey' of rye wrapped in a brown paper bag.

Having acquired two paper coffee cups from the counter on leaving, we located a stretch of poorly-lit sidewalk, and poured ourselves a drink of straight rye. The liquor burned as it went down but provided some warmth. The temperature was close to freezing and I was not wearing an overcoat. At this point, we decided to return to the ship, having spent what little money we had on our bottle of rye, and getting tattooed. Sharing the remains of the rye as we walked back to the dockyard the liquor had started to take effect on me. Disposing of the empty bottle before going through the gate, I found myself having difficulty navigating the numerous pot holes which, filled with water during the day, now had a thin coating of ice. Breaking through the ice on more than one occasion my shoes were soaked and my feet frozen by the time we reached the brow and climbed aboard. The quartermaster informed us that the ship was at four hours notice for sea and the following morning when the hands were called, we were told we would be sailing at 09:00. Secured for sea by 08:30, special sea duty men were piped a few minutes later and we slipped our lines at 09:00. It was March 22, 1941, and *Buxton* had been given the task of providing close escort to the battleship *Royal Sovereign*, who was the covering escort to convoy HX-116. This convoy of twenty-eight ships, having sailed the previous day at 11:00, was already at sea and escorted by the armed merchant cruiser, *Ascania*. In the early months of 1941, German surface ships were considered an even greater threat to our convoys than the U-boat, and the Royal Navy had taken to sailing a capital ship as a covering escort to a convoy in the event that merchant ships were attacked by a surface raider such as *Bismark*, *Scharnhorst*, or *Tirpitz*.

On leaving harbour, *Buxton* took up station on the starboard quarter of the battleship providing those of us on the upper deck a magnificent view of the great ship as she began to bury her fo'c'sle in the broad Atlantic swell. That afternoon, while acting as an extra look-out on the bridge, a lamp on her signal platform began to wink. Picking up his Aldis lamp in order to reply, the yeoman turned and, handing me a signal pad and pencil, curtly said: "Hey lad, make yourself useful and write this down." Somewhat apprehensive and not fully understanding what he was saying, I began to write the words of the signal he was reading. I must have taken it down correctly however, as he seemed satisfied when I handed him the signal pad. Later that night we parted company with *Royal Sovereign* and by the following morning were alongside our berth in Halifax. On the morning following our return to harbour I had fallen in with the hands as usual and was employed on the upper deck with a party of seamen, chipping paint under the watchful eye of a leading hand, when the captain came on deck. He was on his way ashore when he spotted me and exclaimed: "Jones, are you still with us? Has no one made arrangements for you to leave the ship?" When I replied that no one had, he sent for the coxswain and instructed him to contact HMCS *Stadacona* in order to have transport sent to deliver me to the barracks. Later that afternoon, having packed my belongings and said good-bye to my friends on the mess deck, a truck arrived at the jetty, and shortly thereafter, deposited me at the main gate of HMCS *Stadacona*, in front of the regulating office.

CHAPTER VII
Halifax

At the main gate of *Stadacona* stood an armed guard who completely ignored me as I removed my kit from the back of the truck. As the truck drove off a large man in the uniform of a petty officer with a chain around his neck and wearing a pair of green gaiters appeared and, in a loud voice said: "Get that g.... d... bag off the road and report to the RPO in the office on the double." Leaving my kit on the sidewalk, I entered the building where a leading seaman relieved me of the envelope that had been given to me by the coxswain of *Buxton*. Handing it to a chief petty officer, he returned to his typewriter and took no further notice of me while I stood silently waiting for some reaction from the chief. Rising from his chair, he came over to me and said: "So, you're here to join the navy. How old are you lad?" to which I promptly replied: "Seventeen, sir". Glaring at me, he growled: "Don't call me sir, address me as chief." My decision for claiming to be seventeen was made on the spur of the moment and was prompted by the fact that I was not certain the navy could, or would, get me across the Atlantic to join *Conway*.

Having arrived at the gate of a naval establishment on draft from a British warship in the harbour, it occurred to me that perhaps I should consider joining the Royal Canadian Navy instead of continuing to try to make my way to Britain. The fact that I was wearing a naval uniform would require some form of explanation, and this I could provide by stating that I had seen service in the Merchant Navy. Shortly after this initial interview the officer of the watch arrived in the regulating office where I was once again required to provide details of my voyage from Bermuda and how I managed to secure a passage in a ship to Halifax. That evening I found myself assigned to a class of new entry ratings in the barracks, at which time I was issued a set of bedding. After breakfast the following morning, we were marched off to the sick bay to begin our joining routine, starting with a medical and dental examination.

That afternoon we were issued with a complete kit and a hammock and spent the balance of the day marking our clothing and being instructed in the correct way to wear the uniform. We were also taught the art of slinging and lashing a hammock. The next day, during drill on the parade square, our petty officer was interrupted by a messenger who stated that our divisional officer wished to see me.

On being ushered into his office, he began the conversation by asking me to relate once more the story of how I had joined *Buxton* in Bermuda. Having done so, he then asked me to tell him my correct age with an emphasis on the word <u>correct</u>. It was now apparent that somehow he had discovered my true age so I admitted to being only fifteen years and six moths and enquired from him as to how he had learned the truth. He then told me that he was aware that I had tried to join the navy in Vancouver the previous December and been turned down. He was also aware that I had tried to join the army, only to be rejected again, and concluded by stating that I could not be accepted into the RCN for the same reason. Knowing that Canada had previously accepted boys for training as visual signalmen, I asked him if it was possible for me to join that branch, but was informed that this avenue was now closed. In desperation, and in one last appeal, I asked if it would be possible for me to remain in the Canadian Navy and be transferred to the Royal Navy on loan pending my seventeenth birthday. To this suggestion he replied that he would see what could be done, and the interview ended with no firm decision having been made. I returned to the new entry class expecting to be booted out after only two days in the service. The next day I was again called upon to report to the divisional office who then ordered me to return to my quarters and pack my gear as I was about to be drafted to a ship for passage to England. Having informed my instructor of this turn of events, I was dismissed from his class and returned to the barracks to collect my bag and hammock. That afternoon, shortly after the lunch hour I mustered outside the regulating office where I was handed a large envelope addressed to the Master-at-Arms, HMS *Rajputana*, and instructed to load my gear in the back of a van which was to transport me to the dockyard.

On our arrival in the dockyard where *Rajputana* was moored, I stood for a while at the foot of her accommodation ladder and gazed up at her bridge and superstructure. At 17,000 tons I found her immense size to be somewhat intimidating and hesitated for a moment before starting up the gangway with my kit bag on my shoulder. On reaching the promenade deck I was met by a rating who turned out to be the quartermaster on duty. Handing in my draft papers, I returned to the dock to retrieve my hammock, and on regaining the upper deck, was met by the petty officer of the watch who instructed me to follow him below. In the ship's office I was greeted by a second petty officer who, on opening the envelope that I had been given in *Stadacona*, sent a rating to fetch the master-at-arms.

In due course the master-at-arms, Chief Petty Officer Dix, entered the office and, on reading the contents of the envelope, it became obvious that he was annoyed to discover that I was only fifteen years of age. Because of my age I was considered to be a boy rating and the problem was that *Rajputana* did not have any boys in her complement. Where was I to be accommodated? As Chief Petty Officer Dix correctly pointed out, *Stadacona* should have drafted me to a Royal Navy battleship as they carried boy seamen in their complements and it would have been logical to have me take passage on such a vessel. Eventually the matter was settled and the decision made that I should be accommodated in the chiefs and petty officers' mess. My name was added to the watch and quarters bill as follows:

Watch	=	Port
Part of watch	=	1st.Part
Mess	=	C & PO's
Action Station	=	Ammunition party #2 - 6" gun
Abandon Ship station	=	#2 boat, starboard side
Special duty	=	Dayman, C & PO's messman

Having settled into my new surroundings, I was shown where to sling my hammock and introduced to a 'killick' steward who was my new boss. That evening in the mess I overheard a number of the members discussing the news that the Canadian armed yacht HMCS *Otter* had been lost that day not far off Halifax harbour. Details of her loss were not available but it was rumoured that there had been no survivors. Much later, I was to learn that *Otter* had been destroyed by an accidental explosion followed by fire and two officers and seventeen men had lost their lives.

During the morning hours of the following day, a large number of merchant ships steamed out of Bedford Basin on their way through the harbour to the open sea and at 15:30 on March 27, 1941, we slipped from our berth and headed for the gates. I learned that on the previous day prior to my joining the ship, we had embarked a large number of Air Force personnel. Products of the Commonwealth Air Training Plan, these newly qualified pilots consisted of Canadians, Australians, and New Zealanders, together with a good number of British boys. There were even two or three Americans among them who had crossed the border to join the RCAF. Each man, having been issued with a straw-filled mattress on coming aboard, they slept on the deck in what had once been the ballroom in the ship prior to her having been converted to an armed merchant cruiser. During the day they spent a great deal of time playing table tennis in a room that had once been the main lounge. Once we were out of sight of land, the Air Force boys seldom ventured out on the upper deck but, off Chebucto Head shortly after leaving Halifax, word spread through the ship that the large French submarine *Surcouf* was to be seen off our starboard quarter, and along with many of our own ship's company, a number of the air crew boys came on deck to have a look at her. At that time the *Surcouf* was the largest submarine in the world. Built in 1929, she was of 4,300 tons displacement, carried a crew of 150, and mounted two 8 inch guns on her casing. In addition she had a small seaplane housed in a hanger abaft her conning tower. As we watched her sailing past at about 19 knots, rumour had it that she was to form part of our convoy escort, but on the following morning she was not in sight and in her place was a much smaller submarine flying the White

Ensign. This vessel was the British submarine *Tribune* and, together with *Rajputana*, we were the sole escort for the 43 merchant ships in our convoy.

Rajputana was built in 1926 by Harland & Wolff of Greenock, Scotland, and owned by the Pacific and Orient Line. She was originally employed on the United Kingdom Bombay mail service, but just prior to the outbreak of war was in service as a passenger liner on runs to Japan. In September 1939, she was in Yokohama and on being taken up from trade by the Admiralty, was ordered to Esquimalt British Columbia to be converted to an armed merchant cruiser. Armed with eight ancient 6-inch, two 3-inch, anti-aircraft guns, and a Lewis machine gun on each wing of her bridge, she also carried two depth charge chutes, together with four depth charges for each chute. Her after funnel had been removed and most of her passenger cabins and interior fittings had been taken out. Throughout the interior of the ship were thousands of forty-gallon empty oil drums shored up by timbers to provide buoyancy should she be torpedoed or hit by enemy gunfire below the waterline. Manned in part by her original crew (many of whom had joined the navy at the time of her conversion) there were also a large number of ratings from the Royal Fleet Reserve, a few Royal Navy ratings, and some RNR officers. The number of our convoy was HX-117, the letters HX indicating that we were a fast convoy, although our average speed was only eight knots, and steaming at the head of the centre column was the commodore's ship, SS *Sicilian Prince*. The convoy commodore was Commodore R.A. Hornell, RNR. The weather for that time of year in the North Atlantic was relatively mild but three days after leaving Halifax we encountered dense fog for a short while. On our fifth day at sea we had a little excitement when smoke was spotted on the horizon. The ship went to action stations and left the convoy at full speed to investigate, while *Tribune* submerged in the event that the unidentified vessel happened to be an enemy surface raider. It transpired that it was a British ship sailing independently and, after exchanging signals, we quickly rejoined the convoy.

The following day our lookout spotted a drifting lifeboat and our course was altered in order to inspect it. On reaching the boat we found the surrounding sea littered with flotsam but the boat was empty and finding no sign of life, we once again rejoined the convoy. Ten days out of Halifax we encountered heavy seas that scattered the convoy. When the storm abated we spent the next twenty-four hours rounding up the merchantmen and managed to find them all with the exception of one, a Dutch ship by the name of *Prins William II* with a crew of thirty-four.

Eleven days and sixteen hours after sailing from Halifax we arrived at the rendezvous position and were met by escorts from the United Kingdom who took over our job leaving us free to break off and head for Iceland. We had covered 2,196 nautical miles with the loss of only one ship that had straggled. After the war I learned that *Prins William II* had been torpedoed on April 8, 1941, in position 59.50. north and 24.25 west, with the loss of twelve lives. Working up to 19 knots, we set course for Reykjavik, arriving on the morning of April 10, 1941. Shortly after anchoring in Reykjavik, the tug *Jokul* came alongside and transferred our Air Force passengers to a troopship in the harbour. I expected to be disembarked with them on arrival in Iceland, but on asking Chief Dix if this was to be the case, he said: "You'll probably be drafted to the accommodation ship HMS *Baldur* later this afternoon for onward passage to England". Early that evening a small tanker came alongside to refuel our bunkers, but there was no further word as to when I might be expected to leave the ship.

The following morning I was surprised to learn that we had been ordered to sea and at dawn we got under way. On leaving harbour and setting a westerly course I began to think that I might very well be on a return voyage to Halifax. However, shortly after sailing word filtered down to the mess deck that the ship had been instructed to carry out a search for an enemy merchantman suspected of trying to break out in to the Atlantic through the Denmark Strait. I was assured by Chief Dix that we would probably be returning to Reykjavik within a day or two. I have been unable to determine if the report of an enemy ship attempting to break out in to the Atlantic was a ruse by the Germans intended to bring a British ship to that area, but I have since learned that three U-boats were dispatched from a French port on a special mission to the Denmark Strait to hunt for British auxiliary cruisers. One of these Boats was the U-108 commanded by Kapitanleutnant Klaus Scholtz and, after our departure from Iceland at around 06:00 he spotted *Rajputana's* funnel smoke to the north-west of his patrol area. Trying to manoeuvre into firing position, he was thwarted by our constant change of speed and course. At about 09:45 two torpedoes were fired at us at a range of 2,000 meters, but both missed the target.

The following day, April 12, 1941, at 22:46, and 22:48, two single torpedoes were fired at us from a range of 1,000 meters and again, both missed. Finally, on Sunday April 13, 1941, at 06:15, while we were on a reciprocal course, U-108 again sighted us and submerged to attack. A single torpedo fired at 06:00 at a range of 8,000 meters again missed. A second fired three minutes later with the range closing struck the ship on the port side, amidships, causing her to stop dead in the water and take on a list to port of about ten degrees. Having expended five of his torpedoes, Klaus Scholtz had finally scored with his sixth and earned himself the Knights Cross with Oak Leaves for his endeavour.

During the first watch I had turned into my hammock which was slung outside the entrance to the chiefs and petty officers' mess, expecting to be called at 07:00 to prepare breakfast for the morning watchmen coming off duty and the forenoon watchmen getting ready to relieve them at 08:00. Just before dawn I was awakened by a tremendous explosion followed by a blast of air and a ringing sensation in my left ear. For a short moment there was an eerie silence and for a moment I thought I had gone deaf. Gradually I regained my hearing and could make out the sound of the emergency alarm bells ringing. All lights below deck had gone out and the passageway was in complete darkness. Swinging out of my hammock, I groped around for my clothes and while trying to get dressed, was almost bowled over by a number of men racing aft to man their action stations. Shortly after the emergency lights came on and I made my way forward to join up with the ammunition party of #2-6 inch gun. There was nothing for us to do at first and no one in our party seemed to know what was happening. The ship had taken on a slight list to port but as this did not increase as time went on it caused us little alarm. A few moments later our gun fired and continued to fire at erratic intervals for about an hour or more.

We found out later that the U-boat had shown her periscope and that the 6 inch guns had been ordered to open fire, although the prospect of scoring a hit on such a small target was highly unlikely. The ship had been at action stations for almost an hour when the petty officer in charge of our group sent me down to the mess to see if I could obtain anything to eat or drink for none of us had been able to have any breakfast. It was while I was down below that a second torpedo was fired, this time hitting us on the starboard side. I was later told that the U-boat had fired a spread of three torpedoes, two of which had hit, but I can recall only hearing one explosion. For a while it appeared that we might still be able to stay afloat, but with the bulkhead between the engine room and #3 hold gone, the ship was now open to the sea for nearly half her length and she rapidly began to sink. It had been almost three hours since the first torpedo hit us, but due to the thousands of empty drums that had been placed in the ship, we had managed to stay afloat. Now that there was a gaping hole in her hull, many of these drums broke loose and were floating on the surface of the sea. At around 09:00 the order came down from the bridge to abandon ship, and leaving my station I made my way up to #2 boat starboard side only to find that it had already been lowered and that #1 boat had capsized on entering the water.

I was later to learn that most of those who had been in #1 boat were lost. A number of other lifeboats were in the process of being lowered, and I made my way aft in the hope of getting into one of them. Our list to port created a problem for the lowering of boats on the starboard side, and having seen what happened to #1 boat, I was somewhat reluctant to leave the ship that way. While contemplating my next move a group of men, who were attempting to launch one of our life rafts, called out to me to lend a hand. On joining them we succeeded in cutting it loose and dropping it in to the sea which was not more than about ten feet below the level of the deck. Fortunately one crew member had held onto the raft's painter which prevented it from being swept away from the ships side. Securing the painter to one of the guardrail stanchions one-by-one we went over the side using the rope to reach the raft. As it came my turn to leave the deck I managed to work my way down the rope with little difficulty and, on feeling my foot touch the raft, let go of the rope. At that moment the raft rose on the swell and suddenly surged forward causing me to drop into the sea. Luck was with me however, as I entered the water abaft the raft rather than alongside it where I might have been crushed against the ship's side. Clinging to a lifeline I was in the water for a minute or two before someone on the raft gave a hand to haul me inboard where I sat shivering like a drowned rat for some time before one of the seamen took off his watch coat and wrapped it around me as he listened to my teeth chatter. In retrospect it might have been wise to have stayed in the water and clung to a life line as the water temperature was at least four degrees warmer than the atmosphere. This fact did not occur to me and for the next three hours I huddled in the centre of the raft and shivered. Our raft was less than a hundred yards away from the ship's side when someone shouted: "She's going", and as we watched her bow began to rise slowly to a height of about eighty feet still listing slightly to port. Moments later the entire mass slid quickly back into the sea and disappeared below the surface.

Earlier that day, when we had first been hit, the sea had been relatively calm although there had been a long ocean swell running. On abandoning ship, there was a light north-east wind blowing but it was the long swell that caused us the most discomfort. Unlike the lifeboats that could keep their bow on to the seas by using a sea anchor, our raft had a high freeboard and was at the mercy of the wind and waves. One moment we would be lifted high on the crest of the swell and the next would find us falling like an elevator into the trough, causing many of us to become sick. Because of our high freeboard we tended to drift away from the other boats quite rapidly and in a very short while we lost sight of them. For the next four hours we drifted aimlessly not knowing whether we had been able to transmit a distress signal before sinking. At a later date it was disclosed that we had been able to send a signal at 07:00, which had been received by the Admiralty in London, and that we had been advised that help was on the way. Despite the fact that I had wrapped myself in the coat that some kind soul had provided, I continued to suffer from the biting cold. Although I had been in the water for only a minute or two the clothes I had been wearing were soaked through to my skin. The coat gave me some protection from the wind but my hands and face were exposed and felt as though they were frozen. It was my feet, however, that caused me the most discomfort. My boots had filled with water, and unable to stand or move around, they gradually became numb from the ankles down and I lost all feeling in my toes. Some two hours later, as I shivered in misery, I heard some of the fellows talking about having seen an aeroplane circling above and although I never saw it, a RAF Sunderland on patrol out of Iceland had spotted us.

Not long after, two ships were spotted on the horizon. They turned out to be the RN destroyer, *Legion*, and the Polish destroyer, *Piorun*, dispatched by the Admiralty to go to our assistance. *Legion* went by our raft and was almost out of sight before turning to starboard and coming toward us. Stopping on our windward side, she created a lee and on drifting down wind to our raft we could see that she had lowered scrambling nets on her port side. Despite the swell that was running, most of us were able to climb aboard on our own but two of our company were unable to do so and had to be assisted by members of *Legion's* ship's company. At this point my feet were so painful that I was having a hard time standing, but with the aid of two seamen was taken below to one of the mess decks and stretched out on the cushions covering the lockers. Told to shuck my clothing, I was given a wool blanket that I wrapped around my body. In time I gradually stopped shaking. Someone gave me a cigarette and the warmth of the mess deck started to take effect, causing me to become drowsy. I had dropped off to sleep when the coxswain of *Legion*, accompanied by the medical officer came into the mess to check on the survivors. Each man in turn was interviewed by the doctor and on his orders, allowed a tot of rum. After drinking my tot I found myself unable to stay awake and fell into a deep sleep as the ship worked up to 36 knots on her way back to Reyjkavik, some 150 miles from where we had gone down.

The Armed Merchant Cruiser,
HMS Rajputana, sinking in mid-Atlantic
after being torpedoed by U-108 on April 13, 1941   *London Illustrated News*

SS Copeland, the convoy rescue ship in which
I sailed from Iceland to Scotland as a
survivor of the *Rajputana*   *The Macpherson collection*

From this point on my recollection of what happened over the next three days is somewhat hazy. *Legion*, who had picked up 232 survivors, arrived in Reykjavik around midnight and, in the early hours of the morning, a small drifter came alongside to disembark most of them. Those of us who were wounded or otherwise injured were taken to the base accommodation ship HMS *Baldur*, in whose sick bay I found myself the following day. On examination by a medical officer, it was found that both my feet were badly swollen to the point that I was unable to walk without assistance. My left ear was quite painful, but it was my feet that caused the most concern. No one said so at the time, but I think it was feared that I had lost the circulation in both feet which could lead to gangrene. I was told that I would be transferred to a vessel leaving for England, and shortly after I was transferred to the rescue ship SS *Copeland*, which sailed for the Clyde on April 15, 1941.

While I was in *Copeland* I met a merchant seaman who had survived the sinking of the Dutch vessel *Saleier*. She had been torpedoed on April 10, 1941, by the German submarine, *U-52*. The story of how he and fifty-nine other members of the *Saleier's* crew had been rescued by the American destroyer USS *Niblack* on the morning of April 11, 1941, and the subsequent attack on what appeared to be a U-boat by the *Niblack*, was of great interest to all of us who heard it. The fact that an American destroyer had come to the aid of an allied merchant ship, and attacked what was known to be a German submarine responsible for the sinking, was surprising. Those of us who heard the story related by the Dutch seaman were encouraged to believe that it would only be a matter of time before the US would enter the war. Little did we know that we would have to wait for Japan to fire the first shots at Pearl Harbour before we could count on the US joining in the 'fight'.

Three days after being transferred to *Copeland* we arrived in Greenock, Scotland, and from the stretcher I was on, caught my first glimpse of the sheep-studded green fields of that country. Of the twelve officers and eighty ratings aboard who were survivors of *Rajputana* all, except stretcher patients, were placed in regular compartments on a train bound for Glasgow. A special coach with a red cross painted on the side was used for the stretcher patients, which were stacked two high on either side of the centre aisle.

On arriving in Glasgow Central Station, the stretcher patients were taken to a platform where a train was standing waiting to depart for London. There was a lengthy wait on the platform before boarding the train during which time two elderly ladies wearing uniforms of the Red Cross and Salvation Army respectively, visited us. They were handing out small cloth bags containing items that most of us were only too pleased to receive. From the Red Cross I was given a tooth-brush and a tube of toothpaste, together with a compact shaving kit. From the Salvation Army I received a small copy of the New Testament (unfortunately <u>not</u> appreciated at the time), a pair of heavy woollen socks (which I could not wear), and a small note pad and pencil, together with three stamped envelopes. In addition to these gifts they provided us steaming hot, sweet tea, and sticky buns, both of which were greatly appreciated. Before being taken aboard the train a petty officer wearing an arm band indicating that he was a member of the Regulating Transport Office, questioned each of us as to the name of our home depot. Having overheard one of the others reply: "Devonport", I gathered that he was referring to the three main naval bases in England so, when the same question was asked of me, I promptly replied: "Portsmouth". He then questioned me as to my official number, which I was unable to give him as I never recall having been given one. On explaining the circumstances that led to me being aboard *Rajputana*, together with the fact that any documents relating to my being transferred to the RN from the RCN had gone down with the ship, he appeared satisfied and moved on after pinning a tag on my blanket which read 'PORTSMOUTH'. Little did I know that as of that moment, I had joined the Royal Navy and was now a member of the 'Grey Funnel Line'. I was later to discover that my certificate of service in the Royal Navy indicated my actual date of joining to be April 18, 1941, the day I landed in England and five days <u>after</u> *Rajputana* was torpedoed.

Having been duly documented and tagged, our train left Glasgow for London that evening and, after making numerous stops during the night, finally came to a prolonged halt just outside London in the early morning. After sitting motionless for almost an hour, the conductor came through to report the cause of the delay. We were told that the city had suffered a major air raid during the night and that a stick of bombs had destroyed the tracks, which were being repaired before we could proceed. It was early that afternoon before we pulled in to Euston Station where we were then taken by ambulance to a large building to spend the night before continuing to Portsmouth the following day. Judging from the number of army uniforms in sight, it appeared that we were in some form of regimental barracks, but I never did find out the name of the place before leaving the next morning for Waterloo Station.

Having had nothing to eat since leaving Glasgow, we were fed by the army and later on, as a precaution against an air raid that night, were moved to the basement of the building. It had been a long day and having been given medication to relieve the ache in my ear, it did not take long for me to fall asleep. An hour or two later I was awakened by the wail of air raid sirens followed a short while later by the sound of loud explosions. As this was my first experience of an enemy raid, I did not know the difference between the sound of an exploding bomb and anti-aircraft gunfire. As I lay awake in the darkened room I had visions of the building receiving a direct hit and being buried in the ruins. From time-to-time there would be the sound of an extra large explosion and the entire building would shake, scaring me half to death. Eventually the noise subsided, punctuated by an occasional distant explosion, and in the early morning, having fallen asleep for the second time, we were awakened by the welcome sound of the 'all clear' siren. Breakfast was served by the army medics and consisted of oatmeal porridge, sausage, eggs, marmalade, toast, and tea, after which we were taken by ambulance to Waterloo Station to board a train for Portsmouth. It was interesting to look out the window of the ambulance at the Londoners as they made their way to work that morning. The sidewalks were littered with shards of glass and our vehicle had to make a number of detours due to what appeared to be broken water mains. Despite the disruption in their daily lives, and the events of the previous night, the citizens of London were going about their business on that sunny morning in what appeared to be their normal manner. Professional men in bowler hats and pin-striped suits, elderly ladies shopping for groceries, navvies leaning on their shovels having a cigarette, and London policemen walking the beat wearing their traditional helmets, were all calmly picking their way past the shattered store fronts and debris littered sidewalks. The scene was one that had been described previously in the newspapers and on the radio, but now I was witnessing it with my own eyes. Somehow it left one with a mixed feeling of pride and confidence in the people of that tight little island.

There were ambulances waiting to meet our train as it pulled into Portsmouth Station and we were taken to the sick bay at the naval barracks, a short trip of about fifteen minutes. After having been examined by the doctor and allocated a bed in one of the wards, I was again moved to a section of the vast underground shelter that had been tunnelled under the parade ground in the barracks. Considered to be safe from almost everything except a direct hit, these tunnels were where the majority of the barracks personnel slept at night during the height of the blitz. Each evening after supper these shelters would fill up with men carrying their hammocks and spreading bedding out on the wooden bunks that had been built two high along the corridors. Cold and damp even during daylight hours, it was a miserable place to spend the night, but far safer than the barrack buildings on the surface, and that night was no exception.

On my third night in England, and for the second night in a row, I was to experience a massive air raid. Having listened to explosions all night making sleep impossible, we emerged the following morning to find that a large bomb had hit what had been the chiefs and petty officers' mess. The same bomb had caused the western half of the sick bay to fall, leaving the interior of the three story building exposed, very much like the cutaway of a child's doll house. Rescue crews were at work digging for survivors of the mess where it had been reported that a number of men had taken shelter under a billiard table and been trapped when the building collapsed. The exposed side of the sick bay was now protected by a huge sheet made from about fifty blankets pinned together. They were suspended from the roof and now hung down the side of the building in an attempt to keep out the wind and rain. The nightly raids on Portsmouth were devastating. Large areas of the city had been reduced to rubble, particularly in the vicinity of the naval barracks and the dockyard. It was obvious that if the raids were to continue, large numbers of men would have to be evacuated and among the first to go were the sick and wounded.

That afternoon I was on my way to Haslar Royal Naval Hospital, located in Gosport, across the harbour from Portsmouth which had been built in 1746. When completed, it was not only the largest naval hospital in the world, but also the largest building constructed of brick in Europe. On the admitting examination I was found to have a serious infection of my inner ear resulting from a perforated ear drum. My feet, which had caused me so much pain and discomfort, were gradually returning to normal and, three days after undergoing surgery on my ear, I was able to get around on crutches. A day or so later I was shipped off to Park Prewett Military Hospital located in the small town of Basingstoke where I was to spend the next four weeks before regaining the use of my feet and during which time my ear gradually healed.

As a hospital, Park Prewett was one of the best. Originally a civilian hospital, it had been taken over by the military after the outbreak of war but continued to be staffed by civilian doctors and nurses, with the exception of a small number of navy and army personnel required for administrative duties. This meant that the rigid discipline found in service establishments was noticeably absent. The hospital was located in the beautiful county of North Hampshire, a short distance from Aldershot, which lay to the east. The buildings stood on spacious grounds over-looking the market town of Basingstoke set in a small valley to the south. The green fields of the surrounding countryside were studded with small farms, each separated by neatly trimmed hedges. To the west of the hospital, and hidden behind a thick stand of trees, was an RAF station home to a squadron of *Spitfires*. From our ward on the third floor we could hear the sound of the fighters on the airfield as they warmed up preparing to take off, and moments later we would watch as they rose above the tree tops to close up in formation before heading south towards the channel. In this peaceful country setting far removed from the horrors of war it was hard to believe that only a few short miles away the people of Portsmouth, Plymouth, London, and other cities were facing the nightly enemy raids.

One afternoon from the window in our ward the harsh realities of war were brought home to us as we watched the *Spitfires* returning to base. There was a young nurse at the hospital named Joyce whose boy friend was one of the pilots stationed at the nearby base. A few months before my arrival at Park Prewett they had met in a pub in Basingstoke, became engaged, and were planning a summer wedding. Joyce was a beautiful young girl of about twenty and loved by everyone who knew her. We were all aware of her relationship to the young airman and of the fact that on the days that his squadron was in the air, he could be counted on to buzz the hospital while returning to base; his way of letting her know that he had returned safely from his mission. If Joyce was on duty she would run to the window and watch as the fighters prepared to land. Invariably one would break formation and make a pass over the hospital, its wings moving from side-to-side as it zoomed by, before climbing again into formation prior to landing.

One fateful afternoon, Joyce was on duty in our ward when we heard the drone of the fighters returning. As she ran to the window her fiancé's plane swooped low over the building, but instead of climbing at the end of his shallow dive, his plane rolled to the right and side-slipped into the ground. Moments later we heard an explosion, followed by a thin column of smoke rising into the sky. There was deathly silence in the ward as Joyce stood by the window, and without a word and with tears in her eyes, she turned and walked out of the room. Two days later those of us who were allowed to leave the hospital grounds were given permission to attend the funeral which was held at the local parish church.

Of the six or more patients in our ward, the two who occupied the beds on either side of me (whose names I will not disclose) turned out to be quite interesting. The one to my right was an engine room artificer and a member of the submarine branch. He was suffering from chronic sinusitis and spent most of his time bemoaning the fact that he might have to leave submarines and be forced to transfer to general service. His other complaint was that he had married the day before being admitted to hospital and had therefore been unable to consummate the marriage. Those of us who were privy to this information were most sympathetic and, as his wife had taken a room in a local hotel in order to visit him each day, we decided to help out. After morning rounds on a Sunday, patients were left more or less to their own devices. Those who had afternoon passes could go into town and the nursing staff seldom visited the wards before serving the evening meal. We decided that those of us who were in the building would make ourselves scarce, and placing screens around his bed for the sake of privacy, left the newlyweds on their own. All went according to plan and those involved were rewarded by the broad grins on the faces of the happy couple when we later returned.

The chap in the bed to my left was an elderly man from the Republic of Ireland (Eire). He was a member of the Royal Marine Dockyard Police and had served with that force for at least twelve years. I had difficulty deciphering his thick Irish brogue but soon discovered that he had no love of the English. His attitude was all the more puzzling when one considered the fact that for over twelve years he had worn the king's uniform and relied on the money he earned to support his family in Ireland. As an obvious 'Anglophobe', and a citizen of a neutral country where he was probably unable to find gainful employment, he did not endear himself to our company, and on a number of occasions came close to blows with the other patients on the ward. I regret to say that for a long time afterwards I considered him to be a typical Irish republican and, as a result, was apt to tar all southern Irishmen with the same brush. Later I was to serve with many of the boys from Eire who had joined the navy and, with few exceptions, found them to be true and loyal shipmates.

While in Park Prewitt I finally got around to writing to my parents. This was my first letter since arriving in England and the second one that I had written since leaving home some ten weeks earlier. I had written from Bermuda but not from Halifax, and they had no way of knowing that I had been in *Rajputani*, much less that the ship had been sunk. Due to the fact that I had not been a regular member of her crew, the Admiralty had not been obliged to notify my next-of-kin that I was one of the survivors. Now that the British press had carried the news of her sinking, together with pictures of the ship going down, I was in a position to give them details of what had happened to me since leaving Bermuda. In particular, I asked my mother to send me the addresses of Aunt Lorna and others in the United Kingdom, having lost all this information when we were torpedoed. I could see no reason to contact *Conway* as I had now joined the Royal Navy, but was anxious to contact my aunt and other family friends and relatives. Having fully recovered, I turned in my hospital 'blues', was issued with a complete new kit, and told that I was entitled to fourteen days survivors leave together with a return railway ticket to any destination in Britain.

The Furlough issued to me on May 26, 1941,
at Park Prewit Hospital as a Boy Seaman

It had earlier occurred to me that I could probably obtain a refund on the steamship ticket my parents had purchased in Jamaica and I had written to the head office of the Pacific Steam Navigation Company in Liverpool who had replied that a refund was possible. In view of the fact that I had no money, I was most anxious to contact them again and, as a result, asked for a railway warrant for Liverpool. As it turned out I was given what was known in the navy as a casual payment before leaving Basingstoke. A casual payment is a small sum of money advanced to an officer or rating by the paymaster of a ship or establishment while the recipient is away from his own ship. The transaction is entered in the pay book of the recipient and deducted from his wage at a future date. In this case I was given the huge sum of one pound, fifteen shillings, which was expected to carry me over for fourteen days. This was based on the daily rate of two shillings and sixpence, which I was told was the wage of a boy seaman at that time. Leaving my kit bag and hammock at the hospital to be forwarded to Royal Naval Barracks, Portsmouth, I departed for Liverpool via London on May 26, 1941, arriving there the same day. Leaving the train at Lyme Street Station, I made enquiries as to the nearest serviceman's hostel and was directed to a building known as the Royal Sailors' Rest. Located close to the docks, it was probably the worst place for me to find accommodation as Liverpool was being subjected to nightly air raids with the main target being the dock area. Entire city blocks had been destroyed and immediately in front of the hostel was an open area where an anti-aircraft gun and its attending crew had been located.

That first night in Liverpool was one to remember. The sirens started to wail shortly before midnight and the raid that started moments later, lasted into the early hours of the morning. All night long the sound of the guns and falling bombs made it impossible to sleep. At one time during the night I thought of leaving and locating the nearest air raid shelter, but not knowing where one was, and too scared to venture outside, elected to stay put. Once or twice during the night the building shook so violently that I thought we had received a direct hit. Pulling the blanket up over my head to protect myself from dust and plaster raining down from the ceiling, I lay in bed shaking with fright and not expecting to see the light of day.

The 'all clear' sounded shortly before dawn, and after leaving the hostel around 08:00, I went looking for somewhere to have breakfast. Later in the morning, while on my way to locate the Pacific Steam Navigation Company (PSNC) office, I had a strange experience. Walking along the sidewalk of a busy street in the business district of the city, I suffered a blow to my head which almost brought me to the ground. Initially I thought someone had hit me with a heavy truncheon and immediately looked around for my assailant. There were a number of people in the vicinity going about their business and, having stopped dead in my tracks, many came close to running me down as I stood on the pavement wondering what or who had hit me. Unable to understand what had happened, and as no one was paying any attention to me, I continued on my journey not knowing what the cause had been. Locating the office of the PSNC and identifying myself to the receptionist, I was asked to take a seat and told that one of their agents would see me shortly. There were three other people in the room and, after removing my coat and cap, I took a seat across from an elderly couple. A minute or two later I sensed that they were staring at me, and at the same time I felt something trickling down my cheek. Putting my hand to my face I was shocked to find it covered in blood and noticed that the front of my shirt was blood-soaked and the top of my head felt warm and sticky. I then asked the receptionist to direct me to a washroom where I could determine the cause of the bleeding. There was a slit roughly an inch long in the top of my cap which appeared to have been caused by a sharp instrument and I came to the conclusion that I had been hit on the head by a falling object. The only thing it could have been was a piece of roofing slate that had fallen from one of the buildings damaged during the previous night's raid. The lady in the waiting room then suggested that I go to a first aid station located around the corner. There I was seen by a medic on duty who put three stitches in my scalp, leaving me with a sore head for the next few days.

Returning to the PSNC office, I was pleased to learn that someone had been in touch with their agent in Jamaica by cable who had authorized a refund on my steamship ticket in the sum of forty pounds. Forty pounds was roughly equivalent to eight weeks wages in those days and a large sum for a young sailor. I was given the money in five-pound notes (not normally found in circulation) the notes being about four times the size of a pound note and printed in black ink on white paper. This caused me some embarrassment the following afternoon when I presented one of them at the ticket window of a local movie theatre and was told by the girl behind the wicket to wait as she would have to leave her desk to make change. Thinking that I had come by the note illegally she informed the theatre manager who in turn called the police. Fortunately when the police arrived I was able to produce the letter from the PSNC explaining how the money had come into my possession. The police advised me to have the remaining notes changed into smaller denominations in order to avoid future similar incidents.

Enemy bombers raided the city almost every clear night while I was on leave, our only respite being when the weather turned nasty. Although I was under legal age to purchase liquor, I soon discovered that in uniform I had no problem buying drinks, and therefore spent a lot of my time in pubs as there was not much else to do. One night I attended a dance at the YMCA where I met a young lady named Eve whom I offered to escort home after the dance. My offer being accepted, we boarded a bus bound for one of the suburbs of Liverpool and, on leaving the bus, I learned that we still had to walk five blocks to her home. Before we got to the house the sirens sounded and a passing policeman ordered us to take cover in one of the many surface shelters that dotted the residential areas of the city. We entered the shelter and found the building empty so had the place to ourselves. An hour or so later, with the raid still in progress, Eve told me that I had missed the last bus into town so I resigned myself to having to spend the rest of the night in the cold damp shelter. We laid Eve's coat on the narrow bench we had been sitting on and, using my gas mask haversack as a pillow, covered ourselves with my great coat and tried to get some sleep. Needless to say sleep was impossible but we made it through the night locked in each others arms to keep warm.

CHAPTER VIII
Boy Seaman

It was with some relief that my leave finally came to an end and I looked forward to returning to Portsmouth barracks. While passing through London on my final night of leave, I witnessed men, women, and children seeking shelter in the underground stations. Nothing I had encountered since landing in Britain made such an impression on me. Elderly adults and young children settled in for the night on the cold platforms, covered with blankets and quilts brought from their homes. Those who were still awake shared a cup of tea from a thermos flask and talked in subdued tones so as not to disturb the children who were asleep. All of them seemed cheerful and calm, and resigned to whatever fate had in store for them. The entire scene served to inspire those of us in uniform when we realized that Londoners could take whatever 'Jerry' could dish out.

On my return to Portsmouth I learned that due to the continuing raids, many men had been transferred to outlying areas where the navy had established temporary camps. One of these establishments, Camp Stamshaw, was located at the northern edge of the city. After reporting to the regulating office in the barracks, I was first sent to Camp Stamshaw and later that day joined up with a group of about thirty boy seamen who had just been posted to the fleet from HMS _Ganges_, the boys training ship at Shotley. Our group was later transported by lorry to a farmer's field near Cosham where the navy had built a transit camp under canvas. This was to be our home for the next fourteen days and a miserable fourteen days they turned out to be. There were eight boys in each tent, and being shaped like a bell with a pole in the centre, our ground sheets and hammocks were arranged so that we slept with our feet towards the centre. Extra blankets had not been issued and at night I found it extremely cold despite the fact that it was the first week in June. At 06:00 each day, rain or shine, we were turned out of bed for physical training under the eagle eye of our physical training instructor. This 'Adonis' with bulging biceps and a thirty-six inch chest would put us through our paces for a full twenty minutes, after which we had to run through the wet grass around the perimeter of the field for a further ten minutes. Returning to our quarters after physical training we had to strip to the waist in preparation for our morning ablutions. Goosebumps were the order of the day as we washed in the open air over a galvanized trough twenty feet or more in length. Suspended over the full length of this trough was a cold water pipe with twelve taps, hot water not being available. Stripped to the waist, step one consisted of teeth-cleaning (one minute). Step two was to apply soap to a wet wash cloth and quickly pass it over the part of the body located between the waist and shoulders (one minute). The third step was a repetition of the second having first rinsed out the wash cloth (one minute). After rubbing the torso vigorously with a towel to restore circulation one raced back to the tent to dress quickly before the bugler sounded *Cooks to the Galley*.

The entire exercise, known in the navy as a gunner's mate's bath, took four minutes. Breakfast was served at 07:00, a typical meal consisting of two sausages, stewed tomatoes, fried bread to soak up the tomato juice, a slice of bread, margarine, and plum jam, all of which was washed down with lashings of hot, sweet tea, the colour of wood varnish. At 07:45, in answer to the bugle, we formed up on parade for colours and prayers, at the conclusion of which, those in the duty watch were detailed off for working parties while the remainder marched off to classroom instruction or rifle drill. Having been enlisted as a boy seaman, I found myself, for the first time since leaving home, in the company of others close to my own age. It is true that I was actually two years younger than my companions, but they were unaware of this fact, and I wasn't about to tell them.

My new messmates were a mixed lot and came from towns and cities throughout the United Kingdom. They had one thing in common; all having completed fifty-six weeks training in *Ganges*, they had passed out of that establishment and were now considered ready to be drafted to sea. In April 1956, the rating of 'boy' in the Royal Navy was abolished after a period of three hundred years.

During the preceding three centuries that boys had served in the fleet, a number had risen to flag rank, and it was a well-known fact that the best seamen in the world had begun their careers in their teens. *Ganges* was built to replace the old training hulks of a bygone era and was commissioned in 1905. During the fifty-one years of its existence many stories were told of the harsh conditions and strict discipline that boy seamen were subjected to during their training. From what I learned from my new messmates, the life of a boy seaman at Shotley in 1941 was not much different from that of one in 1905. I soon came to realize that the conditions under which we were now living were quite luxurious in comparison to those at *Ganges*. At first my new companions regarded me as an outsider, and there was a tendency to exclude me from their conversation, but as time went on I was accepted as one of the gang and found them very friendly. For my part, I was somewhat intimidated by their year of service in the navy and I suffered from a mild case of inferiority complex. When they learned of my experience in *Rajputani,* the shoe was transferred to the other foot and I got the impression that they were somewhat envious of me. Not only had I been to sea, but I had survived the sinking of my ship.

Enemy activity in the Portsmouth area seemed to have abated slightly during the two weeks that we were in our camp at Cosham but the city was still subjected to the occasional attack. One night a group of us gathered in the open field to watch a heavier raid than usual concentrated on the dockyard area. The night sky was filled with ribbons of tracers that seemed to rise slowly from the ground against a backdrop of searchlights probing the clouds for the enemy planes. From time to time, a large red ball of flame would flare up on the distant horizon where a cluster of bombs had fallen, and the air crackled with the sound of the anti-aircraft shells bursting. One of our lads, Colin, had his home in Portsmouth. Normally an outgoing and cheerful boy with a great sense of humour he now stood quietly and watched with us as his hometown was being destroyed. Dawn was a long time coming and when it did smoke was still rising from the ruins of the homes that had been hit during the previous night's raid. The following afternoon Colin was ordered to report to the regulating office. Our divisional petty officer dropped by later to tell us to pack his clothing and lash up his hammock. We learned that the police had called to say that his mother and thirteen year-old sister had lost their lives in the raid. His father, a dockyard matey, had been on duty as an ARP warden during the raid and found his house in ruins when he came home in the early morning. Word went around that we were to be moved to new quarters, and having spent the past two weeks under canvas, we looked forward to being housed in a warm building once again. Our new home was located on a small island to the east of Portsmouth harbour known as Hayling Island. Before the outbreak of war, Billy Butlin had constructed one of his famous holiday camps on this island. This property had been requisitioned by the Admiralty for the purpose of establishing a training camp for boy seamen and given the name of Coronation Camp. The small cabins, originally constructed for families on vacation, provided comfortable accommodation for those of us who had been sleeping on the cold ground for the past two weeks. The larger buildings were converted for use as a mess hall, officers' mess, administration office, chief and petty officers' mess, kitchens, naval stores, classrooms, etc. The former tennis courts were used as a drill deck, and in front of the administration building, a large mast was erected from which the White Ensign was flown during daylight hours. The entire camp was enclosed by a wire fence and an armed guard was mounted on the main gate.

Hayling Island was basically an armed camp as the threat of invasion still existed and there were a large number of army personnel present to man the guns and patrol the beaches. Many of the civilian residents had been evacuated and the beaches were declared to be out of bounds due to the fact that they had been mined and were strewn with coils of barbed wire. At low tide it was possible to cross to the mainland on foot, but at high tide the island was completely surrounded by water and was connected to the mainland by a narrow causeway. There was a bus service which provided transportation to Portsmouth, but if one missed the last bus at midnight, it was a long wait for service to resume at 07:00 the next morning. This was not a hardship to those of us who were boys as our night leave expired at

20:00 and on our daily wage of two shillings and sixpence we seldom could afford to visit the city. Security on the island was extremely tight, and crossing the causeway when returning from Portsmouth, the buses were boarded by armed members of the Home Guard who required passengers to produce identification. This applied to civilians and servicemen alike. For those of us in Coronation Camp, there was little to be found in the way of entertainment. If we wished to see a movie we had to travel to Portsmouth and, while there was a public house on the island, this was out-of-bounds to us being under age. Many were the rules and regulations relating to boys in the service. Some of these were as follows:

"Boys are prohibited from procuring clothes, knives, lanyards, or other articles of their kit, cigarettes and matches, either from their friends, or by purchase on shore, and all such articles found in their possession will be confiscated. Boys were not to carry knives. Boys were not allowed to wear watches. Watches, articles of value, and any sum of money in excess of two shillings and sixpence had to be taken to the Regulating Office to be turned over to the accountant officer for safe custody. Should a boy receive money, stamps, or money order from his friends or relatives, or wish to save his pocket money, he had to take it to the Regulating Office. He was never to have more than two shillings and sixpence in his possession. During leave on shore, boys were forbidden to enter public houses or clothes shops; they were not to lounge about or assemble in groups, in the streets or pathways. They were not to trespass, but keep to the highways and public paths."

Needless to say, we managed to break nearly all these rules with the exception of entering a public house. Our petty officer instructors frequented the one and only pub on the island and the risk of being caught by one of those gentlemen was very real. The rule about smoking was seldom observed. All of us had wild woodbines, which we carried inside our caps and smoked whenever an opportunity arose. On one occasion twelve of us were being transported by lorry to the naval stores in the dockyard. Having found our seats in the back of the vehicle, the petty officer in charge of our party then went to the cab where he took his seat alongside the driver. Moments after starting off all twelve of us lit up a cigarette and off we went down the highway with a cloud of smoke billowing from the rear of the truck. Had we been caught all of us would probably have been given seven days #11 punishment.

Of all the instructors in Coronation Camp, the one we liked the most was Chief Petty Officer Ernest Herbert Pitcher VC, DSM. Chief Pitcher was fifty-three years of age and considered by us to be an 'old man'. A native of Cornwall, he could be found most evenings enjoying a pint or two of 'scrumpy' (cider) in the local pub. A portly man with a ruddy complexion, he had a friendly disposition and was more like a father than a petty officer when it came to the welfare of his boys. Chief Pitcher had been awarded the Victoria Cross in 1917 while serving as the gun layer of a 4 inch gun in HMS *Dunraven*, one of the 'Q' or mystery ships of that era. As an enemy submarine shelled his ship he and the rest of the crew waited while the battle went on overhead, and all around them. When the magazine below decks caught fire, they took up cartridges and held them on their knees to prevent the heat of the deck igniting them. Finally, when the magazine eventually blew up, they were all blown into the air but later rescued. At the outbreak of the Second World War he had been recalled from the Royal Fleet Reserve and was now our seamanship instructor. I later learned that he passed away in 1946, at the age of fifty-eight. Four hours of each day was spent in the classroom where a warrant officer schoolmaster taught us English, Math, Geography, and Naval History. Before leaving the island I managed to pass the navy's Educational Test 2 (ET2) required in order to be rated ordinary seaman on reaching the age of eighteen.

Another important test that we were required to pass before going to sea was the swimming test. I was never able to understand how a man or boy who could not swim a stroke was expected to pass the swimming test without having taken lessons. Before the war all major naval bases had pools and gymnasiums and if a rating did not know how to swim it was possible for him to learn. A number of the boys who had been at Shotley had already passed their test, but there were a few who had never learned to swim. Despite this our entire class was bussed into Portsmouth one day to be given the swimming test at the navy's Pitt Street Baths. The Admiralty swimming test required us to swim two lengths of an Olympic-sized pool then remain afloat for a further three minutes while wearing a stiff canvas duck suit. As the swimmer made his way through the water he was followed by an instructor walking along the edge of the pool carrying a bamboo pole of about ten feet in length. Should the swimmer start to display signs of distress, the pole would be held out to him only to be withdrawn as he reached out to grab it. This procedure produced a great deal of thrashing around in the water on the part of the swimmer and as the pole was always held at a point which was just out of reach, it generally resulted in his being able to reach the handrail at the end of the pool, only to be told that he had to turn around and do it all over again. Those of us who knew how to swim were able to pass the test without too much trouble and a notation was made on our service certificate to attest to the fact. For those who failed, life was not very pleasant as they were frequently singled out by senior ratings to perform the more distasteful jobs that were a sailor's lot. I should add however, that throughout the war I never knew of a case where a man was not allowed to serve at sea because he did not know how to swim.

Before leaving Hayling Island a most unusual and somewhat frightening event occurred one night that is worth relating. Throughout the camp grounds there were a number of buildings housing trailer pumps, ladders, hoses, and other fire-fighting equipment used by the base. These buildings were constructed of brick but designed to have only three sides, the front of the building being left open for quick deployment of the trailer pump inside. The pumps could be attached to the rear of a truck, but were normally wheeled to the location of the fire by manpower. For this purpose six members of the duty watch were detailed each night and required to sleep in the firehouse in the event of an alarm being sounded. As beds or cots were not provided we spread our hammocks on the floor as we had done when sleeping under canvas. One night, having been detailed off for fire watch, I had turned in early as I had the middle watch from midnight to 04:00. At around 20:30 I was awakened by the sound of air raid sirens as a raid developed over Portsmouth, but as this was a common occurrence I went back to sleep. A short while later there was a tremendous explosion followed by a blast of hot air which swept everything before it. The blast was strong enough to push the mobile pump to the rear of the building where it knocked out most of the wall. At the same time our blankets were stripped off our bodies, along with other small items, all of which ended up in a huge pile of debris behind us. Strangely none of us were hurt by the blast but we all were badly shaken. In the morning we discovered the cause of the explosion had been a parachute land mine designed to explode on the surface, unlike the normal HE bomb that explodes after it has penetrated the ground. The wind had carried the mine across the harbour where it had come to earth at a point about one mile west of our camp, resulting in a blast that had levelled everything in the immediate vicinity.

On July 25, 1941, I was rated ordinary seaman, local defence duties, meaning that, until I had completed my training, I could only be employed in that capacity. In order to be considered a fully-rated ordinary seaman, it was necessary for me to complete the new entry training course which all hostility-only ratings were given on joining the navy, and I had to be eighteen years of age. There were two parts to this course; Seamanship and Gunnery, both of which were taught at HMS *Collingwood*. This turn of events was not to my liking, but there was nothing I could do about it. As far as the navy were concerned, my eighteenth birthday was still a month away, at which time I would loose the designation LDD and be transferred to General Service. What was even more upsetting was that I, who had been wearing the uniform of a seaman since landing in the United Kingdom in April, was now included with a civilian group and forced to attend classes in seamanship that I had already taken at *Coronation Camp* as a boy seaman.

In 1941, the total strength of the Royal Navy stood at 420,100, which included those serving in the Royal Marines, WRNS, and Merchant Navy personnel serving in the Royal Navy under special arrangements. This was an increase of 291,100 from its strength at the outbreak of war and before the war ended in 1945 the total strength of the navy had increased to 861,000. This huge increase in manpower had resulted in a number of training establishments being built in Britain and *Collingwood* was one of the largest, if not the largest, in the country. Situated near the town of Fareham in Hampshire, thousands of young men passed through its main gate during the war years to man the ships of the Royal Navy that were coming off the slips in ever increasing numbers. On arrival at *Collingwood,* new recruits were assigned to classes and each class occupied one of the wooden huts that had been built around a large parade square located in the centre of the camp. At the eastern side of the parade square a long road led to the main gate, on both sides of which were a number of the administrative buildings such as the guard house, regulating office, sick bay, clothing store, and chapel. On the northern side were the officers' quarters, wardroom mess, chiefs and petty officers' quarters, and chiefs and petty officers' mess.

At Portsmouth barracks I joined up with a group of new recruits and travelled by road to *Collingwood.* My former messmates had entered the barracks to await drafts to seagoing vessels, having completed their training as boys and been rated ordinary seamen. As the only one of our group in uniform, I was looked upon as being an 'old hand', but this was of little consolation to me as I contemplated having to repeat most of everything that I had been taught over the past two months. The divisional petty officer assigned to our class was Petty Officer Leadbeater, and after the others had been issued a uniform and taught the correct way to wear it, we spent the next week on the parade square being drilled and learning how to march. Despite my misgivings I learned a great deal at *Collingwood* as there were many training aids available allowing us to experience the practical side of seamanship which I had only been taught in theory. As an example; we were taught to lower and hoist a sea boat, how to correctly swing a lead line with the aid of an excellent simulator, and the correct way to carry out the duties of a helmsman. The last two weeks of the course were devoted to gunnery, and we were taught everything about the 4-inch gun and the various positions and duties of the gun's crew.   My classmates had difficulty adapting to the ways of the navy and were the cause of much of the resentment I experienced. On more than one occasion they refused to quieten down after lights out at 22:00, keeping those of us who wanted to sleep, unable to do so. Their conduct resulted in a visit from Petty Officer Leadbeater who had us fall in on the parade square where we were required to do five laps around the square in double time clad in only our underwear. Three nights of this treatment had the required effect as the innocent who had been punished along with the guilty took matters into their own hands and put a stop to this behaviour.

Having completed the five-week course and rated ordinary seaman on my eighteenth birthday, I expected to be returned to Portsmouth barracks to await a sea draft, but to my disappointment learned that I had been posted to the permanent staff of *Collingwood* to serve on the guard. The guard, which was about twenty strong, were responsible for the security of the ship and providing sentries on the main gate and other sentry boxes located along the extensive perimeter of the property. Throughout the ship, a number of machine gun sand-bagged pits were also positioned. In these were mounted twin Lewis machine guns intended for use against low-flying enemy aircraft which occasionally would sweep in from the sea, shooting at anything that moved.

These pits were manned by the guard at sunrise and again at sunset, when most attacks took place. The gun crews were also required to close up whenever a double red warning was sounded which meant that an air raid was imminent. Members of the guard were billeted in a wooden hut by the main gate directly across from the ship's regulating office. Outside the gate, in a field on the other side of the road leading to Fareham, was located a barrage balloon tended by a crew from the Royal Air Force. Positioned at the very end of the road which led from the parade ground to the main gate, this balloon presented a tempting target to the German airmen who visited us from time-to-time. As they came in from the sea at almost ground level the German pilots would make a ninety degree turn over the parade square and then machine gun the road leading to the gate, and attempt to destroy the balloon. This bit of fancy flying was only possible when the balloon had been hauled down, because when it was raised, its cable presented a hazard to the attacking plane.

One Saturday afternoon we came under attack by a single Messerschmitt 109, as I have described in the foregoing paragraph. It was a few minutes after four in the afternoon and I had been asleep in one of the upper bunks in the guard room having been on watch during the forenoon that day. I was awakened by the marine bugler sounding *Liberty Men* and, a few minutes later, could hear the duty petty officer calling the liberty men to attention in order to be inspected by the officer of the watch. One of my messmates, who had made a pot of tea, offered me a mug which I found too hot to drink so, sitting the mug gingerly on the angle iron that formed the bed frame, I lit a cigarette and waited for it to cool. A moment later the loudspeaker announced a double red warning and the sirens began to wail. As the liberty men ran to take cover, I jumped out of my bunk and tried to find my shoes. In doing so I knocked over the mug of hot tea which began dripping onto the bunk below occupied by a sleeping young marine. As the aircraft flew down the roadway its cannons blazing, the young lad in the lower bunk awakened. As I dived under the bed I heard him scream that he had been hit in the shoulder by a bullet and could feel blood running down his back. When it was all over the young marine had a sheepish look on his face on discovering that what he thought was blood was nothing more than tea. Fortunately no one was hurt and we all had a good laugh.

From time-to-time an officer representing one of the various branches of the navy, such as the Submarine Service, Fleet Air Arm, Coastal Forces, or Combined Operations, would visit *Collingwood*. The purpose of these visits was to encourage newly-trained recruits to consider volunteering in one of these branches. In most cases the guest speaker had previously served with the unit of which he was speaking and we would be regaled with the wonderful benefits that could be ours. Benefits such as extra money earned by submariners and fleet air arm pilots, and the adventurous life led by serving in coastal forces and combined operations. It was all very entertaining and probably successful from the point of view of those who worked in the manning depot, but all that I wanted at that time was a chance to go to sea. While I gave some thought to volunteering for service in submarines, the idea of having to take another course caused me to reconsider as I had spent too much time in classrooms already.

Before leaving *Collingwood*, one of the members of our guard was responsible for an incident which, in retrospect was quite amusing, but at the time embarrassing for the navy. As noted earlier, there was a wire fence, roughly ten feet in height surrounding the camp. On the inside of this fence, at intervals of about 200 yards, were sentry boxes manned day and night by armed guards. Because we used the naval watch system, each spell of guard duty lasted four hours, with the exception of the dog watches, which were two hours. We were provided with .303 Lee Enfield rifles, five rounds of ammunition, a whistle, a torch and, while on guard duty, our bayonets were fixed. During the night the petty officer and officer of the guard did rounds at irregular intervals ensuring that all was well and that the sentry was awake and alert. The main concern and reason at that time for the tight security was the threat of sabotage by enemy agents. Although this may sound far-fetched, our side had been dropping agents by parachute in France for some time so there was every reason to believe that the other side could be doing the same.

One night, approximately half-way through the middle watch, the sentry on duty on the northern edge of the base heard, what he thought to be, the sound of someone approaching his post through the thicket on the outside of the fence. Quite certain that the noise he heard was made by a human being, he called out a challenge: "Halt; come forward to be recognized", while shining his torch in the direction of the noise. Getting no reply, he repeated the challenge, and as he peered through the fence he saw, what he thought to be, a man walking towards him. Dropping his torch and releasing the safety catch on his loaded rifle he aimed at the advancing object and pulled the trigger. A great thrashing around in the bushes convinced him that he had hit someone or something, so he commenced to sound the alarm by blowing on his whistle. On hearing a shot being fired, the duty petty officer and duty officer, who had been on their nightly rounds, came running to the post. On arrival they found a very frightened and shaken lad babbling incoherently and pointing to the bush on the other side of the fence. Back at the guard house, and after the excited lad had calmed down, the duty officer decided to alert the police and a search party was organized to beat the bushes in search of the slain saboteur. Early the following morning this party came across the body of the intruder; a very dead cow belonging to a local farmer. How much compensation the farmer got from the Admiralty for his cow, or what happened to the carcass, I have no idea, but the shaken sentry was cleared of any wrongdoing, and in fact was commended for his action in defence of the ship!

Having served two months on guard duties, and with no indication of how much longer I would be kept in *Collingwood*, I requested to see the commander and asked for a draft to a sea-going vessel. My request, having been granted, I left the establishment for the last time on October 10, 1941, and joined Camp Stamshaw in Portsmouth to await a sea draft. Weeks later I was still billeted in Stamshaw, and on December 3, 1941, an announcement was made over the loud hailer that all Colonial ratings were to report to the regulating office. By Colonial ratings, the Royal Navy meant anyone who hailed from Australia, New Zealand, Canada, or South Africa. On reporting to the office, I was surprised to find that there were quite a number of so-called Colonials in the camp: there were probably about thirty of us, the majority being from Australia, with three from Canada and one from South Africa. The reason for our being gathered together was that King George and Queen Elizabeth would be visiting Portsmouth that day. All Colonial ratings would be taken by bus to Royal Naval Barracks that morning to form a division of their own as part of the large parade planned for the royal visit. We were given one hour to change into our #1 uniform and at exactly 10:00 boarded the bus and were on our way to the barracks. A very large parade was drawn up on the square and the king first inspected the Royal Guard. On his return to the saluting base he was joined by the queen and together they were led by the commander in chief, Portsmouth to our group formed up at the edge of the parade square. Marching in front of the royal couple was a captain of the Royal Marines with drawn sword. Halting in front of our group he informed us that if we were spoken to by either of their majesties we were to reply using the term ma'am, in the case of the queen, and sir, in the case of the king. During inspection, the queen paused for a moment in front of me to enquire how long I had been in England. Having replied "since May ma'am", she then said: "Are we treating you well?" to which I replied: "Very well ma'am".

We arrived back at Stamshaw around 13:00 to find a late lunch provided for our group so we went directly from our bus to the mess hall. Shortly thereafter I realized there was something very wrong with me as I became violently sick and had to leave the mess after having only one mouthful of food. Reporting to the 'killick' of the mess, he sent me to sick bay to see the doctor, who asked if I could recall ever having suffered from chicken pox. On answering in the negative, he smiled and said: "Well son, you certainly have it now." I was then instructed to return to barracks and pack my gear in preparation for a trip to Haslar Hospital. At the same time I was told to break the news to the other occupants of our hut that they would be confined to barracks due to the contagious nature of my ailment. On being admitted to Haslar Hospital, my kit was immediately sent for fumigation, and the following morning I was transferred by ambulance to Winchester General Hospital, a civilian country hospital in Hampshire. At Winchester, servicemen suffering from contagious diseases were housed in a small cottage situated some distance from the main building. The cottage contained about twenty beds, but on my arrival was occupied by only two patients; a young private in the marines recovering from scarlet fever, and a naval rating recovering from mumps. The three of us were left almost entirely alone during the day and our meals were delivered to the cottage on a trolley and left standing outside the front door for us to collect. This resulted in most of our meals being cold by the time we got them as it was now December and the hospital kitchen was some distance from the cottage.

Each day at 09:00 we were paid a visit by a doctor, by which time we had already made our own beds, waxed and polished the floors, and eaten breakfast. A nurse accompanied the doctor and after their morning visit we would be left on our own until after the evening meal. At 21:00 a night nurse came on duty for an eight-hour shift and there was a telephone line connecting our cottage to the main hospital that she could use in the event of an emergency. During daylight hours there was little for us to do other than play cards, read, write letters, listen to the radio, and tend the fire in the open fireplace situated in the centre of the ward. Cut off as we were from all contact with the opposite sex, the three of us looked forward nightly to our nurse coming on duty. Most of the nurses were quite friendly and more often than not they would occupy themselves reading by the fire or knitting. Our favourite was a young and pretty girl named Pam who, much to our delight, was an outrageous flirt. We loved her dearly, and I am sure she enjoyed every minute of it although, in her defence, I have to say that she made it perfectly clear to the three of us that it was all in fun and that she would not tolerate any amorous advances. One night she aroused us when she decided to wash her stockings. She proceeded to sit in front of the fire, raise her skirt, exposing well-formed thighs, and slowly remove her stockings. After rinsing them in the sink, she hung them on the fire screen to dry and the following morning we were treated to a vision of them being replaced before going off duty.

Close to our cottage stood another building which housed a middle-aged woman and her two daughters. The girls were aged fifteen and seventeen and all three family members had been evacuated from their home in London when it was destroyed in the blitz. Unknown to us, the two girls had contracted German measles and, like us, were in isolation. Through the window of our cottage the young marine struck up a conversation with the seventeen year old girl and at her suggestion he slipped out one night to take a walk on the hospital grounds. He returned to the ward in the early hours of the morning and spent most of the day bragging about his amorous conquest the previous night. However, a few days later he was at a loss to explain to the doctor how, on recovering from scarlet fever, he had contracted measles. In addition to coming down with measles, he also became infected with scabies, which led to both the signalman and I being kept at Winchester until January 9, 1942, before returning to barracks.

Christmas Day had been like any other day except that we were treated to a turkey dinner instead of the normal hospital fare. On Christmas Eve, the signalman and I, with the knowledge of Pam, who was on duty that night, managed to leave the hospital grounds for a few hours in order to go to Winchester. Dressed in hospital blues, we made our way across a farmer's field to the main road and managed to get a bus into town. Fortunately we were not accosted by the military police as we had left the grounds without permission and would have been in trouble had we been caught. During our three hours of freedom, we managed to gulp down a few pints of ale before returning to our cottage and without our absence being discovered. Pam, who was aware of what we had planned on doing, turned a blind eye to the entire affair and was quite relieved to see us return safely. The citizens of Winchester were accustomed to seeing hospital patients as it was quite common for ambulatory patients to obtain a pass to go into town; however, this was not available to those with contagious diseases.

It was shortly after my arrival in Winchester that Pearl Harbour was attacked. As I recall, news of the strike against the United States Navy was regarded in a somewhat nonchalant manner. At the time Britain had been holding the fort on her own for two long years and the general feeling was one of relief that the American isolationists had finally been silenced. The signalman in our ward stated: "Someone had to push the 'Yanks' into the pool. Now that they're in, perhaps they'll start to swim and together we'll get the game finished."

Before being discharged from hospital I received my first letter from home since landing in England. It had been written before my parents received my letter sent when I was in Basingstoke. A week later two more letters arrived, together with the addresses of friends and relatives in England that I had lost when my ship went down. The big news from home was that my cousin had married one of the members of the Winnipeg Grenadiers and left Jamaica to live in Winnipeg, Canada. At a later date, when news of the fall of Hong Kong reached us, I feared that he had either been killed or taken prisoner. It turned out that on his return to Canada he had transferred to the RCAF and was taking flight training in Ontario when Hong Kong was over-run. On leaving Winchester and returning to RNB Portsmouth, I learned that I had been granted seven days sick leave. As I now knew the address and telephone number of Major and Mrs. Winter, I called to find out whether I might visit them. They were delighted to hear from me and at their invitation I travelled by train to Bournemouth and then by bus to their home in the village of Blanford in Dorset.

Blandford consisted of a few cottages built around what was referred to as the village square. Most of the homes had thatched roofs and the square was nothing more than a large oak tree enclosed by an iron fence. The main road leading into the village was routed around the tree so that traffic passed on both sides of it and on the tree was a large notice board posting all the local news. The major's home was a small, white cottage with a thatched roof located about a quarter of a mile from the village centre. He and his wife met me at the bus stop with their Austin Minor car and I was treated like a long lost son during my short visit with them. I think they were concerned that I would find their lifestyle boring, but I thoroughly enjoyed their company and the luxury of sleeping in a real bed between sheets once again. Living in a rural area, food rationing was not a problem. There were fresh eggs each morning for breakfast, fresh milk, bacon, cheese, butter, and home-made bread, all of which we seldom saw in barracks. In the cellar was a large barrel of apple cider, and in the evenings the major and I consumed many pints as we sat in front of an open hearth and talked about his former years in the army and the many trips he had made to Jamaica. Despite petrol rationing, my hosts were able to take me on a number of excursions to see points of interest and it was hard to believe that there was a war being waged and on which the outcome of the country's existence depended. The days went by all too quickly and once again I soon found myself caught up in the daily routine of barrack life.

The nightly air raids on Portsmouth were now a thing of the past and a start had been made to clean up the city. Those of us in barracks were in one of three watches: red, white, or blue. This meant that every third day we were duty and called upon to do a variety of jobs. One of these jobs entailed spending the night at a location outside the barracks where we could be called on to fight any fire that might start as the result of an air raid. The navy provided fire-fighting parties to a number of establishments in the city such as the Salvation Army Hostel, as well as numerous buildings in the dockyard. Of great concern to both the navy and the entire nation was the safety of HMS *Victory*, Nelson's flagship at Trafalgar as it would take only one well-placed incendiary bomb to destroy her. *Victory's* top masts had been struck early in the war in the hope that enemy aircraft would not easily identify her and many precautions had been taken to deal with any fire that might have started. When detailed off for fire watch in *Victory*, we marched from the barracks to the dockyard taking our bedding with us. On going aboard we slung our hammocks between the 12 pounders which were run out to port and starboard on the forward end of the upper deck. Here we slept until called during the night to stand a two-hour watch on the quarterdeck abaft the main mast and it was easy for ones imagination to take hold on such occasions. Lying awake at night, I would imagine what it might have been like to serve the very guns that we slept beside, and get an eerie feeling when pacing the quarterdeck on dark nights within a few feet of where Nelson had fallen one hundred and sixty years earlier. At dawn, with our hammocks lashed up, we were marched back to barracks in time for breakfast.

Living in RNB was like living in a capital ship. The rig of the day was #3's with few exceptions. Each morning colours and prayers required the entire ship's company to form up on the parade square along with the Royal Marine band. At the conclusion of the service we would march off the square to the strains of *'Heart of Oak'*. No one was allowed to smoke while working, and at "stand easy" there was always a mad dash to the Navy, Army, and Air Force Institutes (NAAFI) for a sticky bun and cup of tea, joining about two hundred sailors, all trying to be served in fifteen minutes. The parade square was patrolled by a 'belt and gaiter' GI during working hours who ensured that no one walked across the consecrated ground. If the parade had to be crossed, one had to do so, on the double, and failure to comply resulted in being put on the defaulter list.

One Sunday afternoon, having gone ashore without making plans to do anything in particular, I was approached by a well-dressed elderly lady while walking through the park who invited me to accompany her to a social gathering being held in a nearby church hall. On sensing my hesitation to accept her invitation, she went on to explain that every Sunday the ladies in her congregation who had sons or husbands in the navy sponsored an afternoon tea at her church to which all sailors were welcome. Finding her quite persuasive, and being somewhat curious as to what to expect, I agreed to go along. On arrival at the hall I found a group of about fifty people gathered there having what is commonly known in England as high tea. Half the women were middle-aged, but there were a number of girls in their late teens or early twenties along with twelve or more sailors in uniform. During the course of the evening I discovered that the lady who had invited me was the mother of one of the boys who had been lost when the *Hood* went down. A number of others had also lost sons or husbands at sea, and this weekly gathering was their way of keeping the memory of their loved ones alive while giving lonely sailors a home-away-from-home in a strange city. That evening I became friendly with one of the girls whose mother was a petty officer in the WRNS serving in RNB and married to a chief petty officer who was overseas. The family lived in Southsea, a suburb of Portsmouth, and during the weeks that followed I was invited to their home for dinner on many occasions. This girl, Audrey, was still in school and after I had left Portsmouth we corresponded for a short while. However, after one or two letters I lost touch and never met her or her mother again.

During February I received a letter from my father's cousin, Lorna Trollope, who was living in London and to whom I had written while recovering in hospital. In her reply she informed me that she had been corresponding with my mother and was anxious to meet me. As soon as I was able to arrange for a long weekend leave I travelled to London. For the next eight years I came to regard Aunt Lorna as the best friend I had in England and who became a second mother to me. When I first met her she was working as a volunteer hostess at a Service Hostel in London run by the YMCA. The building in which it was located had been a well-known restaurant in London before the war. It had been renovated and equipped with a number of beds, library, reading room, and canteen that served three meals a day at very reasonable prices. Similar to other service hostels like the Beaver Club and the Knights of Columbus, any sailor, soldier, or airman on leave could obtain overnight accommodation and meals at very reasonable prices.

Aunt Lorna was the daughter of Commodore Neville Wilson, CMG, CBE, Royal Indian Navy, and the wife of Brigadier Hugh Trollop, of the Royal Essex Regiment. In 1941 her husband was serving in North Africa with the 8th Army and she had moved to London from their home in Chelmsford to do voluntary war work in the city. About the same age as my father, Lorna recalled: "As a young girl, I remember meeting him when he came over from Canada with his regiment in 1917". In the years that followed our first meeting, I found her to be the kindest, most considerate person I ever met. Typically English, she normally wore expensive tweeds and woollens and was a perfect example of her upper middle class background. She was a lady of strong character, but not in the least bit intimidating. Highly respected by her fellow workers and with a wonderful sense of humour, she got along well with most people, and I thoroughly enjoyed her company.

On my return to Portsmouth after spending the week-end in London, I was informed that I was to be drafted to HMS *Sphinx*, the name given to the Royal Navy's base in Egypt in 1941. Our draft, consisting of about twenty ratings, was given seven days embarkation leave and within a day or two I returned to London where I was able to book a bed for seven days in Lorna's hostel. During my seven days leave with my aunt as guide, we visited many of London's famous landmarks such as Westminster Abbey, St. Paul's Cathedral, Tower of London, and the National War Museum. One day I travelled by the underground to Croydon and visited the cemetery where my uncle was buried in 1918. Before leaving Jamaica I had promised my grandfather that I would do so, and report to him on the condition of the grave which he had not visited for a number of years. Theatre tickets were often made available through the hostels to members of the forces on leave in London, and one evening I was lucky enough to obtain one to see a variety show, featuring Flanagan and Allan.

During my leave in London an incident occurred which I found quite bizarre. One night, having had more than my usual quota of drinks and not anxious to return to the hostel on foot as I normally did, I decided to take a cab. Even in wartime many taxis were available in Picadilly Circus, and having located one in the blackout, I was about to open the door when the driver said: "I've already got a fare lad but I don't mind taking you on if you're going in the same direction. Where do you want to go?" Having answered that I was only going to 'Gatties' in the Strand, he told me to get in. There was nothing unusual about his offer because with wartime petrol rationing taxi drivers often took more than one fare at a time if all passengers were travelling in the same general direction. On opening the taxi door I found an elderly gentleman sitting in the back, obviously highly intoxicated and talking to himself. He was wearing a crumpled tuxedo with a white carnation in his lapel. A fitting companion, I thought, considering my own inebriated state. In a loud voice he turned to me and said: "They don't know who I am, do they? Do you know who I am? I'll tell you who I am. I'm Negly Farson, the best damned war correspondent there ever was. What the hell do these young cubs know about war." A moment later he leaned forward and was violently sick on the floor of the taxi. The driver, having pulled over to the curb in front of 'Gatties', told me that I owed him three shillings and, having handed him the fare,

I hastily exited the taxi. It was difficult to believe that the elderly gent in the cab had been none other than one of my boyhood heroes; a well-known journalist, war correspondent, soldier of fortune, and author of two of my favourite books: *The Way of a Transgressor*, and *The Story of a Lake*. What he was doing in London at that time, where he had been that night, and what happened to him between then and the end of the war, I will never know.

All too soon my leave was over and on March 16, 1942, our draft left Portsmouth by train for Liverpool where we joined the troopship, SS *Almanzora*, for passage to South Africa. When embarkation had been completed on March18, 1942, we slipped our lines and proceeded down river to anchor and wait for the convoy to assemble. Early on the morning of March 23, 1942, we weighed anchor, and taking up our position in the convoy of 31 merchantmen, headed south through the Irish Sea.

CHAPTER IX
Off To War

Almanzora, **owned by the Royal** Mail Line before the war, was of 16,000 GT. She had been converted to trooping in 1939 and was one of the troopships in convoy WS-17 that sailed from the Mersey on March 23, 1942. The letters WS, used for convoy designation between 1940 and 1943, indicated that we were a troop convoy bound for either Suez or Bombay. The WS series of convoys were initially used to transfer troops from the United Kingdom to Suez and the WS designation is generally believed to mean Winston Special. In 1942 the Mediterranean was not considered a safe route for the passage of troop convoys to Suez and reinforcements for the Middle East were therefore routed around the Cape. On sailing from Liverpool, our convoy consisted of 31 merchant ships and was initially provided with an A/S escort of 11 vessels of which eight were fleet destroyers, one was a Hunt class, and two were ex-American four-stackers. Leaving St. George's Channel and with Fastnet Rock to starboard, all ships altered course to the west and headed out into the Atlantic in order to avoid detection by the German _Focke-Wulf Condors_. For the next eight days of our outward journey local escorts were detached singly and in pairs, as the further south we sailed the threat of U-boat attack diminished. By March 31, 1942, all eleven vessels forming our local escort when we departed Liverpool had left us. On our second day of sailing we were joined by the aircraft carrier HMS _Illustrious_, the county class cruiser _Shropshire_, the armed merchant cruiser _Alcantra_, and the destroyers _Lookout_, _Grove_, and _Alderham_.

On joining _Almanzora_, our draft had been allocated space on the crowded troop deck and informed that we would be required to serve as the guns crew for the single 4" inch gun mounted on the ship's stern. Members of the ship's crew normally manned this gun but they were glad to let the navy do the job during the long voyage to Cape Town. Later that same day we met Petty Officer Walter Perry who was to be in charge of our party during the passage. Petty Officer Perry was a dour Cornishman with a face that only a mother could love. During the sixteen days that he was in charge of our draft, he was never seen to smile and became known to us as 'laughing boy'. Daily routine while taking passage in a troopship was quite relaxed by naval standards. Other than normal housekeeping on the mess deck, there was little to occupy the troops during the day. The army spent a lot of time doing physical exercises on the boat deck and conducting classes on the stripping, cleaning, and re-assembling of their weapons. Most evenings a movie was shown in what had been the main dining room of the liner in peacetime, but because of the hundreds of troops on board, only a limited number could see the show each night. Daily work parties were detailed to peel potatoes and assist the cooks in the galley, but there was plenty of free time to play cards, read, and write letters. The days got warmer as we sailed south and many of the troops took advantage of the tropical sun to get a tan. Those of us in the naval draft, who had to stand four-hour watches on the gun, occupied ourselves by watching the Fleet Air Arm pilots practice deck landings on the carrier.

Illustrious was positioned in the centre of the convoy about two thousand yards off our port beam and, unless the wind was directly astern of her, was able to launch and recover her *Swordfish* without altering course. Those of us on duty during daylight hours spent time watching her through binoculars and making bets as to whether the next aircraft to land would 'prang'. We came to the conclusion that the pilots we were watching must have had little or no experience in deck landings, or that landing a Swordfish on the deck of a carrier was the most hazardous exercise in the world. Every third plane seemed to end up with its nose on the deck and its tail in the air.

Eleven days after joining the convoy, *Illustrious* departed along with her destroyer escort and the local Freetown escort consisting of the destroyer, *Wild Swan,* and the corvette, *Hydranger,* together with two French A/S vessels took over the job of escorting us into harbour. On April 6, 1942, we anchored in Freetown harbour and within an hour were taking on fuel and water. The ship was surrounded by 'bum boats' which came alongside to barter and sell African goods in the form of post cards, native masks, oranges, and bananas (a hand of bananas could be had for a package of twenty cigarettes). Two days after our arrival, convoy WS-17 was split into two sections; WS-17A and WS-17B respectively. On April 9, 1942, WS-17A, consisting of 13 ships, sailed for Cape Town escorted by the battleship *Malaya* and nine destroyers. On April 11, 1942, five days after arriving at Freetown and having disembarked a number of army personnel, we sailed in WS17-B along with seventeen other ships on the final leg of our journey. With us were the two cruisers, HMS *Shropshire* and HMS *Devonshire*, serving as ocean escorts. Except for a visit from King Neptune as we crossed the Equator, the remainder of our voyage was uneventful, and on April 23, 1942, we entered Cape Town harbour under the shadow of Table Mountain on which 'mother nature' had spread her table cloth of fleecy clouds.

On disembarking, our naval party travelled by train to Simon's Town where we joined HMS *Afrikanda*, a transit camp under canvas. During the three-day stopover, we were allowed all night leave to visit Cape Town and enjoy the hospitality offered by the South African people. After the austerity of wartime Britain, it was a treat to once again be in a city where there was no blackout and where it was possible to get a full course meal in a restaurant.

I must make mention of my meeting with 'Able Seaman Just Nuisance'. During the short journey to our staging camp, most of us were surprised to find a large friendly dog running throughout the length of the train, his tail wagging and apparently willing to make friends with anyone who would pay attention to him. Asking who he belonged to, we were told the following story: The dog's name was 'Just Nuisance', and he belonged to Mr. Chaney, manager of the United Services Institute in Cape Town, a hostel for sailors ashore. Living at the Institute since 1938, 'Just Nuisance' had come into contact with, and become attached to the many young sailors using the hostel. In fact he had become so attached to any man in naval uniform that he had taken to following sailors everywhere, even on the train, and was often seen on the docks greeting troop ships as they arrived from the United Kingdom. Early in the war, having developed the habit of riding with naval drafts on troop trains, 'Just Nuisance' incurred the wrath of the railway authorities as he insisted on lying across three seats in a carriage with his human companions. On learning that the railway officials had recommended that 'Just Nuisance' be banished or destroyed, sailors of HMS *Afrikander* appealed to their commanding officer to intervene. This evidently sympathetic officer arranged for 'Just Nuisance' to enlist in the Royal Navy, thereby entitling him to a free pass on the train. The new recruit was then issued his own sailor's cap and a special collar to which was attached his official railroad pass. His service certificate stated that he was a 'bone crusher' by trade, his religious denomination was shown as scrounger, and his rank was able seaman.

As a member of the ship's company of *Afrikander*, 'Able Seaman Just Nuisance' was given his own quarters complete with bunk and an attendant sailor to ensure that he was fed, washed, and groomed. He was also reported to have been given a bed at the Union Jack Club in Cape Town. It has been said that his conduct sheet revealed that 'Just Nuisance' was no angel, being guilty of a number of misdeeds such as travelling on the train without his free pass, sleeping on a bed in the petty officers' mess, losing his collar, going AWOL, and resisting eviction from pubs in Cape Town at closing time. His most serious offence was fighting with the mascots of other ships and causing some fatalities. When 'Just Nuisance' married Great Dane, 'Adinda', his fame grew and shortly after the marriage, 'Adinda' gave birth to a litter of five pups. Many years after the war, I learned that 'Able Seaman Just Nuisance' was badly paralyzed as the result of a motor vehicle accident at the age of seven and had to be euthanized. A bronze statue was later erected in Simon's Town in his memory.

During our passage from England, events in the Indian Ocean had resulted in the British Eastern Fleet having to go on the defensive and on April 4, 1942, two days before our arrival in Cape Town, an attack by the Japanese on our base in Ceylon was thought to be eminent. On April 5, 1942, cruisers HMS *Dorsetshire* and HMS *Cornwall* had been sunk. Again on April 9, 1942, the day we left

Free Town, the Japanese raided Trincomalee, and we lost the aircraft carrier *Hermes*. It therefore came as no surprise to those of us bound for Egypt to be told that our final destination had been changed to Bombay, and on April 26, 1942, we embarked in the troop ship *Mauratania* for a fast passage to India. Because of her speed, the *Mauratania* was sailed independently and, after calling in at Durban to embark more troops, arrived in Bombay on May 4, 1942.

While at sea, a great many of our soldiers came down with heat exhaustion. Built for the trans-Atlantic trade, it is probable that the ship's ventilation system was not able to cope with conditions close to the Equator. With her scuttles and deadlights closed, and with the mass of humanity aboard, it was like a furnace below decks. On our second day at sea I was admitted to sick bay suffering from acute pain in my joints and running a very high temperature. My condition was at first thought to be a case of heat exhaustion but was subsequently diagnosed as Dengue Fever and, on arriving in Bombay, I was removed from the ship and admitted to St. George's Hospital. I was to spend the next six weeks recovering from my bout of fever which I had apparently acquired in South Africa. From what I have learned, it is an infectious tropical disease generally contracted by a bite from a certain type of mosquito and that the incubation period is five to six days. My illness kept me in hospital for quite some time, and as my condition improved, I began to take stock of my new surroundings.

The hospital ward contained about twenty beds and was located on the second floor of the building. There were a great many windows which not only allowed an on-shore breeze to keep us cool during the day, but also provided a grand view of the well-kept gardens surrounding the hospital. Being almost in the centre of the city, the pungent aroma so peculiar to the Far East could be detected, and from my bed I could hear the muezzin calling the faithful to prayer from a nearby minaret. Each morning we awoke to the sound of crows in the garden and in the distance one could watch the vultures in the pale blue sky as they circled over the Hindu burial grounds. Our wing had been devoted entirely to the care of Imperial and allied troops and among our patients were members of all three services including one or two American seamen who were members of the United States Navy serving as armed guards on American merchant ships.

One fellow I shall always remember was probably the most seriously ill patient in our ward. He was a chief petty officer, RN, a survivor from the cruiser *Cornwall* sunk by the Japanese the previous month. Having broken his back on abandoning ship, his body was now encased in plaster from the neck down which must have caused him great discomfort in addition to the pain he was in. He was, however, one of the most cheerful patients and a favourite among the nurses. The medical staff was a mixed bag. There were British military surgeons from all three services as well as local Indian doctors who were members of the hospital staff. The nurses were mainly members of the British services but there were also a number of Voluntary Aid Detachment (VAD) personnel and Indian orderlies. Despite the great treatment I received in St. George's Hospital, I was most anxious to be discharged as I had not expected to visit India and hoped to be able to see something of the country and its people before leaving.

Eventually I was considered well enough to be discharged from the hospital, although not fully recovered, and a decision was made that I be sent to a convalescent home for a period of two weeks rest before returning to duty. This home was located in a suburb of Bombay known as Bandra, a forty minute drive from the centre of the city. Before the war it had been the principle residence of a senior executive with the Anglo-American Oil Company who, as his contribution to the war effort, had loaned the property to the navy to be used by sailors recovering from a serious illness or injury. Located a short distance from the coast, the buildings consisted of a large house where the owner, Mr. Sidons, and his family still lived, and three other houses where patients were housed. A high fence enclosed the entire area for security reasons, and a native policeman guarded the main entrance in order to keep out vagrants, hawkers, and the odd fakir or religious mendicant. While living at Bandra naval discipline was very relaxed, but there were a few rules which we were expected to observe and the navy provided a regulating petty officer who lived on the premises to ensure we were on our best behaviour and not an embarrassment to the senior service. Patients were not required to wear uniform unless travelling into town, resulting in most of us dressing in shorts and sandals during the day. We were free to leave the compound whenever we wished on condition that we informed our RPO where we were going and when we expected to return. Leave expired for everyone at 23:00 and we were required to notify the dining room staff if we were going to be absent for meals. Each morning at 06:00 we were awakened by a young lad of about fifteen who served us a large mug of strong tea. Breakfast was at 08:00, a light lunch was served at noon, and our evening meal was at 18:00. The three buildings housing patients were square in shape and constructed around a common room serving as our dining and recreation room. Washrooms were located in the common room and storage was provided for kit bags and hammocks. A wide veranda ran around the four sides of our building and was enclosed with a mosquito screen. It was here that we slept on a bed with a side table and reading lamp.

During the day there was much to do and see. A short path led to the beach where we could go swimming during the heat of the day, and there were two tennis courts, as well as a number of bicycles available to us. About a ten-minute walk from the main gate was the railway station where, for about five rupees, one could get a round trip ticket to Bombay to sight-see, and at a nearby market we could purchase a variety of fresh fruit such as mangoes, bananas, and oranges. The only thing missing was a congenial watering hole where one might get a cold beer. During my stay in Bandra, I became friendly with a young American sailor, Patrick O'Donnell, from Staten Island, New York, who also had been in St. George's Hospital. Pat was a gunner serving as an armed guard on a US merchant ship when he developed an acute attack of appendicitis while at sea. He was fortunate to be alive as, before his ship had docked in Bombay, his appendix had ruptured, and after being operated on in hospital, suffered from peritonitis which almost cost him his life. One day he and I decided to take a trip into Bombay to see the sights and perhaps find a bar. After downing four or five beers, Pat informed me that we were going to find a tattoo parlour as he had always wanted one.

Leaving the bar, we made our way in the direction of the waterfront and eventually found a shop in front of which was a sign that read: 'Tattoo, Excellent Workmanship, Experienced Artist.' Pat chose to have a heart emblazoned on his upper arm pierced with an arrow. Under the heart was to be a scroll bearing the name of his girlfriend, Mary-Anne. Although both Pat and the 'Experienced Artist' tried to talk me into selecting a design for myself, I declined as I was not impressed with the artist's instruments, which I suspected might not be very clean. Unable to examine the finished product because of its location under his left shoulder, Pat paid the sum of ten rupees and off we went in search of another pub. The following day, a scab having formed on his new tattoo, Pat was showing it to one of our messmates who asked: "What does Marry Anne mean? Is it to remind you to propose to your girl when you get home?" The next day we were in town on our way to see the 'Experienced Artist' with Pat muttering: "I'll kill that son of a bitch when I get my hands on him." On entering the shop Pat soon had the terrified owner backed into a corner and it was easy to see that the poor man was completely bewildered. It was some time before we were able to get him to understand what he had done but once the penny dropped, he calmed down and offered to make amends. There was no way that the offending 'r' could be erased, and the only solution was to completely cover up the letters. Subsequently Pat agreed to have a second tattoo in the form of 'Old Glory' placed immediately below the first, the top stripe to the right of the stars covering up the miss-spelled name. The 'Experienced Artist', whose name we had now learned was Abou, was most apologetic and anxious to make amends stating that he would not charge Pat for the second tattoo and even offering to provide me with one free of charge. Throwing caution to the wind I allowed him to do so and ended up with the message 'India 1942' inscribed in ink on my left forearm, and I made sure he spelled the word 'India' correctly.

Another incident involving Pat O'Donnell is worth relating. We had both been told of the infamous street in Bombay called Grand Road, and my friend Pat was anxious to find out if all he had heard about it was true. Grand Road was out of bounds to all allied servicemen. The military police had done a good job cordoning off the area but to Pat that was tantamount to waving a red flag in front of a bull. Reputed to be one of the largest red light districts on earth, we heard that on both sides of the road were houses with iron bars instead of doors and well-lit rooms so that customers could inspect the merchandise from the street. In order to evade the police it was necessary to travel by train <u>into</u> the city instead of <u>out</u>, as the train stations in town were patrolled by the MPs on the look-out for allied servicemen bent on checking out the area.

By riding into town from Bandra, we got off the train at a station located very close to our destination and, hailing a horse-drawn cab, directed the driver to take us to Grand Road. I do not think either of us was prepared for what we were about to see. On entering the street of cages we found the place well-lit, not from street lights, but from the houses themselves. Behind the iron bars which served as doors, were the ladies of the night dressed in bright-coloured saris, their long shining hair in braids and their arms, fingers, ears, and noses adorned with silver and gold. Some were sitting quietly while others engaged in loud conversation with customers on the sidewalk obviously trying to solicit business. The street was a seething mass of humanity and very shortly our carriage slowed to a crawl as our driver tried to get the horse to move into the brown tide that swirled around us. The seats in the carriage were arranged in such a way that one passenger sat facing forward while the other had his back to the driver. I was sitting in the front seat when I saw two men jump onto the rear of the carriage and make an attempt to snatch the cap off Pat's head. Turning around in a flash Pat lashed out at one of them hitting him full in the face and, on taking a swing at the other, both men jumped off and were swallowed up in the mob. At this point I became somewhat anxious and began to think that perhaps our idea to visit Grand Road had not been a wise one. Indicating to the driver to turn the carriage around, which he managed to do with some difficulty, we instructed him to take us back to the train station. In the meanwhile Pat had produced a knife that he seemingly carried under his jumper, and telling me to keep an eye out for trouble in the front, prepared to fend off any boarders from the rear. Fortunately we decided to leave when we did because in relating this story to a reporter from the Bombay Times later on, I was told that shortly before our experience, the bodies of two British merchant seamen had been found by police after they had ventured into the same area.

Our hosts at Bandra, Mr. and Mrs. Sidons, were charming people and Mrs. Sidons often invited us into their home for a cold beer or cup of tea. She had been born in India and was the daughter of an Anglican Bishop who had spent almost all his life in India. The Sidons were the parents of two beautiful girls aged five and seven who were cared for by a young Portuguese amah from Goa. One day while visiting Mrs. Sidons, I happened to tell her that I was born in Jamaica which led to us comparing similarities of being brought up in a British island colony and in British-ruled India. A good twelve years older than I, I found her most interesting and there were a great number of things we had in common. Like most Anglo-Indians she was educated in England and then had returned to India to be with her family. She then met her future husband, an American citizen at the time who was now a British subject.

Relating various incidents in her life, Mrs. Sidons described some of the problems Europeans encountered while living in India. An example of this was that she had gone to great lengths to hire a Christian girl as a nurse for her two children. She claimed it was necessary to do so because there were some native Indians who believed that sexual intercourse with a virgin was a cure for venereal disease. She then told me of a case where one of her friends, the mother of an eight year-old girl, had a young Hindu woman working for her whose boyfriend had contracted gonorrhoea. One night when the child's parents were away, the nurse allowed her boyfriend access to the house where he had raped the eight year-old and infected her. Unable to find someone locally who was both of the Christian faith and a registered nurse, Mr. and Mrs. Sidons travelled to Panaji, the capital of Goa, a Portuguese territory on the west coast of India, where they secured the services of a young nurse who had been trained in that country in a Catholic hospital.

On finding out that I was interested in learning about the caste system of the Hindu religion, Mrs. Sidons arranged for me to meet a young man who worked as a journalist for the Bombay Times. This fellow invited me to go with him to visit an area of the city which was best described as a beggar colony. He explained that if one was born in the hereditary caste of a beggar, one could have no social contact with those of another caste and would be required to be a beggar for the rest of their life. I had seen many beggars on the streets of Bombay over the past week and nearly all of them were deformed. Some were blind and others were without limbs or had limbs that were twisted in a most grotesque manner. I wondered why so many otherwise healthy people were so severely handicapped. It came as a shock when my guide stated that as children many of them had been intentionally deformed by their parents in order to turn them into successful beggars. After all, who would spare a rupee for a perfectly healthy individual? Children born with sound limbs would have their legs or arms broken or bound in such a manner that they would be crippled for life in order that they might follow the same occupation as their parents. I was disappointed in not being able to see the Indian rope trick performed, but was entertained by young boys being taught the art of charming a hooded cobra, having a live mongoose attack and kill a cobra, and in particular, one teen-aged lad who had learned to put a twenty four inch garter snake up his left nostril and pass it out through his mouth. The next best thing to seeing the Indian rope trick was making a small boy disappear into thin air. This was done by having a lad of about six years step into a large basket placed on the ground. Crouching down until his head and shoulders were below the rim of the basket, a burlap sack was thrown over the container, and after a moment or two removed to disclose that the boy had vanished.

My two weeks at Bandra went by all too quickly. One morning I was told that a vehicle would be arriving after lunch to transport me to the barracks of the Royal Indian Navy in the city where the Royal Navy maintained a building to accommodate ratings in transit. The following day found me at my new quarters together with a dozen or so other ratings awaiting transport or on draft to HM ships. Barrack routine was quite relaxed, and due to the hot and humid climate, we were not normally required to turn to in the afternoons. Shore leave was granted every other day, but there was little to see or do other than spend the evenings drinking beer in one of the better hotels. One night in the Taj Mahal Hotel, a messmate and I were seated at the bar when we got into conversation with a well-dressed blonde whom I thought to be in her late forties. As the only two servicemen in the lounge that night she had insisted on buying us a drink, and before the evening ended, had related to us the story of her life. Apparently she was an American citizen originally from Detroit. In the thirties she had been married to a musician who was wanted by the police in connection with an incident involving prohibition in the United States. Leaving the US, she had come to India with him where he found employment as a piano-player in a Calcutta night club. Unfortunately he died at an early age leaving her stranded and penniless in a strange country. In order to survive she moved to Bombay and started up a business proudly claiming it to be the best whore house in town. When the bar closed that night my chum and I were invited to visit her home where she claimed to have a well-stocked bar and, hailing a taxi which dropped us off at her place of business, we continued to party until the early hours of the morning.

At around 08:00 I awoke with a colossal hangover to find myself on the balcony of the house lying on a palisade where I had obviously spent the past few hours. On the mat by my side was a young girl of about sixteen or seventeen who was soundly sleeping. Wearing a knee-length green silk gown, she was lying on her side, and her long black hair, which came almost to her waist, partly covered the fine features of her very pretty face. Without arousing her I went looking for my chum and found him in bed with another gorgeous girl. The mistress of the household was nowhere to be found, and as the two girls, who were now up-and-about, could speak no English, we decided to leave.

Our leave had expired at midnight and we were both therefore charged with being absent without leave for a period of nine hours and placed on the Commander's Report. The following morning, having been duly paraded before the commander and sentenced to seven days #11 punishment, I resigned myself to being confined to barracks for a week. During that week the annual south-west monsoon rains began right on schedule. Having been born in the West Indies I thought I knew what a tropical downpour was, but nothing could hold a candle to what happened when the rains came to Bombay that week. Once it started to rain, it never let up for a minute. The humidity was fierce and almost overnight the clothing in my kit bag, including a spare set of boots, were covered with a grey-green mildew. At this point I was ready to leave Bombay and it was with great relief that I was told I would be joining a ship for passage to Aden within a day or two. On July 13, 1942, I and two other AB ratings were transported to the dockyard where we joined the troopship *Lancashire*.

The 9,500 ton *Lancashire* had been built in 1917 and in times of peace had plied the Indian Ocean in the service of the Bibby Line. Converted to trooping in 1931, she had on board two Indian infantry regiments bound for the Middle East consisting of close to 1,200 troops, plus a lascar crew of roughly 210 seamen and stokers. The Indian troops on board were a regiment of Sikh's from the Punjab and a battalion of the famous Ghurkhas of Nepal. The only Europeans in *Lancashire* were the ship's officers, the British army officers from the two Indian regiments, and the three of us taking passage to Aden. As a result, I and my two companions were given accommodation in a large first class cabin.

As mentioned previously, the monsoon season had begun before we sailed bringing with it gale winds and rough seas. Most of the troops who had never seen the sea before (much less been aboard a ship) suffered badly. I had no occasion to go below to the troop deck but was made to understand that it was truly a shambles and that many of the Sikhs were violently sick. For some strange reason the Ghurkhas seemed to fair better and I frequently came across a group of them making a meal on the upper deck. Each soldier seemed to have a miniature Primus stove in his knapsack on which he could quickly prepare a dish of boiled rice. Needless to say the rice was well-laced with curry which was not the ideal spice to use when suffering from sea sickness. Before long the odour of curry began to permeate the entire ship and one of the ship's officers remarked that he observed the sea water in the scuppers was now yellow in colour. On a more serious note, we were told one morning that one of the soldiers below decks had died during the night. The poor fellow was a Sikh, and from all accounts had been violently sick the previous day. His body had been found in the "heads" in a somewhat undignified position and due to the fact that rigor mortis had set in, he was very difficult to straighten. The cause of death was established as sea sickness leading to heart failure, aggravated by prolonged retching. The following day the corpse, fully dressed in uniform shorts, shirt, boots, turban, and putties, was carried aft and placed on a prayer mat on the gun platform. A religious ceremony followed during which, between the chanting of prayers, his clothing was removed one piece at a time from his body and thrown into the sea. Finally the ship was stopped, and the prayer mat on which the dead man lay was lowered over the side where the body was carried away by the waves.

CHAPTER X
The Mediterranean

Lancashire arrived in the port of Aden on July 22, 1942, and after an overnight stop, sailed through the Straits of Bab-el-Mandeb into the Red Sea. Our destination was Port Taufiq across from Suez at the southern end of the canal. On disembarking my two companions and I loaded our gear onto the back of a truck which delivered us to HMS *Sphinx* located at Kabret, 75 miles south of Port Said on the shore of Lake Timsa. Within the confines of *Sphinx,* living under canvas, dwelt a small army of sailors either awaiting transport to the UK or draft to ships of the Eastern Mediterranean Fleet. Both officers and ratings were housed in tents, as were the messes, stores, offices, kitchens, and canteens. This huge tent city covered hundreds of acres and sat out in the open desert under the scorching Egyptian sun. There were no trees to shade us and on a windy day the blowing sand would cover our bedding and personal belongings, not to mention the sand that was blown into our food. Located throughout the camp were shower stalls enclosed with burlap sacking woven around posts set in the ground. The water in these showers was warm and salty having been pumped from Lake Timsah which forms a section of the Suez Canal. Bathing in the lake was permitted, but it was a long walk in the scorching heat to reach the shore, and the salt water on our bodies, which dried quickly once we emerged, left us with a thin film of salt on the skin and an uncomfortable itch after dressing.

On the second or third day of joining *Sphinx,* nearly everyone suffered from an attack of dysentery, known throughout the camp as 'gippo gut'. This ailment caused a great deal of discomfort, not to mention embarrassment for, when nature called, the latrines were often some distance away making it necessary to answer the call on the spot. For this reason those of us who had reported sick were provided not only with medication, but also a roll of tissue paper and a small entrenching tool in the form of a do-it-yourself kit. It was easy to spot a new arrival in camp as they walked around with a shovel over the shoulder and a roll of toilet paper on a lanyard around their waist. In addition, I might add that these people were frequently surrounded by a swarm of flies and consequently shunned by their shipmates.

Each day after the midday meal, all ranks could purchase two quarts of beer. For some inexplicable reason the brands provided were always Canadian, either Labatt's Black Horse, or Molson's Frontenac. Because the beer was warm when purchased, we buried it in the sand during the day in the hope that it would cool by evening. After the sun set, and having exhumed our treasure, we would scratch a hole on a sandy ridge overlooking an American airfield adjoining the camp and drink our beer while watching USAAF Liberator bombers taking off for their nightly raid on enemy targets to the west. As the heavily-laden planes climbed into the cool night air, we would count them as they became airborne and sometimes make bets on the number that would return, generally sometime after midnight. While the "Yanks" were away dropping their bombs, we would swap yarns and gaze at the stars in the cool desert night. On the odd occasion we would witness a damaged bomber come to a gory end as it attempted to land. Another form of "entertainment" was provided by the Americans who had erected a large movie screen (similar to those found in drive-in theatres) on which the latest films were shown three nights a week. Where we sat drinking our beer we could see the actors on the screen, and the fact that we could not hear the dialogue made little difference. Any torrid or tender love scene in the script was generally greeted by a chorus of catcalls and wolf whistles by an appreciative audience of matelots.

Discipline in *Sphinx* was quite relaxed by RN standards. There were only two watches; red and blue, which meant twenty-four hours <u>on</u>, and twenty-four hours <u>off</u>. Members of the off-duty watch were allowed leave to visit the nearby town of Ismailia and transportation in the form of a two-and-a-half ton truck was provided to take us into town. Few, however, took advantage of this privilege because once in town, there was little to see or do. Along the banks of the

Sweetwater Canal Arabs sold a variety of merchandise, most of which was cheap junk. For ten piastres one could have a photograph taken by a sidewalk photographer while posing in front of a backdrop on which was painted a picture of the pyramids and a smiling sphinx. Young urchins followed us everywhere offering to shine our shoes for five piastres, while others offered to sell pornographic postcards at twenty piastres each, or provide us with a good looking woman (bint) for only one Egyptian pound.

The offer to introduce us to a bint was a way of evading the Military Police who patrolled the streets in the red light district, which was out of bounds to servicemen. The duty watch were required to provide working parties to carry out the essential daily chores required to keep the camp operational. There were new latrines to be dug and old ones to be filled in. Help was needed in the mess tents to peel potatoes and 'gash' buckets had to be emptied. The entire camp had to be policed for blowing refuse and the skirts of the bell tents had to be stopped up each morning in order to allow the tents to air out. Most of these chores were completed before noon and in the afternoons, during the hottest part of the day; we were often left to our own devices. Almost everyone in *Sphinx* looked forward to being drafted to a seagoing ship whether one was an old hand awaiting passage home or a newly-arrived draftee itching to get a berth in one of the ships in the fleet - anything to get away from the flies, dust, scorching sun, and a chance to sleep in a clean hammock once more.

Shortly after my arrival I awoke one morning suffering from severe pain in my left ear resulting from an infection brought on by swimming in Lake Timsah. On reporting to sick bay, I was surprised to find that I was regarded as somewhat of a celebrity. The young surgeon-lieutenant who examined me, together with the other members of the sick bay staff, were delighted to have a patient with a <u>real</u> infection instead of the usual ailments such as blisters, sunburn, scorpion bites, 'gippo gut', and heat exhaustion. Here was a chance for the doctor to look into my ear, and the leading sick berth attendant (SBA) to clean it out (which he did with great gusto) causing me a great deal of pain. At the conclusion of the examination it was decided that I should go to hospital for treatment, a decision greeted by the able seaman who drove the ambulance with much pleasure, giving him an opportunity to run ashore in Ismialia where I was to be admitted to the hospital ship *Maine*. A boat from *Maine* was already at the dock in Ismialia when the ambulance arrived, and after a short trip to where she lay at anchor in Lake Timsah, I was put to bed between clean sheets in one of her air conditioned wards, and later that evening given a wonderful meal. It took eight days for the ear infection to clear, during which time my name came up for a draft to the cruiser, *Coventry*.

The C-class A/A cruiser, *Coventry*, was one of the most effective anti-aircraft ships in the RN at that time, downing more enemy aircraft than almost any other ship in the Eastern Mediterranean Fleet. During the past two years in the Eastern Mediterranean her exploits were legendary and she was considered to be, not only a lucky ship, but a happy one. In March, 1942, she had been in Bombay for a refit and while I had been in *Maine* she had passed through the canal on her way to Port Said. Had I not been on the sick list I would have joined her, and on my discharge from *Maine* was very disappointed to learn that someone else had been drafted other than me. I was even more upset when I discovered that my two friends who had accompanied me in *Lancashire* from Bombay were now members of her ship's company.

In September 1942, the Royal Navy had been fighting the war in the Mediterranean for two years. Early in 1942, after the fall of Tobruk, the German army had advanced to the Egyptian border and were only sixty miles from Alexandria. A decision was made by naval staff to evacuate that port and the ships of the Eastern Mediterranean Fleet were withdrawn to the ports of Haifa and Port Said in the east. The First Submarine Flotilla was moved to Beirut. The destroy depot ship *Woolwich*, together with the repair ship *Resource*, and six destroyers, were moved to the south end of the canal and the battleship *Queen Elizabeth*, which had been undergoing temporary repairs, was undocked and sailed for Port Sudan, and by July was on her way to America for permanent repair. Naval shore staff were re-located to Port Said and, had Alexandria fallen to the enemy, preparations were made to close the canal with block ships. By September, 1942, the situation in the Middle East had improved greatly. General Montgomery had been given command of the Army of the Nile (now known as the 8th Army), Admiral Sir Henry Harwood had taken over as Commander-in-Chief, Eastern Mediterranean Fleet, and the Naval Staff had returned to Alexandria from Port Said. For those of us trapped in *Sphinx* the days went by all too slowly and the monotony became unbearable. It was therefore with a great deal of excitement and curiosity that one day we were called on to clear lower deck in order to be addressed by our commanding officer.

Our commanding officer, Captain Moore, RN, was a fire-breathing individual who, with great pride, informed us that the army had come to the navy for assistance. The information that we were given was that there were a number of trained soldiers in the Nile Delta who were being employed to guard vital strategic locations against possible enemy attack. These troops (fully trained infantry) were considered by the army to be improperly employed and the top brass wanted to use them for more important duties in the field. A decision had therefore been made that the hundreds of idle sailors presently located in the navy's transit camps should be used to replace them in order that these trained men could return to their various divisions as part of the great build up underway in the 8th Army. A naval battalion of roughly 300 strong was to be formed, armed and trained as fast as possible, and while no official name was given to this group, it was to be locally known as the Naval Guard Battalion or, as matelots called it, the 'Sandlocked Navy'. Plans called for our training to take place at a combined operations camp located a few miles north of *Sphinx*, known as HMS *Saunders*.

There were to be three rifle companies and a head quarters company for administration. Our commanding officer was the former captain of *Sphinx*, and our second in command held the rank of commander. The adjutant was a lieutenant commander, and there were a number of RNR, RNVR, and RNZNVR lieutenants appointed as company commanders. In charge of training was the Battalion Gunnery Officer (BGO), a lieutenant commander, RN. Weapons and ammunition supplied to us were drawn from a cache of captured Italian rifles, revolvers, bayonets, and light machine guns stored in a large warehouse near Ismialia, and to make us look like real soldiers, we were issued with khaki shirts, shorts, and gaiters. Steel helmets were issued, but we retained our white naval caps for normal day use. Transportation provided for the battalion consisted of two Chevrolet sedans, an ambulance, two half-ton trucks, and a number of jeeps. The two sedans were allocated to the CO and BGO as staff cars, and on learning that the BGO was looking for a batman/driver, I applied for the job and was accepted. The job came with a number of perks, which included not having to take part in exhausting route marches and being able to trade in my Italian rifle in exchange for a.38 Webley (a much lighter and less cumbersome weapon). I was also granted the privilege of sharing quarters with the officer's cooks and stewards and drawing my rations from the wardroom galley.

Within five or six days of being formed, the entire unit was ordered to move to Alexandria and an advance party consisting of the commanding officer, the adjutant, the battalion gunnery officer, and the paymaster, left for that city by road in the two staff cars. The battalion was to follow by train two days later. En-route to Alexandria we went via Cairo and, much to my delight, the BGO insisted that we break our journey at El Giza in order to visit the Pyramids and the Sphinx. We spent almost four hours sightseeing and took advantage of the break to eat our box lunches before resuming our journey. Arriving in Alexandria late that evening we went directly to the old police barracks at Ras El Tin, which the RN was using as temporary quarters for servicemen requiring accommodation in the city. Here we found the naval staff in a bit of a flap as they were in the process of tending to the needs of the survivors of the ships *Coventry*, *Sikh*, and *Zulu*, who had only that day been landed. Most of the survivors were mobile that night (the wounded having been taken directly to hospitals on arrival) and I was delighted to find that my two former mess mates, who had joined the *Coventry* while I had been in hospital, had survived the sinking and seemed in good spirits despite having lost their kit. That night they told me what had happened during the past forty-eight hours leading to the loss of the three ships, together with the 350 marines which the destroyers had embarked at Alexandria. On approaching Tobruk, in the early hours on the morning of the 14th, the destroyer *Sikh* was the first ship to be hit by gunfire from the shore batteries. The destroyer *Zulu* went to her assistance and tried to take her in tow, but due to accurate enemy fire, was unable to do so, leaving her to sink close inshore where many of her crew and those marines that had survived the landing, were taken prisoners. By 09:00 on the 14th, *Coventry*, which was well clear of the harbour, was ordered to go to the assistance of *Zulu*, but was hit by a bomb which started a fire, causing her to be abandoned. At 16:15 *Zulu*, who had been standing by *Coventry*, was hit by one of the last bombs dropped in the attack and she in turn sank after dark.

My two friends had been rescued from the water by a Hunt Class destroyer of the 5[th.] Flotilla and landed in Alexandria on the very day we arrived from Cairo. We parted company later that evening and had already left the barracks the next morning when the remainder of our battalion arrived in Alexandria. By the end of the day our entire group had been moved to a water treatment plant which served Alexandria, located in the suburb of Siouf. At Siouf Waterworks we relieved a company of Seaforth Highlanders and mounted a guard around the perimeter for the next thirty-three days to protect the plant. Except for the fact that we were allowed all night leave to visit the flesh pots of Alexandria, and that we were no longer required to sleep under canvas, conditions were not much different to that in Ismailia. The former administrative building became the headquarters for the battalion and was occupied by the officers, administrative clerks, and senior NCOs. The ratings were housed in the maintenance sheds and other buildings on the property. Each morning at 08:00 we paraded outside battalion headquarters for colours and prayers, after which the hands were detailed off for routine chores and members of the duty watch were warned for guard duty. Those of us who did not go into town on leave during the dog watches were required to muster for evening quarters and pipe down was at 20:00. There were a number of sentry boxes located inside the chain-link fence surrounding the plant. These were where we mounted guard and emerged from at frequent intervals to patrol the section of fence we were responsible for.

Occasionally there would be excitement during the day when a German reconnaissance plane paid a visit and our bugler would sound the call for *Action Stations,* followed by *Repel Aircraft.* I was never able to understand how we were supposed to repel the enemy as our weapons consisted of 1918 Italian Beretta's and 6.5 mm Breda light machine guns.   In any event, the jerry aircraft flew so high we could hardly see them in the pale blue sky. The army AA guns around the city, together with the high angle 4" inch guns of the fleet, would all be blazing away, and by following the trail of bursting shells which appeared as little balls of cotton, it was just possible to catch a glimpse of the intruder. With both the army and the navy filling the sky with lead, the RAF boys wisely stayed on the ground and one could not blame them as who would want to run the risk of being shot down by friendly fire.

Our commanding officer, who I am convinced suffered from delusions of grandeur, spent a great deal of time trying to persuade the army to allow us to take a more active role in the build-up of their ground forces. He probably thought of his command as being similar to that of the Royal Naval Brigade of World War I which had fought so gallantly in France with great loss of life. He was determined to commit us to battle and was not content to have us employed as guards. Almost every day he would visit army headquarters in order to badger any senior army officer willing to listen to him. We were all a little concerned when his driver informed us that he had taken to carrying a Thompson sub-machine gun around with him. On one occasion he scared the pants off the Military Police outside army head quarters, when his staff car pulled up in front of the building and the 'old man' jumped out of the car and ran up the steps brandishing his Tommy gun. Of course the army had no intention of letting him have his way. The very thought of a mob of untrained seamen and stokers, armed to the teeth, and turned loose in the desert, was enough to make any self-respecting British Army officer shudder. One 'Pongo' was reported to have said: "It's bad enough having to face the Afrika Corps without having to worry about a bunch of rum-soaked sailors in our midst". Despite this lack of enthusiasm on the part of the army, the 'old man's' persistence eventually paid off and reluctantly arrangements were made to have us visit the front. The unofficial explanation for this change of heart was that it would be good for inter-service relations. Plans were made for a limited number of 'Pongos' to go to sea in our ships while those of us in the Naval Guard Battalion were to be introduced to army life in the desert.

On the day of the great experiment, a fleet of Royal Army Service Corps (RASC) two-and-a-half ton trucks picked us up in Alexandria and set out in convoy along the coast road to El Alamein. Due to the size of our contingent we were split into four groups, each being allocated to a specific sector of the line. In the case of Headquarters Company we found ourselves destined for the southern end of the line which was at that time held by 4th Indian Brigade of the 30th Corps. Our arrival at the front created quite a stir among the Indian troops who were unable to understand the purpose of our visit. Fortunately most of the Indian NCOs' spoke some English, as did all their officers. In very short order our new hosts went out of their way to make us feel at home in our new surroundings and taught us how to survive in the decidedly hostile environment. Of immediate concern to the army was our safety during our visit. The entire area was sown with anti-personnel mines, both ours, and the enemy's. Behind the line our mined areas were marked, as were German minefields which had not been fully cleared. What we had to learn was how to recognize the various markings in order to avoid walking in to a dangerous area and should we find ourselves trapped in a mined area, how best to extradite ourselves. We were taught to go down on our knees and to try and retrace our steps while, at the same time, probing in the sand with our bayonets for buried mines. Our hosts also pointed out to us that there were a number of locations behind the lines where a man standing upright was visible to enemy snipers. These locations were well marked and we were warned to keep a sharp look out for them.

As mentioned earlier, the navy had provided us with khaki uniforms, but failed to provide us with matching headgear. Except for our steel helmets, which were most uncomfortable when worn all the time, our only other headgear was our naval issue white caps which the 'Pongos' pointed out was a very dangerous thing to be wearing with enemy snipers around. Not wishing to be on the receiving end of a sniper's bullet, we quickly replaced our white caps with steel helmets and, as a result, stood out like sore thumbs, taking a lot of ribbing from our 'Pongo' friends who all had the standard army khaki wedge cap to wear and who only wore a steel helmet when going into action.

While in the desert our meals came from mobile army kitchens and were not much different from our own rations. However, we were the envy of British soldiers when we lined up for our rum ration at noon each day. As was the custom in the Royal Navy the British sailor never went without his tot, and rum was sent up to us each day from Alexandria. The arrival of the rum meant little to me as I was still U/A, nor were the Indian Sepoys interested. It was the British 'Pongo' who stood around gaping as our lads lined up for our daily issue and it soon became known that almost any British soldier would be willing to part with his daily ration of one gallon of water in exchange for a tot of rum. Despite the fact that most of us were dusty and grimy, and might have been sorely tempted, I do not recall the 'Pongos' having any takers. The one gallon of water per day per man had to be carefully used. After filling our water bottles, what was left was used for brewing tea, shaving, teeth-brushing, and a gunner's mate's bath every other day; i.e. washing the upper part of the body with a wet cloth. Not having our hammocks with us meant that we had no blankets and we soon learned to scoop out a shallow trench in the sand large enough for a man to curl up in. Over this we would spread our rubber ground-sheets which were then weighted down at the corners with rocks to prevent them from being blown away. On turning in for the night one crawled into the trench, covered himself with his bedroll and greatcoat, and tried to fall asleep sometime before dawn. Temperatures during the day were scorching and during the night numbing.

On our second day in the desert a young subaltern in a supporting artillery battery paid us a visit and extended an invitation to our group to inspect his forward observation post. Five of us jumped at the chance and off we went not knowing exactly what to expect. After a hike of about thirty minutes we arrived at a spot where we were told that from that point on we would be visible to the enemy and would therefore have to continue on our hands and knees. We eventually came to the observation post which was built into a mound of sand, and on dropping into this man-made cave, were invited to view the Germans through a periscope which protruded through the roof of the dugout. One at a time we took turns looking at about twenty enemy soldiers, mess tins in hand, apparently lining up in front of a field kitchen for their noon meal. Our young subaltern, in a cultured Oxford accent, suggested that we might like to see some fun. Using a field telephone he placed a call to his battery in the rear of our lines and, giving them the necessary co-ordinates, asked for five rounds of rapid fire. In a matter of seconds we could hear the sound of shells passing overhead and there was a mad scramble to look through the periscope at the 'Jerries' scattering to take cover. Our amusement at their discomfort was short-lived; however, as our young subaltern reminded us that they would likely retaliate. He had no sooner said so when we heard the sounds of shells going the other way! We never did find out where they landed or whether they caused any damage, but we did wonder if our troops in the rear appreciated our little caper.

On the day following this little demonstration by the artillery, we were transported by truck to 'B' Echelon where we visited units of an armoured division. On our way to the front along the coast road from Alexandria, many of us had expressed surprise in the fact that we could see little evidence of the great build-up in arms, ammunition, and equipment that was supposed to be taking place in preparation for a forthcoming offensive. We now had an eye-opener as our small convoy made its way to the rear. The number of armoured vehicles amassed behind the line was nothing short of phenomenal. Together with the heavy guns of the Royal Artillery and the myriad of soft-skinned vehicles, were Bren gun carriers, ambulances, signal vans, tank recovery vehicles, mobile kitchens, vast quantities of fuel, rations, ammunition, and spare parts. It was hard to believe that the enemy were not aware of this huge build-up, but it was pointed out to us that we had now regained air superiority over the Luftwaffe in that part of the world and that German reconnaissance aircraft seldom, if ever, ventured across our lines.

Our visit to the army appeared to be drawing to a close as we were warned to be ready to pull out the following day. I imagined that our hosts would be as glad to get rid of us as we would be to leave for I venture to say that none of us would have willingly changed places with our 'Pongo' friends having witnessed the conditions under which they lived. After spending three sleepless nights in a foxhole we looked forward to sleeping in our clean warm hammocks once again. What we wanted most of all was a shower to wash away the sand and grime that covered us. We soon discovered however, that there was one more job for us to do before we could return to Alexandria.

After leaving El Alamein, our convoy travelled east for a mile or two then made a ninety degree turn towards the sea. On reaching the Mediterranean we were dispersed over an area roughly five miles in length along the shore starting at a point one to two miles behind the front line. It was explained to us that the purpose of this deployment was to guard against, and raise an alarm if the enemy tried to mount a surprise right flank attack against the 8th Army from the sea. Nothing I have read since has indicated that such an attack was contemplated or, for that matter, even possible. In any event I gather that if this were to have happened we would have been expected to hold off any such landing until the army could divert troops to handle the situation. In all probability the true reason for moving us away from the front was that, unknown to us at the time, the great Battle of El Alamein was about to begin and, on orders from General Montgomery, the area was to be sealed off for security reasons on October 21, 1942. All un-necessary travel between Alexandria and El Alamein station had been halted. As a result of this move, those of us destined to patrol the beach during the First Watch on the night of October 23, 1942, were in a position to witness the largest artillery bombardment in history as General Montgomery's gunners, under a full moon, opened the battle at 21:40 with a barrage of over 1,000 guns placed hub-to-hub and backed up by over 1,200 tanks.

The disbandment of the Naval Guard Battalion was now just a matter of time. By October 25, 1942, we had returned to Alexandria and had taken up our original quarters at Siouf. The threat of attack having diminished, many of us were employed as stretcher bearers at the 64th General Hospital in Alexandria during the first few days of the offensive. Shortly after, the entire battalion entrained for Ismailia where we turned in our weapons and returned to *Sphinx*. Within days of re-joining *Sphinx*, I was drafted to the destroyer depot ship, *Woolwich*, and joined her in Port Taufiq on November 5, 1942. *Woolwich* was a ship of 8,750 tons and had been built in 1934. She had a compliment of 350, was armed with four inch AA H/A guns, and was the depot ship of the fifth destroyer flotilla consisting of approximately eleven ships. Earlier in the year, when Alexandria had been evacuated, she had sailed for Suez with her brood of destroyers and was making her way back through the canal to her former berth, flying the flag of Commodore Destroyers. The day after joining *Woolwich*, we started through the canal and travelled as far as Lake Timsah where we anchored for the night. Resuming our journey the following day, we arrived at Port Said on November 7, 1942, docking astern of the cruiser, HMS *Dido*.

Having been rated able seaman in April, 1942, my pay had increased slightly from that of an ordinary seaman but the prospect of further promotion in the immediate future was somewhat slim. I was therefore very interested when I saw a notice on the ship's bulletin board seeking a volunteer bugler. Anyone interested in applying for the job was asked to report to the ship's office. Having been taught to play a bugle while in the Jamaica Reserve Regiment and knowing that the job of bugler would mean an increase in pay of over three shillings a week, I decided to apply. The fact that I could not read a note of music did not deter me as I felt confident in my knowledge of the various calls to be able to play them by ear. On being paraded before the commander I was invited to audition for the job. Leaving the ship's office, the commander led the way to the quarterdeck, where I was given a bugle and asked to play *Reveille*. Having done so, he then asked me to sound *Up Spirits*, then *Cooks to the Galley*, both of which I played with no difficulty. Satisfied that I could indeed play a bugle, my application was approved and I became the official bugler in *Woolwich*. Apart from the increase in pay, the job came with other perks. For example, I was now considered to be a dayman, and as such excused from normal shipboard duties and not required to muster with the hands each morning. While I continued to be a member of the seaman's mess and ate my meals there, I was instructed to sling my hammock in the wardroom flats at the foot of the accommodation ladder leading to the quarterdeck. The reason for this was that as the only bugler in the ship, I had to be readily available to the officer of the watch during the night. During daylight hours I was considered a member of the gangway party consisting of the officer of the watch, quartermaster, and duty messenger. These three were all required to do regular four-hour watches, but as bugler I spent the entire day on the quarterdeck.

As *Woolwich* wore the Flag of Commodore 'D', our quarterdeck was a busy place and those of us on the gangway had to be on our toes at all times to man the side for visiting captains of other ships in the harbour, dipping our ensign to merchant ships as they passed our stern, answering other warships as they saluted our flag in passing, and calling boats alongside from our lower boom to either embark or disembark staff officers as they came and left. On a typical day I would be called by the quartermaster half-an-hour before *Reveille*, which was sounded at 06:00, followed by *Cooks to the Galley* fifteen minutes before breakfast. During the balance of the day I was required to make the following calls: *Divisions, Colours, Defaulters, Request*

Men to Muster, Stand Easy, Out Pipes, Up Spirits, Secure, Liberty Men, Evening Quarters, and finally *Sunset*. Occasionally there were other calls to be made such as *Repel Aircraft, Action Stations*, and if the ship was getting under way, *Special Sea-Duty Men Close Up*. Due to the fact that *Woolwich* was not equipped with an electrical broadcast system, each of these calls had to be repeated throughout the ship as many as four times. This meant that I got plenty of exercise walking forward, walking aft, and descending and ascending ladders. Having memorized all the above calls, all went well until one day when I was ordered to make a call I was not familiar with. The occasion was as follows: The ship had been in dry dock undergoing a minor refit. Having been re-floated she was on her way back to her normal berth in the harbour. A strong westerly breeze was blowing and because of our high freeboard the crew on the fo'c'sle were having trouble securing to our buoy. The captain, having turned down the offer of a tug by the dockyard, was determined to moor the ship on his own, but was getting no co-operation from the wind. Two buoy jumpers had gone into the drink in the space of twenty minutes and the commander, who at the best of times was a most excitable man, was having an epileptic fit on the fo'c'sle.

The ship had left the dock shortly after 09:00 and at 11:45 we still had not been able to secure to our buoy. Needless to say, all parties were suffering frustration, nerves were frayed, and the air on the fo'c'sle was starting to turn blue as "Jimmy" would vent his wrath on the mooring party. Those of us on the quarterdeck were unaware of the situation forward, although we had been told that the hands on the fo'c'sle were still at work. At 11:45 I turned to the officer of the watch and asked whether or not I should sound *Cooks to the Galley* and *Up Spirits* as the fo'c'sle party had not yet secured. Making a command decision he replied in the affirmative adding something to the effect that "if the fo'c'sle party can't get their act together, that's their problem. There's no reason that the rest of the ship's company should suffer because of them". Having been given the green light I started off up the starboard side of the upper deck sounding both calls and on arriving on the fo'c'sle was about to repeat them when I was suddenly attacked by an irate commander brandishing his telescope which appeared to be aimed at my head. The poor man was red in the face and looked as though he was about to explode. "Who gave you the order to call the hands to dinner?" he screamed, charging at me like a maddened bull and with the perspiration streaming down his cheeks. Backing away I answered that I had been told to do so by the OOW. "Then cancel it. Sound the *Belay*" he ordered. All hands on deck were looking at me by now, and I felt about six inches high. My problem was that I had no idea what the *Belay* sounded like on the bugle, not ever having heard it played before. For a moment I hesitated, not quite sure what to do, then, putting the bugle to my lips, sounded the first five bars of the *Blue Danube Waltz*. Much to my surprise, no one said a thing. 'Jimmy' lowered his telescope and returned to the task at hand and the hands all started working again. I in turn returned to the quarterdeck and reported to the OOW that he had incurred the commander's wrath. I never did learn to play the *Belay*, and to this day am not sure that such a call exists.

There was one other occasion when I found myself in trouble as a result of not being able to read music. One of the ship's company had been hit by an automobile and killed while on shore leave in Alexandria. Following the accident I was told by the master-at-arms that I would be landed with the firing party on the day of his funeral and that I would be required to sound the *Last Post* at the graveside. Once again I was to be called upon to play a tune that I had not learned by ear, but on this occasion I had twenty-four hours in which to do so. Having been told that there was a Maltese steward aboard who had been a professional musician before the war, I went looking for him, and on explaining my problem he agreed to help. That evening, having obtained the sheet music, we secluded ourselves in the chain locker and thanks to his instruction I was able to take part in the ceremony the following day.

On November 28, 1942, twenty-one days after our arrival in Port Said, we sailed for Alexandria. On leaving harbour my station was on the bridge in order to return the salutes paid to our flag. Standing on the port wing I was able to see all that was going on as we slowly pulled away from the dock. As we passed *Dido* her marine bugler sounded the *Still* and everyone on her upper deck stood to attention and faced outboard. Ordered by the OOW to reply, I did so, and felt very important when, as the last notes of the salute died away, everyone on our upper deck did likewise. Before the hands had been dismissed from harbour stations we sailed past a merchant vessel which was on fire from stem to stern. She was a small ship of about 2,000 tons and as we past her on our port side it was obvious that she was not underway. Through our binoculars we could see no sign of life aboard and I was quite surprised that no one on our bridge appeared to be too concerned about her fate. As we worked up to our full speed of fifteen knots she was soon lost to sight and I never did find out who she was or what had caused her to be on fire.

On our short voyage to Alexandria we sailed independently and when the word went around that we would have no escort a number of the old hands were heard to remark: "Hope we don't end up like the old *Medway*." The reference of course was to the fate of the submarine depot ship, HMS *Medway* which had been torpedoed off Port Said on June 30, 1942 by U-372 while on her way from Alexandria to Haifa. Despite the fact that the overall situation in the eastern Mediterranean had improved, German U-boats were still active in the area and only two months earlier U-83 had torpedoed and sunk the troopship *Princess Marguerite* just north of Port Said. It was therefore not surprising that a number of the ship's company slung their hammocks on the upper deck that night. On entering Alexandria the ship was moored in the same location that she had occupied prior to the evacuation.

In the harbour on our port side were the interned French warships of Force X; the battleship *Lorraine*, cruisers *Tourville*, *Duquesne*, *Duguay*, *Trouin*, and destroyers *Basque*, *Fortune*, and *Forbin*. All these ships still wore the red, white, and blue tricolour of France but were manned by skeleton crews and were unable to fire their main armament due to the fact that the breech-blocks of the guns had been removed. They had been allowed to retain their light anti-aircraft weapons however, for self defence and we kept a close watch on them at all times. During the three years that these warships rode at anchor in Alexandria their crews were allowed ashore nightly and their liberty boats would pass our stern with their seamen dressed in civilian clothes. Those of us who were still engaged in fighting the Germans had little use for them, least of all the matelots of the Free French Navy who still wore their uniforms proudly and whose ships formed part of our fleet. I have often wondered what thoughts must have gone through the minds of the French seamen who manned these once proud ships of the French navy as day after day they watched our battle scarred ships sail past them, returning from sea to bury their dead while they swung around the anchor safe in harbour.

Christmas Day 1942 (my second Christmas since leaving home) was uneventful. After a meal of turkey, mashed potatoes, and traditional plum pudding, the hands were given a make-and-mend in the afternoon. After lunch some of our boys visited a Greek destroyer which lay alongside and returned later in the evening in great spirits. It turned out that the Greeks had provided them with numerous glasses of ouzo which they quickly learned does not mix well with rum. On New Years Eve the same Greek destroyer was the cause of a great deal of excitement, not only in *Woolwich*, but throughout the entire fleet. I had turned in early that evening in my usual billet by the ladder leading to the quarterdeck, when at the stroke of midnight I was awakened by the quartermaster sounding sixteen bells. Moments later, I heard the sound of gunfire and was called by the messenger to report to the officer of the watch. Dressing quickly, I arrived on deck and found the night sky lit up with tracers and flares. A very excited sub/lieutenant ordered me to sound *Action Stations*. The destroyer on our starboard side was blazing away with all of her 20 mm Oerlikons and it appeared that every other ship in the harbour was doing likewise. A few moments later, there was a tremendous explosion a short distance ahead of our bow, which was thought to be a bomb going off. Going directly to the mess deck I sounded *Action Stations*, and within minutes our guns had been manned and the gun crews were awaiting instructions. Whoever was firing the Oerlikon on the Greek ship came close to mowing down everyone on our topside. The stops on his gun prevented him from firing in to his own ship but lying as he was, well below our upper deck and some distance forward of our beam, we were well within his arc of fire. No one seemed to know exactly what was happening and I heard someone say that the French ships were trying to break out of the harbour.

Our captain arrived on deck wearing his greatcoat over his pyjamas and demanding to know of the gangway staff what was going on. Signals were being sent between ships in the harbour and from ships to shore asking the same question. Eventually, as officers took charge of the individuals involved, it became apparent that there was no air raid in progress that the French ships in harbour had not turned on us, and that Italian or German frog men had not penetrated the harbour defences. The firing died away and order was restored. The massive explosion that we had heard earlier turned out to be the sound of a torpedo exploding on hitting the jetty at the foot of the Ras El Tin lighthouse. It had been fired by one of the nest of motor torpedo boats moored on our starboard side. It was later determined that the entire affair had been started by sailors on the Greek corvette celebrating the birth of the New Year. Fortunately no one was killed that night and I never learned whether the blame was laid on any one individual.

While serving in *Woolwich* hardly a week went by without one of our destroyers returning from sea showing signs of having met the enemy. Frustrated at not being involved in the action I requested to be relieved as the ship's bugler in the hope that I would be drafted to a sea-going ship. My request was granted but instead of being drafted I ended up working in the chief boatswain's stores where I was to learn more seamanship in a month than I might have learned in a year working part of ship. I was fortunate to have as an instructor, an elderly three badge AB who had close to fifteen years of service under his belt. From him I learned the art of rope and wire work which I found most interesting and of great help to me in the future.

One of the responsibilities of the chief buffer was care and maintenance of the captain's skiff. Captain Bailey, our CO, enjoyed small boat sailing and would call his boat away whenever he had some free time on his hands. I was given the job of looking after this boat and on a number of occasions he would take me along to tend his jib. Captain Bailey was without a doubt one of the finest officers I had the pleasure of meeting in my nine years of service. Having served as a midshipman in the first war he was probably in his late fifties and epitomized all the qualities of a British naval officer. A mild-spoken gentleman, he had a great sense of humour and was respected by both officers and men. As a young lieutenant between the wars he had spent a great deal of time on the China Station and had many stories to relate of his experiences in the Far East which were not only interesting but often humorous. He was very interested to learn of my life-long determination to join the navy and my experiences since leaving home. In turn I learned a lot from him about sailing and thoroughly enjoyed the hours spent in his company.

While in *Woolwich*, I met two fellows with whom I developed a long-lasting friendship. They were both deep sea divers with the rank of able seamen and both hailed from London. These two men, whose personalities were vastly different, had joined the navy before the war as boy seamen. John Bull was about six foot two in height, well-built, and an amiable character. The other chap, Roy Cullen, was a rough and ready individual, quite a bit shorter, stocky, and apt to loose his temper easily. Roy was also known to have a problem with liquor and had spent time in cells on more than one occasion. Having been moved from the boatswain's store, I now found myself billeted with the members of the ship's diving party, all of whom occupied a compartment on the upper deck known as the diving locker. This was where the diving equipment was stored and maintained and where we slung our hammocks. As divers in the depot ship, both John and Roy were employed on all jobs that required underwater inspections or underwater repairs to ships in the flotilla. As part of the diving team, I was away from the ship during working hours and employed in the diving cutter. The diving officer was an elderly commissioned gunner by the name of Mr. Carpenter and on one occasion, having expressed a desire to learn more about deep-sea diving, he gave me permission to put on the gear. All went well as John and Roy got me suited up until the copper helmet was locked onto the collar of the suit and I attempted to stand up. At five foot six, and weighing only 145 lbs., it must have been quite comical as I tried to move towards the ladder at the side of the boat and at that moment I gave up all thoughts of becoming a diver. Johnny Bull and I frequently went ashore together and generally ended up at the Alexandria Fleet Club where it was possible to get a great meal and draft beer at reasonable prices. The city did not provide much in the way of entertainment and, apart from the pretty expensive bars and cabarets, there was little to do other than visit one of the three military operated brothels. These brothels were supervised by the services as a means of controlling the spread of venereal disease and were quite successful. Originally there had been only one of these approved establishments in the city for the use of all members of the armed forces, but with the influx of military personnel in the area from 1941 onwards, it became apparent that additional facilities would be required.

Old hands told tales of Australian soldiers on leave in Alexandria standing in queues over two city blocks long for the privilege of paying twenty piastres in order to spend fifteen to twenty minutes with one of the girls. Sailors whose ships might be in harbour for a matter of hours resented having to wait in line with hundreds of 'Pongos' who had perhaps two or three days leave from the front and consequently all the time in the world to satisfy their carnal desires. True to the traditions of the Senior Service, the navy established its own exclusive facility and reportedly recruited only the youngest and prettiest girls available. Regardless of what the prudish may think, this solution to a problem which has confronted warriors over the ages, served to reduce the high incidence of sexually transmitted disease within the fleet. This was proven later in the war when, supposedly on the orders of General Montgomery, the brothels were closed, causing the venereal disease rate to soar. It is interesting to note that any British sailor contracting VD was punished by having his leave stopped, loss of pay, stoppage of rum etc., unless he was able to produce a receipt indicating that he had taken the precaution of using one of these establishments and had not been infected as a result of a casual encounter. These receipts provide the medical staff with information as to the date of the encounter and the name or number of the girl involved. The girl could then be traced and examined by the authorities and if found to be infected, removed from the system.

The Alexandria Fleet Club was first started in May, 1939 to provide food, drink, entertainment, and accommodation to men of the Mediterranean Fleet. The amenities of the club included a well-equipped bar, lounges, reading and writing rooms, library, concert hall, billiards, and table tennis. In June 1940, the grounds of the original club, which already covered four acres, was extended to provide a summer and winter beer garden capable of seating 2,000 men and, in the spring of 1942, a garrison theatre known as the Globe was opened. A typical evening ashore involved a visit to the beer garden where a nightly tombola session was conducted. Four or five of us would sit around a table generally cluttered with beer bottles, marking our tombola cards as the numbers were called over the microphone. With a thousand or more sailors playing, some of the jackpots were a considerable size, and on one occasion I was the fortunate winner of a full house netting me close to 100 Egyptian Pounds. It was in the Fleet Club that I had a chance encounter with one of the Hollingshead boys who had lived at my grandparents' home when we were under the care of Miss Sheldon in our kindergarten years. Philip Hollingshead was about three years my senior. Both he and his younger brother, Michael, had attended Jamaica College in their teens and, after leaving school, had gone overseas to enlist. Philip joined the RAF and I believe 'Mick' enlisted in the Canadian Army.

On this occasion, after having spent the night ashore, I was in the process of morning ablutions in the club's washroom, when I heard the unmistakable sound of someone suffering from the effects of a monumental hangover. You can imagine my surprise when the cubicle door opened and out stepped Philip looking like the wrath of God! I recognized him immediately despite his green complexion and blood-shot eyes. He was wearing an air force battle dress which gave the appearance of having been slept in, and while I had seen people in worse condition, they had all been dead for a number of days!! Over breakfast we compared notes and I found out that he was on leave from his squadron which was located at one of the many desert air strips strung out along the coast at that time. After joining the RAF in England, he had taken his training in Canada and been commissioned as a pilot officer. Returning to England, his squadron had been sent to Egypt and he had been in the Middle East for just over six months. We parted company later in the evening and I never did learn whether he survived the war.

One Saturday afternoon, Johnny Bull and I decided to take a run ashore but for some reason that I can not recall, he was unable to accompany me when the first liberty boat left the ship at 16:00. We agreed to meet later in the evening at a watering hole known as Cobber's Long Bar and from there we would walk to the Flect Club to play tombola. After landing in the dockyard I took a cab to Mohammed Ali Square and, with lots of time on my hands, went for a walk along the busy streets window-shopping. The sidewalk cafes were crowded with Egyptian citizens drinking cups of strong sweet coffee and puffing on their hookahs. As it was a warm day, I looked around for a place to have a drink. Finding a vacant seat on the side walk in front of a wine merchant's establishment commonly known to matelots as a "Boiled Oil Shop", I was approached by a waiter who could not speak English. Through sign language I was able to convey the message that I was thirsty and wanted something to drink, whereupon he disappeared into the shop and returned with a bottle of wine and a glass. The label on the bottle provided no clue as to the contents as it was in Arabic, and on tasting the liquid I was not impressed. Having paid what I considered to be a high price for the drink, I was reluctant to leave it unfinished and sipping it slowly managed to empty the bottle over a period of about half-an-hour.

As it was now close to the time that I had agreed to meet John,

I set course for Cobber's Long Bar about a block or two away, a favourite haunt of ours mainly because the proprietor was an expatriate Australian of doubtful vintage. I never did learn his true name, but Cobber had served with the ANZAC during the first war and was wounded in Gallipoli. While recovering in hospital in Egypt he had met, and later married, an Egyptian girl and settled in Alexandria. His establishment was located on the ground floor of a very old building and occupied a huge room with a vaulted ceiling. The highly polished mahogany bar ran the entire length of the room, hence the name Cobber's Long Bar, and the place was generally crowded with 'Aussies' and 'Kiwis' on leave from the front. On my arrival, I could see no sign of John, but expecting him to turn up momentarily, sat on a stool at the bar and ordered a pint of beer. The bottle of wine I had consumed at the "Boiled Oil Shop" started to take effect and I doubt that I finished the pint in front of me.

For the rest of the story I have to rely on what I was told later by John, who claims that he arrived just as I was about to fall off the bar stool but was able to catch me before I crashed to the floor. Unable to revive me, and not willing to leave me in the state that I was in, he hoisted me onto his shoulders and carrying me out of the bar hailed a passing gharry. Not wishing to forgo his game of tombola, he took me to the Fleet Club and on promising the petty officer of the shore patrol that he would be responsible for getting me back to my ship, I was laid out on a table in the beer garden where I spent the evening while the game went on. Still unconscious at closing time, my faithful shipmate hoisted me on to his shoulder once again, and was able to get me back to the dockyard and into the waiting liberty boat. At this point I was vaguely aware of where I was and what was going on around me, but for some unexplainable reason I seemed to have lost the use of my legs. The liberty men in the boat were all in a jolly mood and as our boat approached the *Woolwich* they were singing like members of a Welsh miners' choir, much to the displeasure of the duty officer of the watch. Calling down to the coxswain in the boat, he ordered the poor man to take the cutter around the ship once more before coming alongside and when that did not do the trick, around the ship we went for the second time.

Eventually order was restored when it became apparent that the boat was liable to be sailing around the ship until sunrise if the returning liberty men did not quieten down. Unable or unwilling to carry me aboard over his shoulder, Johnny left me in the boat where I lay on the bottom boards unable to move. On being asked by the OOW if the boat was clear, I heard the coxswain reply: "No sir, one man is still here; seems to be out like a light." Finally realizing that I was not capable of moving under my own power the long-suffering OOW sent for the duty LTO and ordered him to hoist me inboard by means of the port electric crane. Thirty minutes later, strapped in a Robinson stretcher, I was deposited on the upper deck at the foot of the OOW who then gave the order to have me carried to sick bay for examination. Discharged by the medics the following morning, having had my stomach pumped out, I was placed on charge and paraded before the commander as a defaulter. This little man who had once tried to crush my cranium with his telescope appeared sympathetic as I related to him the events of the previous day and for a moment I thought that he might consider dropping the charge against me. However, I was mistaken and, with a smile on his face, and having lectured me on the seriousness of returning to the ship under the influence of alcohol and unfit for duty, promptly awarded me seven days #11 punishment.

Early in January 1943, I applied to take a short ASDIC course to be held in *Woolwich*. This two-week course was designed to train prospective ASDIC ratings in the operation of the Type 144 ASDIC set, and was very basic in nature. Our instructor was a young petty officer whose name I do not recall, but I was told he had been awarded the DSM for having been the ASDIC operator in HMS *Wolverine* on March 8, 1941, when she sank the U-47 commanded by Gunther Prien, the terror of Scapa Flow. On Jan 16, 1943, having qualified as a Submarine Detector Untrained (SDU), I was drafted to the destroyer *Kelvin* and sailed in her for Malta the same day. *Kelvin* was a 'K' Class destroyer assigned to the 14th Destroyer flotilla. She had come out to the Mediterranean in May of 1941 and been damaged by a near-miss off Crete during the evacuation of that island. After undergoing a five-month extensive refit in Bombay from August to

December 1941, she had returned to the Mediterranean and been re-assigned to the 14th DF. Despite the fact that the Afrika Corps were on the run in the east, and the Americans and British were advancing from the west, our ships operating along the entire North African coast at this time from Libya to Algeria were still subject to air and submarine attack.

We seldom left Alexandria for more than 24 hours before coming under attack and on one occasion were forced to repel aircraft off Mersa Matruh about 250 miles west of Alexandria. As the 8th Army advanced and airfields fell in to our hands, the RAF was able to provide us with increased fighter cover. Early one morning off Sidi Barrani, the pilot of an RAF *Spitfire*, which had been covering us, reported that he was about to bail out due to engine failure. Assured by our skipper that we would pick him up, we altered course and headed in the direction of the parachuting airman. As the sea was quite calm we stopped up-wind from the downed pilot and drifted down in order to throw him a line. A number of us off watch gathered on the upper deck to witness the rescue and as he was hauled inboard our navigator, who was on the quarterdeck, was heard to say: "Tough luck old boy. Would you like to come with me to the wardroom to get you out of those wet clothes and have a shot of brandy?" to which the young pilot replied: "Thanks for the offer old boy, but I've just finished breakfast." Within twenty minutes another *Spitfire* had been sent out to take his place.

On my first day in *Kelvin* the ship went to action stations at dusk and in accordance with my station on the watch bill, I hastened to join up with those of us who were detailed off to pass ammunition from the fo'rad magazine to 'A' gun. Until the guns opened up using ready-use ammunition we were not required to enter the magazine and a number of us sat around in the dimly-lit mess deck waiting for the action to commence. With some embarrassment I realized I was the only one in the party wearing a steel helmet. Not wanting to draw attention to myself going into action for the first time, I removed the helmet and tried to act as though I was an old hand at the game. A minute or two later, as a stick of bombs fell towards us, the ship heeled sharply to port as we took evasive action, and at the same time, our main armament opened up. The vibration created by a sudden burst of speed, the alteration of course, and the guns going off, dislodge a metal cap box stowed on the deck head which came crashing down, hitting me on the head and scaring the wits out of me. The laughter of my shipmates at my expense was soon cut short as the PO in charge ordered us into the magazine.

Down in the powder room where the brass charges were stacked in racks, my job was to load the charge on to an electric hoist which carried the round up to the gun turret above. The hoist was in the form of a continuous belt to which was attached a number of steel trays. As these trays moved upwards they tripped a lever which automatically opened a sliding steel door built in to the base of the hoist. The sliding door opened for a matter of seconds only. The trick was to place the charge on the tray and quickly get the hand out of the way before the door closed. In the event that the charge was not correctly placed on the tray, the door would not close, but the belt would continue to move upwards, causing the brass casing containing the charge to buckle like an accordion. When this occurred, the hoist had to be stopped and the damaged casing removed. Suffering from a bad attack of nerves, the very first charge that I tried to load on the tray jammed the hoist. With an oath, the PO in charge stopped the hoist, and on extracting the damaged round, said to me: "Carry it to the upper deck and throw it over the side". Climbing vertical ladders from below the water line to the upper deck with a thirty pound weight on the shoulder, while the ship rolled and pitched, I do not recommend. On returning to the magazine I took care to ensure that I would not have to do it again.

HMS Kelvin photographed in action in 1942.
Note the size of her bow wave and elevation
of her guns, which are repelling enemy aircraft   The author's collection

Early in February 1943, while we were at Malta, *Kelvin* and *Javlin* were tasked with intercepting German and Italian ships attempting to escape from Tripoli. Our commanding officer, Commander Townsend, met with the commanding officer of *Javelin*, Lieutenant Commander Alliston, DSC, to discuss the forthcoming operation. Both agreed that there was a danger of their ships shooting at each other in the confusion of battle, even though a bright moonlight night was expected. It was therefore agreed that in the likelihood of this happening *Kelvin*, as the lead ship would switch on her navigation lights and *Javelin* would follow suit. It was also recognized that the small ships the enemy were using could not easily be sunk by gunfire as armour-piercing shells would often go right through them without exploding, so the two commanding officers intended to use high explosive shells. As it was anticipated that the action would be fought at close range, both destroyers might also be able to lob depth charges at the enemy. As previously related, my job at action stations was in the magazine; therefore I had little knowledge of what occurred the following night until the 'old man' cleared the lower deck and addressed the ship's company on our return to Malta.

On my return to the United Kingdom later in the year, a report of this action was printed in the newspapers which read:

"Two Clyde-built destroyers, Kelvin (built by Fairfields, Goven) and Javelin (built by John Brown, Clydebank) are in the news. Together they sank 11 small ships including a torpedo-boat and a Corvette in a three-hour attack on a Mediterranean coastal convoy from which only one ship escaped. As Javelin dashed across the bows of the enemy escort at only ten yards range her gunners threw a depth charge on each side of her blowing her right out of the water. It was a brilliant example of eye-shooting with depth charge thrower. The first enemy ship sighted, a coaster of about 600 tons, was hit by Kelvin's second and Javelin's first salvo. She blew up while trying to beach herself. The next two ships were chased at over 30 knots before being engaged and sunk. A merchant vessel of 2,500 tons was taken by surprise, hit at over two miles range and blown up with her torpedo-boat escort by the Javelin, while Kelvin destroyed another ship. While in the middle of the convoy the guns' crews were swinging their heated guns round-and-round onto different targets and cheering like mad every time a new one was engaged. Only the Corvette replied to the British fire. A schooner hit by the Javelin turned three full circles before bursting in to flames. Shortly after 0300 the action was broken off and the two destroyers headed back to Malta."

Judging by this newspaper report, it would seem that an exciting time had been had by all!! It was a pity that I should have missed all the excitement, confined as I was to the magazine of *Kelvin*.

On one occasion when we were in Alexandria, I was quite surprised to find about a dozen letters that had finally caught up with me, a number of which had been mailed as much as six months previously. Among them were letters from my mother which she had sent to my Aunt Lorna in England to be forwarded. These letters had originally been sent to HMS *Nile* after I had left the UK, but because of my extended stay in Bombay had ended up in the 'dead letter file' of the fleet post office in *Sphinx*. One of these letters was from my Aunt Lorna's father, my Great-Uncle, Commodore N.F.J. Wilson, who was living in Kenya. Having learned from his daughter that I had joined the RN, he apparently expected that I would eventually be considered for a commission and was most anxious to help me in any way that he could in that regard. With this in mind he had deposited in my name at the Alexandria branch of Barclays Dominion, Colonial, and Overseas Bank, a considerable sum of money in order to assist me in purchasing the necessary trappings of a naval officer such as a sword and other uniform items not provided by the crown. In writing to thank him for his generous gift, and to assure him that the money would be used for the purpose intended, I refrained from saying that the possibility of my being commissioned as a naval officer was extremely remote.

Another letter from Aunt Lorna indicated that she had correctly guessed that I was in the Middle East. She had written to suggest that I should pay a visit to her husband Hugh, a staff officer attached to 8th. Army headquarters in Cairo. Apart from the fact that I was serving in a sea-going ship with no means of getting to Cairo, I had little desire to meet this gentleman. At the time I believe he held the rank of brigadier general and the thought of Able Seaman Jones seeking an audience with General Trollope at army headquarters in Cairo was too ludicrous to imagine. I decided to pass on the offer.

There seemed to be no end to the tasks we were given in March and April 1943, and we continued to be on guard against E-boat and U-boat attack, especially in the Strait of Pantelleria. Between March 19 and May 15, 1943, we visited the ports of Valletta, Benghazi, Tripoli, Phillipville (Skikda), Alexandria, Port Said, Tobruk, and Bone (Annaba). On May 13, 1943, Marshal Messe ordered the surrender of all German and Italian troops in Tunisia. We later learned that 250,000 men had surrendered to the allies during the last days of the campaign. While in Alexandria harbour on May 14, 1943, the "old man" cleared lower deck and announced that the following day we would be sailing for Tripoli, our first port of call on our way back to Britain. The entrance to Tripoli harbour had been blocked by the enemy by sinking two ships. Underwater demolition divers had made a gap wide enough for a destroyer to enter, but it was a tight squeeze requiring careful navigation. I recall standing on the upper deck as we entered very slowly, looking down through the clear water to see the wreck of the block ship only a few feet from our hull. From Tripoli we sailed to Malta for the last time, and during our short visit, were once again witness to an attack on shipping in the harbour by German and Italian aircraft. As the sirens warned of the impending attack, the harbour filled with smoke from numerous canisters along the waterfront, ignited in order to hide the ships at anchor from the bombers overhead.

Our next port of call was Bone where we were to meet up with a number of American liberty ships and escort them to Algiers. The American freighters were being loaded with German and Italian prisoners of war and, while waiting for the convoy to form up, we anchored outside the harbour. During the forenoon I was one of the crew of the motor cutter when it went into the harbour to collect the mail. While waiting for the truck that was to deliver our mail I, with other members of the boat's crew, had an opportunity to study our recent enemies at close range. There were four Landing Craft Infantry (LCI) alongside the jetty filled with Hitler's 'supermen' waiting to be ferried out to the waiting American ships. The majority of these prisoners appeared to be under twenty years of age. There were a few seasoned veterans and it was interesting to note that while the older men appeared to be somewhat dejected, the younger ones gave the impression that they were about to embark on a holiday cruise. The Military Police guarding the prisoners did not object when we tried to strike up a conversation with the Germans, many of whom seemed only too willing to try out the few words of English that they knew. A number of them wanted to trade items such as buttons and badges for cigarettes, and there were one or two who could speak English quite well. They promptly informed us that the war was far from over and that the defeat of the Afrika Corps was only a temporary set-back for the German army which would eventually be victorious.

On returning to the ship we learned that we would not be sailing before nightfall and *Hands to swim, port side aft* was piped. As it was a very hot day, a number of us took advantage of the chance to cool off in the Mediterranean. There were approximately forty of us in the water that afternoon when an air raid developed and bombs began falling in and around the harbour. All available anti-aircraft guns opened up and the ship went to action stations before we were able to scramble back aboard, but not before a stick of bombs exploded in the water some distance from where we were anchored creating a tingling sensation throughout the body as we swam back to the after gangway. The following day we arrived in Algiers where we secured alongside an American destroyer in the harbour. The American 'gobs' were quite friendly and a great deal of trading in souvenirs took place between our boys and theirs. The matelots drew the line however, when 'tot time' came around and the "Yanks" offered to trade a gallon of ice cream for a tot of rum, and found no takers. That evening we sailed for Gibraltar where we anchored two days later. Two days in Gibraltar allowed both the port and starboard watch one night ashore and on May 30, 1943, we joined up with a convoy heading for 'Blighty'. While in Gibraltar we were provided with an impressive demonstration of the army's anti-aircraft defences, as a high flying enemy reconnaissance plane approached the rock. As we gazed at the aircraft in the sky the entire rock seemed to explode as hundreds of guns threw up a curtain of steel in front of the aircraft, creating a noise greater than the loudest clap of thunder ever heard.

Our homeward bound convoy had originally sailed from Casablanca with a strong A/S escort, and while crossing the Bay of Biscay we had a number of U-boat alarms resulting in at least three attacks by the escorts but with no apparent results. As we came abreast of the coast of France we were shadowed by a German Condor, which hung around for an hour or two before being either chased off or shot down by a Spitfire flown from a CAM ship in the convoy. We were too far from the action to see what really happened. Arriving in Greenock on June 4, 1943, we left the Clyde two days later, and after sailing north around Scotland were off Sheerness on June 8, 1943, and alongside Chatham dockyard on June 9, 1943. *Kelvin* was long overdue for a re-fit and was to spend the next six months in dockyard hands before she again went to sea. The ship was paid off and most of the hands went on Foreign Service leave. In the fifteen months I had been away from Britain a great deal had happened throughout the world. The Battle of the Atlantic still raged, but the Germans had lost 31 U-boats during the previous month and the air gap in the Atlantic was about to be closed. Shortly after our return to England, the King paid a visit to Malta and the allies were about to invade Sicily. The last major German offensive on the Eastern Front, the Battle of Kursk was about to begin. In Britain the fear of invasion was now a thing of the past, air raids were few and far between, and the RAF and USAF continued to fly massive air strikes against Germany. Within three months Italy would surrender and the Italian fleet would lie at anchor in Valletta harbour.

CHAPTER XI

Return to 'Blighty'

On paying off, *Kelvin's* **ships'** company entered the Royal Naval Barracks in Chatham, HMS *Pembroke*, from where all members went on Foreign Service leave. I was granted fourteen days and travelled to London where I stayed at the YMCA Hostel in the Strand where my Aunt Lorna worked. On returning from leave and, reporting to *Pembroke*, I was drafted to HMS *Osprey*, the anti-submarine school in Dunoon, Scotland where I began the qualifying course as a trained ASDIC operator.

Although having landed in Greenock when I initially arrived in the UK, I had always been stationed in England and now looked forward to visiting Scotland for the first time. The train from London left Euston Station at roughly 21:00 and arrived in Glasgow Central Station the following morning at around 07:00. From the railway station we went by lorry to the ferry which took us across the Clyde to the beautiful little town of Dunoon. Night train journeys in wartime Britain were not very enjoyable. Normally eight people were jammed into a carriage compartment, four on one side facing four on the other. As almost everyone smoked, the air would become quite thick as the journey progressed and it was necessary to open a window. Because of the black-out this required the light in the compartment to be switched off so we travelled mostly in the dark. In the summer the fresh air was a blessing, but during the winter months it could be decidedly cool and servicemen would doff their greatcoats and use them as blankets. If one was lucky enough to be seated beside a girl this could lead to a very interesting and pleasurable experience as boy and girl snuggled under the greatcoat to keep warm in the darkened compartment.

On this occasion, the long journey to the north turned out to be both memorable and pleasant. Minutes before we pulled out of Euston Station an elderly brigadier, whose red cheeks matched the tabs on his collar, came puffing and panting down the platform accompanied by a rather pretty girl wearing an ATS uniform. The guard on the platform had raised his green flag and was about to blow his whistle, when this officer came abreast of our coach. There was no time to loose as the train was about to leave. Opening the door of our carriage, he passed a suitcase to helping hands, and moments before the train started to move, managed to assist the young lady to enter the carriage. While the train was slowly moving out of the station, she leaned out of the window and called out: "Goodbye daddy; I'll write as soon as I get there". There was room for one more person on our side of the compartment and, as the 'Pongo' seated beside me stood to place her suitcase on the luggage rack, she wedged herself into the space he had vacated with the result that she now sat next to me. On close inspection, those of us in the service realized that this young lady was a commissioned officer in His Majesty's Forces as she wore two pips on her shoulder indicating that she was a lieutenant in the ATS. Normally officers travelled in first class compartments and I assumed that her reason for being in our carriage was because of her nearly missing the train.

As we sped through the night, the spirited conversation in our compartment gradually subsided as one-by-one we tried to get some sleep. Because there were a number of smokers in our group, we had opened the window and turned off the light due to the blackout. In conversation with the charming lieutenant I learned that she was twenty-three years of age and had been in the ATS for over two years. Her father had seen her off at the station as she had been posted to an establishment near Falkirk, Scotland. She told me that her father, who had served in WWI and retired from the army as a colonel, had been called to the colours at the outbreak of WWII and, much to his disgust, was chained to a desk as a staff officer in Southern Command. Before long, most of us had fallen asleep and the lieutenant was breathing softly in my ear, her head having come to rest on my shoulder. When the train came to a brief stop at Rugby, she drowsily asked where we were, then linked her arm around mine, cuddled up closer and fell back to sleep. Later, after dropping off to sleep, I was aware of an exploring hand on the inside of my thigh, sending me that unmistakable signal that every sailor dreams of, but all too seldom receives. There was only one conclusion. Quietly, we slipped out of the compartment and went along the corridor to the lavatory. Fortunately, no one in the compartment saw us leave or return, and we were all asleep before the train arrived at Crewe.

On arrival at Glasgow Central Station the following morning, the 'Pongo', who had put the lieutenant's suitcase on the luggage rack in Euston, retrieved it for her and insisted on carrying it own the platform. She spoke briefly to me saying goodbye and wishing me luck on my forthcoming course. At the end of the platform she was met by two members of the Military Police who saluted smartly and relieved the 'Pongo' of her suitcase. She was then led to a waiting staff car parked at the front of the station. I can reassure any 'Pongo' who happens to read this that the young lady was returned to the army by the 'senior service' in exactly the same condition as when she had first boarded the train.

It has been said that the building then known as *Osprey*, where theory of ASW was taught, had been a maternity hospital in pre-war days. Requisitioned by the Admiralty it was the main school of the ASDIC branch of the navy, previously located at Portland on the south coast of England. The Submarine Detectors course lasted eleven weeks. The first four weeks of theory were taught at *Osprey*, after which a further seven weeks of practical training was conducted at HMS *Nimrod* located in the little town of Campbelltown on the Mull of Kintyre. I was to spend the next four and-a-half months in bonnie Scotland where I developed a love for that country, which I retain to this day.

While I admired the English and had made a lot of friends south of the border since my arrival in 1941, there were times when the inhabitants of that tight little country could be somewhat condescending. Those of us who had come to England from far-flung outposts such as Canada, Australia, New Zealand, and the many colonies, were often reminded that we were colonials, the intimation being that as such, we were somewhat inferior to the true bloodied Englishman. The Scots, on the other hand, never gave one that impression. Canadians in particular were regarded as one of their own, and perhaps rightly so, for the Scots had played a major roll in the shaping of Canada, and it was amazing how many Canadian servicemen on leaving Canada had been given the names and addresses of family members in Scotland with the instructions: "Be sure to look them up when you get over there". I was no exception, as I had been given the address of a long-time friend of our family, Christine Featherstone, who resided in Stirling.

Christine had been a teacher at St. Andrews High School in Jamaica and a colleague of my Aunt Cynthia. She had returned to Britain shortly before the outbreak of war and had later married a naval officer. On being granted weekend leave, I decided to pay her a visit. Having travelled to Stirling by bus from Glasgow, I had little difficulty in finding her home, where I was met at the door by a lady who turned out to be her housekeeper. Unexpected as my visit was, I was made to feel welcome, and during the next two days was given a tour of Stirling and the surrounding countryside, including Stirling Castle and the Wallace Monument. Christine, whose husband was a paymaster commander in the RN with the surname of Dickson was, at the time of my visit, at sea and she had not seen him for many months. As a paymaster commander, his ship was probably a cruiser or battleship, although I never did find out the name of it. In any event, a week or so later I wrote to thank her for her hospitality and in replying she informed me that only four days after my visit she had received word from the Admiralty that her husband's ship had been torpedoed and that he was not one of the survivors.

Dunoon was a great little town and I thoroughly enjoyed myself while serving in *Osprey*. Situated across the Clyde from Gourock, it had been a busy holiday town for the people of Argyle in pre-war years. Despite the war it still attracted a large number of holiday makers and that summer it was filled with visitors, many of whom were young girls from the Glasgow factories. Naval personnel in Dunoon were very much in evidence. In addition to the large compliment in *Osprey*, the submarine depot ship HMS *Forth* and her flotilla of operational submarines were only a few miles to the east of town in the Holy Loch. During my time in Dunoon I came to know many submariners who were partly responsible for my deciding to join the submarine service in later years. My claim to fame while in Dunoon came about one night after the pubs had closed and a gang of us were walking back to the ship having consumed copious amounts of beer. There was a statue in town of a lady erroneously known as Mary of Argyle who seemed to hold a fatal attraction to the average British sailor, particularly when he was under the influence of liquor. On many occasions passing sailors had risked life and limb to climb this work of art in order to adorn Mary's likeness with bits and pieces of naval uniform. It was not uncommon for the local police to find Mary wearing a sailor's collar or cap as they patrolled the town in the early hours of the morning. On this particular night some 'wag' suggested that the navy would never have allowed a good-looking girl like Mary to remain a virgin while in Dunoon. A plot was therefore hatched on the spot to rectify the situation. In the wee hours of the morning, having obtained the use of a ladder, a pillow, and a ladies dressing gown, the poor girl was de-flowered and the citizens of Dunoon awoke the next day to find that Mary appeared to be eight months pregnant. Being one of the smallest members in our group it was I who had been selected to climb the ladder to do the dastardly deed, hence my claim to have been the sailor who made Mary of Argyle pregnant. With the help of the Fire Brigade, the local constabulary were able to 'deliver' the unborn child the next morning and restore Mary's good name.

On July 17, 1944, the theoretical portion of our course having been completed, our class was drafted to HMS *Nimrod* for practical instruction. From Dunoon we sailed in a Caledonian MacBrayne ferry northwest through the Sound of Bute to the small town of Tarbert then south along the eastern shores of the Mull of Kintyre to Campbelltown. The small bay which forms the harbour of Campbelltown is sheltered from the southwest by a brae which is covered with broom and heather. The entrance to the harbour is guarded by a small island called Davar and the town itself lies at the northwest corner of the harbour. In 1944 there were two cinemas, two pubs, and two hotels in Campbelltown, the largest hotel being the Royal. The films shown in the cinemas were changed every six days and as they did not change on the same night it was possible to see a total of two movies each week or eight in a month. Apart from the cinema, the only other recreation or entertainment was to be found in the pubs. Occasionally a dance would be held in the church hall and if one wished to take the bus to Machrihanish, the Fleet Air Arm operated a wet canteen at the air field which we were allowed to use. At the foot of the High Street in Campbelltown was a small park where the war memorial stood. Beyond the park was a long pier on both sides of which were moored the local fishing boats, a number of naval trawlers, and about four antiquated submarines all, except the fishing boats, being used for A/S training.

The ASDIC School occupied a modern building at the northeast corner of the harbour and was about a fifteen minute walk from town. As the preceding class had not completed their course when we arrived, our draft was employed in a variety of jobs during working hours, and on my second day at the school I found myself working in the flower garden located outside the Wren's quarters. Stopping work to light a cigarette during stand easy one morning I heard a girl's voice say: "Would you like a cup of tea with your cigarette sailor?", and on looking up, an arm was extended from the window holding a mug of tea and at the other end of which was a bonnie Scottish lass. This was how Marjorie and I first met, and on the offer of a second cup of tea that afternoon, I made a date to meet her outside the main gate that evening to go to the cinema.

The week following our arrival we started practical training at sea. Each morning after breakfast the twenty-four members of our class would form up in groups of six and, dressed in sou'westers, oilskins, and sea-boots, with box lunches in hand, would march to the harbour and board one of the four armed trawlers which would take part in the days exercise. The submarine(s) taking part in the exercise, having sailed earlier in the morning, would have reached the exercise area before we did and would have already dived by the time we arrived on the scene. Within the boundary of each exercise area the submarine would dive to a safe depth of eighty or ninety feet, and throughout the duration of the dive would tow fishermen's buffs (air inflated spherical buoys used to mark fishing nets) on the surface to indicate her position. The duration of the dive and course to be steered was predetermined and known to the surface vessel. There were a number of ways that the vessel on the surface could communicate with the submarine during the exercise including tapping hulls, Morse messages by means of ASDIC transmission, smoke candles, and underwater grenades.   As the exercise got under way the ASDIC operator would be given a compass bearing and instructed to carry out a sweep on either side of the bearing. On contact being made a mock attack would be carried out culminating in the dropping of an underwater grenade simulating a depth charge. The submarine commander would then judge if the attack had been successful. During the course of the day four such attacks would normally be conducted, and by 16:00 we would be back in harbour and secured for the night. With the exception of Saturdays and Sundays this was the routine we followed for six weeks regardless of weather conditions. Some days were dry and calm, but more often than not we encountered rain and gale force winds. We envied the submariners who had nothing to do all day but sit around in a steady platform drinking tea and playing cards while we tossed around on the wet and windy surface eating soggy box lunches.

The submarines based in Campbelltown were from the 7th flotilla and consisted of a variety of obsolete vessels. Among them were the H-Class boats H-32, H-33, H-34 and H-44, all of which had been built in 1918/1919. There was also one of the L-Class, L-27, built in 1919, and two Dutch boats, the O-9 and the O-10, both built in 1925. Although obsolete in 1939, many of these boats had been pressed into operational service during the first year of the war, but having been replaced by more modern vessels, as time went on, were now relegated to ASW training. Occasionally these old boats would be joined by one of our more modern submarines for a short period of time as they joined the fleet and began the work-up to operational readiness. As with any operation involving submarines there is always an element of danger involved and only a month before my arrival in Campbelltown the submarine *Untamed* had been lost with all hands while on A/S exercise off the Mull of Kintyre.

One of the members of my class with whom I had become quite friendly was a South African by the name of John Peard. John, who hailed from Durban, had joined the South African Defence force at about the same time that I had joined the RN. As was often the case during the war when two or more commonwealth sailors met, they tended to join forces against their English shipmates and our relationship was no exception to this rule. John and I were complete opposites. He was six feet four in height and a handsome blonde. He was an Olympic class swimmer, and had made a name for himself in his native country as a rugby player. Our friendship began in Scotland and lasted for many months, and I will have more to say about John as my yarn unfolds. Neither of us ever having been inside a submarine, we were both curious to see what they were like and with this in mind one evening we went for a walk on the pier where they were moored. The trot sentry that day happened to be a member of the crew of one of the Dutch boats and was delighted to find that he and John could communicate as a result of John's knowledge of Afrikaans. As a result, we were invited aboard the O-9 and, after being shown around the vessel, ended up in the seaman's mess where we were treated to a glass of schnapps. Later that evening we were introduced to the officer of the watch who promised to try and arrange that we go to sea with them for a day. He was as good as his word for about a week later it was announced that a small number of our class would be able to go for a day sail in one of the submarines. John Peard and I entered our names and later in the week spent a day at sea in H-33. It was an interesting experience involving my first dive in a submarine which I found to be something of an anticlimax.

Since my first date with Marjorie on joining *Nimrod*, she and I had been seeing a great deal of each other and our relationship had begun to take on serious overtones. I didn't recognize the symptoms at the time but I was falling in love. As already stated, Campbelltown had little to offer in the way of entertainment but somehow the two of us were never at a loss in finding things to do when we were together. Hardly a week went by when we did not visit the cinema, and regardless of what the weather was like, we enjoyed going on long walks in the evenings. We seldom visited the pubs, but after returning to town from one of our walks our favourite haunt was the lounge of the Royal Hotel where we would warm ourselves in front of the fire and enjoy a drink before heading back to the ship.

While still in *Osprey*, Aunt Lorna had written to say that she had rented a house in Lochranza on the Isle of Arran. She and her children, Sarah and Charles, were to spend the summer holidays there, and she hoped that she would be able to pay me a visit. Knowing that my birthday fell on August 21, she wrote to say that she had made reservations for herself and the two children at the Royal Hotel for Friday August 20, and hoped that I could arrange to get leave to coincide with her visit. Having previously written to tell her of my girl friend Marjorie, she mentioned that she was looking forward to meeting her. Both Marjorie and I managed to get weekend leave and were lucky enough to find accommodation in the Royal Hotel for two nights. Aunt Lorna and the children arrived by ferry from Arran at 19:30 on the Friday and later that evening all of us sat down to a wonderful dinner in the hotel to celebrate my birthday. Marjorie surprised everyone by producing a small cake that she had talked one of the cooks in *Nimrod* into making to mark the occasion.

Saturday was a bright sunny day and after breakfast all five of us went for a walk to the top of the brae overlooking the harbour. We had taken a picnic lunch and after eating, lay on blankets in the warm sun watching the fishing boats and other vessels as they sailed in and out of the harbour entrance. Lorna showed me a telegram she had received from my father before leaving Lochranza. In it he reported that my mother's health was generally good but that she was in Toronto waiting to travel to New York for an operation. I had known for more than a year that my mother had suffered from a malignant growth in her throat but had no idea that she was seriously ill and would require surgery. Lorna questioned me at length as to what I knew of her illness but I was unable to give her much information, knowing only that she had been taking radium treatment for what I had been told was an enlarged thyroid gland. Lorna and the children left for Arran on Sunday, and after checking out of the hotel, Marjorie and I climbed the brae once more to our favourite spot overlooking the harbour. The weather had changed as a front moving in from the Atlantic brought with it a steady drizzle and low clouds. Chilled to the bone and somewhat damp, we slowly made our way down the path leading to town. As the day drew to a close a lone piper played the *Lament* in front of the war memorial, as he did every Sunday at sunset. To this day whenever the *Lament* is played on the pipes it brings back memories of that evening as it was on that day in August that my mother passed away in Toronto. It was as though the lone piper that evening was playing for her.

On the afternoon of August 24, I visited the sick bay for an appointment with the dentist to have my wisdom teeth extracted. On leaving the dentist's office I was met at the door by Marjorie who was holding a sheet of paper. Without a word she handed it to me as tears welled up in her eyes and she began to sob. It was a telegram informing me of my mother's untimely death. The following day Lorna wired to say she had managed to book a room at the Royal and would be arriving at 19:30. That evening she showed me the telegram she received from my father in which he stated that my mother had died in New York following an operation. I learned at a much later date that the operation had taken place in Toronto, not New York.

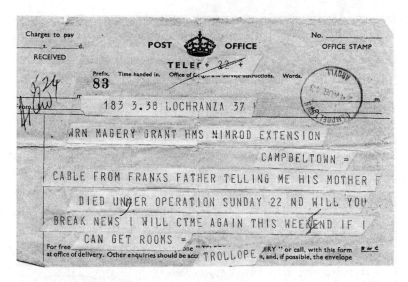

The telegram sent to Marjory in *HMS Nimrod*
informing her of my mother's death,
August 24, 1943

Two weeks later our ASW course ended and I returned to *Osprey* in Dunoon as a fully qualified Submarine Detector. Within twenty-four hours I was told to hold myself in readiness for an overseas draft, and on September 20 was granted fourteen days embarkation leave. Having decided to take the plunge, I phoned Marjorie to give her the news and to propose marriage. I suggested that we might get married while I was on leave. My proposal was accepted but she insisted that we wait until my return to Britain before setting a wedding date. Although disappointed at the thought of a long engagement, I was nonetheless overjoyed with her answer and decided to travel to Campbelltown to spend my fourteen days leave with her. Stopping off in Glasgow just long enough to purchase an engagement ring, I boarded a bus to Campbelltown the following day. Having previously travelled to Campbelltown by ferry, I thought it would make a welcome change to make the journey by road. However, this turned out to be a great mistake as it took about twelve hours to do the trip.

Leaving Glasgow early in the morning we headed north to Balloch then along the west bank of Loch Lomond before heading north-west to Oban. From Oban we travelled south along the Mull of Kintyre arriving in Campbelltown late in the afternoon. On enquiring at the desk of the Royal Hotel I was told there were no rooms available, but on explaining to the young lady at the desk the predicament that I was in, I was informed that there was one small room available but that it was not equipped with anything but a single bed and a chair. Desperate for some place to lay my head, I agreed to take it sight unseen and asked for the key. I then learned that the so-called room was actually a broom closet located on the landing of the hotel staircase and that there was no key to the door. On moving in I found that there was literally no room to swing a cat. The single bed occupied ninety percent of the room and the only other piece of furniture, the chair, was wedged between the wall and the bed. There was nothing else in the room and the one window set in the north wall provided a scenic view of the brick exterior of the building next door. This was where I was to spend the next thirteen days of my leave and where Marjorie and I would retreat to when we required some privacy.

Despite my sparse accommodation, the days that followed were most enjoyable and my only complaint was that there was little for me to do during the day while I waited for Marjorie to come ashore on the first liberty boat in the evening. I spent a great deal of time reading by the fireplace in the hotel lounge and was also able to get caught up on my letter-writing. It was a luxury to be able to lie in bed in the mornings as long as I wished and I often slept in until lunchtime. Each afternoon I would meet Marjorie outside the gate of *Nimrod* and walk with her to the base at midnight when her leave expired. Despite my pleading, she would not agree to our getting married while I was on leave but assured me that if I were willing to wait we would get married immediately after my return. We promised to write regularly to each other and all too soon the time came for us to part.

The journey to Glasgow by bus was not something that I was looking forward to and on learning that I could return by Scottish Airways for the sum of about five pounds, I elected to do so. On leaving Machrihanish Airport early one morning I landed in Glasgow twenty minutes later and that evening reported to the regulating office in *Osprey*. On October 31, 1943, I joined a draft which travelled to Glasgow where we boarded a south-bound train to Liverpool. Still unaware of our final destination, we embarked in the troopship *Andes* which was moored alongside in Gladstone Dock. The *Andes,* owned by the Royal Mail Line, was a relatively modern vessel having been built in 1939. She had never seen service as a passenger liner having been taken up from trade at the outbreak of war to be converted to trooping. At 26,435 tons, she had a speed of 21 knots and as a troopship was capable of carrying over 4,000 personnel. Shortly after embarking we learned that she was bound for New York and would be sailing independently. At 21 knots, it did not take us long to span the Atlantic and on the morning of November 9 the skyline of New York unfolded as we sailed past the Statue of Liberty. John Peard, my former classmate and friend from *Nimrod* who was also a member of our draft, speculated as to the type of ship that we would be joining. There were a number of Royal Navy ships in American ports under refit or repair but most of the members of the naval draft expected to join one of the many escort vessels that were being made in the United States for Britain.

On disembarking, we boarded a fleet of buses, and after a journey of little over an hour, were deposited on the parking lot alongside a large brick building located in the town of Asbury Park, New Jersey. This building, which had been a hotel before the war, was being used by the Admiralty as an accommodation barracks for RN personnel in the United States and known as HMS *Asbury Park*. The base accounting ship located in New York was known as HMS *Saker,* also a former hotel. The daily routine in *Asbury Park* was quite relaxed and rather like living in a hotel. Frequent runs ashore were allowed and almost every night saw us taking in the sights of the "Big Apple". The one problem facing every British sailor in the United States was a shortage of cash. Despite this handicap there were various ways and means that could be employed to ensure that a trip to the city was worthwhile. For example, it did not take us long to discover that the American Red Cross was willing to part with a five dollar bill in exchange for a pint of Royal Navy blood. Donors were supposed to give blood once a month but on arriving in Manhattan our first port of call was usually the Red Cross clinic. After two or three weeks in the United States I suspect that most of us were suffering from anaemia, but for some unexplainable reason we got away with it.

I have often wondered whether the copious pints of beer that we consumed after receiving our five dollars replenished the blood that we sold. A visit to the Stage Door Canteen was next on the list. With a bit of luck one could obtain a free ticket to a Broadway show and if all the tickets had been distributed it was always possible to obtain free coffee and doughnuts at the canteen. Most nights there was an orchestra on hand and a dance in progress well-attended by United Services Organisation (USO) hostesses, US servicewomen, and showgirls from Radio City Music Hall. Occasionally one might encounter a stage or screen celebrity in the crowd, as I did on one occasion when, at the conclusion of a dance, John Peard, who had been watching from the sidelines, asked me whether I was aware of the fact that I had been dancing with Claudette Colbair. One night while visiting a night club on Broadway, the lights were dimmed and the master of ceremonies announced that the orchestra was going to play a few bars of the national anthem of each of the allied countries. On hearing their national anthem played, allied servicemen in the house were invited to stand for a round of applause. Having worked their way through the alphabet from Australia to Yugoslavia, there was a roll of the drums, the lights were turned off, and a spotlight was aimed at the swinging doors leading to the kitchen. A scantily dressed young lady then emerged pushing a trolley laden with bottles of champagne and all allied servicemen in the house were presented with a glass. Although I am not all that keen on champagne, on learning from the waiter that this was a nightly occurrence at midnight, John and I made sure that whenever we were in town we dropped in for a glass of beer at eleven forty-five in time for the nightly ritual.

Generally, the average American was quite friendly and we had been admonished by the navy to be on our best behaviour. As a result, with few exceptions, I do not recall any violent clashes with our gallant allies. I think that most of us were somewhat overwhelmed by the experience of being in a country which was supposed to be at war but where the population as a whole seemed to have no conception of what war was like. For most of us it was difficult to sympathize with the citizens of New York when we heard their complaints about rationing of food, clothing, and petrol for their automobiles. In this wonderful fairyland, the streets were brightly lit at night and we could walk into any restaurant and order steak and eggs, enter any department store and purchase silk stockings and other items of clothing without coupons, and wonder at the never-ending stream of traffic in Manhattan both night and day. Occasionally one would encounter an American serviceman who had seen service overseas but many of their men in uniform had never been out of the country and had never heard a shot fired in anger. Most of them with two or three months of service sported two or three medal ribbons on their jackets and were regarded by their fellow citizens as heroes. One could not help but compare the citizens of New York with the long- suffering citizens of London who, for almost four years, had endured the horrors of war without flinching. All good things have to come to an end, and before the month was out, John Peard and I were drafted to Brooklyn Navy yard where we joined a Kill Class patrol sloop built by the Pullman Standard Car Company of Chicago, Illinois and which had been transferred to the Royal Navy under 'Lend Lease'.

Before sailing from Brooklyn, John Peard and I had an encounter with an Irish American longshoreman which is worth relating. It reflects the attitude of some Americans at that time towards anyone or anything connected with the British. With only a few dollars between us John and I went ashore one night with the intention of downing a pint or two at a pub located close to the dockyard gates. Entering the premises we found the place almost deserted. Apart from the bartender there was only one other person present. At the far end of the bar stood a giant of a man, gloomily contemplating his glass of draft. We parked ourselves on a couple of stools well-removed from the other customer and ordered two glasses of beer. Having served us the bartender entered into conversation with the man at the end of the bar leaving us to enjoy our drinks. Looking around I spied a juke box in the corner of the room and inserted a quarter, selecting a popular tune of the day, *Pistol Pack'n Mama*. As the music started the big bruiser at the end of the bar called out in a loud voice: "Shut that damn thing off". When neither John nor I made a move to comply, he arose, walked over to the machine and pulled the electrical cord out of its socket. I then called the bartender over to where we were sitting and asked for an explanation. He suggested that we finish our drinks and leave as his friend did not like "Limeys".

Both John Peard and I were wearing shoulder flashes on our uniforms which read CANADA on mine and SOUTH AFRICA on his. Pointing this out to the bartender I made a remark suggesting that the big oaf at the end of the bar was probably illiterate otherwise he would have seen from our shoulder flashes that we were not English. At this point John warned me to keep my big mouth shut, but it was too late. The giant Irishman had overheard my remark and, rising from his stool, made a beeline towards me. Grabbing me by the front of my jumper, he yanked me to my feet and duck-walked me to the swinging doors of the saloon. Holding me at arms length with his left hand, he drew back his right, and drove his fist into my face. On my way to the door I appealed to John for help, but with a smile on his face he made no attempt to interfere, as I was unceremoniously thrown out of the bar. Later that evening, nursing a bloody nose, I cursed him for sitting idly by while I was almost murdered. "What's the point in having a big hulk like you as a shipmate if you can't give me a hand when I get into trouble?" I asked. "At six foot three and almost two hundred pounds, I thought that an old time rugby half-back like you with mitts like sledge hammers would have come to my assistance". Smiling, he reminded me that I had asked for it and added that shortly before entering the pub he had seen a US Navy Shore Patrol standing at the corner of the street. The last thing he wanted to happen was for us to get tangled up with the "Yanks" on our last night in the "States", and I had to agree that he was probably right.

CHAPTER XII
Bermuda

Our new ship had not yet been given a name. Known only as _British Escort Craft #5 (BEC-5)_ when we joined her, she was later named HMS _Kildary_ and saw service off the west coast of Africa as a member of an A/S Escort Group. As an American-built vessel, she was equipped with bunks and had a number of amenities not found on British warships, such as electric washing machines, shower stalls, and drinking water fountains. Unfortunately, neither John nor I were destined to enjoy these luxuries as, on our arrival in Bermuda a few days later, we were informed that we were to be drafted to the anti-submarine school in the dockyard as instructors.

Located on the naval base, known as HMS _Malabar_, the A/S school was housed in the ruins of the old fort, which had served to guard the northern tip of Ireland Island. My first reaction on being posted ashore in Bermuda was one of elation. After two and-a-half years of war the prospect of living on a semi-tropical island where there was no shortage of food, no nightly black out, and away from the constant threat of danger, was quite appealing. I had visions of sandy beaches, pretty girls, rum and coca cola, and all the other pleasures associated with a tourist paradise. Bermuda is actually a collection of approximately 150 small islands situated in the Western Atlantic off the coast of North Carolina. Because many of these islands are connected by bridges there is very little sense of crossing from island to island while on shore.

In 1943, the use of automobiles on the island, other than a few official government and military vehicles, was prohibited. Public transportation was by boat or horse-drawn carriage, and nearly everyone owned a bicycle. In 1809, after the American War of Independence, the Royal Navy began construction of a fortress and naval dockyard on one of the islands known as Ireland Island North. The work on this fortress, which covered over 25 acres of Ireland

Island North, continued into the mid-nineteenth century and was carried out by slave labour and hundreds of convicts sent out from England. Within the walls of the old fort, which were made of stone three feet thick, the navy had constructed barrack rooms, store houses, mess halls, and classrooms. It was here on the high ground overlooking the dockyard that the ASDIC School was located and where those of us who worked in the school as instructors lived. Stretching away to the southwest of Ireland Island North, in the form of a big arc, were a string of islands connected by bridges and respectively named Ireland Island South, Boaz Island, Watford Island, and Somerset Island.

The large body of water within this arc separating these islands from the capitol city of Hamilton to the east was known as Great Sound. The distance by water from the naval dockyard to Hamilton was about four miles and a liberty boat ran at regular intervals throughout the day between these two points, a trip of about an hour-and-fifteen minutes. The last boat at night returning to the dockyard departed Hamilton at midnight. As a result of the 'Destroyers for Bases' deal, the United States maintained a naval presence in the form of a naval air station built on a peninsular jutting out from Somerset Island into the southern end of Great Sound. From this station the US Navy flew A/S patrols far out into the Atlantic using giant PBY-5 flying boats. The headquarters of the Commander-in-Chief, American and West Indies Squadron, was located in Bermuda and it was to Bermuda that the warships being built in North America came for trials before crossing the Atlantic.

The A/S school was commanded by a lieutenant commander, RNVR (Special Branch) and his 2 I/C, a lieutenant RNVR. The senior rating in the school was Chief Petty Officer Goldic, an RN Submarine Detector Instructor (SDI) assisted by two petty officer Higher Submarine Detectors (HSD). A total of fifteen other ratings: leading seamen, able seamen, and ordinary seamen, made up the balance of the staff, all being qualified submarine detectors. ASW training provided by the school was confined to attack table exercises conducted in the classrooms and familiarization of underwater acoustics by ASDIC operators through the use of electric recordings. ASDIC teams of ships involved in work-ups would arrive at the school at 08:00 each morning for four hours of instruction, returning to their ship for lunch. Afternoon sessions were from 13:00 to 17:00. In addition to theoretical classroom instruction, the school also provided a team of experts in the form of Electrical Artificers (EA) and Higher Submarine Detectors (HSD) which could be made available to any vessel experiencing technical or electrical problems. Accommodations for the staff were both comfortable and airy. Each rating had a bed and locker, and the thick stone walls of the fort, together with the prevailing sea breeze from the west, resulted in pleasant temperatures in our living quarters, even on the hottest of days, and there were a number of options for recreational activities.

A theatre in the dockyard showed two movies each week, many of them new releases. The chiefs and petty officers had their own wet canteen in *Malabar*, while about two miles down the Malabar Road across from the Watford Bridge was a large wet canteen which served the lower deck ratings on the base as well as ratings from visiting ships. I suspected that the navy had intentionally built this canteen two miles from the base, for, when the bar closed at midnight, the two mile walk back to the dockyard resulted in most of the matelots being sober when rejoining their ships. Going to Hamilton for an evening run ashore was hardly worth while for two reasons. Firstly, there was very little to see or do in Hamilton other than to sit at a bar or visit the Fleet Club, where a dance was held every Friday night. The dances at the Fleet Club were not very popular from a matelot's point of view. The majority of women available as dance partners were middle-aged or elderly married women from Britain who worked for the government as mail censors. (All mail from North America destined for the UK was channelled through Bermuda where it was censored before being forwarded across the Atlantic.) If one wished to stay overnight in Hamilton, accommodation could be had at the Sailors' Rest on Front Street (the same Sailors' Rest where I stayed in 1941 on my way to England).

In the dockyard were a number of small sailing dinghies available for those who wished to learn to sail. As there were never enough boats for everyone, John Peard and I devised our own craft. In a small cove on the western side of the island we came across a pair of floats and the undercarriage of a wrecked *Swordfish* aircraft. With the aid of a hacksaw and a pair of tin-snips we were able to cut away the struts attached to the floats and, after hours of work, we were able to cut the floats in half. Our next task was to cut an opening in the top of the float to serve as a cockpit. Having done that, we fashioned a double bladed paddle to propel the craft and the finished product had the appearance of an Eskimo kayak. Our kayaks required a great deal of ballast to keep on an even keel, and this was provided by two or three sand bags, which also served as a seat. In true naval tradition John Peard named his kayak *Afrikaner*, while I named mine *Eager Beaver*. We moored them on the seaward side of the fort some ninety feet below the ramparts, presenting us with a challenge when we wanted to use them. Having discovered a passageway leading from inside the fort to a gun port overlooking the beach, we were able to 'break out of ship' and reach the beach by rappelling down the fort's walls with a sheer drop of about eighty feet to the rocks below. On learning of our project, our shipmates became interested and the little cove behind the fort became the focal point for the entire ship's company for holding picnics, fishing from the rocks, swimming, sunbathing, and sailing.

On one of the rare occasions when I visited Hamilton, I struck up a conversation with an American chief petty officer from the US Naval Air Station whom I happened to meet in one of the local watering holes. In the course of the evening I mentioned that I would give just about anything to get away from Bermuda, if only for a few days. On hearing this, he claimed that he would be able to arrange a trip for me if I could manage to obtain two days leave. He apparently was one of the crew of a PBY-5 that flew from Bermuda to Miami every Friday, returning to Bermuda late the following Sunday. This weekly trip was referred to in the USN as the milk run, as one of the items brought back to the islands from the mainland was fresh milk for the US admiral and wardroom officers. I was told that if I made myself available at the US Air Station by 16:30 on any Friday afternoon, I could go along for the ride to Miami returning on the same aircraft late the following Sunday. Taking him up on the offer, I applied for a weekend pass to start at 16:00 the following Friday. My request having been granted, I arrived at the US base at the appointed time. Unable to locate my host and, due to a failure in communication, I was issued a life vest and invited to board one of the many PBYs sitting on the tarmac. Shortly after take-off I realised a mistake had been made and that the plane I was in was not bound for Miami. For that matter it never left Bermuda air space that day as the pilot, who was a rookie lieutenant, had been instructed to practice his landings. For the next hour and-a-half we went around in circles taking off on Great Sound and landing on Little Sound. Altogether we must have taken off and touched down at least eighteen times after which, on the aircraft being hauled out of the water, one of the crew asked me how I had enjoyed the flight. If I recall correctly I was too dizzy to form a polite reply! Some time later I was able to contact the old chief and explain what had happened and a few weeks later he was able to arrange another flight, this time on the right aircraft. I was well aware that what I was doing could have landed me in a lot of trouble if anything had gone wrong. I did not have permission to leave Bermuda and, had the plane not been able to return on the Sunday, I would have been adrift on the following Monday and had a lot of explaining to do.

As it was, all went well. On landing in Miami two members of the air crew accompanied me into town where we indulged in a monumental pub crawl ending up in a lively joint which I remember was named the *Golden Palms*. The following day two of the American sailors obtained a car and, rounding up three girls, we travelled to a resort a few miles out of town where we spent a great day on the beach followed by a fantastic sea food dinner. Shortly before noon on the Sunday we were airborne again on our way back to Bermuda. The following Monday, having caught the first liberty boat out of Hamilton, I reported aboard by 08:00 and had difficulty convincing my messmates that I had been to Miami over the week-end.

One morning, as the first class of the day marched into my classroom, I recognized a New Zealander who had been on course with me in *Osprey*. I learned that he was one of three 'Kiwis' in his ship that had been built in the US and that they were on their way to the UK after completing work-ups. Delighted to meet up with John Peard and me in Bermuda, he invited us to 'drop around' the following day for 'sippers'. John and I accepted the invitation and, having been given permission by the OOW to come aboard, spent a couple of hours with the 'Kiwis' and made plans to meet again the following day. They informed us that their ship carried a sailing dinghy which they were sure they could get permission to borrow. The plan was that four of us would take the boat for a picnic and combination fishing trip in Great Sound. The 'Kiwis' had a bottle of 'pusser's' rum and had obtained fishing tackle from an unknown source. The ship's galley provided us with roast beef sandwiches for lunch and strips of pork fat for bait. Permission to use the boat having been granted, John and I arrived at the jetty early that Sunday morning to find that a cooler containing ice, cola, and a dozen bottles of beer had been loaded into the boat.

Equipped with a 5-HP outboard motor and a tank of gas, we pushed off from the ship and headed out into the bay. It was a clear day with not a cloud in the sky. As the sun rose it became very hot and four thirsty sailors made short work of the beer. By mid-day we came to the conclusion that the fish were not biting so hauled in our lines, cut the motor, and got down to the serious business of consuming the rum and sandwiches. As we drifted in the bay we gazed with interest on a beautiful bungalow situated in a clump of trees and in front of which a well-manicured lawn sloped down to the beach. The house appeared to be deserted and we speculated as to who the owner might be as a very large American flag was flying on a flag-pole by the driveway. The sea was flat calm and as we came close to shore it was possible to see the bottom of the bay through the clear water. It was one of the 'Kiwis' who first noticed that a short length of bamboo floating on the surface was attached by a length of rope to an object on the sea bed. Using our boat hook we hauled in the bamboo and noted that it was secured to what appeared to be a fish trap. Our curiosity aroused, all hands set to and hauled on the rope. On reaching the surface we discovered that the trap, which was constructed of wire mesh, contained about six brightly coloured fish. Quickly removing our catch, we returned the trap to the sea bed and, sighting two other markers on the surface, repeated the exercise with the same results. Engrossed in what we were doing, we were initially unaware of the presence of an individual on the lawn of the bungalow, running toward the shoreline. He was dressed in white, and waving what appeared to be a white flag to attract our attention. Having succeeded in doing so, the individual turned out to be an elderly oriental gentleman and, what at first was thought to be a white flag, turned out to be a cook's apron. Unable to understand what he was saying, but recognizing the fact that he was somewhat irate, we avoided further confrontation and headed back to the dockyard. Contemplating the fourteen or more fish in our possession, and elated at the success of our fishing trip, it was our intention to have one of the ship's cooks prepare us a dish of fish and chips on our return. We also decided not to reveal how they were caught. You can imagine our embarrassment when we arrived alongside the ship to find a US Navy Shore Patrol wagon parked on the jetty and three burly 'gobs' having a heated discussion with the officer of the watch. It turned out that our party had been accused of stealing the contents of fish pots, the property of an admiral in the United States Navy. The elderly oriental gentleman on the lawn of the admiral's house was none other than his Filipino mess boy who was responsible for having set the traps with the intention of providing his master with freshly-caught fish. Having confiscated our catch, the shore patrolmen departed and our 'Kiwi' friends were placed on charge to be paraded at Commanders Defaulters the following day. John Peard and I bid them farewell and wished them good luck as we slowly climbed the hill leading to our barracks.

Early in the New Year, an American USO group visited the islands to entertain US servicemen and they offered to put on a show for the British sailors in *Malabar*. The three stars of the show were a Broadway dancer named Nancy Kelly, a vivacious and curvaceous blonde singer named Paddy Barnes who, it was said, had been a female vocalist with Bob Crosby's band, and the beautiful Hollywood actress, Lynda Darnell. Coincidental with the arrival of this group in Bermuda, John Peard and I had planned to take a bicycle tour of the islands. Having been granted three days leave we made arrangements to stay at the Sailors' Rest in Hamilton where we rented our bicycles. Not wishing to appear conspicuous in uniform, we wore Bermuda shorts and sports shirts. Leaving Hamilton, the first leg of our journey took us to Tucker's Town located to the south of St. David's Island. From there we crossed to the north side of St. George's Island before travelling along the north shore road of that island to Flatts Village. At Flatts Village we visited the Bermuda Aquarium and Zoo after which, while riding across the bridge at Flatts Inlet which connects Harrington Sound with the Atlantic, we could hear the sound of band music coming from a pavilion overlooking the inlet. Curiosity getting the better of us, we parked our bikes and entered the building which turned out to be one of Bermuda's exclusive supper clubs and from which a dance floor had been built over the water in Harrington Sound. The music was being played by a United States naval band rehearsing with the cast of the USO show scheduled to open on the US naval base that night. Ordering a round of drinks, John and I parked ourselves at a table on the dance floor and watched the cast go through their numbers while enjoying the music.

As the afternoon wore on we were joined by some US service men in the audience and, on learning we were RN ratings, they insisted on ordering a round of drinks. At the conclusion of the rehearsal, a number of the girls in the cast joined our group and, as the band continued to play, many of the US sailors started dancing with them. The three stars of the show had joined the party and were in much demand as dance partners. Handsome six foot tall John Peard, with blonde curly hair, danced with both Lynda and Nancy while I, who had never learned to dance properly, had to settle for Paddy Barnes. True to their word, the troupe gave a performance in *Malabar* dockyard theatre the following week after which they were entertained by the chiefs and petty officers' mess located in the dockyard.

Before our short leave expired, John Peard and I paid a visit to the old Royal Naval Cemetery located on Ireland Island South. The purpose of my visit was to attempt to locate the grave of my Great-Great-Great-Grandfather, Vice Admiral Sir William Charles Fahie, KOB, KSF, RN, formerly Commander-in-Chief, North America and Lakes of Canada Station during 1821 to 1824. I had been told by Aunt Lorna that after his retirement from the navy he settled in Bermuda where he died in 1833 at the age of 72. With no other information as to where he might have been buried, I thought that the logical place to look would be the Royal Naval Cemetery. Unfortunately, my search proved unsuccessful.

After the war, I was to discover that he had resided in the Parish of Paget, located directly across Hamilton harbour from the city of that name. There is a monument to his memory in St. Paul's Anglican Church in Paget which on the western face reads:

"Sacred to the memory of Vice-Admiral Sir Wm. Chas. Fahie, KCB, KSF, formerly Commander-in-Chief of this Station who departed from this world 11 January AD 1833."

The Eastern face of the monument is inscribed as follows: "To record a life of honourable enterprise in the service of his country, and a death which attested the strength of a faith moored on the rock of ages, this monument was erected. Ne Forte Chedas Interitura"

In May 1944, I had been in Bermuda for about six months and was beginning to tire of the place. My expectation of warm seas, sandy beaches, beautiful girls, and a carefree lifestyle had not been realized. Big events were taking place in Europe, and a feeling of guilt at being away from the action began to creep in. There were no beautiful girls to be found in Bermuda, the day-to-day ASW classroom sessions had become boring, and I had the general feeling that I had seen and done everything in that semi-tropical paradise. Another reason for my desire to leave was that I desperately missed Marjorie. We had been engaged a little over eight months and she had promised that we would be married on my return. During my absence she had been drafted to a shore establishment in the small town of Balloch and was no longer in Campbelltown. We wrote each other weekly and I got the impression that she was looking forward to seeing me again. Before the end of May, I made a request to see my commanding officer and asked to be returned to England or drafted to a sea-going ship. On being paraded before the CO, my request was denied on the grounds that I was doing an essential job for the navy and I could not come up with a good reason for wanting to leave Bermuda. In June, I made a second request to return to England using as my reason the fact that I wished to attend the ASDIC School in order to qualify as a HSD. Once again my request was turned down, but I was assured that an entry would be made on my papers that I should be given a chance to qualify as an HSD on my eventual return to England.

When news of the Normandy landings was announced on June 6, 1944, I was having a drink in the wet canteen with a shipmate bemoaning the fact that I had been twice refused a request to be drafted. Turning to me he asked: "Have you ever given any thought to volunteering for service in submarines?" I admitted that the thought had crossed my mind, only to be put on the back burner because I thought I was too young to die. He then went on to point out that the navy were always looking for submarine volunteers, and that if I was serious about wanting to leave Bermuda I should consider volunteering. That night I lay awake for some time thinking about his suggestion, and before dropping off to sleep, made up my mind to give it a try. Two days later, standing before the CO once more, my request was granted, and on July 14, I left *Malabar* and joined HMS *Mary Rose*, an Algerine minesweeper which had arrived in Bermuda in early July and was preparing to leave for the UK on completion of her 'WUPS'. My new ship had been built for the Royal Navy by the Redfern Construction Company of Toronto, Ontario. She had been exchanged for the British built Corvette HMS *Buddleia*, which had been renamed HMCS *Giffard*. I was to be in her for exactly ten days before she sailed. At 900 tons displacement, she was the smallest vessel I had ever served in but with a speed of 16.5 knots the Algerines were regarded as the fastest and largest minesweepers in the RN at that time.

The ASDIC team in *Mary Rose* consisted of the A/S Officer (a RNVR Sub/Lt), a RN Petty Officer HSD, and five ratings including myself. I found the PO HSD a little strange in that he considered himself something of a poet, producing four line stanzas which he liked to pin on the notice boards in the ship for all to read. Two of these were as follows:

"The trouble with this ship,
it seems,
is streaky bacon
and beans."   *And*

"Mary Rose sat on a pin
Mary rose"

These 'words of wisdom' were always signed with the name 'Ping', which is of course the sound that the ASDIC transmission makes as it travels through the water. Hence the term 'ping happy', indicating that the person so labelled is suffering from a mild form of insanity brought on by too much pinging. Apart from the HSD, who was not a bad chap, the other members of the team were fairly normal although the A/S officer, who had only recently been commissioned, was completely out of his depth when it came to understanding his job.

Nine days after joining the ship it was announced that we would be sailing on Sunday, July 23 for England. On the eve of our departure my watch was granted shore leave which expired at 01:00. Those of us who intended to go ashore were warned that we were under sailing orders and that the last liberty boat to leave Hamilton departed at the stroke of midnight. As I wanted to do some last minute shopping before leaving Bermuda I decided to go into town on the 16:00 liberty boat. While in town I made a number of purchases including twelve pairs of silk stockings for Marjorie and a rather nice, locally-made brooch, for Aunt Lorna. Having completed my shopping, I dropped in at the Army and Navy Club for a pint or two where I met a young Canadian matelot from Vancouver serving in one of the Canadian MTB's operating out of Hamilton. After consuming two or three pints we decided to continue our drinking in the fresh air. Slipping into the grocers next door, we purchased a pint of dark rum, a dozen bottles of cola, two plastic cups, four pork patties, and headed for the park in the centre of town. Finding an empty bench, we sat down to enjoy our picnic and watch the local entertainment.

By nightfall we had consumed our supplies and, on somewhat unsteady legs, we set forth to locate the boat landing on Front Street. En route to the harbour my companion and I became separated and when last seen he had mounted a policeman's podium at one of the main intersections and was attempting to control traffic by means of very confusing hand signals. On arriving at the landing, I found the liberty boat moored alongside and made my way down a flight of stone steps to board her. The tide being out, the steps were covered with green, slimy algae and I had to be very careful not to slip. There were still fifteen or twenty minutes before the boat, which was crowded with liberty men, was due to depart, and discovering that it was imperative that I relieve myself, I remembered that there was a public lavatory at the head of the steps. Thinking that I would have plenty of time to slip ashore to use this facility before the boat shoved off, and leaving my purchases on my seat, I scrambled up the steps to locate the urinal. Having carried out the evolution, I returned to the landing and was dismayed to find that the picket boat had slipped her lines and was getting under way. Calling out: "Wait for me", to the coxswain, I started to race down the steps only to find myself falling head over heels to the landing below, loosing my cap in the process, and landing in a heap on the pier. Covered in mud and seaweed, and with the stern light of the boat disappearing in the distance I sat upright and surveyed the situation. There was a throbbing pain in my right knee which I first thought I had broken. On close inspection I found that there was a large hole in my pant leg around which the tropical uniform that I was wearing was slowly turning crimson.

Returning to the street, the following facts became apparent: (1) the last boat to the dockyard had left and there was no other way for me to get to *Malabar* that night; (2) I would probably miss the sailing of the ship, which in wartime was a court martial offence; and (3) I was in great pain, had difficulty walking, and was uncertain as to the extent of my injuries. With great difficulty I set out in the direction of the Sailors' Rest on Front Street. On ringing the door-bell, I was met by a bleary-eyed superintendent who, having previously seen sailors in my condition, made no comment regarding my appearance and did not have the slightest interest in learning what had happened to me. When I asked if I might get a bed for the night, he gruffly replied: "There aren't any beds available." He then offered to let me sleep on the billiard table in the games room and provided me with a pillow and a blanket, which I was only too pleased to accept. The following morning, after a most uncomfortable night, I awoke to find that I had rolled over on the table during the night and the blanket was no longer under me. Blood had clotted and the wound on my knee was now firmly attached to the green beige of the billiard table. Unable to sit up without taking the beige with me, it was at least two to three years later that the green fibres of the beige finally disappeared from under the skin of my knee cap!! Leaving the Sailors' Rest around 07:00 on Sunday, I made my way down to the waterfront in the hope of finding a vessel that might take me to the dockyard. Out in the bay were two Canadian MTBs about to get under away, both moored about one hundred yards off shore. Signalling franticly, I managed to attract the attention of someone on one of them which slowly came within hailing distance. On explaining my situation to the young 'sub' on her bridge, he obligingly offered to give me a lift and, coming alongside, I stepped aboard.

As we approached the dockyard, I was elated to see that *Mary Rose* was still at her berth, and for a moment even dared to think that I might be able to sneak aboard without being seen. This was not to be the case for, as I crossed the brow, who should be standing there to greet me but the coxswain. Informing me that I had been placed on the First Lieutenant's Report for being absent over leave, he sent me below to put on a clean uniform, and within the hour I was called to muster at the defaulters table. Pleading guilty to the charge, I was pleasantly surprised when later that day the 'old man' handed down a comparatively light sentence in the form of fourteen days number eleven punishment. This meant that my leave and tot would be stopped for fourteen days and that I would have to turn out half-an-hour before the hands and perform extra work during working hours. The fact that my leave was stopped did not concern me, for we were about to sail across the Atlantic and it would be well over fourteen days before we were granted shore leave again. My only explanation for this lenient treatment was that the captain, who was a regular officer, had been commissioned from the lower deck and could empathise with someone in my situation.

The following day, in company with HMS *Thisbe*, another Algerine, we sailed for St. George's Harbour at the eastern end of the chain of islands that make up Bermuda. Here we patrolled off the mouth of the harbour while our convoy of miscellaneous craft took up stations in three columns in preparation for crossing the Atlantic. It was a motley collection of vessels that came out to meet us. Hopper barges loaded with coal and being towed by coal-burning tugs, a giant floating crane, two dredgers, and a large floating dock with two ocean-going tugs in attendance. All these vessels appeared to be coal burners, and columns of black smoke rose in the calm air from their various shaped funnels. Taking up station on the port side of the convoy, and with *Thisbe* on station to starboard, this mass of ungainly scows rode out to sea like a herd of turtles, headed for the Azores at a maximum speed of close to four knots. Those of us in *Mary Rose* gazed with dismay at our charges and wondered aloud how many of them would manage to complete the voyage that lay ahead. Apart from the fact that the entire convoy was shrouded by a large cloud of black smoke which could be seen by any prowling U-boat beyond the horizon, there was also the prospect of these ungainly vessels foundering if we encountered bad weather. Fortunately, during the fourteen days that it took for us to reach the Azores the sea was like a mill pond, and during August, 1944, only one merchant ship had been reported as lost in the North Atlantic. During the same period, the U-boats had been destroyed, indications that we were finally wining the battle of the Atlantic.

The Azores, located at 38 degrees, 44 minutes north and 29 degrees west, maintain an average temperature similar to that of Bermuda which is 32 degrees, 45 minutes north, and 65 degrees west of Greenwich. In that summer of 1944 we experienced warm sunny days and calm seas as we crawled across the ocean but time hung heavily on our hands under such conditions. Our 'buffer' (chief bo'sun's mate) who had been in the navy since 'Adam was a boy', was not at all pleased with the dark red colour of his upper deck. He seemed to think that it could be made to look like the gleaming white decks of teak that were common on British built vessels and with which he was familiar. Despite the fact that it had been pointed out to him that the ship had been built in Canada using an unknown type of Canadian wood for her deck, he insisted on trying to holystone it to an almost white condition. The seamen were therefore put to work each day scrubbing decks with salt water and, on our hands and knees using holystone and 'pusser's' soap, in an attempt to achieve the desired result. Needless to say, the colour of the deck was not altered, and the poor 'buffer' in his frustration almost became a basket case by the time we reached the UK.

The average speed of our convoy was four knots, if all went well, but on a number of occasions one of the tugs would lose its tow and everyone had to mark time while a new line was passed to the drifting vessel. Furthermore, the tugs could not carry enough coal in their bunkers to cross the Atlantic without re-fuelling at the hopper barges which had been loaded with the extra fuel required. When a tug was about to run out of coal she cast off her lines and went alongside her charge to replenish the bunkers while the convoy treaded water waiting for the exercise to be completed. Despite all these handicaps we turned over the convoy to an RN escort group operating out of West Africa and finally entered the harbour of Horta in the Azores fourteen days after leaving Bermuda.

My period of punishment having expired, I was looking forward to night leave in Horta but was informed by the coxswain that only those who were First Class for leave would be allowed ashore. As part of my punishment I had been placed on the Second Class for leave list for a period of two months. Not to be deterred, I immediately volunteered to be part of the shore patrol and was accepted. Thus, on our first night in harbour, attired in tropical rig with the traditional web belt and wrist bands, sporting the letters 'SP' on our left wrists to signify our authority, I and four others, with a stoker petty officer in command, were landed and charged with maintaining the good order and discipline of our liberty men. We started our patrol on the main street of Horta and slowly made our way to the centre of town. On the way we passed a large open area where a soccer match was under way between two local teams and we took time to join the local inhabitants in rooting for the home team. Continuing in to town along a narrow street, we encountered a marching band of about twenty musicians on their way to the soccer match, followed by a large crowd of football fans of all ages. This mob surged down the street with a complete disregard for anything or anyone in their way. Our patrol was swept to one side and forced to take refuge in the doorways of the shops lining the street. The band having passed, we regained some semblance of order and continued into town at a leisurely pace, checking out the merchandise on display in the many shops that were open.

As I had lost the gifts bought in Bermuda for Marjorie and my aunt, I persuaded our petty officer to allow me to make a purchase or two and was surprised to find that I was able to buy genuine silk stockings at a price well below that which I had paid in Bermuda, and in a small jewellery store I found a gold wire brooch made by a local goldsmith in the shape of a Spanish galleon which the shopkeeper assured me had been modelled after Christopher Columbus' *Santa Maria*. The exchange rate on the British pound with the Portuguese escudo was very much in our favour which made us feel somewhat like millionaires in comparison with the local inhabitants. A large bottle of champagne, for example, cost about five shillings and the gold brooch was less than one pound. Having passed through the centre of town without encountering more than a handful of our liberty men, we found ourselves in an area close to the sea front where a number of taverns were located. Entering one we found it occupied by a number of our shipmates in varying states of sobriety. The local wine, which sold for roughly two shillings a bottle, had started to take its toll, leaving many of our ship mates incapable of navigating on their own. At every table those who were still relatively sober were enjoying the company of the numerous hostesses on hand, employed by management to entertain the clientele. These ladies charged five escudos for a dance and all appeared to be suffering from an unquenchable thirst as they downed numerous glasses of wine. Although our boys plied them with drinks it was remarkable to note that they appeared to be in no way affected by the quantity of booze that they consumed, which was obviously coloured water. For the sum of one hundred escudos 'Jolly Jack' could obtain the services of one of these charming ladies for a period of anywhere from twenty minutes to half an hour. The young, good looking girls were in great demand, making many trips to the rooms upstairs while leading an unsteady matelot by the hand.

The arrival of the shore patrol in the tavern had little or no effect on our shipmates who were thoroughly enjoying themselves. In fact, we were all invited to sit down and quench our thirst. The stoker petty officer in charge of the patrol didn't raise an eyebrow when a couple of our lads knocked back a glass of wine and in no time at all we had divested ourselves of our webbing and our wrist bands and had joined the party. Leave for everyone expired at midnight, and with about forty minutes required to return to the ship, it was necessary to close things down around 23:00. Regaining some semblance of responsibility, and in fear of being reported, our fearless leader had us replace our gear, and with the aid of those who could still navigate, we rounded up anyone who needed assistance and set course for the docks, singing loudly as we wend our way through the town. Across the harbour, which was shaped like the letter 'U', we could see our two minesweepers berthed on the far side: so near and yet so far. Unknown to us one of our group, obviously under the influence, made the decision that it would be faster and easier to swim across the harbour to the ship rather than taking the long way by road around the basin. No one missed him as he undressed and slipped in to the water. When he failed to return that night he was listed as being adrift, and on the following day around noon, the local police reported to the authorities that a British sailors uniform, complete with cap, stockings, and shoes, had been found on the beach opposite the tavern that we had visited the previous night. His body had not been found by the time we sailed and it was generally accepted that he had been attacked by a shark while swimming across the basin. On arrival at the jetty where the two vessels were berthed side by side, there was some confusion as to which was which, and a number of us (myself included) found out on going below to the darkened mess deck that we were in the wrong ship much to the disgust of those who were asleep in their hammocks and who were awakened by irate individuals enquiring as to: "Who the f--- has slung his 'mick' in my billet?".

Eventually everything got sorted out and those who were incapable of slinging their hammocks ended up sleeping fully clothed on the mess deck cushions. Despite the fact that most of the watch ashore had returned, three sheets to the wind, in true RN tradition, no one was placed in the 'rattle'. Providing a rating caused no trouble when coming aboard and was able to muster with the hands the next day, he was not charged. One of our ship's company did, however, incur the wrath of the officer-of-the-day and was placed on charge for coming aboard minus his shirt and wearing a lace trimmed black brassiere liberated from a young Portuguese lady as a souvenir of his run ashore. No one reported the conduct of the shore patrol PO, but when I volunteered to serve on the patrol on the following night, the coxswain growled at me and replied: "No bloody way Jones, you've had your run ashore and you are lucky that you are not in the rattle". Discretion being the better part of valour, I made no comment and let the matter drop.

Mary Rose sailed independently for the Clyde a few days later and after an uneventful passage arrived in Greenock, where I left her to join *Osprey* in Dunoon. Having been granted fourteen days Foreign Service Leave, I boarded the ferry for Glasgow and sent off a wire to Marjorie in Balloch informing her of my return and asking her to apply for leave in order that we could get married. Stopping in Glasgow only long enough to purchase a wedding ring and apply for a marriage licence, I travelled by bus to Dumbarton and knocked on the door of her parents home. I had hoped that when the time came to meet her parents I would have Marjorie with me but this was not to be the case and I was a little concerned as to how I would be received.

Marjorie's father, a warrant officer in the Cameron Highlanders, was overseas with his regiment and had been away from home for a number of years. Her younger brother, Dan, lived at home with his mother and was employed by William Denny and Bros. Ltd., the entrance to whose Clydebank shipyard was located a block or two down the street from their home on Dumbarton Road. Any concerns that I might have had were quickly dispelled, for the lady who answered the door greeted me like a long lost son, and made me feel most welcome. Marjorie's mother was everything I expected her to be. A typical Scottish housewife, she was about five feet four inches in height and her long black hair, which was streaked with silver, was rolled tightly in a bun at the nape of her neck. Her countenance belied the hardships that she must have endured as a working class housewife who had been forced to raise her family during the lean years leading to the outbreak of the war for she had a twinkle in her dark blue eyes, a wonderful smile to accompany her keen sense of humour, and a soft-spoken voice with just a hint of a Glaswegian accent. Their home had three bedrooms, one of which was occupied by Dan. I was informed that I would be using Marjorie's room. She in turn would share her mother's room while I was on leave.

The day following my arrival, a telegram from Marjorie was delivered to the house telling me that she had been granted seven days leave and asking me to meet her train at Glasgow Central Station the following day. That night I had a hard time dropping off to sleep as I thought of our meeting the next day. While I had been away, we had written to each other on a weekly basis, and in my letters I had reminded her of her promise that we would get married as soon as I returned to Britain. At no time had she ever suggested that this would not be the case.

The allies appeared to be well on their way to final victory in Europe, and although no one would guess as to when Japan would be defeated, there was a general feeling abroad that it was only a matter of time, perhaps less than a year, before the war would be over. In the year that we had known each other we had often discussed our plans for the future and I had taken it for granted that the day would come when I would leave the navy and that we would then make our home in Canada. I had given some thought of a transfer to the RCN after the war with the intention of continuing my naval career, but both of us had felt that it was too early to make such a decision. These were some of the thoughts that went through my mind as I rode the street car to Glasgow the following day to meet her train. Moments after the train had pulled into the station I caught sight of her as she came down the platform and a minute or so later we were in each others arms. That evening, as the four of us sat down for supper, we discussed our plans for the wedding and agreed that we would have a civil ceremony in Glasgow as soon as I could make the necessary arrangements. I asked her brother Dan, if he would act as my best man, to which he agreed, and Marjory informed me that she had asked her best friend Jean, who was also in the WRNS to be her maid of honour.

During the course of the conversation, I happened to remark that I would have to report to the Submarine Headquarters in HMS *Dolphin* when my leave expired as I had volunteered for service in submarines. This information was greeted in silence as I went on to explain that I had done so as a way of getting off Bermuda. Later that night after her mother and brother had gone to bed, Marjorie and I sat and talked and I discovered that she was most unhappy about my decision to volunteer for service in submarines. As time went by I began to realize that she was very upset, but not wishing to get involved in an argument on the subject, we both decide to retire and talk about it in the morning. Kissing her good night I went to bed and quickly fell asleep. In the early morning hours I was awakened as someone entered the room and came towards my bed. Turning on the light I glanced at my watch and saw that it was close to 03:00 and, standing by the door in her night dress and slippers (sobbing uncontrollably), was Marjorie. Putting out my hand, I drew her to the edge of the bed where she sat for a moment in silence while I tried to get her to tell me what was wrong. Reaching for the switch she turned out the light and slipped into bed, wrapping her arms around me and continuing to sob convulsively for what seemed to be an eternity. Eventually she quietened down and told me that it was due to me having told her that I had joined the Submarine Service that was bothering her. She dreaded the thought that I might not survive the war and thought it best that we wait until it was over before we got married. She went on to say that she wanted us to have children, but that she was scared to think of having to bring up a child by herself if something were to happen to me. I tried to convince her that there were probably thousands of couples in the same situation, but that waiting for the war to end was not the answer.

The fact that life was so uncertain was the very reason that two people in love should try to find what happiness they could when they had the chance to do so. Somehow I got the feeling that she wasn't being honest with me and that what she really wanted to say was that it was the thought of getting married that really frightened her, not the prospect of my getting killed. I questioned her as to whether she had met someone else while I had been away, but she assured me that she had not and insisted that she still loved me. As if to convince me that she was telling the truth she became very passionate and within moments we were locked in each others arms making love as we had never done before. Just prior to dawn, she slipped out of my bed and returned to her room. When I awoke, Dan had already left for work and, on entering the kitchen I found that Marjorie and her mother were already up and making breakfast. If Mrs. Grant was aware of what had happened during the night, she gave no indication of it, and after breakfast she left the house to go shopping. Over a cup of tea I raised the subject of our conversation during the night and asked her if she had changed her mind about calling the wedding off. When she told me that she had not, I asked her if she wanted us to break off our engagement, to which she replied: "I still love you Frank." I said: "As far as I'm concerned, if you still love me, there's no need for anything to change." That evening after supper Dan suggested that we all go down to the local pub for a drink and Marjorie decided to call on her friend Jean to join us, which she did. During the course of the evening Marjorie broke the news to Jean and her brother that our wedding would be postponed. When pressed by Jean to explain why, all that she would say was: "We're still engaged and will probably be getting married at some time in the future." What had started out as an enjoyable evening was spoiled for everyone by Marjorie's announcement which put a damper on the conversation, and after seeing Jean home the three of us returned to the house in a somewhat sombre mood.

That night, an hour or two after I had gone to bed, she once again came into my room and without a word pulled back the covers and slipped in to bed with me. The following morning it became obvious that Mrs. Grant was aware of what had happened. Whether Marjorie or Dan had told her I do not know, but she must have known that her daughter had spent the past two nights in my room and was probably as confused and upset as I was at what had transpired. That day I came to realize that a decision had to be made one way or the other. There was no way that I could spend the remainder of my leave in her company not fully understanding what she really wanted me to do. On the one hand she insisted that she still loved me, and on the other, informed me: "I don't want to get married just now", reasons I had difficulty understanding, for during the past two nights she had shared my bed and given herself to me without reservation. I was having difficulty understanding the workings of the female mind. Later, taking a long walk through the park, we discussed our problem. I wanted to understand how she felt about our relationship and tried to explain to her how much I loved her, but it was to no avail. All that I could get out of her was that she thought that we should wait a while before getting married. She saw no reason that we could not continue our engagement, but felt that we should not rush in to marriage. Eventually I came to the conclusion that there was no way that I could get her to change her mind. I could not bear the thought of losing her, but under the circumstances thought it best that I should leave. That night, for the third time, she came into my room after I had gone to bed, leaving just before dawn. Having made up my mind to return to the ship, I broke the news to her after breakfast. If I had thought that she would try to make me change my mind, I was mistaken. She agreed that we should separate in order to think things over, but when she offered to return her ring, I asked her to keep it. Before leaving I talked to Mrs. Grant and tried to explain what had happened between us. The poor woman was very upset and at a loss to explain her daughter's behaviour. As I was leaving the house Marjorie came to the door and kissed me good bye. She also handed me an envelope but made me promise not to read the note inside until the next day.

Returning to Glasgow, I booked into the Overseas Club for the remainder of my leave, which did not expire for another eight or nine days. In the envelope given to me by Marjorie, was a silver ring engraved with the image of Saint Andrew. The note inside asked me to wear it as a token of her love for me. She went on to say that some day she would be my wife if I would only be patient and wait a while. She promised to write, once again declaring her love for me, and ended by saying that she hoped I could understand how she felt. As stated earlier, Glasgow had become my favourite place to spend my leave. On this occasion, however, I took no pleasure in being there and was feeling sorry for myself. A few nights later I met a bunch of Canadian sailors on leave from HMCS *Niobe* and accompanied them to the Paisley Dance Pavilion which was a favourite hangout for Canadian servicemen. There were scores of girls at the dance and my new-found friends were soon paired off, but I was in no frame of mind for female companionship and long before the dance ended I rode a bus back to town and retired for the night. Deciding to cut my leave short, I returned to *Osprey* a number of days early.

Ten days after my return to Dunoon, I was drafted to HMS

Forth, for a short torpedo course. *Forth* was the submarine depot ship for the 3rd. Submarine flotilla based in Holy Loch. The purpose of the course was to familiarize members of the A/S branch with the basic workings of the Torpedo branch. Both branches at a later date were combined to become the TAS branch. While on course in *Forth* I had the opportunity to meet members of the submarine branch which I was about to join. I was very impressed with those that I came in contact with and began to understand the difference between submariners and the ratings in general service. As a sailor explained to me: "The biggest misconception held by general service ratings is that submariners <u>think</u> they're better than others. This isn't true as submariners <u>know</u> they're better."

CHAPTER XIII
Submarines

On September 28, 1943, I was accepted for service in submarines and fifteen days later left *Osprey* for *Dolphin* in Gosport, Hampshire, home of the Submarine Service of the Royal Navy. In 1904, when first occupied by the navy, *Dolphin* (Fort Blockhouse) located at the entrance to Portsmouth Harbour had formerly been the home of the army's mining engineers. On being taken over by the navy it meant that the senior service was relieving the army of the responsibility for coastal protection against invasion with locomotive torpedoes.

On joining *Dolphin* all new entries were given a thorough medical examination. Just as I had feared, the medical officer took one look at the scar tissue in my left ear and questioned me at great length as to what had caused it. Realizing that he was on the verge of rejecting me, I assured him that it had caused me no trouble over the past four years and that I was confident I would be able to go through the escape tank without rupturing my ear drum. Reluctantly he agreed to allow me to try, on the condition that on completing the escape, I return to sick bay for a further examination. Fortunately, the first part of the following day was spent in a classroom where we were introduced to the mysteries of the Davis Submarine Escape Apparatus (DSEA). In the afternoon, wearing a pair of swimming trunks, three of us at a time, along with our instructor, entered a small chamber at the bottom of a thirty foot tank. After closing the door to the chamber a valve was opened allowing water to flood the chamber until the air became compressed to the point that water stopped entering the compartment. At this stage the pressure inside the compartment was equal to the pressure on the outside and the outer door could then be opened. One-by-one we began breathing oxygen from our DSEA sets as we climbed the ladder leading to the outer hatch and slowly rose to the surface of the water in the tank. One man had to remain behind to close the hatch and drain the chamber so that three more men could repeat the exercise. At the moment when the pressure in the chamber equalized I was subjected to a stabbing pain in my left ear and, on ducking my head under the surface to climb the ladder, was alarmed to see the surrounding water change colour to a shade of pink. Fortunately, no one else seemed to notice my discomfort, but having been ordered to report back to sick bay on completing the course, I went off to see the medical officer, fully expecting to be rejected due to a ruptured ear drum. On reporting to the SBA on duty, it being quite late in the afternoon, I was told that the medical officer had already left for the day. Questioned as to why I wanted to see him, I explained that he had wanted to know if I had been able to pass the course successfully. Locating my documents he asked: "Have you?" Having assured him that it was a piece of cake, he stamped my papers: 'Fit for Submarine Service', and told me to: "bugger off". I went off to the mess deck feeling very pleased with myself for having put one over on the service.

Submarine training consisted of two parts. The first part was entirely theoretical and taught in a classroom with the aid of a blackboard. New entries were required to learn everything about the mechanical workings of a submarine. Over a period of two weeks we made notes and drawings of virtually every piece of electrical and mechanical machinery to be found in a boat. The batteries, main motors, engine room clutches, main salt water line, high and low pressure air lines, hydroplanes, tube spaces, periscopes, and above all, the location of the ballast tanks and how and when they were opened or shut. Having passed the first part of the course, we were then introduced to a simulator which had been designed to represent the interior of a control room. In this room equipped with periscopes, hydroplane wheels, compass and steering positions, together with a mock up of the blowing panel, it was possible to enact the entire sequence to be followed in order to dive and surface the boat. It was so realistic, that on the command 'dive', the steel deck that we stood on took on a three or four degree slope as we dived and reversed itself as we surfaced. The next stage of our training was what we had all been looking forward to; finally being allowed to go to sea in a real submarine and spend day after day diving and surfacing the boat. For our new entry training we had been sent to HMS *Elfin*, the submarine training school located in Blyth, Northumberland. In *Elfin* our living quarters were the typical war-time Nissen huts used throughout the United Kingdom in all types of military establishments. These huts were heated by a coal-burning stove located in the centre of the hut from which dense clouds of smoke normally poured but with little radiant heat.

North-eastern England can be cold and damp at the best of times, but the fall and winter of 1944 was exceptionally wet and miserable. The well-worn paths between the huts were ankle deep in mud and, on days when we had to go to sea, we often sailed from Blyth shrouded in a blanket of damp fog which rolled in from the North Sea. As budding submariners we were glad of the white woollen sweaters issued to us on joining the submarine service and which were the trade mark of both the submariner and the coastal forces sailor. Recreational facilities in *Elfin* were few and far between. There was a wet canteen on the base and a movie theatre but little else. The nearest large city was Newcastle which we seldom visited, and Blyth itself had little to offer. As entertainment, the wardroom officers (both male and female) had formed a musical appreciation club where one could go and listen to classical music played on a very old phonograph. Three nights a week music lovers would sit in freezing Nissen huts wearing heavy overcoats, mitts, and scarves, listening to scratchy recordings of Straus, Brahms, Mozart, or Chopin. As a form of entertainment this did not appeal to the average sailor but if one pretended to be a music lover and indicated a desire to improve one's knowledge of the subject it was sometimes possible to talk a snobbish member of the WRENS into escorting her to one of these concerts. Once inside the freezing hut she was more often than not only too willing to accept the offer of sharing your great coat which would then be used as a blanket to keep warm. With the lights turned low, all the better to enjoy the music, many an hour could be passed cuddled up to an attractive WREN under a 'pusser's' greatcoat listening to the London Philharmonic Orchestra.

One should never underestimate a matelot. Where there is a will there is always a way.

One of the submarines used for training in Blyth, and in which I had trained, was the old Oberon Class *Otway*, one of the three 'O' class boats. Built by Vickers-Armstrong of Barrow in 1926, she and her sisters, *Oberon* and *Oxley*, were originally intended to be employed in the Far East. Both *Oberon* and *Otway* survived the war, but *Oxley* was unfortunately torpedoed in error by the RN submarine, *Triton*, off the cost of Norway in 1939. Other submarines of the 6th Flotilla employed in training at the time were *Sportsman*, *Taku*, *Tuna*, and *Unbending*.

As a training flotilla we had no reason to venture far out to sea. It was nevertheless impressed on us that once we cleared harbour we were subject to all the hazards that accompany any submarine at sea, in wartime, or in peace, whether operational or training. Enemy surface vessels, other than E-boats, were the least of our problems but we were always on guard against U-boats, particularly when surfaced. Another danger that we faced was attack from the air, either by enemy planes or by friendly aircraft. There was, of course, the ever-present danger of collision with a surface vessel, which almost always resulted in the submarine holding the short end of the stick. Having qualified as a submariner I was granted a few days leave at Christmas and decided to spend it in Glasgow. While on leave I went to Dumbarton to visit Mrs. Grant who told me that Marjorie was unable to obtain leave for Christmas but that she hoped to be able to get home for New Year. I was invited to stay with the family while on leave, but declined the invitation and returned to my room at the Overseas Club.

Three days after Christmas I reported back to *Elfin* and on December 29, 1944, was enrolled in a submarine ASDIC operator's course which lasted until February 23, 1945. On surface vessels the ASDIC operator is trained to use the instrument to detect a submerged submarine for the purpose of destroying it. On the other hand submarines use the instrument in a number of different ways. In certain circumstances torpedoes can be fired at a surface or underwater target using the ASDIC beam to indicate range and bearing. Other uses are to detect mines when passing through a mine field, a navigational aid (taking a bearing from land), a hydrophone (to detect the presence of ships on the surface) and, as a means of communicating with another submarine or surface ship by using the ASDIC sound wave to transmit a message in Morse Supersonic Telegraphy (SST).   At an earlier date I had thought of changing my term of engagement in the navy from Hostilities Only (HO) to Short Service engagement (SS). On re-engaging as a SS rating, previous time served (with the exception of boy's time) counted towards the seven years of the term. At the end of seven years I would then have the option or continuing on for five more years for a total of twelve years or being transferred to the lists of the Royal Fleet Reserve for a period of five years. Once I made the decision to re-engage my request to do so was quickly granted and, on completing my course, was given fourteen days re-engagement leave.

It had been almost six months since I had seen Marjorie and, although we had written to each other during that time, our relationship was obviously in trouble. I therefore decided to confront her one final time in the hope that she might have had a change of heart. At the conclusion of my leave I had been ordered to report to *Dolphin*, but chose to go to Glasgow first in order to meet with Marjorie for what was to prove to be the last time. In Glasgow I discovered that Marjorie had been unable to get leave which meant that I had to go to Balloch. Taking the bus from Glasgow, I met with her the following day and was disappointed to learn that she had no intention of changing her mind. Feeling very dejected, and having come to the conclusion that there was no point in prolonging our discussion, we parted company. That evening she handed me the ring I had given her, and having said good bye to her for the last time, boarded the bus to Glasgow, never to see or hear from her again. Feeling utterly miserable, I spent one more day in Glasgow before deciding to take the train to London where I intended to spend the balance of my fourteen days leave.

On arriving in London, I checked in to the Union Jack Club located near Waterloo Station and, after pawning the engagement ring, set out to drink the town dry. It was in a small pub in the Haymarket, the Coach and Horses, that I first saw her. Sitting alone at first, she was joined later in the evening by an unsavoury character in civilian attire with whom I gathered, judging by her actions, she was not on friendly terms. After a heated ten minute argument during which I got the impression she was being threatened in some way, he abruptly rose and stalked out of the pub leaving her in tears. Intrigued by this turn of events, I went over to where she sat with the intention of asking if I could join her. Having accepted my offer of a drink, she invited me to pull up a chair, and before the bar closed that night she had explained who her former companion was and why she was so upset. Her name was Alice, and four weeks before she had left home after having a heated argument with her father. For the past six months she had been employed on the production line of a company engaged in the manufacturing of electrical equipment for the armed forces. Finding the job boring, she had decided to join the Army Territorial Service (ATS) but her father refused to allow her to do so, leading to her decision to leave home. On leaving, she had moved in to the city where she had met the young man that I had seen earlier. This character had befriended her and offered to find her a place to live. Having accepted his offer, and after moving in to a small flat in Kensington, he now expected her to support him by becoming a street-walker. Refusing to go along with his wishes, he had threatened to use physical violence to force her to do so, at the same time claiming that she owed him one months rent on the flat, which of course she was unable to pay.   Having heard her story, I agreed to help on condition that she returned home to her parents after we had managed to retrieve her personal belongings from her flat. She agreed to do so and on leaving the pub I hailed a taxi and together we went to the address that she gave me. Having secured her clothes I explained the situation to the taxi driver and asked for his assistance in finding a place where she could spend the night.   At 04:00 in wartime London this proved impossible and having dismissed the cab we spent the next four hours drinking numerous cups of coffee in Lyons Corner House in the Strand, an all-night restaurant. After breakfast we checked into a small hotel as a married couple, the desk clerk no doubt accepting our story in view of the fact that we had with us her suite case. Having been up all night we were both completely exhausted and, on lying down on the bed, fell asleep for hours.

Later in the day she gave me the address of her parent's house and I made her promise to stay in the hotel while I went to call on them. She claimed that she was afraid to face her father who, according to her, had a violent temper. Assuring her that everything would be all right, I took the Underground to Greenwich and on locating 10 Park Street, with some trepidation, knocked on the door. The man who answered was of medium height with a florid complexion. His sandy hair was short and curly and his stern features matched the tone of his voice as he enquired as to the purpose of my visit. After giving him my name I explained the reason for my call, ending by saying: "I have a message for you from your daughter." Closing the door behind him he stepped out of the house and, after listening to the story of how I had met Alice, he said: "If you're not telling the truth, I'll have you arrested for abducting her." Assuring him that everything I had told him was the truth, I went on to explain that his daughter regretted having left home but was afraid to return to face the consequences. Giving him my word, that if he promised not to punish her I would have her back home before nightfall, reluctantly he agreed to let me go into the city to fetch her and promised not to report me to the police if I were willing to leave some form of identification with him as security. Handing Mr. Honeysett my naval pay book and taking the chance that Alice would still be waiting for me, I left him standing at the door of his home and returned to the city to find his daughter. To my great relief Alice was still in the hotel and I was able to convince her that both her parents wanted her home and that they were willing to forgive her for running away. Leaving the hotel we arrived at her home late that evening. On entering the house she was met by both her mother and father who welcomed her with open arms while I stood on the sidelines watching. Feeling somewhat embarrassed by the outpouring of emotion that I was witnessing, all I wanted to do was retrieve my pay book and leave the house. However, when I suggested to her father that I should be on my way, both he and his wife insisted that I stay for supper.

After we had eaten, we went across the street to a pub and later that evening I was informed that I was expected to spend the night as a guest of the family. It was some time before I got the message, but it eventually dawned on me that Alice's parents, Mr. and Mrs. Honeysett, were under the impression that I had fallen in love with their daughter. I was to learn later that she had planned to marry a fellow in the navy, but that he had been sent out to the Pacific and that shortly after his leaving the UK, the engagement had been broken off. Since our meeting in the Coach and Horses, I had given no thought to having any kind of a lasting relationship with her. At the age of eighteen, one tends to act impulsively. Having recently been rejected by a girl I had hoped would be my wife, my ego had suffered quite a setback. On the rebound, and with little thought to the future, I decided to take the plunge, and before I knew it had made a commitment to marrying Alice, much to the delight of everyone in her family.

Alice was the fifth child of Bertha and Arthur Honeysett who had raised four daughters and one son. The eldest girl in the family, together with her husband Bert (who had been on leave from the army at the time) had been killed earlier in the war when the family home had been demolished by a German bomb. After the death of their daughter and son-in-law, Mr. and Mrs. Honeysett had moved to their present address on Park Street in Greenwich, along with the three younger girls. The boy, Jim, left home to join the Air Force, and Alice and her two sisters, Doris and Barbara, continued to live with their parents until Doris left to get married. When I arrived on the scene only Alice and Barbara were living at home and Jim, who had since made his home in Maidstone, was now married with two children. Mrs. Honeysett suffered from chronic asthma and sought the sympathy of anyone she came in to contact with by making sure they were aware of her condition. She spent most of her day puffing on foul-smelling Turkish cigarettes which she claimed helped her condition, and in the evenings would send her long-suffering husband off to the local pub to get her a pint or two of Guiness stout, which she claimed was required to maintain her strength. In class-conscious Britain, Mr. Honeysett, who was employed by the Post Office, would have been considered a member of the working class. He was a mild-mannered man, obviously resigned to the fact that he was married to a hypochondriac. In his youth he had served as a cook in the Merchant Navy and become a proficient baker. Before wartime rationing came into effect, and sugar and other ingredients were still easily available, he had used his talents to supplement his income by making wedding cakes at home which he sold. He now announced that if he could round up the necessary ration coupons he would produce one of his masterpieces for Alice and me. The Honeysetts did not own an automobile, but Mr. Honeysett was the proud owner of a motorcycle equipped with a side-car.

Earlier in the war he had joined the Home Guard, and I was told that he and another member of his platoon, both of them armed with shot guns, had used this vehicle to patrol Hampstead Heath on the look-out for enemy paratroopers. With the threat of invasion having passed, the motor cycle and side-car were now used for an occasional trip to the country if petrol was available. It was an unforgettable sight to see Mr. and Mrs. Honeysett setting out on one of these jaunts. He, with his motoring coat, cloth cap, leather gauntlets and goggles, sitting astride the saddle, while Bertha, in the side-car with a long scarf wrapped around her neck and barley able to see over the side of the car, headed out of town for a Sunday drive in the country. As there were only a few days left before my leave expired it became necessary to move quickly if we were to be married. A wire was dispatched to Jim in the Air Force informing him of the forthcoming event, and on our meeting the next day I prevailed on him to act as my best man. Alice's younger sister, Barbara, was to be the maid of honour, and I was persuaded to visit the vicar to make arrangements for us to be married in the Parish Church. Bearing in mind that I had been doing my share to keep the breweries in business since arriving in London, I thought it best if I first sobered up before talking to this man of the cloth.

Our meeting took place in the vestry of the church and for one fleeting moment he seemed to have given me the excuse that I was looking for should I wish to call the whole thing off. He reminded me that the Church of England required that the details of the marriage be read for three successive Sundays in the church before a ceremony could take place. With my leave about to expire this condition could not possibly be met. Here was an ironclad reason for backing out if I wanted to take it. I was soon brought down to earth however, when he went on to say, that as a member of the armed forces the law of the land had been changed to allow a serviceman to obtain a 'special license' on twenty-four hours notice. There went my avenue of escape!

My brother-in law to be was two or three years older than me and before the war had been an auto mechanic. He and his wife Phyllis had two young children, Jill and William, aged five and seven. The family had made their home in Maidstone, Kent and it was from that town that Jim had joined the RAF. During the first year of the war he had seen service in France, but on returning to England just before Dunkirk, had been stationed in Britain ever since. Jim was a happy-go-lucky type, and he and I became good friends, and remained so until I left England in 1948. We both enjoyed a pint of beer and prior to marrying his sister he and I spent many evenings holding up the bar. All arrangements having been made, our wedding was scheduled to take place at Christ Church, Greenwich at 14:00 on March 3, 1945 (the fourth anniversary of my leaving home).

As soon as the pubs opened on the day of the wedding, Jim and I left the house intending to walk to the church in time for the ceremony, but also with the idea of celebrating the occasion by having a few drinks along the way. At each pub we visited, Jim made it known to everyone that we were on our way to my wedding and that he was the best man. Both of us being in uniform, this announcement was normally met with an offer by the landlord to have a drink on the house, and quite often the same offer was extended to us by perfect strangers standing at the bar. Needless to say, having called in at about six pubs along Trafalgar Road we both arrived at the church somewhat inebriated, much to the disgust of the bride's family. As the wedding ceremony began, I realised that I should have gone to the washroom before leaving our last port of call but it was too late. In no time at all I looked down the aisle to see Alice coming towards the altar on the arm of her father. At a certain point during the ceremony we were required to kneel on a cushion in front of the altar. The moment I knelt on the cushion I remembered that the sole of my right shoe was almost worn through. Embarrassed to think that everyone could now see the hole in the sole of my shoe, I tried desperately to hide them under the bride's veil which lay in folds on the floor behind us. In doing so, the veil became entangled and ended up at a jaunty angle on the right side of Alice's head, causing her to deliver a sharp jab in my ribs with her elbow. At this point in the proceedings my bladder felt as though it was going to burst, but fortunately I was saved from embarrassment when the enemy came to my rescue.

Earlier in the war, Christ Church had suffered damage from German bombs which had never been fully repaired and it was possible to see the sky through a gaping hole in the roof. As the vicar droned on and I fidgeted, the proceedings were interrupted by the wailing of air raid sirens, followed a few seconds later by the unmistakable sound of a German V1 flying bomb as it passed overhead on its way to the centre of the city. Since June of the previous year London had been subjected to constant attack by these wonder weapons which were later superseded by the V2 rocket. By the end of the war over 8,500 V1's had been launched against Britain and here was one of them coming to my rescue. All heads in the church were now looking at the sky through the hole in the roof and there was a slight pause in the ceremony as the bomb passed overhead and everyone waited with bated breath for the engine to cut out. When it did there followed a dull explosion some distance away. The vicar was now anxious to conclude the service and, speaking at a much faster pace, ended by stating: "I now pronounce you man and wife". It did not matter that having made the greatest mistake of my young life, my only concern at the time was to locate the nearest toilet.

Much to my relief I was able to do so before signing the marriage certificate in the vestry. Before leaving for home, a photograph was taken of us outside the church, after which we climbed into a taxi and were driven home in grand style. A small collection of relatives and neighbours had gathered for the reception. Those who had contributed their monthly ration towards the baking of the cake were able to recover some of the sugar they had donated by eating large portions of the finished product which had turned out rather well. That evening Jim and Phyllis, together with Alice and I, left for Maidstone by train where we were to spend a couple of days before I had to report back to *Dolphin*.

Alice returned to Greenwich a day or two later and it was agreed that she should join me in Portsmouth as soon as I could find somewhere for us to live. Before I was able to do so, however, I was sent by train to my favourite village of Campbelltown in Scotland to join the submarine training flotilla for a short course in super-sonic telegraphy (SST). Two weeks later, having been drafted back to *Dolphin*, I was given week-end leave (Friday noon to Monday 08:00) and went to London by train to see Alice. On my first night in town we went into the city to meet Aunt Lorna and introduce her to my new wife. Dinner that night was in an up-scale restaurant off the Strand, followed by dancing until around shortly after midnight. The following morning we were still in bed when, around 09:00 we were awakened by an enormous explosion which shook the house to its foundations. As the sirens had not sounded prior to the bang we came to the conclusion that it was a V2 rocket that had landed and, as there was nothing we could do about it, turned over and went back to sleep. Little did we know it at the time but the exploding rocket was one of the last two to fall on England during the war and it had hit a block of flats in Stepney killing 134 people.

As I was about to undergo a radar course in *Dolphin*, I rented a room in Gosport from the parents of one of my mess mates and Alice came down from London to join me. Now that I had a local address I was considered by the navy to be a 'native' and as such was able to go ashore almost every night. The house we lived in was located quite close to the base and by taking a short-cut through a small park on the edge of town I could cover the distance in about twenty minutes. In the mornings I usually had a light breakfast of tea and toast before leaving for the base at about seven thirty in time to be aboard by eight. The park that I used as a short-cut to reach the base had a shallow wading pool located in it. The water in the pool was about fourteen inches in depth and local children could often be seen sailing model boats on it.

One evening on my way home, I was approached by a well-dressed, middle-aged woman who wanted to know how deep the water was. I told her that it was quite shallow and she then said: "Is it possible for someone to drown in it?" Thinking she was concerned for the safety of the children wading in the pool, I assured her that they were in no danger but stated: "Anyone can drown in shallow water if they are stupid enough to submerge their head and continue to try and breathe." On my way back to *Dolphin* the following morning I was surprised to see a neat pile of clothing on the grass alongside the pool together with a lady's hand bag, shoes, and hat. On looking around I caught sight of what turned out to be the body of the lady I had met the previous evening. She was face down at the bottom of the pool and obviously dead. At that time of day, and with no one else in sight, I felt obliged to go into Gosport and report my discovery to the police. It was well after 09:00 before I was allowed to continue on my way. I had to wait until an ambulance crew recovered the body, deal with the police who questioned me at length, and sign a statement regarding my conversation with the woman the previous evening. On entering the main gate and surrendering my leave ticket I was charged with being adrift and ordered to report to the regulating office. The master-at-arms in the regulating office appeared downright disappointed when later in the day he had to drop the charge against me as the Gosport police backed up my story as to why I had been detained.

My radar course came to an end on May 4, 1945, and at that time it was apparent that the war in Europe was drawing to a close. On May 8, 1945, I had an appointment to visit a dentist in Haslar

Hospital to have a tooth filled. Armed with a chit from the sick bay I presented myself at the victualing office in order to have the supply PO stop my tot. The drill was, if a sailor was not going to be in his mess at 11:30, which was when the rum was issued, he was required to have the issue stopped until, on returning on board, it could be obtained by going to the supply office. It was eleven forty-five before I returned from the hospital, and on reporting to the supply office was told that while I had been out of the ship it had been announced that the war had been officially declared over. It was Victory in Europe! A make-and-mend had been declared as of noon, and the king had ordered the navy to 'splice the main brace'. Instead of <u>one</u> tot of neat rum being held for me, I was now entitled to <u>two</u>. Accepting the rum I then went to my mess to change into my # 1's before going ashore. On entering the mess the rum bos'un admonished me for being late in drawing my tot. He then proceeded to measure me out <u>two</u> tots, which I readily accepted. It was obvious that a mistake had been made but I did not feel that it was up to me to correct it so said nothing; therefore, I was probably the only member of *Dolphin's* ship's company to have received a total of <u>four</u> tots on VE Day!

A petty officer friend of mine who had the duty watch that day and therefore was unable to go ashore, offered to loan me his bicycle. However, I had to promise that I would take great care of it and ensure that it would not be stolen, and he insisted that if I had reason to leave it unattended on the street, it should be securely chained to a post or fence. On riding into Gosport I found the main street swarming with civilians and servicemen bent on celebrating the victory. The pubs were doing a roaring business and it was almost impossible for a man or woman in uniform to purchase a drink. In those days there were a total of fourteen pubs on the High Street in Gosport and that afternoon I must have visited all of them. No sooner did I enter a tavern but I was handed a glass of liquor by a perfect stranger and told to: "Drink up Jack". On visiting the first two or three taverns I took great care to chain the borrowed bicycle to the nearest lamp post, but as the afternoon wore on I neglected to do so and left it standing outside the pub. Fortunately for me it was not stolen, but there came a time when I found myself incapable of riding and ended up pushing the darn thing home where I arrive at around 19:00. The celebrations in both Portsmouth and Gosport continued well into the night. People were dancing in the street and bon fires were lit on almost every vacant lot.

In Portsmouth a gigantic fire was started by sailors in the town square across from City Hall. At the height of the blaze the trolley bus wires became red hot and parted, bringing the buses to a halt. Some well-intentioned citizen then called the Fire Brigade and on their arrival the fire trucks were quickly stripped of their ladders and hoses which were all combustible. Sailors could also be seen carrying benches out of the adjoining park which were then added to the bonfire, along with anything else that would burn. In practically any other country in the world the festivities of that night would have become riotous, but despite the revelry, I do not recall reading of any cases of murder, rape, arson, or injury in Portsmouth. Apart for some minor damage to city property, the boys of the Royal Navy behaved very well considering that nearly every one of them were 'three sheets to the wind' at the height of the festivities. Nothing they did came close to the behaviour of the matelots of the RCN who ran amok and ransacked Halifax, Nova Scotia that same day. The sailors in Halifax may have had some justification for their actions because of the idiotic decision made to close the bars, restaurants, cinemas, and theatres, leaving them nothing to do and nowhere to go to celebrate. It has also occurred to me that around the world, places such as Times Square, New York, and Sydney, Australia, where people had suffered the least from the dangers and horrors of total war, were where the citizens were most vocal and jubilant. I wonder how many of those in Times Square on VE Day had ever heard a shot fired in anger, heard a bomb explode or lost a relative or friend to enemy action during the past four years of war.

CHAPTER XIV
Australia

Early in June, 1945, I was drafted to HMS *Cyclops* as a member of the spare crew for the training boats under the command of Captain S/M7. Located in Rothesay, the 7th. Submarine Flotilla consisted of the three submarines: *Safari* (recently returned to the UK from the Far East), *Truant*, and *Trusty*.

Alice, who was now pregnant, returned to London and was living with her parents. Late in July I returned to Portsmouth and rejoined *Dolphin* where I was warned for a draft to the Pacific. On August 9, 1945, the war came to an end with the dropping of the second atomic bomb on Nagasaki, and on August 15, 1945, we celebrated VJ day in Britain which was somewhat anti-climactic when compared to VE day. Despite the fact that the war had ended, the movement of personnel to the Pacific was in no way affected, and having been granted seven days embarkation leave, which I spent at home in London, I joined a large draft of submariners from *Dolphin* on August 22, 1945, and embarked on the troopship *Otranto* in Southampton for passage to Australia.

Otranto, which belonged to the Orient Steamship Line, was a vessel of 20,000 gross tons, built by Vickers in 1924. In peacetime she was capable of carrying 1,700 passengers and her crew numbered 420, but as with all troopships during the war, she was crammed with troops for our passage to Australia. Of the 3,500 souls on board when we sailed, 600 were Australian servicemen recently released from German POW camps, 350 were WRENS, and the remainder were from the Royal Navy and the Royal Marines. Despite overcrowding on the mess decks all seemed well as we sailed south through the Bay of Biscay. As the temperature increased the further south we sailed conditions on the troop-decks became most uncomfortable due to the heat. Banned from using the promenade and boat-decks, which were reserved for the use of the officers and WRENS aboard, the troops only access to fresh air was on the forward or after well-decks of the ship. On both of those decks, however, there was little room available for the Australians, many of whom with four years of back pay in their pockets, spent their waking hours gambling in what came to be known as the 'Otranto Casino'. From sunrise to sunset the ex-POWs would gather around the various games being played such as Crown and Anchor, Fraz, Poker, Crap, and that uniquely Australian game of chance known as Two Up. Those of us who were still poorly paid members of the service stood around to watch as the 'Aussies' placed bets of hundreds of pounds on the throw of the dice. Incredibly, the officer commanding troops and the ship's master-at arms appeared to turn a blind eye to what was going on and it became apparent that they were intimidated by the 'Aussies' whose discipline, as the master of the *Otranto* later put it: "Was not all that could be desired". To make matters worse, after leaving Port Said, and on entering the Suez Canal, water rationing was introduced. The troops were allowed water for two hours in the morning and two hours in the evening, and in some of the washrooms, six taps had to serve 400 men.

On entering the Red Sea, the situation worsened when as many as 1,000 of the troops reported sick suffering with stomach complaints. Most of those admitted to hospital blamed the food and it was noted that very few of the officers or the WRNS who were reported to have been given better meals were affected. As far as the food was concerned, I found it to be little different from what we had grown accustomed to in wartime Britain. The 'Aussies', who had spent many years behind German barbed wire, had probably eaten worse but they were now being supplied with Red Cross parcels containing delicacies seldom seen during the war. They later claimed that they only survived the passage because of the Australian Red Cross. This of course was a lot of rot and most of those reporting sick were in fact suffering from heat exhaustion. Each day, after sunset, the gambling continued on the troop-decks and, on one occasion, I recall watching a group of 'Aussies' engrossed in a game of Fraz when the officer-of-the-day and the master-at-arms came through their mess on nightly rounds. As was the custom in the navy, the officer on rounds was preceded by a marine bugler sounding the 'G' note. On hearing the 'G', all ranks were required to stand to attention in silence as the party went by. Those RN ratings in the mess that night were shocked to see the 'Aussies' disregard the rounds party completely as they continued to deal the cards and lay their bets on the mess table. What was even more of a shock was the fact that neither the master-at-arms nor the duty officer said anything; they merely looked the other way and continued on through the mess as though nothing had happened.

As already mentioned, the promenade and boat decks were out of bounds to everyone except officers and WRNS. To ensure that everyone was aware of this order, ropes had been slung across the ladders which led to the forbidden land, from which signs were suspended reading: "Out of Bounds to all Troops". This was tantamount to waving a red flag in front of a bull as far as our 'Aussie' friends were concerned and somewhere in the Indian Ocean all such ropes and signs were cut and thrown overboard. Thereafter, the 'diggers' roamed freely on the upper decks much to the delight of the 'Brits', although few, if any, of them were brave enough to follow their example. This then was the state-of-affairs when we arrived at Bombay to take on oil and water. Prior to entering the port it had been announced over the PA system that our stay in harbour would only be a matter of hours and consequently no one would be allowed ashore. On anchoring in the stream we were visited by the usual bum-boats which came out to the ship selling a variety of goods. Some of the boats carried fresh fruit which was purchased by the troops aboard, many of whom had not seen a banana or an orange for quite some time. During the course of the day three of the 'Aussies' made a deal with one of the boatmen to be taken ashore. Unseen by anyone in authority, they managed to slip over the side with the aid of a length of rope and when last seen by those of us on deck were on their way to the Bombay docks. On sailing the next morning the trio had not returned and we resumed our voyage without them and I never did learn of their fate; however, suspect they eventually reached Australia. After leaving Bombay the ship called in at Colombo, Ceylon, where she remained for thirty-six hours but no leave was granted. On crossing the equator (the third time for me) there was no crossing the line ceremony observed and I suspect that the 'Brits' did not want to be held responsible by King Neptune for returning the 'diggers' on board to the Southern Hemisphere.

On October 9, 1945, forty-nine days after sailing from Southampton, we arrived in Freemantle, Western Australia, where those of the Australian contingent who lived in the Western states disembarked. The day following our arrival we were allowed to go ashore until midnight. Going into Perth from Freemantle by bus we discovered that the city was without electric power, the public utility workers having gone on strike. After dark the stores that remained open conducted their business by the light of gas lanterns. Most of the pubs remained open and I recall visiting one of them that had a number of candles placed along the bar. Sitting on a stool beside me was one of the local citizens with whom I struck up a conversation and was surprised to find that he was drinking Scotch and milk, which I was told was a popular drink in that part of the world. This explained the numerous pitchers of milk I had seen sitting on the bar earlier in the evening. Having never heard of this combination of liquids before, I was curious to find out what it tasted like and decided to order one. This was a great mistake on my part as I had been drinking rum up until that time and had not had much to eat since leaving the ship that afternoon. As soon as I put the glass down I realized I had a problem for I had no idea where the washrooms were. Unable to restrain myself I exploded where I sat, spraying the individual sitting to my right of me and probably everyone else sitting at the bar. Fortunately, my eruption had extinguished all the candles on the counter and the room was temporarily plunged into darkness. This allowed me to escape through the front entrance before the lights were restored and no doubt saved me from being skinned alive by the irate 'Aussies' that had been subjected to a shower of Scotch whiskey and milk.

The following day *Otranto* left for Sydney, New South Wales, having disembarked a number of submariners slated to join the submarine depot ship HMS *Maidstone*. *Maidstone,* having recently arrived from Macassar with 450 RN POWs, turned these repatriates over to HMS *Exeter, Encounter,* and *Stronghold,* who left Fremantle on October 25, 1945, to return to the UK. On our way around the south coast to Sydney, it was announced over the ship's loud speakers that we would be making an unscheduled stop at Melbourne to land one of our company who needed emergency medical treatment. News of our unexpected arrival was broadcast later in the day to the citizens of Melbourne by a local radio station along with the information that those members of the Australian contingent on board who lived in Victoria were to disembark. The radio announcer urged his listeners to drive to the docks after supper and turn on the headlights of their automobiles as a signal of welcome to the returning 'diggers'.

Shortly after 19:00, *Otranto* moved slowly into Melbourne and attempted to berth alongside one of the many large piers in the harbour. Those of us who had come up from below to witness our docking were amazed to find the entire waterfront ablaze in light. Hundreds of autos were parked facing the harbour with their headlights on turning night into day. Furthermore, the dock we were attempting to berth at was a seething mass of humanity, most of whom, to our experienced and well-trained eyes were women. It appeared that the patriotic citizens of Melbourne, with a little encouragement from the local radio stations, had decided to head for the docks to welcome home their fighting men. News of the welcome quickly spread throughout the ship and in a matter of minutes practically everyone on board had crowded to the port side to get a better look at what was going on. This caused the vessel to take on an alarming list to port and hindered the efforts of the pilot to bring her alongside. In frustration, a command was given for all personnel to return to their respective messes in order to get the ship back on an even keel. Those of us in the port side messes took turns looking through the half dozen or more scuttles which were more or less on the same level as the pier. As the ship's side came closer to the dock, the troops were calling out to the girls on shore asking for souvenirs of any kind. The girls in turn were willing to hand over just about any object in their purse, such as book matches, cigarettes, combs, lipstick tubes, and compacts, providing they were given something in return. It did not take the lads very long to give away every knife, fork, and spoon in the mess, and when these had all disappeared the cups, saucers, and dinner plates followed. The closer we came to the pier, the bolder everyone became. One of our boys, his body halfway out of the scuttle, started things off by asking for a kiss. Immediately his request was granted by a girl on the dock whose friends hung onto her legs as she stretched out across the water to join hands with the sailor. As soon as we were secured alongside the pier it was only a matter of time before one of our lads was physically pulled out of the ship and swallowed up by an excited crowd of young females and spirited away. When the officers on the bridge became aware of what was happening orders were passed to the Military Police to close all the scuttles on the port side. By the time this was carried out 370 British sailors, including me, had made it ashore, most of us dressed only in coveralls and without any form of identification with us. Finding myself standing on the dock surrounded by a bunch of hysterical girls I was seized by the arm and propelled towards the dockyard gates by about four of them. Going directly to a car parked outside the gate I, along with another matelot and all four females, piled into the auto and in a flash we were off heading for downtown Melbourne. For the next two hours we must have visited at least three taverns and consumed a dozen beers before any thought was given to our returning to the ship. Remembering that we had been told that the ship was to sail at midnight we prevailed upon the girls to take us back to the docks, which they eventually did around 23:00. When our car arrived at the head of the pier we found the gates closed and the huge mob of two hours earlier had been dispersed. The Military Police, along with members of the Melbourne Police Department, had taken charge. On entering the gate our names were taken by a petty officer from the ship's regulating office who ordered us to go aboard immediately and informing us that charges would be laid the following day.

Otranto sailed at midnight and amazingly, of the 370 matelots who had broken out of the ship, each and every one had apparently returned aboard. During the forenoon watch all ratings whose names had been taken the previous night were ordered to fall in on the forward well deck. Of the 370 men who were expected to parade, only 11 showed up. The ship's police were really not to blame for it must be remembered that on leaving the ship most, if not all of us, were not properly dressed and we carried nothing in our pockets that could be used as identification. On returning aboard it was impossible for the naval police to escort each and every man below in order to have him produce his pay book to verify his identity. Unable to punish everyone, the charges were dropped against the slow thinkers who had used their real names and the matter was closed.

On October 20, 1945, *Otranto*, berthed at No. 9 pier in Woolloomooloo, Sydney to the cheers of relatives and friends of the 216 Australian troops still on board. An Australian army band playing *Waltzing Matilda* was on hand to welcome the prisoners of war (POWs) who lined the rails of the ship and pelted the band with copper pennies. All were aiming at the kettle drum and the poor fellow playing the drum had been repeatedly hit on the head, finally giving up as he ran for the cover of a nearby shed. The news media had turned out in full force and the press made much of the fact that the 'diggers' had hung a sign over the side of the ship for all to see and which read: 'HELL SHIP - RMS BELSEN'. For the next two days, Sydney papers were filled with dire tales of those claiming to have been mistreated en rout to Freemantle. Men complained of the sleeping accommodations, cramped conditions, food, and the ban on leave while on passage. One man was reported to have said that the treatment he received was a disgrace to the British Admiralty. Those of us who worked for the Grey Funnel Line, found the whole event highly amusing as we were in a position to know how the British Admiralty, owners of the Grey Funnel Line treated their employees.

On disembarking, the naval draft was billeted in a converted warehouse on the waterfront which went by the name of *Woolloomooloo*. Those of us in the submarine branch were later sent to the old Australian light cruiser HMAS *Adelaide,* anchored off the north shore of the harbour and used by the RN as the submarine depot ship for the three 'V' class submarines *Vox, Voracious* and *Virtue,* all of whom were attached to the Royal Australian Navy for ASW training. I was only to spend two months in Australia before returning to the UK, but during that time thoroughly enjoyed my stay and have always had a desire to some day return. For those of us in *Adelaide,* our daily routine was in no way strenuous. The submariners were divided into four separate divisions, three of which provided the crews for the three submarines, and the fourth being considered the spare crew. All the ratings and officers were victualed and accommodated in *Adelaide* as the three subs, normally operated during daylight hours, returning to harbour at nightfall. Those of us in the spare crew could be called upon at short notice to replace a man in one of the boats who, for whatever reason, was unable to go to sea, and providing that the man being replaced was of equivalent rank and trade. This situation occurred frequently; for example, someone away on leave, being hospitalized, or having to go into Sydney to see a doctor or dentist. *Adelaide* lay at anchor in one of the many picturesque inlets on the north shore of Sydney harbour. She was moored at a distance of less than a hundred yards off shore, parallel to the beach, and with her bow facing south towards the harbour. Between the ship and the beach a catamaran provided a stage for the embarking or disembarking of provisions and stores and the three submarines were moored in a trot on her port side. On her starboard side a small boat was secured to the catamaran which was used to take individual officers and men to a landing on the beach, and from where they could walk to the ferry which crossed the harbour to Circular Quay in the city.

On joining *Adelaide* as a member of the spare crew, I was often required to go to sea in *Vox* on daily A/S exercises, but early in December I was approached by the coxswain of the spare crew who asked if I would like to take on the job of ship's postman. When I learned what the job entailed I was only too glad to accept the offer as there were a number of appealing 'perks' that came with it. The Fleet Mail Office was located in downtown Sydney which meant having to take the ferry across the harbour to the main ferry terminal at Circular Quay. Mail was landed from the ship twice daily at 08:00 and at 13:00, the procedure being as follows:

At 08:00 I would present myself to the officer-of-the-watch and ask his permission to carry on ashore with the ship's mail. Permission being granted, the duty quartermaster would then row me over to the small dock on the beach where I walked about half a mile to catch the ferry. Arriving at Circular Quay I would board a street car which dropped me off outside the Fleet Mail Office. After delivering the outgoing mail I would receive the incoming mail in a sealed mail bag and set out on the return journey, arriving back at the ship at about 11:30, in time for 'up spirits'. The afternoon delivery left the ship at 13:00, and was a repeat performance of the morning run with one slight difference. After dropping off the outgoing mail I was free to carry on ashore, picking up the incoming mail the following morning on my way back to the ship. This arrangement was very much to my liking as it allowed me to spend my nights ashore while continuing to draw my tot, eat two meals on board each day, and answer to no one in authority except the coxswain. Without a doubt, I had landed the best job in the ship and was the envy of all my mess mates. The spare crew coxswain (whose name I shall not disclose for reasons that will become apparent) was a tall and handsome young man of about twenty-five years of age. As a submarine coxswain he was one of the younger ones but had obviously proven himself at an earlier date as he wore the ribbon of the DSM. I had only held the job of postman for about a week when he again asked me to visit his cabin to discuss a matter which I might find of interest. At our meeting he confided that he had devised a scheme to make some extra cash and wanted to know if I would be interested in hearing his proposition. My curiosity aroused, I asked him to continue. He went on to tell me that there were approximately 178 submarine ratings being carried in *Adelaide*. This number included the crews of the three subs and those carried as spare crew. As coxswain of the depot ship, he was responsible for ordering the tobacco ration for these 178 men; each man being allowed one pound of duty-free tobacco every month per Kings Rules and Admiralty Instructions

(KRAI). Duty-free tobacco, both pipe and cigarette, as supplied by the Crown, was normally issued in one pound cans and commonly known in the navy as 'ticklers' because it was supplied by the Firm of Tickler whose company also supplied the navy with jam.

Submariners, who were paid more than General Service ratings, preferred to purchase tailor-made cigarettes rather than roll their own. As a result only two or three of our ship's company took advantage of the monthly duty-free allotment. With almost 175 pounds of cigarette tobacco available to be drawn from dockyard stores at a cost of two shillings and sixpence per pound, it seemed almost criminal to ignore the fact that a pound of tobacco could be sold ashore in Sydney for twenty shillings, a profit of seventeen shillings and sixpence per pound. With this in mind the coxswain suggested that we should combine our recourses and purchase all the tobacco not used by the ship's company and turn a handsome profit by selling it ashore. All we would have to do was figure out a way to get it past customs. It now became apparent why the coxswain had previously asked me to be the ship's postman. It was his intention to use me to help him get the tobacco ashore. What better way to land contraband than in a sealed Royal Mail bag carried over the shoulder of one entrusted to deliver the king's mail! My thoughts were confirmed when he went on to outline details of the scheme. The plan was as follows: on each trip ashore with the mail I would take a minimum of four pounds of tobacco in the mail bag. This bag was sealed before leaving the ship and could not be opened by anyone other than by those authorized to carry the mail.

On my arrival at Circular Quay, instead of going directly to the Fleet Mail Office, I called first at the bus depot where there were lockers for rent and in which I would keep an empty suit case. Seeking the privacy of a booth in the public lavatory located in the depot, I was then to break the seal on the mailbag, remove the paper labels on the cans of tobacco, disposing of them by flushing them down the toilet. On re-sealing the mailbag with a spare seal carried in my pocket, the suit case which now contained the tobacco would then be returned to the locker and I would continue on to deliver the mail at the Fleet Mail Office. Repeating this routine in the afternoon would result in a total of eight pounds of tobacco being deposited in the bus depot locker ready to be sold each night. At a selling price of 20 shillings a pound, our profit would amount to 7 pounds Australian or three pounds ten shillings for each of us. Not bad considering that the average worker in those days earned about five pounds a week. Needless to say, the prospect of making this much extra money interested me greatly. The legality of what he proposed was never questioned and it did not take me long to make up my mind, I told the coxswain that he could count me in. I should point out to anyone reading this, that neither the coxswain nor I considered what we were about to do as illegal, for traditionally, the Royal Navy (meaning all who served in it) were of the opinion that, throughout its history, we had encountered only five enemies in the world: Spain, France, Germany, the United States of America, and Customs and Excise Officers. Having defeated the first three, we pretended that the fourth did not exist, and were still at war with the fifth.

Once our smuggling operation got underway and the money began coming in, the coxswain rented a one-bedroom apartment in town, found himself a female companion to share it with and spent most of his weekends at the race track. I, on the other hand, continued to use the facilities provided by the British Centre, the largest and best recreational club in Sydney, designed for the exclusive use of British sailors. The British Centre was located adjacent to Hyde Park, within walking distance of the dock area. Overnight accommodation was available at a reasonable price, and the centre contained, among other things; a large library and reading room, barber shop, tailor shop, theatre, restaurant, and huge ballroom in which dances were held twice a week. In short, they were able to offer everything that might interest a sailor on shore leave except alcohol, and that was available in one of the many pubs in downtown Sydney. Saturday night dances were well-attended and very popular with the matelots. Volunteer civilian hostesses were in abundance in addition to the numerous 'Aussie' WRANS who turned out in droves on dance nights. At one of these dances I had the good fortune to meet a young lady by the name of Valerie who hailed from Melbourne and with whom I was to share many pleasant hours during my time in Australia.

Valerie worked at the RAN Signals Office in Sydney and had been in the WRANS for about two years. She was one of the most beautiful and interesting girls I had ever met. A year older than me, she was about five feet in height with light brown hair and blue eyes. Like many Australian girls, she was sun-tanned with just the right amount of freckles on her nose to enhance her natural beauty. She enjoyed all types of sports, was an excellent swimmer, and could handle a sailboat better than anyone I had ever met. For some unexplainable reason she appeared to enjoy my company and was only too willing to provide me with her telephone number. This was the start of a friendship that I will long remember and cherish to this day. From the outset she was aware that I was married and as a result our relationship was platonic. It remained that way as a result of her integrity, not mine. I had already begun to regret my hasty leap into the sea of matrimony but accepted the fact that I had made my bed and would now have to lie in it.

The months of November and December in Australia are similar to July and August in the Northern Hemisphere. Each afternoon hundreds of sail boats could be seen on the blue waters of Sydney Harbour and the wide sandy beaches of Manley and Bondi were crowded with sun worshipers. Both beaches were located quite close to the city centre and Valerie and I were frequent visitors. On one occasion we spent an entire day at Taronga Park on the north shore of the harbour. The park is home to one of the finest zoos in the world, and after inspecting the koala bears, wombats, wallabies, wallaroos, platypus, and other native species, we found a site overlooking the water where we enjoyed a picnic while watching the myriad vessels which ply the waters of beautiful Sydney harbour on any given day during the summer.

Valerie's love of the outdoors prompted her to suggest that we should visit a secluded beach located a few miles up the coast from

North Sydney. This beach was on private property and reputedly owned by the Governor General of Australia who, at that time, was Field Marshal Lord Alexander of Tunis. Whether this was true or not I had no way of knowing, but on leaving the bus which dropped us off in a little hamlet at the end of the line, we walked for about a mile along the shore before arriving at a small bay. There wasn't a cloud in the sky and the bright sun made the blue waters sparkle as we stood and surveyed the scene. A broad beach of snow white sand separated the shore line from the sea, and close to the land stood a cluster of large boulders, some the size of a small house. As far as the eye could see there was not a soul in sight and we had the beach all to ourselves. Under the shade of one of the large boulders we spread a blanket and laid out the contents of our picnic hamper. Before leaving town I managed to scrounge a bottle of Gordon's gin from an American GI, and having brought along a bottle of ginger ale, we stretched out on the sand and enjoyed a cool drink before going for a dip. Finishing our drink, we decided to change into our swimwear. It was then that Valerie came up with a marvellous idea. With a mischievous smile on her face she said "there's no one else around so why don't we go skinny dipping?" Needless to say I needed no urging, but having made the suggestion she now insisted on undressing behind the large boulder in front of which we had been sitting. Choosing a spot to disrobe out of sight of each other, I heard her call out: "Ready or not, here I come. The last one in the water is a stinker", and in a matter of seconds we were both on the open beach racing towards the water wearing nothing but a smile on our faces. You can imagine our shock when, on emerging from behind the rock and halfway to the water we encountered four nuns who had appeared out of nowhere and were slowly walking in our direction. Too late to do anything about it we both kept on going straight into the water where, by submerging ourselves up to our necks, we were able to cover our nakedness until the quartet were out of sight. To this day I have no idea where these Sisters came from, or for that matter, why they were on the beach. For the next four hours we had the beach to ourselves but later in the afternoon a number of other people turned up and when it began to cloud over we decided to call it a day and head for home. Walking back to where the bus had dropped us off in the morning it began to rain and by the time we got to the hamlet a full thunderstorm was raging. The only shelter that we could find was in a telephone booth while we waited for the bus to arrive. Soaked to the skin, we broke out what was left of the bottle of gin and without either ice or mix, finished it off. Later that night I found out that drinking neat gin was not a wise thing to do, for it came back to haunt me and I have not been able to stomach the stuff since.

A week or so later, having spent the night ashore, I returned to the ship early one morning just in time for breakfast. As was the custom the 'sparkers' had tuned into a local radio station and through the speaker on the bulkhead we heard the announcer begin to read the first news broadcast of the day. Little attention was being paid to what was happening in the world that morning until we heard the word Admiralty, at which time a hush fell over the mess deck. It was then we learned that it had been announced by Buckingham Palace that: "The king has been graciously pleased to approve the award of the Victoria Cross for valour to Lieutenant I.E. Fraser, DSC, RNR, and Acting Leading Seaman James Joseph Magennis". The announcer then went on to add that two other members of the crew of the submarine XE-3 had been decorated; Sub. Lieutenant (Kiwi) Smith RNZNR and ERA Charlie Reed had been awarded the DSO and the CGM respectively. All eyes turned on 'Mick' Magennis, who was in the mess that morning, and it became obvious that he was just as surprised as we were at what we had just heard. A short while later the coxswain came into the mess to congratulate 'Mick' and inform him that Lt. Fraser wished to see him on the quarterdeck.

'Mick' had been the diver in the midget submarine XE-3 when, on July 31, 1945, under the command of Lt. Fraser, she had slipped into the anchorage where the Japanese heavy cruiser *Takao* was moored. The cruiser was still under repair from the damage earlier inflicted on her by the US submarine *Darter* who had scored two hits on her on October 23, 1944. As the diver in XE-3, 'Mick's' job was to attach limpet mines to the hull of the enemy vessel which was heavily overgrown with barnacles. With great difficulty, due to the shallow water in which the cruiser lay, he was eventually able to do so but damaged his breathing gear on leaving the submarine. For over half-an-hour he worked, managing to secure six mines along the keel of the ship before returning to the sub. With 'Mick' safely aboard, completely exhausted, and his hands lacerated by the crustaceans on the hull of the enemy ship, Lt. Fraser attempted to leave the area. It was then that he discovered that the empty limpet container could not be released and was making the craft unmanageable. It then became necessary for someone to leave the boat once more. 'Mick' volunteered to go out in order to correct the problem, and having succeeded in doing so, XE-3 was finally free to set course for the open sea.

Born in Belfast, Northern Ireland October 27, 1919, 'Mick' joined the Royal Navy as a boy seaman in 1935, and entered the Submarine Service in 1942. Those of us who were his messmates knew him as a quiet type who got along with almost everyone. He could best be described as a typical British sailor; amiable, carefree, and somewhat mischievous on occasion. Despite his Irish temperament, I never knew him to loose his temper, although I have no doubt he was quite capable of holding his own if push came to shove. At the time of the award he was a member of the ship's company of the *Voracious*, but was immediately transferred to the spare crew mess in *Adelaide* and relieved of all duties pending his return to the UK by air. The coxswain stated that 'Mick' and Lt. Fraser were to meet Admiral Sir Bruce Fraser (Commander-in-Chief British Pacific Fleet) that afternoon. 'Mick' subsequently changed into his #1 uniform and landed with me at Circular Quay when I went ashore with the mail that morning. On our way across the harbour I noticed that, instead of the regulation tapes that were part of the British sailor's uniform, 'Mick' was wearing, what appeared to be, an ordinary boot lace which he had cut to the required length. When I questioned him as to what had happened to his tapes, he told me that on putting on his jumper he realized that they were missing. In a hurry to get dressed he had fashioned the tapes that he now wore by taking a pair of scissors to one of his boot laces. At the time I wondered how he expected to get away with it on meeting Admiral Fraser, but to the best of my knowledge he did, and in a picture of him in the paper that evening, the substituted boot lace can be clearly seen. That afternoon the lower deck was cleared and as 'Mick' stood beside the captain looking most uncomfortable, the official citation issued by the palace was read to the ship's company. Having been relieved of all duties, 'Mick' was granted indefinite leave on the condition that he kept the authorities informed of his whereabouts daily. He and Lt. Fraser were to be in London by December 11, 1945, for the investiture at Buckingham Palace, and flown home as soon as a flight could be arranged. At loose ends in Sydney, 'Mick' decided to make a trip to Newcastle to visit with friends but neglected to inform the authorities of his whereabouts.

A day or so later word was received that a flight to the UK had been arranged to leave Sydney at 23:00 that night, but by then no one knew where Leading Seaman Magennis was. The Sunday Telegraph dispatched a reporter to track him down, and all radio stations in New South Wales joined in the search by issuing bulletins on the hour, every hour, asking him to report to the nearest police station. At 19:00 that night the Sunday Telegraph reporter dropped into a small café for something to eat. He sat on a stool at the counter and struck up a conversation with a sailor sitting beside him who was eating a hamburger. During the conversation the reporter realized he was talking to the man he had been looking for all day. At 23:00, a BOAC Sunderland flying boat took off for Darwin on the first leg of a flight to the UK. On board were Lt. Ian Fraser and 'Mick' who were given an opportunity to inspect the wreck of the *Takao* when the aircraft landed in Singapore. On arrival in the UK, they landed at Poole and travelled by train to London. 'Mick' Magennis was the only surviving junior rating in the navy to be awarded the Victoria Cross during World War II. Swept up in a whirl of publicity he found himself somewhat out of his depth when called upon to attend functions where gin, champagne, and cocktails were served instead of beer or rum, which were more to his liking. Although he was proud of the decoration, he was, by nature, a shy person and at times embarrassed by all the attention being paid to him. Little did he know then the price that he was later to pay for having received his country's highest award for valour. After he left Australia, I did not meet up with 'Mick' again until late in 1947, when we were both serving in *Dolphin*. I will have more to say about him in due course.

Christmas Day 1945 was spent in the company of a friend whom I had met at the British Centre in Sydney. His name was Roy and he was the owner of the barbershop located in the Centre. Valerie had gone home to Melbourne to be with her parents over the holiday season and I had no plans to do anything out of the ordinary. I had met Roy soon after my arrival in Sydney when I had gone to his shop for a hair cut. He was a man in his late twenties and at the time was in the process of getting a divorce from his wife of five years. Over a period of time we had become good friends and often went into town for a drink after he had closed up shop in the afternoon. In order to buy a drink at a bar in Sydney in those days one had to be in the pub before 18:00 as all licensed premises closed at that time. This archaic law was later changed, as were the idiotic laws governing the sale of liquor in Canada. Most offices in Sydney closed at four in the afternoon and anyone wanting a drink had two hours in which to reach his favourite watering hole, order a drink and consume it before they closed for the night. Needless to say bars that were almost empty all afternoon were filled to capacity a few minutes after four. Everyone tried to catch the eye of the barmaid and order as many drinks as possible in the two hours remaining. If one were lucky enough to be served, the waitress expected a handsome tip, and if this was not forthcoming, it would be the only drink that you would be served that day. Sharp at 18:00 the bars closed and anyone who wished to continue drinking would then have to find one of the many bootleggers that abounded in Sydney in those days. Roy had been invited to attend a Christmas party at the house of a friend. He in turn asked me to tag along and I agreed to meet him at his shop on Christmas Eve and accompany him to his flat. On closing his shop he pulled the blinds and produced a bottle of rum which we finished before leaving. On our way out of the building we passed the kitchen where the cooks were preparing food for Christmas dinner the next day. We watched as the meat was removed from dozens of turkeys and the bird's carcasses were disposed of in a large oil drum. Remembering that Roy owned a small dog, I asked one of the cooks if I could have a turkey carcass to take home for the pup, to which he replied: "Take as many as you want". Selecting one of the larger ones which had a lot of meat on the bones, I wrapped it in an old newspaper, and tucking it under my arm, we set off to board a street car to Roy's apartment.

The pubs, having just closed, we found the streetcar filled with happy drunks on their way home to their wives. As all the seats were occupied, Roy and I, along with many other passengers, were forced to stand in the aisle hanging on with one had to an overhead strap. A man standing next to me, obviously inebriated, kept staring at the turkey under my arm, the neck of which was protruding from its newspaper wrapping. The sight of the bird, or to be correct, what he thought to be a fully roasted bird, must have triggered a remote corner of his inebriated brain, for he suddenly remembered it was Christmas Eve and he had forgotten to purchase a turkey for his wife. In a loud voice he bemoaned his thoughtlessness and wondered aloud what his wife was going to do to him when he got home. A second drunk, overhearing the conversation, made the suggestion that: "Maybe the sailor will sell you **his** turkey, Bill. Why don't you ask him?" Bill's face brightened at the thought, and pulling out his wallet offered me two pounds for the bird tucked under my arm. When I declined his generous offer he increased the sum to three pounds, and when I had once more turned him down, he pulled out two more notes and waving them before my eyes informed me that this was his last offer. Sensing his mounting hostility I caught sight of Roy who had one eye closed and was nodding his head. In a matter of seconds the deal was closed. Turning over the carcass of the bird and accepting the five quid, Roy and I made our way to the exit door of the car, wishing the now smiling owner of the bird a Merry Christmas and continuing our journey on foot.

I spent most of Christmas day on Manley beach soaking up the sun and relaxing in an attempt to recover from the effects of the night before. Judging from a photograph that appeared in the paper the next day, I gathered that I had not been the only sailor in town who had been celebrating. The picture showed a dozen or more matelots stretched out on the grass in Hyde Park sleeping off hangovers brought on as a result of the previous night's activities. If the Christmas celebrations were somewhat boisterous they did not come close to the events that took place in Sydney one week later when the citizens, with the help of hundreds of British sailors, welcomed in the first new year after six years of war. In my opinion, Australians are true party animals, and on the Eve of 1946 they proved it without a doubt by turning out in the thousands to celebrate. New Year's Eve celebrations in Sydney 1945 were reported to be the gayest since 1938 and are best described by quoting reports from a newspaper published on the following day:

"From nightfall until the early hours of the morning about 30,000 people wearing coloured paper hats, false noses, or grotesque masks, paraded the streets at King's Cross. About 50.000 people welcomed the New Year in at Manley with dancing, singing and fireworks, and at Bondi 10,000 people thronged the promenade and entertainment centres. The police reported that the huge crowds were good humoured and well behaved despite the fact that British sailors took a leading part in the celebrations. One British sailor walked up and down Macleay Street dressed in a bed sheet, wearing a long dunce's hat, and carrying a cardboard scythe. In Springfield Avenue, a woman's shoe was torn off at 22:30 p.m. then raffled amongst the crowd. It was sold to a British sailor for ten shillings. Later in the evening a pair of women's scanties was thrown over the trolley bus line on Macleay Street. At midnight tens of thousands of people linked hands and sang Auld Lang Syne, while revellers blew whistles, hooted car horns and beat on improvised drums. Soon after midnight a naked woman ran across Macleay Street into a block of flats to the cheers of British sailors standing nearby."

Throughout the night thousands of couples made out in the entrances to shops and offices and at King's Cross groups of more than one hundred people formed a single line and danced along the roadways and sidewalks. Australian servicewomen formed a Congo line in Hyde Park and led hundreds of sailors on a wild serpentine dance through the park, wading through the fountains and ponds in their bare feet. At 02:00, I joined a group of apartment dwellers who were having a party on the roof of their apartment building and dancing to music played on a portable gramophone. Unfortunately, the party came to an abrupt end when one of the tenants in the building complained angrily that the noise was keeping his baby awake. Dressed in his pyjamas he appeared among us and, picking up the offending gramophone, hurled it over the edge of the roof where it shattered into a thousand pieces on the street below.

It is perhaps fortunate that at the time there were few American servicemen remaining in Australia. 'Aussies' as a rule had high regard for the British matelot, despite the fact that he was often referred to as a 'pommy' or 'kipper'. On the other hand both 'diggers' and 'kippers' universally disliked the 'Yanks' and had there been many of them around it is doubtful that the night would have passed without incident. Despite the general feeling of good will extended to the British servicemen, a small minority of Australians (I suspect of Irish origin) frequently voiced their dislike for the 'pommy'. Evidence of this anti-British sentiment is expressed in letters to the editor of a Sydney newspaper after printing a story related to the sailing of the Aircraft Carrier HMS *Indomitable* for the UK. With the dismantling of the British Pacific Fleet, one after another the large ships of the RN sailed from Australia bound for England with troops and former prisoners of war going home to be demobilised. On the day that *Indomitable* sailed from #2 dock at Woolloomooloo, over 300 women gathered at the gates to the wharf to bid farewell to the British sailors, many of whom had married Australian girls.

Just prior to the ship's departure, scheduled for 10:00, the crowd outside the gates became hostile when an armed guard informed them that they were not going to be allowed admission to the wharf. "What would you do if we rushed the gates?" taunted the women. The sentry's reply is not recorded, but it is safe to say that he implied that he had no intention of using his rifle, which probably wasn't loaded anyway. On the carrier orders were given to man the rail for departure and some of the women at the wharf entrance became hysterical. The crowd then swept the guard aside and raced to the edge of the dock. A Royal Navy lieutenant in charge of the berthing party then lost his cool. Ordering the matelots in his working party to get a hose and to keep the crowd back from the mooring lines, which were about to be cast off. As the sailors kept the hose playing in front of the crowd one woman dashed through the spray and slapped the officer's face, knocking his cap into the harbour between the ship and the wharf and almost causing him to follow his cap into the water. Matelots on the flight deck who witnessed the incident, burst into cheers as the lieutenant ran up the wharf and took cover behind a large packing crate. The crowd then surged along the pier, many of the women weeping and others shouting hysterically to sailors on the ship. With a 400 ft. paying-off pennant trailing over her stern, *Indomitable* pulled out in the stream to start her long journey home while the crowd slowly dispersed and a number of ratings, using a boat hook, fished for the lieutenant's cap which was still floating in the harbour.

The day following the departure of *Indomitable,* Sydney papers were inundated with letters to the editor. Some defended the action taken by the RN lieutenant; others condemned the hysterical women, while a number of writers used the incident as an excuse to vent their wrath against the British in general. British seamen wrote to apologise for the conduct of their countrymen per the following example:

APOLOGY: "We the members of this mess, apologise for the conduct of the lieutenant who ordered the hose to be turned on the crowd when the *Indomitable* left. His action wasn't typical of the lower deck ratings' feelings towards a kind and hospitable people. We are disgusted that one of our countrymen should have done this: Signed, #5 Mess."

One of their countrymen, however, obviously did not share their sentiments towards a "kind and hospitable people" for his letter read as follows:

"Advance Australia fair, by name,
Your land of heat and sudden rain
With deadly ticks, snakes, and spiders,
Where Englishmen are ranked outsiders.
But though you say the country's grand
Give us our own congenial land.
So, 'dinkum' 'Aussies' fare thee well
I love you all my friends like hell!"
Signed,
Yorky, RN.

Another nasty letter written by an Australian WRAN in reply to a civilian female who had upheld the virtues of the British sailor read as follows:

To RN Forever:
"I am a WRAN, holding a position in which I come in contact with RAN and RN personnel, and have yet to see an RN sailor who reaches the standard of cleanliness, decency, and manners of the average Australian sailor. You are probably the type who does not warrant the respect of any Australian, certainly no Australian would want you to weep over him."

Finally, an Australian sailor wrote:
"The women who howled and screamed when the *Indomitable* left would have richly deserved having a fire hose turned on them. They weren't the ones who really felt sorry the 'kipper's' were leaving. A similar mob did the same with the 'Yanks".

From the above, it can be seen that RN matelots were either hated or loved by the residents of Sydney. As far as I was concerned my shoulder flashes read 'CANADA' and wherever I went in Australia I was regarded as one of the family. There weren't many Canadians 'down under' at that time.

Early in the New Year I was relieved of my job as postman in

Adelaide due to the fact that there was a shortage of A/S ratings in the spare crew. Those of us who were qualified were required to go to sea on the daily A/S exercises. In my case, I was part of the ASDIC team in HM S/M *Vox*. Valerie returned from leave during the first week of January, but as a result of being at sea almost every day, there was little opportunity for us to get together. One evening, after securing alongside, a messenger from the ship's office came on board with orders for me to report to the First Lieutenant's cabin. On doing so I was handed a copy of a letter sent to the ship by the welfare office in *Dolphin*. From it I learned that Alice had contacted the authorities in Portsmouth to seek their assistance in having me returned to the UK on compassionate grounds due to a series of domestic problems at home. When I left England in August the previous year, she had gone to live with her parents in Greenwich being about six months pregnant. Upon my arrival in Sydney I received a number of letters from her but at no time had she indicated that all was not well at home. Our baby was due in February and she had written to say that she would continue to stay in Greenwich until I returned, at which time she thought that we should make application to the London County Council for a house of our own. The housing shortage in Britain was critical during the years immediately following the end of the war, but it was expected that ex-servicemen and serving members of the Armed Forces would be given priority in obtaining their own home once the situation improved. The domestic problems referred to in the letter from the welfare officer indicated that my in-laws intended to move from Greenwich to Mottingham, Kent in the near future, and as a result Alice and the baby would have to find other accommodation. Of a more serious nature was the fact that due to Alice's mothers asthmatic condition she would not be able to help her daughter after the baby was born. Finally, the doctors indicated that there might be delivery complications therefore the welfare officer recommended that I should return to the UK as quickly as possible. Based on this, I was informed that arrangements were being made to have me sent home by air and that I should expect to leave Sydney within a day or two.

The following day I left *Vox*, and on rejoining the spare crew mess, prepared to leave the *Adelaide* at short notice. Weight restrictions on the aircraft meant that my hammock and the bulk of my personal gear would have to travel home by sea so, having packed a steaming bag containing my best uniform and the barest of necessities, I was confined in the ship pending an immediate draft. I managed to place a call to Valerie before leaving, promising to write as soon as possible. Recalling that I had seen a silver pendant in a jewellery store in town which had been fashioned in the shape of an aboriginal boomerang, I prevailed on one of my mess mates to purchase it and have it engraved with the words; 'I shall return'. I mailed it to Val before leaving, along with a note in which I told her how much I had enjoyed her company. I also intimated that should circumstances change in the future, I would definitely consider returning to settle in Australia.   Informed that I would be leaving the ship at 16:00 the following day (which happened to be a Saturday) I found myself cooling my heels on the mess deck during the early afternoon, the majority of the crew having gone ashore on liberty. At around 13:00 the duty quartermaster entered the mess and asked for volunteers to help unload a motor cutter that had come alongside with fresh provisions. Having little else to do I joined with two or three members of the duty watch to lend a hand. One of the lads went aboard the cutter and started passing its cargo to willing hands on the catamaran from whence we carried it aboard the ship using the after brow. Reaching for a 50 lb. bag of potatoes being handed up to me, the boat drifted away at that moment. Unable to hang on to the burlap sack and in order to avoid falling overboard myself, I let it go and watched as it sank to the bottom, leaving a trail of bubbles as it descended. Watching us from the quarterdeck was the officer-of-the-watch, sword belt hanging from his waist and telescope tucked under his arm. Having witnessed this heinous crime being committed, he called out to the 'killick' of the work party: "Have that man charged and brought before me immediately." Within the hour I was paraded aft, and being called upon to remove my cap, stood in front of the OOW to listen to the charge being read. It appeared that I had been negligent in my duty in that I had allowed 50 lbs. of spuds, property of the King of England; i.e., the Crown, to slip from my hands and fall into the clutches of King Neptune;

i.e., Davy Jones' locker. Pleading: "Not guilty, sir", the young sub glared at me and in a squeaky voice I heard him say: "Commanders Report", at which the 'killick' screamed: "On cap; about turn; double march." At 16:00 a boat arrive alongside to fetch me, and saluting the new office of the watch (the sub had been relieved at eight bells) I showed him my draft chit and sought his permission to carry on ashore. I mention this episode as an example of how the long arm of the service can reach out to ensure that the admiralty gets its pound of flesh.

Three years later, having left the navy, and living in Toronto, I received my RFR pay cheque from the British Naval attaché in Ottawa. On opening the envelope I was amazed to see that the sum of five shillings had been deducted to compensate the Crown for the 50 lbs. of potatoes lost in Sydney harbour in January 1946!!

The motor cutter landed me at Circular Quay where I found a small van waiting to take me to an RAAF base on the outskirts of the city. Our flight, scheduled to depart early that evening had, for some unknown reason been delayed and we did not take off until the early hours of the next day. On boarding the aircraft, each of the passengers was handed a woolen blanket, the purpose of which became apparent as we climbed to an altitude of ten thousand feet. The plane was not fitted with individual seats for the comfort of the passengers. Two very uncomfortable metal benches were located on either side of the centre aisle on which we were expected to sit for a very long flight. Once airborne we found it far more comfortable to wrap our blankets around us and sit on the floor of the compartment rather than on the bench. Because the aircraft was not pressurized we were forced to fly below eleven thousand feet, but even at that altitude it was unbearably cold and the blankets were put to good use. Operated by RAF Transport Command, our kite was a consolidated *B-24 Liberator* long range bomber. In addition to the normal crew, there were a total of five passengers of which three were commissioned officers, the other two being myself and an RAF corporal. One of the officers was a group captain in the RAF who I was later informed had been the personal pilot to the

Governor General of Australia, HRH the Duke of Gloucester. The other two were a lieutenant commander, Royal Navy, and a captain of the Royal Marines.

After leaving Sydney our first stop was Adelaide, a distance of about 770 miles. In Adelaide the RAF corporal left us, and on topping up with fuel we took off for Perth, some 1,400 miles to the west. Our flight path took us north of the Great Australian Bight on our port side, while to starboard was the Nullarbor Plain which borders on the Great Victorian Desert of Western Australia. After leaving the coast the landscape began to change and shortly before flying over the gold mining town of Kalgoorlie, the terrain had taken on the appearance of the surface of the moon. From a height of ten thousand feet one looked down on a myriad of craters which, during the rainy season held water, but were now dry. The soil around these craters was alkaline encrusted, white in the centre, with concentric circles radiating outwards in various shades of red, blue, or purple. From these dry craters, tracks radiated outwards made by the animals of the desert seeking water. One wondered where these same animals now had to go to find water in the dry season. On landing in Perth we were informed that there would be a four hour delay before resuming our flight. After a hearty meal in the station's mess hall the RAF group captain suggested to the other passengers that in view of the long hop to our next destination, it might be a good idea to consider taking some refreshments with us. He proposed that if he could persuade the station transport officer to lend him a Jeep he would go into town and purchase a few dozen beers to help us through the night.

The next leg of our journey would take place that night as we crossed the Indian Ocean to the Cocos Islands 1,750 miles to the west. Everyone thought that his suggestion was a good one, and true to his word he obtained the loan of a Jeep from the transport compound and returned to the airfield a short while later with four dozen bottles of Fosters ale. The Captain of Marines, not wanting to be up-staged by the RAF, then managed to scrounge enough cheese and crackers from the officers' mess to feed our party during the long flight. Throughout the night, my three companions and I huddled in the belly of the aircraft feasting on cheese and crackers and drinking beer. Disposing of the empty beer bottles was no problem as these were dropped through the aircraft's flare tube leaving a trail of dead marines in our passage across the Indian Ocean. In the early hours of the morning I managed to get some sleep despite the fact that the aluminium floor was most uncomfortable and the interior of the fuselage very drafty.

Just before dawn one of the crew came aft with a large thermos of strong tea and announced that we would be landing in about one hour. Prior to setting the plane down our pilot informed us that on approaching the air-strip we would be flying directly above the wreck of the World War I German cruiser, *Emden*. As we flew over the barrier reef of North Keeling Island the outline of the German ship could be seen through the crystal clear water where she had been beached after her running fight with HMAS *Sydney* on November 9, 1914. The final approach to the runway, which was almost the full length of the island, was very low over the water. As we descended I thought for a moment that we were going into the sea, but at the last second our wheels touched down, and we eventually came to a stop in front of a low building with a roof thatched with coconut palms. At the time I gave little thought to the fact that we had arrived safely, but in later years I came to realize the importance of having a good navigator. The Cocos Islands were a mere speck in the ocean, roughly half way between Perth and Colombo. The slightest error in navigation could have led to our missing them completely, and without enough fuel to reach the nearest land, we would have been forced to ditch in the sea.

Our flight was scheduled to resume later that day, but after breakfast we were informed that this would not be the case due to adverse weather conditions existing in the vicinity of the Equator. An Australia bound BOAC plane, which had landed shortly before us had experienced excessive turbulence after leaving Ceylon and as a result we were grounded until the tropical storm abated. The Cocos Islands, also known as the Keeling Islands, are a group of twenty-seven small coral islands in the Indian Ocean with, at that time, a native population of about 400. Used as a re-fuelling stop on the air route between England and Australia, a distance of over 10,000 miles, they provided an important link in what was probably the longest commercial air route in the world in 1946. Lying only 12 degrees and 15 minutes south of the Equator the daytime temperature was unbearable. None of the buildings were equipped with any form of air conditioning other than a 'punkah' suspended from the ceiling and kept in motion by a small boy in one corner of the room pulling on a rope. Having disembarked from our aircraft we were given breakfast in a building which served as both the officers mess for those stationed on the islands as well as a rest stop for BOAC passengers. The mess hall was a large, airy room, open on all four sides from about four feet from the floor to just under the ceiling. Despite mesh screens, which covered all openings to the building, there were swarms of what appeared to be sand flies in the room and although an on shore sea breeze gave some relief to the occupants, it was so hot that the butter on the table had turned to liquid and was quite rancid. After breakfast, having been issued with bedding for our overnight stay, we were shown to our billets. The heat was so oppressive that there was little else to do other than to strip down to a minimum of clothing and try to catch up on the sleep that we had missed the previous night.

That evening, the sun having set, it cooled off considerably and after dinner a number of us went for a walk along the sea front under a canopy of stars, the like of which I had never seen before. Those of us who had Australian money were later able to purchase a beer in the mess before turning in, a limit of two bottles per person being allowed. After a restless night we were awakened at six in the morning by one of the native mess-boys coming into our quarters to help us get the day started by handing out cups of steaming hot tea. Shortly after breakfast we were informed that we had been given clearance to take off and by 10:00 were once more rolling down the runway headed for the Island of Ceylon. Our flight to Colombo was uneventful and boring except for the last half hour as we flew over the tea plantations on the southern tip of the island. The mountainous terrain that was crossed created a great deal of turbulence as we came in for a landing and I was quite glad when we finally touched down. On leaving the plane, which had come to a stop some distance from the terminal building, a coloured piece of paper was carried by the wind across the tarmac where it came to rest on the concrete a few inches from my shoe. On reaching down to pick it up I was pleasantly surprised to find that it was a Ceylonese bank note in the sum of five hundred rupees; a very welcome find for someone who did not have any of the local currency. From Colombo our *Liberator* was scheduled to fly on to Delhi, India, and while waiting to continue my journey I was billeted in the RN barracks. The RAF group captain continued on to Delhi while the lieutenant commander and the captain left to join ships in the harbour. I was not given any idea as to how long I would have to wait before continuing my journey, but it was pointed out to me that I had been travelling on a Priority 3 air transport ticket which meant that I could be bumped by anyone holding a Priority 1 or 2 ticket. This was the priority that most officers were given, and it looked as though I might be in for a lengthy stay.

Two days after my arrival, having spent the five-hundred rupees that I had found, I was in need of further funds to purchase gifts for home. Locating the RN pay office in the barracks, I was able to obtain a 'casual payment' in the sum of five pounds from the paymaster. My intention was to purchase tropical fruits such as bananas, oranges, etc. on the eve of my departure for England and hope that they would not spoil en route. Two days later I was informed by a messenger from the ship's office that I was required to report to Admiralty House immediately. On doing so, I was ushered into the presence of a WRN officer who enquired of me why I was being returned to the UK by air. Explaining that there were compassionate reasons for my draft, she asked me where I would be going after landing in England. When I replied that I would be travelling to London she seemed pleased and handed me an envelope, informing me that I would be required to deliver it to the Admiralty in Whitehall from the Flag Officer Ceylon. Along with the letter for the Admiralty I was also given a second letter which read as follows:

2nd February 1946
Able Seaman F Jones
P/SSX 747185
Is carrying a very urgent non-secret letter, addressed to Admiral
Commanding Reserves, from Flag Officer, Ceylon.
Signed; Assistant Secretary to
Flag Officer, Ceylon.

On pointing out to her that my air ticket was only Priority 3, and
that I was uncertain as to how long I might have to wait for a seat
on a plane, she informed me that I was being upgraded to a Priority
level 1 and that I would be departing the following day in a BOAC
Avro York Lancaster for London. That evening I went into town and
purchased a large quantity of fresh fruit which I packed carefully
in a large biscuit tin, and the following morning was driven to the
airport where I joined a number of other passengers in boarding
the converted bomber. The Avro York 1101 was then part of the
BOAC fleet and was actually a modified *Lancaster* bomber. Unlike
the old *Liberator* that had carried me from Sydney to Colombo, the
York was a pressurized aircraft with a crew of nine, including two
charming stewardesses and seats for twenty-four passengers. The
majority of the passengers were officers in uniform and all three
services were represented. There were about six men and two women
in civilian dress and I was the only enlisted man in the group. I
could not help but notice that on boarding the aircraft the cabin
attendants seemed to be regarding me with what appeared to be
more than usual interest. At first I thought that this was perhaps
due to fact that I possessed a priority 1 ticket which, as an enlisted
man, was most unusual. It was much later in the flight, after landing
in Cairo that I learned the true reason for the curious glances in my
direction and the VIP treatment that I had been receiving from the
flight crew. One of our passengers, a young RNVR Lieutenant, in a
conversation that we had in the Cairo airport, informed me: "I've
been told by the stewardess that you're being returned to England to
receive an award from the king." This young officer was anxious to
learn what the award was and what I had done to receive it. When
I told him that there was absolutely no truth to the story I got the

impression that he did not believe me. The more I protested that the story was false, the more he was convinced that embarrassment and modesty were the real reasons for me not admitting the truth.

After arriving in England I discovered how the rumour had started. On the train to London from Holmsley RAF station where we landed, I shared a compartment with the BOAC officer who had been our engineer on passage. He told me that one of the girls on the plane had been the cabin attendant on the *Sunderland* in which 'Mick' Magennis and Ian Fraser had returned to the UK. Both VC winners had been flown home on a Priority 1 ticket and the cap tally on 'Mick's' cap had proclaimed that he was a submariner. On joining the *Avro* in Colombo with a Priority 1 ticket, and noticing from my cap tally that I was also a submariner, this girl had jumped to the conclusion that here was another hero on his way home to be decorated. I never found out how many of the other passengers were aware of the rumour that she started. If others on the plane had heard the story they were either too polite to ask me questions or inclined to take it with a grain of salt. In any event, the only one to broach the subject was the brash lieutenant in Cairo. I must admit, however, everyone on that plane treated me with the greatest of respect in marked contrast to the type of treatment normally given to one 'below the salt'.

Our first stop on leaving Colombo was Karachi where we de-planed for a meal while the aircraft was re-fuelled. On leaving Karachi, the next leg of our journey took us to Basra, Iraq; a distance of about 1,250 miles. This portion of the trip I found most interesting due to the changing terrain. The barren and inhospitable land below, void of all vegetation and human habitation, conjured visions of camel caravans, Marco Polo, and more recent heroes such as T.E. Lawrence, whose campaign against the Turks in 1916 had taken place only 900 miles west of the very land that we were flying over. Due to some type of mechanical problem we were on the ground in Basra for almost four hours. While waiting for repairs to be made to the aircraft we were given a meal in the BOAC cafeteria located on the airfield. There was little to see in Basra other than oil tanks, warehouses, aircraft hangers, and acres and acres of desert sand. Everyone was pleased when it was announced that the necessary repairs had been completed and we were ready to resume our journey. It was dark by the time we became airborne, and other than isolated lights on the ground as we crossed over Saudi Arabia, there was nothing to see until we were flying over Jordan where one could see a glow on the northern horizon from the lights of Jerusalem. It was after midnight when we touched down in Cairo where we were allowed to disembark and stretch our legs. In the small hours of the morning we left for Malta where we landed at around 09:00 the following day in time for a breakfast of bacon and eggs in the RAF mess on the George Cross Island.

I left Sydney wearing my blues and on arrival in the Cocos Islands had changed into tropical gear, stowing my blues in the 'steaming bag' I carried. Now in Malta, my last stop before landing in England, I wanted to change back into blues, but because my bag was now in the luggage compartment of a civilian aircraft, I was unable to retrieve it. There was nothing I could do other than hope for mild weather on touching down in the UK. Leaving Malta shortly before noon, we settled down for the five-hour flight that would take us across Sardinia, the French Alps, and the English Channel to our final destination, London. Over the south of France the weather changed for the worse and leaving the mountains we encountered severe winter conditions as we approached England. As we crossed the channel it was snowing heavily, visibility had reduced to zero, and it was doubtful that we would be allowed to land in London. We were not at all surprised then, when our pilot announced that due to the weather we would be landing at Hounsly RAF Station in South Hampshire, and I lost no time locating my bag and changing into my blues. Not only was I attracting the attention of everyone on the station dressed in tropical shorts, but I was starting to turn blue with cold. Before transport could be provided to take us to the nearest railway station, I had to undergo a medical inspection, be issued with a railway warrant to London, and pass through Customs.

While in Australia, one of our ships had arrived in Sydney from

Singapore with well over a million dollars in Japanese government occupation bank notes. These notes, which ranged in denominations of five cents to ten dollars, did not have the value of the paper that they were printed on and were freely distributed among those of us in the fleet who wanted them as souvenirs. Having obtained about six or seven hundred dollars of this phoney money, I came up with the idea of using some of it to avoid paying duty to British Customs on the gifts I had purchased overseas. Packing the small attaché case in which I had my gifts of silk stockings, watches, broaches etc., I spread about one hundred dollars in Japanese money over the packages. When I opened the case at the request of the custom's officer, the poor man's eyes began to bulge on seeing the phoney notes. "What have we got here?" he asked. Replying quite truthfully that it was Japanese occupation money, he then asked: "Are they worth anything?" When I assured him that they were worthless and only souvenirs, I suggested that he might like to have one or two hundred dollars to pass around to his children or friends. With a smile on his face he winked at me, and handing him a handful of bills, he reached across the table and closed the lid on my case. Having cleared customs we were then interviewed by the station medical officer who wanted to know what country we had come from, how long we had been away from the UK, and whether we had any medical complaints. Having answered all his questions, we were given a card which stated that, in the event of becoming ill any time after twenty-one days of arrival, it should be shown to a doctor (civil or service). Producing the letter I had been given in Colombo, I was issued with a railway warrant and transportation was provided to take me to the nearest railway station. On my way to London I shared my compartment with the BOAC flight engineer (as previously mentioned) who told me the origin of the rumour started by the stewardess on my joining the plane in Colombo. From Waterloo station I went by tube to Trafalgar Square, and on being admitted to the Admiralty by a commissioner at the door of the Spring Gardens entrance, handed over to the officer on duty the envelope entrusted to me in Colombo. Learning that I had been flown home on compassionate grounds and that my wife lived in London, the duty officer suggested that I might want to see her before reporting to *Dolphin*. Accepting his offer, I was issued a long weekend pass which meant I would not have to report for duty until 08:00 the following Monday morning. Making my way back to Charing Cross, I took the tube to Greenwich and shortly before midnight was let into the house by Alice who was unaware that I was coming home.

My unexpected arrival created quite a stir in the household. Having disturbed everyone from sleep, Alice made a pot of tea and her parents joined us in the kitchen where the four of us sat and talked until early in the morning. I learned that Mr. and Mrs. Honeysett had rented a London County Council house located in Mottingham, Kent, on the outskirts of greater London. Alice had also made application on our behalf to obtain a place of our own in the same housing development. While our application had not yet been approved, her parents were scheduled to move in early March meaning that we would have to find somewhere to live at that time. As the baby was expected to arrive in late February, in all probability the family would still be in Greenwich at the time of its birth. Alice intended to have the baby at home and would only be admitted to a hospital in the event of an emergency during delivery. Apart from the fact that we would have to find somewhere to live, I was unable to understand how Alice had been able to convince the authorities that the situation at home was serious enough to warrant my return to the UK by air. In any event, regardless of how she had managed to do it, I was now in England and there was nothing that could change that fact. Having spent the weekend in London, I caught an early train to Portsmouth on Monday morning and reported on board *Dolphin* by 08:00. Two days later, having completed my 'joining routine', my case was reviewed by the Welfare Office in RNB and I was provided with a letter addressed to the London County Council (LCC), requesting that I be given priority in obtaining a council house. The following day I left for London on fourteen days Foreign Service leave.

On February 24, 1946, I went to London for the day with the intention of visiting Aunt Lorna who was still serving with the

WVS as a receptionist at the YMCA services club at *Gatties* on the Strand. She was not aware that I had returned to England and was quite surprised to see me. I had hoped that she would be able to give me news from home, but was told that since my mother's death she had received only two letters from my father and a couple from my aunt in Toronto. I learned that her husband had been returned to the UK from Italy after having spent a considerable length of time in a military hospital in that country. He had come close to losing his life as a result of a serious accident involving his Jeep and another military vehicle shortly before the end of the Italian campaign. That evening she and I went to a theatre in the Strand to take in the movie "Gone with the Wind", at the conclusion of which we had dinner together. It was late in the evening when I bid her good night and caught the 'tube' to Greenwich. On entering the house I was surprised to find that Mr. and Mrs. Honeysett were not at home and, on going upstairs to the bedroom, found Alice lying on the bed in great pain. She told me that her mother and father had gone to visit her sister at around noon and that shortly after they had left the house she had started to experience intermittent spasms of pain. Fearing that she might be going into labour, she had placed a phone call to Mrs. White, the local midwife. This elderly lady was one of many midwives employed by the health authorities throughout the country for the purpose of assisting women in childbirth. Mrs. White, who at one time had been a registered nurse, made regular monthly calls on her patients and had been calling on Alice since the third month of her pregnancy. That afternoon, after learning that Alice was experiencing periodic spasms, she arrived at the house on her bicycle (her normal means of transportation) and over a cup of tea assured her that she had nothing to worry about. "It's false labour dearie", she said. "Your baby is not ready to be born. When the time comes, you'll know." Having delivered her verdict, she mounted her bike and left.

Alice had not had anything to eat since noon, and although she said that she was not hungry, I made a fresh pot of tea. Taking her up a cup of tea and biscuits, we discussed the events of the day. As the evening wore on we kept track of her contractions and noticed that they were occurring at regular intervals of fifteen minutes then more frequently and lasting longer. It was now very close to 22:00 and I was on the verge of panic. Here I was alone in the house with my wife who was about to give birth and I had no one to call on for help. There was no telephone in the house, her parents were not at home, there were no neighbours on the street to call on, and any first aid courses that the navy had given me had not included delivering a baby. My only course of action was to contact Mrs. White. Telling Alice that I would only be gone a few minutes, I left the house and ran to the phone booth located at the end of our street. On answering her phone, Mrs White was quite indignant when I identified myself and explained the reason for my call. "I saw your wife earlier today" she informed me, "and I told her that she had no need to worry as she was not in labour." When I insisted that the situation had changed since the previous afternoon and that Alice was having contractions only ten minutes apart, she accused me of being a panicky husband and berated me for having disturbed her rest. Despite her virulent tirade, I managed to convince her I was telling the truth and she reluctantly agreed to come as soon as possible. I ran all the way home and entering the bedroom discovered that Alice's water had broken and she was about to give birth. For the next half-hour or more all I can recall was that I was at a complete loss as to what to do. Without going into detail, I can remember seeing the top of the baby's head starting to emerge and what seemed to be hours later (but in actual fact was probably only a matter of minutes,) I was looking down at a fully formed baby lying at the foot of the bed, wet, red in colour, moving his arms and legs, and squawking at the top of his lungs. Opening a large roll of cotton wool, I was in the process of bundling him up when I heard a knock on the front door and was relieved to see Mrs. White standing there with her little black bag. Entering the bedroom, she ordered me out with instructions to wash my hands and boil a large kettle of water. She then cut the umbilical cord and delivered the placenta, while I sat shaking in the kitchen trying to light a cigarette. I was still there when Alice's parents arrived home, and having related everything that transpired since noon the previous day, Mr. Honeysett went to a cupboard and, producing a bottle of brandy, proceeded to pour me a stiff drink, which I gratefully accepted. It was after four in the morning before Mrs. White made her departure. Mother and baby having fallen asleep a short while later, I settled down on the sofa in the living room where I slept like a log until awakened by my new-born son the following morning. We decided to name the baby Colin Donald, and two days later, my leave having expired, I was able to return to *Dolphin*, satisfied that all was well at home.

Before leaving London I called in at the local LCC office and was informed that our application for a council house had been approved. Our new home was located in Mottingham and it was expected that we would be able to take possession at the end of March. On re-joining the ship I was delighted to learn that I had been selected to take a Higher Submarine Detector (HSD) course to be conducted in Portsmouth and which was scheduled to start in about three weeks. On qualification as a HSD, I would be only one level below the highest ASDIC qualification available, namely Submarine Detector Instructor. Apart from the increase in pay that this promotion entailed, I would be considered as a department head and given every consideration for advancement to leading seaman. Unfortunately, the events of the past three months were about to take their toll.

On March 25, 1946, I was admitted to Haslar Hospital suffering from infectious hepatitis. Possibly the flight home from Australia, together with the situation at home, had left me in poor physical condition. Eight days later I was transferred to an isolation ward in the Sherborne Naval Auxilliary Hospital where I spent the next three weeks. During my hospitalization, Alice and Colin moved into our new council house in Mottingham and on being discharged from hospital, I left for London to visit my new home for the first time. The district of greater London known as Mottingham was actually located in the county of Kent. Typical of the suburban developments that had been started in Britain just prior to the outbreak of war, the houses were all of brick construction, identical in appearance in the front, with small, narrow yards at the rear where most occupants planted a vegetable garden. During the war many of these homes had been provided with an Anderson shelter (an underground bunker built of corrugated steel, covered with earth, and equipped with bunk beds and wooden benches) and our new home was equipped with one of these. By North American standards these houses would have been considered primitive, but in post-war Britain they were regarded as quite modern in comparison to the average working class family home of that time. On the ground floor there was a living room with a coal burning fireplace, at the rear of which was located the combination kitchen and dining room. Upstairs were two bedrooms and a two-piece bathroom containing a wash basin and an indoor flush toilet. This was considered to be a real innovation as older homes still had outside toilets although connected to an underground sewage system. Despite the fact that these homes had central heating, they were nonetheless damp and cold during the winter, and in the early morning it was necessary to light the fireplace in the living room to warm the house. Taking a bath was a major undertaking. The water heater located in the kitchen provided hot water for the entire house, but the water had to be first heated by gas. The tub, which was also in the kitchen, was normally covered by a hinged wooden board which served as a counter when the bath was not in use, and raised when it was. When in use the kitchen then became the bath room and could not be used for its intended purpose. Needless to say having a daily bath was normally out of the question, and Saturday nights were generally considered family bath night. A commercial area was located in the centre of the housing development, and along with other places of business were a grocery store, cinema, chemist shop, and the local pub. The pub was the centre of social activity, and during warm summer evenings young couples would often go walking with their children and partake of a pint on the terrace outside the tavern while the youngsters played on the swings in the adjoining park. Mr. and Mrs. Honeysett acquired a house within walking distance of ours and Alice visited them frequently. Mr. Honeysett enjoyed a game of darts, and when I was at home on leave he and I frequently met at the local pub for a game and a pint of beer. While in hospital I had written to Aunt Lorna informing her of the baby's delivery and on learning that I was at home on sick leave, she offered to let Alice and I have the use of her house in Aldershot for a week.

Earlier in the war she and her husband, Hugh, had purchased a house in Aldershot where he had been stationed at the time. On his posting overseas, Aunt Lorna had taken up her wartime job in London and the house had been let. Having returned to the family home in Chelmsford after the war, the house was now up for sale and had been sitting empty for a number of months. Accepting her kind offer, the three of us arranged to meet in London one morning where she met Alice and Colin for the first time. That afternoon, having been given instructions as to how to find the house and armed with the keys, we took the train from Waterloo Station and arrived in Aldershot that evening. The Tudor style house was fully furnished with three bedrooms on the upper floor; a far cry from our own little council house in Mottingham. Alice and I occupied the master bedroom, and as Colin's pram could be detached from its undercarriage, we were able to utilise it as a crib. Spring had come to Southern England and the weather that week was perfect. The crocuses in the garden were already out and the lush lawns were an emerald green. During the day, after we had done our shopping, we went for long walks along the narrow country lanes of Surrey, and in the evenings would take Colin with us while visiting the local pub where we sat around the fire enjoying a pint and chatting with the locals. One afternoon, while walking along the main road leading to the Army camp, a staff car came towards us at a high rate of speed escorted by four members of the military police riding motor cycles. On both fenders were red pendants on which were emblazoned five gold stars. As the cavalcade swept by us we were surprised to see that the lone occupant of the staff car was none other than Field Marshal Viscount Montgomery of Alamein, easily recognized by his famous black beret with its two badges. The week went by all too quickly and soon we were back in London, but our short holiday had done us a world of good and both Alice and I had enjoyed a good rest. Having missed my HSD course due to illness, I was slated to join the next class at the end of May. This four-month course consisted of eight weeks theory, followed by eight weeks practical exercises carried out in training boats operating out of Portsmouth and Portland. At the end of September the course ended and having passed both theory and practical exams I was rated as a Higher Submarine Detector. During October I was employed in the maintenance of ASDIC equipment in a number of submarines belonging to Reserve Group "R" mothballed at *Dolphin*, and on November 5, was drafted to the submarine *Sportsman* as her HSD.

H.M. S/M *Sportsman*.The first 'Boat'
that I served in as an HSD   *The authors collection*

CHAPTER XV

Sportsman

Sportsman **was an "S" class** submarine built in HM Dockyard, Chatham and launched in April 1942. Originally given the number P79, she was named *Sportsman* in 1943, and had seen service in the Mediterranean during that year. Her armament consisted of a 3 inch HA/LA gun, seven 21 inch torpedoes (6 forward and 1 aft) and a 20mm. AA gun behind the bridge. With a displacement of 814 tons, she carried a crew of 48 officers and men and had a diving depth of 350 feet. Within days of joining her we sailed for Chatham dockyard to undergo a major refit, and on the boat being taken in hand by the dockyard, all members of the ship's company were returned to *Dolphin* with the exception of those regarded as heads of departments. Those of us who were to stand by her during the refit were billeted in two Quonset huts located in the dockyard, while a third hut was allocated for our use as an office. Bus transportation was provided between the naval barracks and the dockyard at meal times, but other than the noon meal, was seldom used. Most of us preferred to use the NAAFI canteen in the dockyard rather than subject ourselves to the 'pusser' atmosphere within the confines of RNB where submariners were looked upon with a jaundice eye by general service 'crushers', 'jaunties', and 'GIs'.

The Quonset huts were equipped with two large coal-burning iron stoves which were never allowed to go cold in winter. They not only heated our quarters but were used for drying laundry, making toast, warming cans of soup, and brewing tea. Our working day started at 08:00 and ended at 16:00, with a break of fifteen minutes for stand easy in the morning and afternoon. For those of us entitled, we drew our tot at the ship's office at 11:30 each day, our commanding officer, allowing us to draw neat rum instead of the regulation grog, a privilege that we all appreciated and which was never abused. Each day a small number of hands were required to form the duty watch. These people served as sentries on the boat at night, stoked the fires in the huts, and scrubbed out our quarters in the morning prior to the first lieutenants rounds at 10:00. Our boat, which had been parked in one of the many basins in the dockyard, was reached by a short walk from our billets. The water having been pumped out of the basin, she sat high and dry on wooden chocks and was held in the upright position by stout timbers wedged between her hull and the basin wall. It was expected that our refit would take at least nine months to complete, meaning that for the most part of a year I would be able to commute to London by rail practically every day. By train the journey to Mottingham via Dartford was a little over an hour, providing I was able to make the necessary connections without delay. From the Dockyard gates to Chatham station was a matter of minutes by bus, and on arrival in Dartford a second bus dropped me off almost at my front door. With the ship's company in four watches, I was able to go home three nights out of four, and would normally arrive in Mottingham shortly after 17:00. On returning in the morning it was necessary to leave home no later than 06:00. in order to be sure of reporting aboard by 08:00.

Travel between Chatham and London created something of a problem for those of us who did so daily. To save time when leaving the dockyard in the evening, we seldom changed into full uniform. Wearing a raincoat over trousers and jersey, it was possible to fool the naval police into believing we were fully dressed as we left the gates, and most of us had learned the hard way never to try and go ashore wearing sea boots. During winter months large areas of the dockyard were inundated with water from melting snow and where the roads had not been paved, standing water often resulted in a muddy quagmire, in some instances six or more inches in depth. As a result of these conditions, we normally wore rubber sea boots during working hours, but as this form of dress was frowned upon by the 'Gestapo', we ran the risk of being charged if we set foot outside the dockyard gates in anything other than leather boots or shoes. Strangely enough, the wearing of sea boots and working rig was acceptable within the walls of RNB and the dockyard. It was the fifty or more yards separating the two gates that created the problem. As far as the navy was concerned, once a man was between the two gates he was considered to be in the public eye and therefore required to be properly dressed.

As earlier mentioned, it was because of this type of thinking that submariners were reluctant to go anywhere near the barracks. We would rather use the NAAFI canteen in the dockyard to purchase our lunch than run the risk of entering RNB during lunch hour. On returning to the dockyard one morning, after having spent the night at home, I and two others of our ship's company were stopped at the gates by a 'killick' of the Naval Police. Having first been ordered to produce our identity cards, we were then questioned as to whether we were correctly dressed under our coats. Forced to admit that we were not wearing jumpers, collars, or silks, we were then escorted to our ship's office where formal charges were duly laid. On being paraded before our commanding officer later in the day we found him somewhat sympathetic for he knew only too well the conditions under which we were living in our Quonset huts. Unable to completely dismiss the charges against us, he did the best that he could under the circumstances and handed down severe reprimands. At the start of our refit there were three officers attached to our group; our commanding officer, his first lieutenant, and an engineer lieutenant. The various department heads all came under the torpedo coxswain and ranged in rank from able seamen to chief petty officer. During daylight working hours the boat swarmed with dockyard 'mateys' and within days of our arrival the interior of the vessel was a shambles. Electrical cables, air hoses, and oxyacetylene hoses were strung throughout the compartments and the deck was as black as the ace of spades as oil, grease, and mud on the boots of the workers was tracked between the fore-ends and the after tube space. The smell of fresh paint mingled with the acrid gasses of the acetylene torches, and the natural odour of shale oil, which is common to all diesel submarines, produced an indescribable fug within the pressure hull. As no major changes were to be made to the ASDIC instruments in the boat there was little for me to do at first in respect to the electrical equipment in my department.

Towards the completion of the refit I became involved in the few changes that were made, but during the early weeks found myself working with the other seamen, swinging a chipping hammer or wielding a paint brush on the casing. On the days that we were required to stand a duty watch, those of us who were living up the line would normally bring our own food from home for our evening meal. The alternative would be to pay for a meal in the dockyard canteen where it was also possible to obtain a pint of beer. There were about six ratings in the duty watch, of which one was the petty officer in charge, and one or two others were 'killicks'. One of the 'killicks' was our signalman Peter Jennings who, over a period of time, became one of my best friends, and remains so to this day. In the course of his duties it was necessary for Peter to visit the mail office in the barracks on a daily basis and also make numerous trips to the main signals office. Because of the distances to be covered the first lieutenant arranged for him to obtain a bicycle from naval stores. This machine was duly delivered to our ship's office and signed for by Peter, who took pride in keeping it in pristine condition. At the end of the day the bicycle was housed in our hut and Leading Signalman Jennings made it known that under no circumstances was anyone allowed to ride it in his absence. Despite warning us of the dire penalty to be paid for ignoring his order, it became common practice when Peter was ashore for members of the duty watch to mount the bike in order to get around the dockyard or visit the canteen. One night Able Seaman Brooks borrowed the bike for a trip to the wet canteen in order to have a pint or two. Hours later, mounted on the bike and, having consumed about fourteen beers, he was on his way back to our quarters when he accidentally went off the road. Riding directly into one of the dockyard basins he wound up swimming for his life, while the bicycle came to rest on the bottom of the basin in about fifty feet of water. On finding everyone asleep and the lights out when he entered the hut, he quietly undressed, and having hung his wet coveralls up to dry, crawled into bed. The following morning no one at first noticed that the bike was missing. It was not until after the hands had fallen in, and when Peter was about to make his first trip to the barracks, that he discovered his means of transportation had disappeared.

The investigation that followed the loss of our signalman's bicycle lasted almost a week, during which time the Naval Police, Royal Marine Dockyard Police, and the City of Chatham Police Department, were all involved. Suspicion centred on Able Seaman Brooks as he was the last person seen riding the missing bike. Unable to solve the case, the Naval Police called in the Dockyard Police, and when they too failed to come up with an answer, they called on the Chatham Police for help. Eventually the excitement died down and out trusty 'bunting tosser' was issued with a second bike which he kept chained and padlocked when not in use. I was unable to learn whether or not the cost of the bike was ever deducted from his pay. Many months later, while drinking beer in *Dolphin's* canteen I met up with Brooks who filled me in on what had happened to Peter's bike and exactly where it could be located. Two years were to pass before I had an opportunity to tell Peter what Brooks had told me. It was Christmas Eve 1948, and Peter and I were drowning our sorrows at a bar in Toronto when he brought the subject up. Just as I had suspected all along he was convinced that I had been involved in the disappearance of his bike, and when I related to him what Brooks had told me in *Dolphin*, I do not think he believed me.

As 1946 drew to a close I realized that for the first time since leaving home I would probably be spending Christmas in some place other than a naval establishment or a serviceman's hostel. Some time around the end of August, Alice had told me she was expecting our second child. With the baby due around late March or early April, I was fairly certain that I would still be in Chatham when the child arrived. I was looking forward to being with her and Colin over the holidays, and on instructions from our commanding officer, the coxswain had listed the names of those who would be going on Christmas and New Years leave. The ship's company had been divided into two groups and the first group consisted mainly of the married men in the crew. This group would be the one that would be away at Christmas. The second group consisting almost entirely of single men would be on leave over the New Year festivities and each group would have a total of five days leave. On the day that my leave started I was on my way to the dockyard gates when the little green MG Roadster, owned by our first lieutenant, pulled up alongside. Shouting at me over the noise of the engine he asked: "Are you travelling to London Jones?" Replying in the affirmative, he beckoned to me to throw my steaming bag in the back of the car and hop in. Our 'Jimmy-the-One' was a handsome chap in his mid twenties. Of fair complexion, he sported a neatly trimmed naval beard, was around five foot eight in height, and reputed to be something of a ladies man. In the six or more weeks that I had been in *Sportsman* I do not imagine I had spoken to him more than once or twice, other than over the defaulters table or in reply to a direct order. I therefore found his offer of a ride to London somewhat surprising, and was even more surprised when he offered me a cigarette and we became engaged in lively conversation. I learned that he had entered the navy as a cadet on leaving public school, and joined the Submarine Service on passing out of Dartmouth College as a midshipman. His father sat in the House of Commons as an MP, and I gathered he was quite well off financially for, although the family home was in Essex, he maintained a flat in Mayfair which he used when in town. A flat in Mayfair must have cost him a pretty penny and most RN lieutenants could not afford to drive an MG and rent a Mayfair flat - even on a submariners pay.

Our trip to the 'Smoke' that day was most interesting and ended all too soon. Dropping me off in Deptford, he wished me a Merry Christmas and was on his way as soon as I stepped out of the car. Contrary to what others may believe, I found Royal Navy officers to be perfect gentlemen and not apt to act condescendingly when dealing with members of the lower deck. Officers of the Royal Naval Reserve were really Merchant Navy sailors and were not normally pretentious. They had the highest respect for anyone that they considered to be a real seaman, be they officer or rating. On the other hand, officers of the Royal Naval Volunteer Reserve (RNVR) were more often than not the ones that were despised by the ratings who were regarded by them as being 'below the salt'. Many of these young gentlemen adopted an air of superiority the moment that they were commissioned and were often regarded by their shipmates as insufferable bores. There were exceptions to the rule of course, but far too many of them appeared to think that they were God's gift to the Navy, and intellectually superior to the common matelot.

There was little to celebrate in the UK that first Christmas after the war. Food rationing was still in effect, beer was still weak, and there was a shortage of coal throughout the country, making it difficult to keep a warm house. Despite the austere conditions, everyone made the best of what we had and looked forward to the coming year convinced that now the war was over things would begin to improve. During March, the new 'A' Class submarine, *Acheron*, being built in the dockyard, was scheduled to be launched. On the day of the ceremony, March 25, 1946, 'Jimmy-the-One' gave us a make-and-mend in order that we might attend her launching, which was performed by the wife of Admiral G.B. Middleton, Admiral Superintendent of the Dockyard. It was a beautiful day as *Acheron* slipped into the Medway to the cheers of a very large crowd. This was my first look at one of the new 'A' class boats which I hoped one day to serve in.

Our refit continued into the spring of 1947, and on April 9, I was told to report to the ship's office where I was met by the coxswain and informed of a phone call just received. My sister-in-law had called to say that Alice had given birth to a girl and that mother and baby were doing well. That evening I arrived home to find a house full of relatives, including my brother-in-law, Jim, who had driven up from Maidstone. After supper he and I paid a visit to the local pub to celebrate the birth of my daughter, Valerie. By the end of May, *Sportsman* had once more begun to take on the appearance of a submarine. Most of the work inside the pressure hull had been completed and the outside was being prepared for painting. Early in June, I received a telegram from Aunt Lorna advising that her father, my Great Uncle Neville, the Commodore, had cabled to tell her he was about to return to England.

As noted earlier, during the war years Uncle Neville, now 81, had lived in Kenya, East Africa. Now that the war in Europe had ended, he informed his daughter that he planned to return to England for, to use his own words: "I don't want to die in Africa and I feel that I should die in my own home". Finding it difficult to book a passage home by sea from the east coast of Africa, he had travelled overland to Uganda, where he had started out on a journey of almost four thousand miles down the Nile to Cairo. This gruelling trip, most of which was made in an Arab Dhow after leaving Khartoum, had take him many weeks to complete and must have been very tiring for a man of his age. On his arrival in Cairo, he had travelled by train to Alexandra and booked a passage in a British collier about to sail for Newcastle in ballast. After landing in Newcastle, his intentions were to spend a few days with his daughter in Chelmsford, then continue to his home in Sidmouth. Before doing so however, he had expressed a desire to meet me, and he and Lorna, having booked in to the *Savoy* in London, extended an invitation to Alice and I to join them for dinner. The doorman at the *Savoy* appeared somewhat flustered when our taxi dropped us off in front of the hotel. I suspect that Alice was not the cause as she was dressed in a plain white dress in the style of the day which I believe was referred to as the 'new look'. On the other hand I was in uniform and I gathered that young matelots were not frequent visitors to the *Savoy*. Aunt Lorna and Uncle Neville greeted us as we entered the lobby, and at the entrance to the Grand Ballroom we were met by the maître-d who escorted us to our table. A quick survey of other guests made me aware that of all those wearing uniform, I was the only one present not holding a commission. If for a moment I was somewhat self-conscious, I need not have worried for Uncle Neville very soon put me at ease with his friendly manner and animated conversation. During the course of the evening he regaled us with yarns of his early days at sea under sail culminating with his being appointed as the Director of the Royal Indian Marine in 1914. He then told me of his dealings with Admiral Lord Jellicoe who was the driving force behind the Royal Indian Marine (RIM) becoming the RIN. When he was not holding forth on his favourite subject of ships and the sea, he was on the dance floor with Alice. It was obvious that he had taken a liking to her as he asked her to dance on numerous occasions throughout the evening and I marvelled at his energy, finding it difficult to believe he was close to 82 years of age. In the small hours of the morning

Aunt Lorna was finally able to convince her father that he should call it a night. We said farewell in the lobby, and the following day he left London for his home in Sidmouth. Approximately three weeks later a letter arrived from Lorna enclosing his obituary from the Times of London reporting his death on June 20. True to his word, Uncle Neville had returned to his home to die.

As July came to a close, we began cleaning up the boat in preparation to taking it over from the dockyard. By August 1, we had moved our gear inboard and a draft had arrived from *Dolphin* bringing our compliment up to strength once more. During the first week in August our dock was flooded, and a day or two later we carried out a test dive in the basin. All went well and as no leaks were detected, we departed Chatham on August 5, sailing down the Medway to Sheerness where we spent the next few days conducting sea trials off the Isle of Sheppey. Our trials completed, we set a course for Spithead and rejoined the 5th S/M Flotilla at Gosport. On August 9, 1946, I set out for 'The Smoke', having been granted 22 days long leave. The start of my leave also coincided with my being drafted from *Sportsman*, which meant 1 would not be re-joining her on my return to *Dolphin*. Later, *Sportsman* was transferred to the French Navy and re-named *Cibyl* based at Toulon. She went to sea one day in 1947, and disappeared off Porc Rolles in approximately 1,000 feet of water, lost with all hands.

One afternoon, shortly after returning to *Dolphin* from leave, lower deck was cleared and the ship's company mustered to witness punishment. Once assembled, we were brought to attention as the prisoner, under escort, was paraded before Commodore Bryant. We were about to see my former shipmate, L/S 'Mick' Magennis, deprived of his Good Conduct badge and sentenced to serve twenty-one days detention. Having been convicted of being drunk (among other serious charges) he now stood cap in hand, before the commodore that afternoon to hear his warrant read. As his rank, Christian name, surname, and official number was read, there was a look of utter disbelief on the faces of assembled officers when the prisoner, calling out in a loud voice, complained that the punishment warrant had not been correctly prepared. He pointed out that, as a recipient of the Victoria Cross, it should be so stated in the document. As a result of his outburst, the ceremony was held up while the necessary correction was made to make the warrant read Leading Seaman James Magennis, VC. On completing his sentence of twenty-one days, 'Mick' was later discharged from the submarine service and returned to general service on September 1, 1947.

CHAPTER XVI
Artemis

In August 1946, having celebrated my twenty-first birthday, I gave serious thought to what I wanted to do when my present engagement expired. For some time I had contemplated transferring to the Australian Navy and even discussed the possibility of doing so with Alice. On the other hand, I had heard great things about the Canadian Navy which had grown considerably since I left Halifax in April, 1941 for England. The Admiralty were obligated to return me to Canada at the completion of my engagement, and Australia had made it known throughout the RN that any naval personnel wishing to transfer to the RAN would be welcomed with open arms. On my return to *Dolphin* from leave, I learned that one of the new 'A' class boats, HM S/M *Artemis,* was about to depart for Halifax for a period of three months ASW exercises with the RCN. Submitting a request to be drafted to *Artemis* for compassionate reasons, I pleaded my case before the commander, pointing out that I had not been home since joining the navy in 1941. If I were to join her I would more than likely have an opportunity to spend a week or two at home on leave. The drafting officer pointed out to the commander that an HSD had already been posted to *Artemis,* but the commander stated that he could seen no reason why a second HSD could not be carried and granted my request. I subsequently joined *Artemis* on September 10, 1946, and five days later we sailed for Halifax, Nova Scotia.

Artemis had been built by Scotts of Greenock and launched in August, 1946. The majority of her compliment of 61 had been with her since her commissioning, and although she had been accepted from the builders by the Admiralty almost twelve months previously, she had not yet completed all her sea trials. The 'A' class submarines were basically an improved 'T' class but of all-welded construction and a displacement of 1,620 tons. With the war in Europe about to end, and the expected shift of operations to the Far East, the

Admiralty had placed orders for 44 of these boats. The 'A' class had a 10,500 mile radius at 11 knots on the surface and carried one 4 inch gun, one 20 mm AA gun, three .303 machine guns, and ten 21 inch torpedo tubes (6 fwd. and 4 aft) with twenty torpedoes. Of great interest at the time was the air warning RDF which could be operated while submerged and habitability was greatly improved by the installation of special air conditioning equipment which re-circulated air in the boat and, if required, adjusted the carbon dioxide and oxygen content.

On joining *Artemis*, I was pleasantly surprised to find that for the first time since becoming a submariner, I not only had my own bunk, but also a foot-locker to stow my gear. Of the forty-four 'A' boats originally ordered, the unexpected end of hostilities with Japan resulted in thirty being cancelled. *Artemis* was commanded by LCdr. J.B. Kershaw DSO, RN, who had served with the famous Fighting 10th Flotilla in 1941. As a young lieutenant in command of the submarine *P31* (later HM S/M *Uproar*), his boat had involuntarily dived off the coast of Tripoli. As the conning tower submerged Lt. Kershaw was thrown off his feet and knocked unconscious. Two other officers on the bridge were washed over the side. One of them, the fourth hand, managed to climb back aboard but the third hand was drowned. Down in the control room, the First Lt., P.J. Oakley, RN, called for the switches to be thrown full astern, grouped up, while the ERA on the blowing panel, Chief Petty Officer Townsend, blew all 'main ballast tanks'. With water cascading down the conning tower hatch, the boat slowly rose to the surface. Lt. Kershaw went on to distinguish himself in *Uproar* by attacking an Italian merchant ship off the island of Lampione on March 5, 1942. The 5,081 ton ship, *Marin Sanudo*, was being escorted by two Italian Destroyers when first sighted, and because of enemy aircraft cover, *Uproar* was forced to carry out the attack with the use of ASDIC at a depth of 40 feet. As one of the enemy destroyers passed directly overhead, Lt. Kershaw fired a salvo of four torpedoes, all of which hit the target. He then took *Uproar* down to lie on the sea bed at 240 feet while the enemy destroyers carried out a counter attack, dropping a total of thirty depth charges on the submerged boat. For this action Lt.

Kershaw was awarded the Distinguished Service Order. All five of the officers in *Artemis* were Regular Navy; "Jimmy-the-One", the third hand and the engineer officer being lieutenants, while the fourth hand, who was also the navigator, was a S/Lt. RN There were a handful of hostility only ratings on the lower deck still awaiting discharge, but the majority of the ship's company, including the chiefs and petty officers, were regulars.

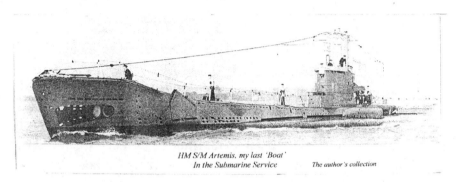

HM S/M Artemis, my last 'Boat'
In the Submarine Service   *The author's collection*

A unique situation also existed in *Artemis* in that <u>every</u> member of the lower deck from the coxswain to the most recently joined AB drew their tot. To the best of my knowledge there was not a teetotaller in the ship's company, including the officers. This somewhat unusual situation produced what I came to think of as being the happiest vessel I ever had the privilege to serve in.   In order to elaborate, I should point out that discipline in *Artemis* was of the highest standard and I do not recall a single incident where any member of the ship's company betrayed the commanding officer's trust or let his shipmates down as a result of overindulging. The fact that we all enjoyed a drink brought us together as a team. We worked together and supported each other in everything we did, whether as individuals or a group. An example of this was a ship's company party that was thrown a day or two after I had joined the boat and to which I was invited. It was explained to me that when accumulated money in the ship's fund had reached a certain level, a committee of two would reconnoitre the surrounding countryside in search of a secluded village pub in which to hold a party. On finding such a place, arrangements would be made with the landlord for our entire ship's company (less those who were on duty or wished to volunteer for duty) to be wined and dined on a particular night. Once a date was set, a coach capable of seating forty or more would be hired to transport us to and from our destination. In most cases the pub selected would be off the beaten path, allowing the submariners to eat, drink, play darts, and sing to their hearts content without outside interference. My first ship's company party was held in a pub near Hook, Hampshire, the village consisting of about two dozen homes, one public house, and a small post office. The main street was illuminated by one gas lamp and the local inhabitants were protected from any form of crime by an elderly policeman who did his rounds on a bicycle. A most enjoyable evening was had by all and at closing time we boarded our bus with varying degrees of difficulty, leaving the village more or less intact, and the publican well-pleased with having made a handsome profit with no damage to his property. The local constable might not have been too pleased, however, when, before departing, one of our stokers latched on to his helmet, climbed a lamp post in the village square and hung it by its chin strap from the top of the lamp, while another member of our crew borrowed his bicycle and tested its road worthiness.

Of all the officers serving in *Artemis,* the one that I liked the most was the third hand, Lt. Bagley, our gunnery officer. The son of a banker, Bagley had entered Dartmouth at about the same time that I had joined the service. He was slightly overweight, of average height, and had a cheerful disposition. Well-liked by all the crew, I never ever saw him loose his temper. In the months that followed he and I had many interesting conversations during the middle or morning watches that we shared on the bridge. We talked about everything except religion and women, and as a member of a staunch Tory family, I soon learned that he had little use for the socialist government of the day. He was intrigued on discovering that my family had lived in the West Indies and questioned me at length on what it was like to have been born and raised in a British colony. The average British matelot was not a political animal and politics were seldom ever discussed on the mess deck. The one exception to this rule was when Clement Attlee had ousted Winston Churchill in

1945, at which time the service vote was considered one of the main factors leading to the upset.

Our captain, LCdr. Kershaw, was an enigma and considered by many of the ship's company to be somewhat eccentric. Many attributed this to his wartime service in the Med. and the stress he must have been under as commanding officer of *Uproar* in those hectic days. He was a big man with a solemn countenance who seldom smiled, and when angry his appearance took on an almost maniacal expression when he stared at one with steel grey eyes. A stern disciplinarian, he did not suffer fools gladly and made it quite clear to everyone that he would not tolerate incompetence on the job. Our first lieutenant, on the other hand, was a nondescript individual, so much so that I do not even recall his name. He carried out his duties in a quiet and efficient manner, apparently to the captain's satisfaction and with the aid of a very astute and likeable coxswain, Chief Petty Officer Rennie, who hailed from Glasgow. I found our fourth hand, the navigator, to be very shy and got the impression that he was terrified of incurring the captain's wrath. He was accepted by the crew as a necessary member of the Wardroom, but to a large extent was ignored by everyone from the commanding officer on down. The fifth member of the Wardroom was our engineer lieutenant who can be best described as a 'dour' Scot. As a seaman I seldom came into contact with him and consequently knew little of his disposition.

Among the chiefs and petty officers, the ones that I got to know very well were the coxswain and the second coxswain, a likeable young petty officer. As already mentioned, an HSD had been posted to the boat prior to my joining, and as a result I found myself carrying out the duties of an SD. Our HSD, Petty Officer Paul, gave no indication that he objected to my being aboard. However, I noticed that he quite often had me carry out routine maintenance on the equipment that he was responsible for. Other members of the mess that became good friends of mine while serving in *Artemis* were, Leading Signalman (Mac) McAllister, Leading Telegraphist (Lofty) Hanson, A.B. Jack Pope, A.B. Doug Little, Seaman

Torpedoman (Rattler) Morgan, Leading Torpedo Operator Victor (Claud) Raines, A.B. Patrick (Paddy) Fegan, A.B. Ken Hallet, A.B. (Buck) Taylor, A.B. Jack Wren, Petty Officer Len Baker, Tel. Ken Creaser, Stoker Bert (Knocker) White, and A.B. Jack (Slasher) Scar, a Canadian from Saint John, New Brunswick.

Sailing from Portsmouth on September 15, 1947, we arrived in Halifax eight days later after an uneventful voyage. The weather was near perfect for the North Atlantic at that time of the year and we were on the surface for the entire trip across. The only event worth recording was a chance encounter with a merchant ship two or three days out of Halifax. I was on the bridge with Lt. Bagley during the forenoon watch on a bright sunny day when I sighted the masts of a ship, hull down on our starboard quarter. The sea scale was about 4 (moderate) but there was a long Atlantic swell running which caused us to loose sight of the distant horizon whenever we were carried into its trough. While riding on the crest of one of these rollers I noticed that the vessel was trying to raise us by lamp and reported the fact to the OOW. Lt. Bagley called down to the control room for McAllister to report to the bridge and we then learned that the message being sent was: "Are you a submarine?" The following exchange of signals then took place:

> Artemis: "We are indeed, and who are you?"
> Stranger: "I'm an American ship. I go to New York. I belong to Panama. Who do you belong to?"
> Artemis: "Congratulations, I go to Halifax, I belong to the British Navy."

A short while later we crossed her course far to the south west and she had dropped out of sight, this being the only ship sighted on our way across.

CHAPTER XIV
Final Year in the Navy

On entering Halifax Harbour we secured alongside jetty 5 and before the day was out had transferred our gear from the boat to the large brick building at the north end of the dockyard which was HMCS _Scotian_, home of the Halifax Naval Reserve Division. During the next forty-eight hours we refuelled, took on water, a limited quantity of provisions, and were ready for ASW exercises with the RCN. For the next six days we went to sea each day at dawn, returning to harbour at around 16:00. Once clear of the harbour entrance we dived and the accompanying Frigate or Destroyer attempted to locate us with the intention of carrying out a mock attack.

Nine days after our arrival, having placed a call to my brother in Toronto to advise him that I was in Canada, I applied to see the skipper for seven days leave. To my surprise he gave me ten days in order that my return to Halifax would coincide with the return of the boat from Saint John, New Brunswick, where it was expected that she would be while I was away. Armed with a leave pass and having obtained the huge sum of twenty-five dollars advance in pay, Lt Bagley arranged for Stadacona Barracks to provide me with transport to the Canadian Naval Air Station in Dartmouth, HMCS _Shearwater_. On making enquiries of the Regulating Transport Officer, I was informed that Transport Command had no flights to Toronto scheduled for that day but that I could go as far as Montreal in a _Dakota_ that was due to leave within the hour. Early that afternoon we landed at Dorval Airport in Montreal, and on finding that I could not get a flight to Toronto, decided to hitchhike. It took me almost an hour to get from the airport to the main highway between Montreal and Toronto, but within minutes I was able to flag down a large transport truck whose driver informed me that he was on a direct non-stop run to Toronto. Much relieved at the prospect of covering the more than 300 mile trip in one vehicle, I sat enjoying the scenery while engaging my trucker friend in conversation. He informed me that he had served in the army during the war but had not gone overseas. On his discharge from the military he had become a long distance trucker, thanks to having served in the Royal Canadian Army Service Corps. He went on to tell me that he made it a habit to pick up any serviceman that he came across hitchhiking. When I mentioned that I would probably be returning eight days later, travelling in the opposite direction, he assured me that I would not have any trouble getting a ride. As the miles slipped by we passed through Cornwall, Brockville, Kingston, Napanee, Port Hope, and Oshawa.

Having covered the trip in a little over three hours I was dropped off almost in front of Union Station where I was able to board a Yonge Street streetcar. Leaving the streetcar at St. Clair Avenue, I had about a block to walk to the corner of Heath Street and within half an hour of my arrival in the city found the home of Aunt Betty. My cousin Penny, who was home from school, answered the door bell and told me that my aunt was working but expected home shortly. The only other member of the family at home at the time was my grandfather, my cousin Don, Penny's brother, still being at work. As my brother had informed the family that I might be showing up in Toronto, they were expecting me. My otherwise un-announced arrival, however, created something of a flap as Penny immediately began phoning anyone and everyone informing them that her cousin had just arrived home from the war. Most of those she spoke with must have thought it was about time, as the war has been over for two years. On being told by Penny that I had arrived, my grandfather lost no time coming out to greet me, and before long Aunt Betty and cousin Don had shown up. My brother phoned to say that he and his fiancée, Jean, would be over after dinner and plans were being made to have Aunt Betty's sister, Aunt Molly, and her husband, Cole, drop by for a drink. At dinner that night five of us sat down to eat but before the table was cleared the house started to fill up with relatives and friends of the family who wished to meet me. By midnight there was a party in full swing at 17 Heath Street which did not break up until three in the morning; two and-a-half hours after grand-dad, who was in his eighties, had gone to bed.

My grandfather had retired from his job as Public Trustee for the Province of Ontario and recently come to live with his daughter, Betty, having given up his bachelor flat on Walmer Road. He informed me that he had found a way to keep busy by serving as a bailiff for the Court of Queen's Bench three or four times a week. For many years he had been involved with the Ontario branch of the Navy League of Canada and was about to retire from that organization in which he had served as their Provincial Treasurer. During my visit to Toronto, he persuaded me to accompany him one evening to HMCS *York*, where I was introduced to the commanding officer of the local sea cadet corps. and asked to speak to the cadets on the subject of what it was like to serve in submarines. During the rest of the week I was entertained by almost everyone who had come over to the house starting with Dennis and Jean, who invited me to have dinner with them on the second night of my arrival. The three of us spent an enjoyable evening dining in Toronto's Chinatown. The following night I was the guest of Aunt Molly and her husband, Cole Peterson, who took me to dinner at the Toronto Tennis Club.

My aunt's house had four bedrooms, and I refused to let anyone give up their room for me while I was on leave. Rather, I insisted on being allowed to sleep on the couch in the living room which meant that I was unable to turn in before all visitors had left the house and the occupants had retired. Each morning I arose as early as possible in order to fold my bedclothes and use the bathroom before any of the others began to stir. I generally had the coffee on and toast made by the time the rest of the family came to breakfast. My grandfather did not stir until the others had left the house, which allowed us to talk at length in the forenoon before going into town for lunch. Each day we ate lunch in one of the many clubs he belonged to in the city and he made a point of introducing me to individuals whom he thought might be able to help me get a job when I finally came out of the service. At the Albany Club I was introduced to Mr. John C. Hall, a senior executive of George Weston Ltd., the biscuit manufacturer, and Mr. Ernest Milling of Saturday Night magazine. At the Toronto Press Club I had the pleasure of meeting the night editor of the Evening Telegram, Lieutenant Commander RCNVR (R'td) Ernest Bartlett who had been made a prisoner of war by the Germans and only recently returned to Canada to take up his former position with the paper. He had many interesting stories to tell and suggested that he might be instrumental in helping me obtain employment with the Toronto Harbour Commission. At the luncheon room at Osgoode Hall I met Mr. Kenneth Stratton KC, and Chief Accountant of the Office of the Public Trustee, Mr. R.G. Marner, both of whom told me to contact them should I leave the navy the following year and decide to settle in Toronto.

Before my leave expired, Dennis and I visited our mother's grave in Mount Pleasant Cemetery. Four years had passed since I learned of her death while stationed in Scotland. Standing in front of her grave that day, I realized that I never really accepted the fact that she would not be there to greet me when I eventually came home. Quite clearly, I recalled the last time I had seen her as she waved to me while I stood on the deck of the *Lady Rodney*. Now, suddenly I was overcome with guilt at the thought of how much pain I must have caused her. Only now did I fully understand what she must have given up to have allowed me to follow my dream. Even then, in 1941, she must have known that in letting me go she would probably never see me again. My eight days leave ended all too quickly and my last night at home was reminiscent of my first night in town.

Everyone had too much to drink and it was about two in the morning before I was able to turn in. On leaving the house after breakfast the following morning, I made my way to the lakeshore then to the main Toronto to Montreal highway. It was almost 11:00 before I arrived in Oshawa after a series of short rides offered by motorists going to work. On the outskirts of Oshawa a small truck picked me up and took me as far as Kingston where I dropped into a roadside diner for a bite to eat and encountered a number of RCAF personnel. When I told them that I was hitch-hiking to Montreal, one of the airmen informed me that there was an RCAF *Dakota* at the airport scheduled to leave for Dorval that afternoon. The aircraft had been employed towing a drogue for a local anti-aircraft army unit and was about to return to its squadron. Accepting their offer of a ride to the local airport, we arrived on the tarmac just in time to see the old *Dakota* getting ready to depart. A few words exchanged with the pilot and I was allowed to climb aboard. Within a matter of minutes we were given clearance to take off and I found myself sitting on the metal deck of the DC-3 bound for Montreal. There were no seats in the fuselage of the aircraft but two airmen sat on what I presumed to be their parachutes which lay on the deck. Following their example, I stretched out on the aluminium floor of the cabin using my steaming bag as a pillow. Shortly after we were airborne, I was startled to hear a loud noise coming from outside the plane at a point near the tail. This frightening noise sounded as though someone was on the outside using a jackhammer to open the cabin door. Doing my best to appear cool, calm, and collected, I inquired of the two airmen as to what was causing the noise, only to be given a long-winded, and most improbable story about loose rivets in the fuselage, which were probably as a result of metal fatigue in the frame, creating a situation whereby the rudder and the elevators might even drop off while in flight. Presuming that my leg was being pulled, I went along with their little joke while doing my best to appear outwardly calm. After a while I noticed that the noise only occurred intermittently after running into a pocket of air turbulence which caused the aircraft to veer slightly off course. On landing in Montreal my two 'light blue' comedians explained that there was a length of weather-stripping at the top of the cabin door which had worked its way loose and now hung outside. Whenever the aircraft altered course, the slipstream would cause this to flap against he body of the plane, which sounded like a drummer beating on a bass drum.

As my return flight was now running behind schedule, I learned that I might not be allowed to continue on to Halifax. A harassed air transport officer explained that he had been ordered to load a large number of wooden crates containing aircraft parts destined for Greenwood which had created an overweight problem. Unless one of his high priority passengers failed to show, I would not be allowed to fly that day. This sort of thing often happened on service flights where hitchhikers had no priority and could be bumped at a moment's notice by anyone who out- ranked them. Of little concern at the start of the leave period, the implications of being bumped off a return flight were far more serious if it resulted in the hitchhiker being unable to return to his or her unit on time. Fortunately I was paged at the last minute and told I could board as one of the priority passengers had failed to show up. Later that afternoon, when about to land at *Shearwater,* we were over-flying George's Island when I spotted *Artemis* on her way in from sea. Thinking that it would be a lot of fun to make a low-level pass over her bridge as she was entering harbour, I asked our pilot if he would do so. Unfortunately, we were already cleared to land, and having entered the flight path on our approach to the field, he was unable to grant my request. An hour or two later an Air Force utility van dropped me off outside *Scotian* where I reported to the regulating office and was welcomed back by the coxswain and the officer of the watch.

While I had been away, *Artemis* had visited Saint John, New Brunswick where she carried out ASW exercises with a number of RCN ships in the Bay of Fundy. Everyone was singing the praises of Saint John where I was told the ship's company had been royally treated. The other event that occurred during my absence was the dramatic disappearance of Able Seaman 'Paddy' Fagan, followed by his subsequent apprehension by the RCMP and his eventual return to the Royal Navy. However, before relating in detail the events leading to 'Paddy' going AWOL, I should set the stage with a brief account of an earlier adventure of his during the war. Born in Dublin, Ireland, 'Paddy' was the youngest in a family of five boys and three girls. At the age of fifteen Patrick Fagan left home to seek fame and fortune in a foreign land. Unlike so many of his fellow countrymen the foreign land he chose was not America, but England, and it was there that he joined the Royal Navy as a boy seaman in 1938. At the time of the attack on Pearl Harbour in December, 1941, 'Paddy', who was then an able seaman and qualified anti-aircraft gunner third class, was serving in a minesweeper based in Singapore. On

February 14, 1942, the day before Singapore fell to the Japanese, the commanding officer of 'Paddy's' vessel cleared lower deck and announced to the assembled ship's company his intention to scuttle the vessel in order to prevent it from falling into enemy hands; there was no way that the ship could escape. Her bunkers were empty and with the enemy at the gates of the city fuel supplies were being put to the torch.   The little sweeper was sailed into the stream where scuttling charges were placed in her engine room and set to explode after the crew had been landed. It was a case of every man for himself and many of the sailors decided to arm themselves and join up with the army who were gradually being pushed into the sea by the sons of Nippon. Left on his own with no one to answer to, 'Paddy' armed himself with a service revolver, a hundred rounds of ammunition, and six hand grenades. Setting off in the direction of the city he found the streets almost deserted and most of the shop windows boarded up. Eventually he came to a watering hole that he had frequented in happier days and on finding the door locked, used his service revolver to unlock it. Inside, the refrigerator was still running and stocked with food and beer. Behind the bar the shelves were filled with alcohol of every description, including a variety of wines and liquors. What more could a thirsty sailor ask for?   Making himself comfortable, 'Paddy' opened a bottle of beer, made a sandwich, and set about re-arranging the furniture in the lounge to serve as a bed. Fully intending to keep track of all food and drink consumed, he started recording each item taken from stock in a meticulous manner. Unfortunately, as the hours slipped by and the empty bottles started to pile up, he stopped writing chits and concluded that when the owner showed up he could estimate the bill by counting the empty bottles. Throughout the night heavy fighting in the city continued and the following day Singapore surrendered. Unaware of what was happening in the city, 'Paddy' sobered up long enough to make breakfast on February 15, resuming his binge after preparing and consuming a hearty meal of steak and eggs in the restaurant kitchen. Later that day he was drawn to a window overlooking the street below by the sound of loud voices. In an alcoholic haze he surveyed the scene below and, coming to the conclusion that he was looking at enemy troops, foolishly drew his revolver and fired into the street.

In a matter of seconds the Japanese returned the fire, but 'Paddy' had moved away from the window and was not hit. Minutes later the troops stormed the building and on breaking down the door leading to the lounge, found our hero, flat on his back, out like a light and stinking of gin. Had he not been blind drunk it is almost certain he would have been shot. It is hard to understand even now, why they spared his life. Twenty-four hours later, Able Seaman Fagan, RN, regained consciousness in a filthy pool of his own making, lying on the floor of a Singapore police station. To all intents and purposes one would have to presume that 'Paddy' Fagan's war was over. As a prisoner of war, 'Paddy' was held in Singapore for over a month during which time he was severely beaten and almost starved to death. In telling me his story he claimed that he and other prisoners were so hungry that they actually ate rats while in captivity. After the fall of Singapore there were more than 50,000 British POWs held by the Japanese on the island, including 14,000 Australians. The main POW camp was located at Changi, the former home of the British peacetime garrison and it was to Changi that 'Paddy' was transferred from his cell in the city police station.

Early in April, 1942, the Japanese began to use this very valuable source of cheap labour to clean up and restore the damaged naval dockyard. Work parties were formed and transported to the city and it was while employed in one of these work parties that 'Paddy' was able to elude his guards and make good his escape. At the end of the day, while waiting with about five hundred fellow prisoners for transportation back to Changi, 'Paddy' and two of his mates were able to give their guards the slip and submerge themselves in Singapore Harbour. Taking refuge under one of the wharves with only their heads above water they waited until dark before swimming out to where a number of coastal sampans were moored. Later that night, they slipped their moorings and, along with other local craft, managed to clear the harbour entrance under the nose of the Japanese guard ship. A survey of provisions in the sampan disclosed a bag of rice, a cask of rather foul smelling water, and a basket of fruit that had seen better days. It became evident that a lengthy sea voyage was out of the question. All three men agreed that their only chance of evading the enemy would be to sail south-east along the coast of Sumatra and Java during the hours of darkness and keep out of sight during daylight hours by running into shore and hiding in the jungle.

Surabaya, having fallen on March 7, 1942, and Dutch Forces in Sumatra having surrendered on March 17, all of Indonesia was virtually in enemy hands by April and the chances of reaching New Guinea safely were quite remote. All went well during the first week although progress was slow, and after five nights they had managed to cover a distance of only 250 nautical miles. On the sixth night an off shore wind carried them fifty or more miles to the north-east, and a day later they were fighting to stay afloat in heavy seas off the coast of Borneo. Unable to find adequate shelter from the sun during the day, and slowly dying from hunger and thirst, they drifted aimlessly for three days before being rescued. On the morning of the fourth day, a Dutch submarine heading for the Lombok Straits on passage to Western Australia spotted them and drew alongside the Sampan. Mistaken for Japanese seamen by the Dutch, they were on the verge of being abandoned to their fate when 'Paddy' was able to convince the submariners that they were British sailors and were eventually taken inboard. The Dutch Submarine was either the K12 or the K11, both of which survived the war and were paid off in Australia in 1944 or 1945.

The ongoing saga of 'Paddy' Fagan does not end here, however. Shortly after the fall of Singapore, Mr. and Mrs. Fagan in Dublin received word that their son was missing and presumed dead. After his arrival in Australia the authorities should have informed the grieving parents that 'Paddy' was still alive and well, but for some unexplainable reason, this information never reached them. The fact that the Republic of Ireland was a neutral country may have been one reason, but it was more likely due to the fact that 'Paddy's' parents had moved to a different address during the year and the Admiralty was unable to locate them. In any event, young Fagan was not the world's greatest correspondent and it was some time in December before the doctors declared him well enough to return home. The trip back to the UK via the Cape of Good Hope took another six or eight weeks which meant that it had been almost a full year since the family had received word that he was missing. Once back in England, 'Paddy' was granted a total of eight weeks leave; two weeks sick leave, two weeks survivors leave, and four weeks foreign- service leave. Obliged to wear civilian clothing before crossing the border into Erie, he purchased a suite in Belfast and, learning of his parents' new address from an old neighbour, arrived home to find a house-full of relatives and friends gathered to celebrate his demise. His arrival in England had coincided with the statute of limitations running out on the life insurance claim. Only a few days had elapsed since he had been declared legally dead and a cheque had been received by his mother and father. That evening, 'Paddy' was able to take part in his own wake which then became a welcome home party before the night was out. Unfortunately the insurance money had to be paid back when the party was over.

'Paddy's' earlier adventures, described above, might explain his weird conduct while serving in *Artemis*. There were those who claimed that his treatment by the Japanese and his subsequent escape, combined with his near- death experience, had left him a bit unbalanced. My personal belief was that 'Paddy' was trying to 'work his ticket' and that his unorthodox behaviour was designed to make everyone think that he was insane. Close to twenty-five years of age, he was a gangling individual with a chalky complexion and freckled face. His rusty-coloured hair was close cropped and his pale green eyes were set wide apart. Overall, his countenance was that of an Irish leprechaun wearing a perpetual grin. The incident in Saint John which led to him being apprehended by the RCMP while I was on leave in Toronto came about as a result of his exposure to an American radio show. At that time there were hundreds of radio quiz shows being broadcast in the states, and one of the more successful ones was Doctor IQ. Contestants were paid large sums of money in US silver dollars to correctly answer general knowledge questions. In Britain the BBC had nothing to compare with these shows and 'Paddy' was fascinated by the thought that someone could actually earn large sums of money merely by correctly answering questions that he considered simple. The more he thought of it, the more determined he became to go to New York and earn himself some of those silver dollars the Americans were giving away each night. Ashore in Saint John one evening after consuming a skin-full of beer, 'Paddy' enquired of a fellow drinker the best way to get to New York. On being informed that one option was a Greyhound bus, he went looking for the bus depot and with no conception of the distance involved purchased a one way ticket to New York. On crossing the border at Eastport in the State of Maine, the bus was boarded by US immigration officers who, on taking him into custody, turned him over to the RCMP. Within twenty-four hours of leaving Saint John, 'Paddy' had been returned to his rightful owners, the Royal Navy. LCdr. Kershaw, needless to say, was not amused.

Between October 13 and November 7, 1947, *Artemis* spent practically every day at sea on ASW exercises with the RCN. During this period we normally operated from Saint John, but occasionally would spend the night at anchor in Seal Cove on the southern tip of Grand Manan Island in the Bay of Fundy. On November 7, 1947, while on exercise with HMCS *Haida,* a mechanical defect in our engine room forced us to cancel the exercise. Taken in tow by *Haida,* we returned to Halifax where the dockyard was able to carry out the necessary repairs in time for us to take part in the Remembrance Day parade in Saint John on November 11, 1947. At the conclusion of the parade, in which a large number of the ship's company participated, the public were invited to visit the boat and that afternoon over a thousand citizens of Saint John took advantage of the invitation to tour *Artemis.* The following Sunday, while alongside in Halifax, the boat was again open for visitors and once more invaded, this time, by hundreds of 'Haligonians'. During the afternoon of this open house, an incident ocurred which, while regarded as humorous at the time, could easily have been otherwise and might have had a tragic outcome.

It all began during the forenoon watch on the Sunday that we were open to the public. Those of us who were duty watch that day were expected to be in our #1 uniforms and in the boat by noon to greet the many visitors who were expected to come aboard. Earlier that day a work party had scrubbed out the boat, washed down the mess tables, squared away the bunks, and cleaned the decks using a cleaning solution obtained from the second coxswain's stores and commonly referred to by matelots as 'spirit of wine', which was in fact methyl alcohol, otherwise known as methanol. Despite the known danger of consuming this product, there were those in the mess that maintained that it was relatively harmless if diluted with large quantities of fruit juice. Unable to go ashore that day, and compelled to act as hosts to a hoard of civilians, the boys on the mess-deck decided to make a punch using the coxswains 'spirit of wine' as the main ingredient. Drawing off a pint of this potent liquid, they diluted it with four large cans of grapefruit juice, four large cans of pineapple juice, and topped it off with a sprinkling of maraschino cherries and slices of lemon. The 'brew master' of this concoction was a young telegraphist by the name of Ken Creaser who happened to sport a truly magnificent naval beard, similar to that worn by the sailor pictured on a package of Players cigarettes. During the course of the afternoon, having consumed three or four cups of punch, Ken produced a package of cigarettes, and placing one of them between his lips, turned to one of his mess mates requesting a light. His mate obliged by striking a match and holding it out at arm's length. Ken, whose beard was saturated in punch that had spilled from his glass, lurched forward to accept the proffered light and a moment later his dripping beard ignited. A quick-thinking bystander threw a towel over Ken's head, smothering the flames, but not before the seamen's mess was permeated with the odour of singed hair. Shortly after mid-day our visitors started to arrive on the jetty. At that time the tide was high and the angle of the brow was a mere five degrees or less. The brow was a twenty-four inch wide wooden plank with cleats fastened at twelve-inch intervals across it. On one side of the plank were stanchions supporting a handrail made from rope. As visitors came down the brow from the jetty to the casing they were met by one of the members of the duty watch and escorted below to the fore-end by way of the forward torpedo hatch. After touring the boat they returned to the casing through the engine room hatch and then crossed the brow to return to the jetty. One of our visitors that afternoon was a young constable from the RCMP who arrived on board dressed in full ceremonial uniform of scarlet tunic, blue breeches, leather jack-boots, and Stetson hat.

As a member of a quasi-military organization representing the crown, he was given VIP treatment and on his way through the boat was invited to take a seat in the mess, meet the boys, and to try our home made punch. Somewhat sceptical at first he eventually agreed to accept a small glass of our brew and on drinking it, held out the glass for a refill. Three hours and five glasses later our young 'mountie' was experiencing trouble walking and would certainly have been incapable of mounting a horse had he had one. With great difficulty he climbed the ladder leading to the casing and having thanked us for our hospitality, attempted to cross the brow leading to the jetty. Unfortunately the tide had ebbed and the brow, which had been at a five degree angle when he arrived, was now at about forty-five degrees. Furthermore, the outgoing tide had caused *Artemis* to pull away from the jetty, leaving a wide gap of water between the saddle tanks and the dock. To make matters worse, a light shower had left the brow both wet and slippery and as our guest made his way up the steep incline his large, highly polished cavalry boots caused him to slip and over the side he went. Falling into the harbour feet first, he went completely under while his Stetson came off and floated on the surface, marking the spot where he had submerged. Had the boat not been straining at her moorings due to the ebbing tide, he would have hit the saddle tanks and probably been badly hurt. As it turned out he rose to the surface like a wounded whale and was helped up on to the saddle tanks by members of the ship's company. It was a very sad looking 'mountie' that eventually made it ashore. A thin film of bunker oil on the surface of the water had left his once immaculate scarlet tunic black and when last seen, his wide-brimmed Stetson was floating out to sea with the tide. Silently he turned and walked toward the dockyard gate where it was presumed he had left his car. The week following our open house, we prepared to leave for home having spent two months on loan to the RCN. During our two months in Canada we had been treated very well by the RCN with the result that many of our ratings acquired a new sense of respect for the Canadian Navy and a number of them were seriously considering the possibility of transferring from the RN. I suggested to those considering such a move that they had better get used to eating Canadian food.

On our arrival in Halifax we had been billeted in HMCS *Scotian*, and except for short periods of time during our stay, had been fed Canadian rations cooked by Canadians. The average British seaman, accustomed to eating roast beef, potatoes, and peas, followed by a heavy dessert such as 'figgy duff', was not impressed by Canadian meals of which green salads, light luncheon meats, fruit, and copious quantities of fresh milk were the norm. It was impossible to convince a British matelot that corn was a consumable vegetable. As far as he was concerned it was food fed to chickens in England and rice was a food Asians ate except when the Royal Navy put raisins in it and produced a dish known on the lower deck as Chinese wedding cake. Apart from myself, there were three others of our ship's company with ties in Canada. Our Ldg. Tel., 'Lofty' Hanson, had married a Nova Scotia girl while in Halifax on a previous visit. His wife hailed from Sydney and after our arrival they were able to get together in Halifax when Mrs. Hanson arrived to stay with relatives in town. 'Lofty' also spent a week in Sydney on leave from which he returned to the boat with a shoulder roast of moose meat as a present for his mess-mates, the moose having been shot by his brother-in law while he was in Sydney.

Another rating who managed to go home on leave was Able Seaman Jack Scar who hailed from Saint John, New Brunswick. Jack had joined the navy in the UK and had not been home since 1939. Finally there was Ken Creaser who met and married a young lady by the name of Mary while we were in Halifax. Ken's wedding was a momentous event and an occasion that called for a wild party, attended by most of his mess mates. The wedding reception was marred slightly when a vicious fight broke out between 'Paddy' Fagan and a leading stoker, who could not hold his liquor. Order was soon restored, however, and the offending Stoker removed from the grounds. Mary Creaser was a wonderful girl. After her marriage to Ken, those of us who were friends were frequently invited to visit them at their apartment in town where some memorable parties were held. With Christmas just a few weeks away, all members of the ship's company went shopping to purchase gifts for wives and sweethearts back home. The coxswain made sure that the boat's stores were fully stocked. We filled our freezer with sides of beef, hams, and turkeys. The fore-end and our food lockers contained Christmas puddings, canned fruit, and the myriad food items that were still in short supply in war-weary Britain.

Before leaving Canada, a Halifax group known as 'Boxes for Britain' entrusted us with 150 food parcels containing 1,000 pounds of Christmas cheer for distribution by WVS Headquarters in the UK to needy families of London. Our CO, LCdr. Kershaw, having been told that the cost of mailing a five dollar parcel to the UK was one dollar, approached the secretary of the group and volunteered our help in order to save them postage. On our arrival in Portsmouth we received word that a further 155 parcels had been dispatched by freighter after our departure. A letter of thanks received from Mrs. Beata Fortune, Secretary of the Halifax Group, expressed the hope that these parcels would do a little to brighten the Christmas of a few people in Britain. While in Canada, members of our ship's company, including the members of the Wardroom, had enjoyed the hospitality of the Canadian Navy. On the eve of our departure, the officers of *Scotian* made a somewhat unusual gift to the captain and officers of *Artemis* in the form of a five gallon keg of Newfoundland 'screech'. This gift came with the provision that it was only to be breached on an auspicious occasion, and as a result, Lt. Bagley gave instructions that it was to be stored with loving care in the magazine pending such an event taking place. Having bid a final farewell to our Canadian hosts in *Scotian*, we stored our personal gear aboard the boat and sailed the following morning at 06:00, clearing the harbour and setting a course for the UK.

Twenty-four hours after departing, a radio signal was received from *Scotian* to the effect that an 8 mm movie projector was missing from that establishment. While this message did not suggest that anyone in *Artemis* had stolen this item, it was implied that it might have been <u>borrowed</u>, or to use a true naval term, <u>liberated</u>. On receipt of this signal the captain called the coxswain to his cabin and a short while later addressed the ship's company over the PA system. In all fairness to the skipper, he could not bring himself to believe that anyone in *Artemis* would have deliberately taken the missing projector. On the other hand, having spent most of his life in the navy, he was fully aware of what sailors were capable of doing. In addressing the members of his ship's company he suggested that someone might have taken the missing item as a joke. If that were the case he would be willing to overlook the matter if the guilty party were to own up to having done so. As no one came forward in response to his appeal, he must have felt reasonably sure that the missing projector was not in his boat, but before sending a reply to Halifax he had to make sure. Addressing the ship's company for the second time, he assured his listeners that he would not take disciplinary action against anyone who admitted to having taken the projector, providing that it was returned immediately. In order to convince us that he meant what he said he intended to turn off the lights for five minutes in all compartments of the boat except the engine room, control room, and motor room. The guilty party would then have ample time to produce the missing item and place it in the passageway. When the lights were turned on and the projector had not materialised he seemed somewhat relieved. At this point he had almost convinced himself that it had not been brought aboard *Artemis* and that no one in his ship's company was guilty of theft. Nevertheless, before sending a reply to *Scotian* he had to make quite certain that this was the case. For the third time that afternoon he addressed the ship's company over the PA system announcing that he and the coxswain would conduct a thorough search of the boat. Armed with a torch, the captain and the coxswain then started their search in the forward torpedo tube space. Having searched every nook and cranny in that compartment, including the empty torpedo tubes, they then moved on to the fore-ends. On moving aft through the next compartment, they carried out a thorough search of the seamen's mess, stokers' mess, petty officers' mess, ERA's mess, and even the wardroom. In the control room they searched the

ASDIC cabinet, looked down the periscope well, and the chart table stowage.

Next came the radio room and galley. They checked the heads, magazine, auxiliary machinery compartment, engine room, motor room, and after tube space, even lifting the floor plates in the engine room. Finding nothing, the 'old man' was finally convinced that the missing projector was <u>not</u> in *Artemis* and that no member of his band of pirates was guilty. Calling the PO Tel. to the control room, he dictated a signal to be sent to *Scotian* which stated in unequivocal terms; firstly, that he resented the implication that anyone in his ship's company would have unlawfully removed such an item from the barracks and, secondly, that he had conducted a thorough search of his boat and the missing item was definitely not aboard. As I had the first watch that night I was on the bridge with Lieutenant Bagley when a voice from the control room called up the voice pipe requesting: "Permission to ditch gash." This was a nightly routine that the duty watch performed at 19:00 prior to the first lieutenant doing his rounds.

In each of the messes there was a five-gallon pail which served as a 'gash' bucket. In the course of the day these buckets were used to dispose of all forms of garbage including tea leaves, coffee grounds, cold tea, cigarette buts, empty food cans, etc. Each bucket was constructed with a handle to which a slip hook could be attached. When permission to 'ditch gash' was given by the officer of the watch, the duty hands brought the 'gash' buckets into the control room and positioned them under the conning tower hatch. Two or three seamen would then climb the conning tower to the bridge then, lowering a rope to which was spliced a slip-hook, one-by-one the cans would be hauled up to the bridge and emptied over the side. That evening, as Lt. Bagley and I stood watch, each of us deep in our own thoughts while the duty watch ratings 'nattered' in the background, we were both startled by the sound of a loud clang which came from the vicinity of the saddle tank on the port side. Thinking that perhaps we had hit an object in the water, Lt Bagley called out to me: "Jones, what the hell was that noise?" Before I could reply one of the ratings on the bridge spoke up saying: "I'm not sure sir, but I think it was a movie projector hitting the tank as it went into the drink." For a moment there was silence on the bridge; all that could be heard was the wind whistling through the periscope standards. Finally Lt. Bagley said: "Very well, carry on." I am not sure if anyone ever told the captain what happened on the bridge that night, but it seems highly likely that he found out. Within minutes word spread throughout the boat and all hands were aware that the projector had been concealed in one of the gash buckets and tossed over the side. In any event the subject was not brought up again and if the RCN is still looking for their lost 8 mm projector, I would suggest a search of the Grand Banks.

Our passage home was one of the roughest trips I ever experienced. On leaving Halifax we ran before a tropical hurricane that had formed in the Caribbean and after lashing the New England coast, had turned east into the Atlantic. It was moving to the east faster than we were and we were gradually being punished with a following sea which eventually built up to gigantic proportions. On the Beaufort Scale the strength of the wind went from a strong gale force 9 to force 11 with a velocity of between 56 and 65 knots. The sea state increased in ferocity from 6 to 8 which produced waves of from 20 to 40 feet in height from crest to trough. Looking astern as these monstrous waves threatened to overwhelm us was quite frightening. Bearing in mind that those of us who were on the bridge were only fourteen feet above the waterline, the crest of one of these monsters might be as much as twenty- six feet above our heads. One moment we were riding high on the crest and seconds later the horizon disappeared as we dropped into the trough. It became necessary for the officer of the watch and all others on the bridge to secure themselves by means of a safety clip to the eye bolts welded to the inside of the tower. As each wave came crashing down it would inundate the entire boat and those of us on the bridge would find ourselves completely submerged and holding our breath. As the boat rose from the trough of the wave and the water drained from the bridge and casing, one of us would have to very quickly release his safety belt and re-open the conning tower hatch which had been slammed shut by the force of the water. With both of our diesels running it was important that the conning tower hatch remained open as an air intake for the engines. Each time that the hatch cover closed a vacuum was created in the boat as the engines consumed the air inside the pressure hull. This constant fluctuation in pressure resulted in a painful condition in the middle ear leading to severe headaches over a period of time. Down below in the control room, gallons of water came cascading down the hatch and a 'bird bath' had to be erected at the base of the conning tower hatch to prevent it from sloshing around on the deck. A bird bath was nothing more than a tub made of canvas roughly sixteen inches high with a fire hose attachment in its base allowing the collected water to be drained into the bilges. The motion of the boat in this type of sea was something akin to a roller coaster. Everything that was not tied down, screwed down, or nailed down, was liable to break loose. When turned in, it was necessary to rely on straps across the bunk to avoid being thrown out of bed and our cook was unable to prepare any kind of a hot meal in the galley. As a result, for days on end, all we had to eat was sandwiches and tea. Old hands in the boat claimed that it was one of the roughest passages that they had ever undertaken. When we eventually arrived in the Solent and were about to enter Portsmouth harbour, the 'old man' instructed the signalman <u>not</u> to bend on a new ensign. He wanted all hands in Blockhouse to be aware of the weather we had encountered on our way across. The ensign that had been new on leaving Halifax had been reduced to half its size on our arrival, due to the hurricane winds we had experienced. We arrived in Portsmouth on December 5, 1946, and on the week-end following I was able to go home for thirty-six hours.

Since joining *Artemis* in September, 1946, I had not received a letter from Alice despite my having written her on at least four occasions while in Canada. I have to admit that on arriving home I was not entirely surprised by the welcome I received. Ever since *Sportsman's* refit in Chatham, during which I had been at home almost every day, I had suspected that there was something bothering Alice. I was now to learn that during my absence she had met someone with whom she claimed to have fallen in love with, and intended to ask me for a divorce. It is not necessary to relate in detail the circumstances leading to the failure of our marriage other than to state that it had been a mistake from the beginning. I should relate, however, that prior to my joining *Artemis* we had discussed our plans for the future and it was with the intention of testing the water that I had wanted to go to Canada. As I saw it there were three options open to us; (1) I could continue to serve in the RN and make our home in England; (2) I could request a transfer to the RCN and make our home in Canada; or, (3) I could request a transfer to the RAN and make our home in Australia. Having discussed all three of these options with her, I had been under the impression that she intended to leave the final decision entirely up to me, and that she had no objection to moving to either Canada or Australia. I could of course have taken my discharge in England and found employment there, but we never considered this as a fourth option.

It was now obvious that our marriage was on the rocks and continuing to remain in Mottingham would serve no purpose. I therefore returned to Portsmouth before the weekend was over. On the following Monday I met with my Divisional Officer, Lt. Bagley, in order to seek his advice as to what my next course of action should be. It was arranged that I should meet with the Legal Aid Officer in the barracks and on doing so a day or two later, I was advised that the Navy would assist me in obtaining a divorce. In due course the Admiralty would appoint a lawyer in London and I was told that it would probably take about seven to eight months for my case to be processed. *Artemis* was required to enter Portsmouth dockyard the following week for minor repairs and while in dockyard hands, half of the ship's company were to be sent on leave. For those of us who were still on board on Christmas day we enjoyed the usual turkey dinner and Christmas pudding. On Boxing Day, 1947, I went ashore with my friend 'Lofty' Hanson, took in an early movie, and spent the remainder of the night in a tavern on Queen Street. The first leave party returned on December 30. Those of us going on leave over the New Year were on our way the following day. With no desire to stay in England for the holidays, and having heard of how the Scots celebrated Hogmanay, I elected to visit Edinburgh in order to find out if everything I had heard was true.

Leading Seaman Raines, our LTO, was married to a Scot and lived in Glasgow. Earlier he had invited me to spend my leave with him and his wife but, while I was grateful for his kind offer, I explained to him that I had never been to Edinburgh before and my reasons for wanting to do so now. He made me promise that before our leave expired I would travel to Glasgow in order to spend a few days at his place prior to our having to return to Portsmouth. Promising to do so, I set off for the capital of Scotland in high spirits and arrived in Waverley station early on the morning of New Years Eve, 1947. On leaving the station, I questioned a policeman on Princess Street as to where I might find the nearest serviceman's hostel and, having been directed to the Salvation Army located only a few blocks away, I booked a bed and then went in search of a restaurant to have breakfast. After a meal of fried eggs, sausages, and toast, I set out to explore the city and to discover for myself what went on in the land of the heather at the start of each New Year.

I have since found Edinburgh to be a windy city, and the morning of December 31, 1947, was no exception. The temperature, however, was quite mild for December and I really did not need the greatcoat I was wearing. Starting on Princess Street in the vicinity of the Scott Monument, I walked towards Carlton Hill where I stopped to view the city from the Nelson Monument. Continuing on to the east, I took the Abbey Hill road which brought me to Holyrood Palace. From there I headed west towards Edinburgh Castle along the Royal Mile and on reaching the Waverley Bridge, ended up once more on Princess Street, where I had a late lunch. After lunch, still seeking information on what to do in Edinburgh on New Year's Eve, I sought the advice of a young lady on duty in a tourist information booth at the station and was told that I would find what I was looking for at a public house which went by the name of the *Auld Hundred*. On entering this establishment a short time later, I was disappointed to find it virtually empty. It was now close to four in the afternoon and the only people in the pub beside myself were the bar-tender and three young men seated at a table in the centre of the room. After ordering a whisky and soda, I engaged the bar-tender in conversation. Having explained to him why I had come to Edinburgh, I went on to say that I was very disappointed to find little or no excitement in town on Hogmonay.   On over-hearing what I had said to the bartender, one of the three fellows at the table arose, and joining me at the bar, introduced himself in a broad Australian accent. He insisted that I join them at their table where I learned that they were newspaper reporters visiting Edinburgh to celebrate the eve of the New Year. They had met in London the previous week and, having heard as I had, of how the Scots celebrated New Year, had decided to stop off in Edinburgh on their way to Glasgow. All three were scheduled to fly to the US the following week in order to cover one of the first sessions of the United Nations about to take place in New York. On being introduced to the other two chaps, I learned that one hailed from South Africa and the other from New Zealand. I found my new companions a spirited lot, as they ordered round after round of drinks. I was informed early in the evening that under no circumstances would I be allowed to order drinks. Not only was I in uniform, but I was the first Canadian any of them had met. Even more important was the fact that they were all on very generous expense accounts from their respective newspapers and were quite certain that the Navy did not provide expense accounts for sailors. At around seven or eight that evening a few more patrons drifted in, and by eight-thirty or nine the *Auld Hundred* had started to come alive. When it became known that the four of us represented the four major countries in the Commonwealth we were treated like VIPs and there were numerous suggestions as to where we could go to have fun that night. A number of the locals suggested that we go to a night club located at the west end of Princess Street and reputed to be the liveliest spot in town.   Acting on this advice, my new-found friends and I left the *Auld Hundred* and, having caught a cab, were dropped off in front of a large, barn-like building from which the sound of music and loud laughter spilled into the street. Inside the building, which seemed to be more like a dance hall than a night club, were numerous tables surrounding an open area in the centre of the room which served as a dance floor. The tables around the dance floor were laden with empty bottles and glasses and at one end of the hall was a bar where patrons were lined up in threes waiting to be served. The air in the building was thick with smoke and an orchestra was pounding out the latest hits for a crowd that was well on its way to being inebriated by 23:00. Thanks to my well-heeled Commonwealth friends, we had been able to purchase a bottle of rum by greasing the palm of our waiter, and having exited the building, the four of us were swept up by a human tide ending up on the Royal Mile, where it seemed that the entire population of Edinburgh had gathered. At the stroke of midnight, the crowd started to sing *Auld Lang Syne* and, on joining hands, perfect strangers were invited to partake of a 'wee dram' to welcome in the New Year.

Separated from my friends in the surging crowd, I found myself being propelled across the North Bridge once more, eventually ending up where it all began: on the sidewalk outside the Post Office. Having been imbibing for the best part of the previous day, and not having had much to eat, I found myself incapable of walking. Unable to think clearly, and uncertain as to which direction would lead me to the Salvation Army Hostel, I wrapped myself around a lamp post which seemed in danger of falling down, and contemplated my predicament. I might possibly have been there for the remainder of the night had not a sailor and his girl passed by. Unable to speak coherently, I tried to attract their attention by making a whistling sound. Unfortunately, my whistle was mistaken by the 'matelot' as being directed at his girl. Letting go of her arm, he pried me loose from the lamp post and proceeded to make a good job of re-shaping my nose. I must have presented a pathetic sight after he departed, holding up the errant lamp post, blood flowing from both nostrils, and my lip swollen. Gradually the crowds dissipated, leaving me in sole possession of an otherwise empty street!

It was in this condition that I was found by a native of Stornoway who, along with two lovely ladies, were on their way home after a night of celebrating. The gentleman from the Isle of Lewis, himself a man of the sea, had no trouble recognizing a fellow sailor in distress and immediately came to my assistance. Unfortunately I had no way of knowing what he was saying as he addressed me in his native Gaelic tongue. It was obvious that the two lassies were greatly distressed at the state that I was in and, on prying me loose from my 'iron crutch', had me place my arms on their shoulders. With one on each side for support we set off down the street with the gentleman from the Isle of Lewis marching ahead singing loudly in Gaelic. Shortly thereafter we arrived at a block of flats, and having ascended two flights of stairs, entered an apartment which I later discovered consisted of nothing more than two rooms and an indoor toilet. The larger of the two rooms served as both kitchen and dining room and built into the wall was a bunk style bed hidden from view by a curtain. The smaller room served as both living room and bedroom, and a second bunk style bed was also built into the wall. I recall one of the women helping me to undress, removing my 'gun shirt' that was covered with blood, and placing it in the kitchen sink to soak in salt water.

From that point on my memory fails me and my next recollection was awakening to the sound of what I thought were bees swarming. Coming awake slowly in unfamiliar surroundings, I lay on my back and tried to figure out where I was, and how I had got there. I realized that I was in a comfortable and warm bed but could not recall having retired the previous night. My head throbbed, my mouth was dry, and my nose was quite sore. The sound that awakened me was coming from the other side of the curtain that hung from the ceiling along the length of the bed. Supporting my aching body on one elbow, I gently pulled the curtain back to reveal a brightly-lit room in the centre of which was a large round table cluttered with soiled dishes, empty glasses, stale food, and dirty ashtrays. At the far side of the table was a giant of a man in full highland dress. As I watched, he flapped his left arm like a duck about to rise from the surface of a pond, a motion consistent with priming a bag-pipe with air, prior to playing it, hence the sound that I had thought were bees swarming. Catching sight of me as I peered around the curtain, he winked, then breaking into quick time, commenced to stride around the table to the tune of *Scotland the Brave*. As he played I became aware of something moving in the bed and on pulling the curtain back to let in more light, was startled to discover there was a woman under the sheets clad in nothing more than her underwear. She was a fine-looking, buxom girl of about twenty years of age with long straight blonde hair that fell below her shoulders. She appeared not the slightest bit concerned that I was staring at her and in fact seemed to be amused at the expression on my face, which must have been one of sheer amazement. Slowly I began to recall the events of the previous day and wondered if this first day of the new year was a harbinger of things to come. It occurred to me that perhaps my luck had already changed for the better. After all, the sailor who hit me the previous night could have broken my teeth, and how often did I awake to find a good-looking girl in bed with me? Having given up on *Scotland the Brave*, the piper began to play *Highland Cathedral* and the occupants of the next room, who had obviously been aroused by the sound of the pipes, now joined us in the kitchen.

This gentleman, from the Isle of Lewis, presented quite a picture. Wearing a knee-length night shirt, his bandy legs were shown to full advantage, and the night cap on his head gave him the appearance of a gnome. I was to learn later, that the elderly lady was the mother of the girl in my bed and also the unofficial spouse of the gentleman from the Isle of Lewis. She too wore a flannel night gown, but instead of a night-cap, her hair was in curlers which were almost two inches in diameter and held in place by a silk bandanna wrapped around the head and knotted on her forehead. The piper, having broken in to a lively reel, the couple began to dance. Taking the man from the Isle of Lewis by the arm, his companion whirled him around the table in a lively jig and in a matter of minutes a full-blown ceilidh was under-way in the kitchen. Eventually some sense of sanity was restored in the room. The piper announced that he would be leaving as soon as the gentleman from the Isle of Lewis poured him a 'wee dram', his only reason for having come by was that he was first foot in, and he had a long day ahead of him. My companion of the previous night had modestly covered herself in a scarlet dressing gown and, having located my trousers and jumper at the foot of the bed, I too managed to get dressed. My shirt that had been placed in salt water in an attempt to wash out the blood stains, was now dry, but still badly soiled. I was, however, able to use it by putting it on back to front. The two ladies of the house then cleared the table in the kitchen and made breakfast, while the man from the Isle of Lewis went off to shave and to get dressed.

Breakfast consisted of a large plate of oatmeal porridge, kippered herrings, toast, and marmalade, washed down with lashings of strong tea. During the meal my host informed me that as soon as we had eaten he and I would set off for the town of Leith in order to observe the tradition of 'first foot in'. Apparently he had decided that I would be a great companion as a result of my dark complexion and black hair. Having worked out of Leith for years with the fishing fleet, he had many friends in that port and it was his intention to visit as many of them as he could that day. Promising to return home in time for supper, we boarded a streetcar on Princess Street and set a course for Leith. By 16:00, we must have knocked on at least a dozen doors and been invited into as many homes. At each visit we had been offered a wee dram, which more often than not ended up being a number of 'wee drams' and as a result of this hospitality neither I nor the man from the Isle of Lewis were too steady on our feet. My recollection of our return to Edinburgh is of the gentleman from the Isle of Lewis leading a chorus of happy Scots on the streetcar in the singing of: *I'll Cling to the Old Rugged Cross*, and *Rock of Ages*.

We arrived back at the flat to find a party in progress. Mother and daughter were entertaining other tenants in the building, most of who were three sheets to the wind. Unable to keep pace with the others, I decided to thank my new-found friends for their hospitality over the past twenty-four hours and find my way back to the Salvation Army Hostel in order to get a good night's sleep. The following morning, on taking stock of my finances, I was shocked to discover that I had a mere four pounds left to last me for the next eleven days. Despite the hospitality of my media friends I had insisted on paying my share of the bill on more than one occasion and had forked out a substantial sum of money on the drinks purchased the previous evening. Having accomplished what I had set out to do, I came to the conclusion that my best course of action would be to return to the boat before I was completely broke, but decided to stay in Edinburgh for as long as the four pounds held out. I recalled the invitation from Claude Raines to visit him in Glasgow before returning to Portsmouth, but could not bring myself to do so in my penniless condition. Cutting my expenses to the bone, I managed to survive for five more days before leaving for London.

Four days later I took the 21:00 train from Waverley Station and arrived in London the following morning. Checking into the Union Jack Club outside Waterloo station, I took in a movie that evening and the following day slept in until 10:00 before checking out. Down to a few shillings in my pocket, I was able to afford one more meal in London before catching the Portsmouth train at 20:45 and, *Artemis* still being in the dockyard, reported aboard before midnight. The following morning, after I had turned to with the hands, Lt. Bagley sent for me and questioned why I had returned to the boat five days before my leave was due to expire. On being told that I had run out of funds, he pulled out his wallet, handed me five pounds, and ordered me to go ashore and not return until the following Friday. Although I protested he insisted that I accept the money while, at the same time, reminding me that it was a loan which I could re-pay in my own time. Having checked into the Sailors' Rest, I spent the next four days in Portsmouth, but time hung heavily on my hands and I was glad to re-join the boat at the end of the week.

Our stay in the dockyard was drawing to a close and all hands were put to work cleaning up the mess that the dockyard 'mateys' had made. I was kept busy carrying out the monthly maintenance checks on the ASDIC stores and equipment and five days later we crossed the harbour and laid-up alongside the jetty in *Dolphin*. Five days before the end of the month, our HSD, Petty Officer Paul, left the boat to be admitted to hospital and I replaced him as the official HSD in *Artemis*. Due to the fact that I was still an Able Seaman, but now responsible for the A/S department and the four AB operators, I made a request to be rated Leading Seaman. The 'old man' agreed and I was informed that I would sit the exam for Leading Hand at the next opportunity.

On January 27, 1948, *Artemis* sailed from Portsmouth, and after a rather rough passage, went alongside the submarine depot ship HMS *Maidstone* in Portland, Dorset. For the next six or seven weeks the boat was to undergo a series of trials and exercises which had not been completed at the time of her commissioning. While alongside *Maidstone,* our ship's company was accommodated in the depot ship although we were called upon to go to sea almost every day. Throughout February, 1948, our daily routine varied little. When we were not loading torpedoes alongside *Maidstone* we were at sea firing them at targets. These practice torpedoes were then recovered, re-fuelled, re-loaded, and fired again. In addition to exercising the torpedo branch, we carried out mock attacks on surface vessels using ASDIC, and gunnery shoots with both the 4 inch and the 20 mm A/A guns. The weather did not co-operate and we spent many miserable days both in harbour and at sea.

On a number of occasions when exercising with surface vessels the exercise had to be cancelled due to severe winter gales. On February 11, 1948, having loaded three 'fish' the previous day, we slipped from *Maidstone* and sailed for the torpedo range to fire them. On our first dive we lost our trim and the boat, having taken on a bow-down angle, came to rest on the bottom in about 25 fathoms (150ft.). With our bow stuck in the mud and the boat at an angle of roughly 35 degrees, 'Jimmy' shut main vents and blew main ballast tanks, but *Artemis* refused to budge. After sitting on the bottom for fifteen or twenty minutes the 'old man' tried once more, and with both motors going full astern group up, we finally freed ourselves and regained an even keel. There was no apparent damage to the boat after this incident but in view of what happened to us three weeks later in the Bay of Biscay, one can only wonder if our hitting the bottom that day had not in some way damaged the ASDIC dome. Shortly after we arrived in Portland, I received a letter from Australia. As stated earlier, I was undecided as to what I wanted to do when my engagement expired and had written to Valerie asking her advice with regard to my settling in that country. I now received a letter from her that caused me to have second thoughts about migrating to the island continent. Having lost her address after leaving Sydney, I had come up with the bright idea of writing to the chief of police in her hometown of Geelong, seeking help in finding her. On the assumption that the police would be more inclined to help a lovesick sailor, my letter implied that I wished to propose marriage but had mislaid her address. The boys in blue had lost no time in locating her but instead of writing to tell me so, had contacted her personally and apparently caused both her and her parents a great deal of embarrassment. The whole sad story of what happened was related to me in her letter. After being discharged from the navy, she had been living with her parents in Geelong and obtained employment in Melbourne. One Sunday afternoon, while she and her parents were entertaining friends, a police cruiser had pulled up in front of the house. In answer to a knock on the door, her mother was confronted by a very large constable in uniform wishing to speak to Miss Valerie Jewel. When Valerie came to the door the constable explained the reason for his visit in a very loud voice which was overheard by all of her friends. He had scolded her for having broken a poor sailor's heart by not answering his letters and implied that she was a heartless woman. Despite her protest that I had not corresponded with her since leaving Australia, and that we had never discussed the prospect of marriage at any time, the policeman refused to listen to her side of the story and departed after saying to Mrs. Jewel: "Make sure your daughter writes to that poor heartbroken sailor in England." Naturally, Valerie was angry and I was given the blame for the whole series of events. I therefore came to the conclusion that I would not be welcomed with open arms by Valerie Jewel should I decide to settle in Australia.

February passed quickly and the weather slowly improved. Since arriving in Portland on January 27, the boat had spent 19 days at sea, loaded and fired 16 torpedoes, and conducted a number of other A/S exercises. We still had two major trials to complete, one of which was a deep dive, and the other a series of sound trials to determine the extent of our cavitation level. On the last week-end in February, having been granted four days leave, I travelled up to London with the intention of visiting Alice and the children. Being unable to obtain a railway warrant, and short of cash, I hitch-hiked to London passing through Dorchester, Bournemouth, Southampton, and Portsmouth. That night, having checked into the Union Jack Club, I went pub-crawling in the area of Kings Cross and awoke the following morning suffering from a colossal hangover. On going out to Mottingham later in the day I found Alice suffering from a bad cold and, having spent the afternoon with the children, returned to the city late in the evening. Repeating the previous night's performance, only this time in Piccadilly Circus, I awoke early on the Sunday morning once again suffering with a sore head. Taking the 14:00 train to Weymouth, I reported aboard at 23:45. The following morning we embarked a 'boffin' (a scientific expert) and sailed from Portland in company with the submarine *Trespasser* and the frigate HMS *Helmsdale* for the Bay of Biscay. Over the next three days we carried out a series of dives starting at 100 ft. and gradually increasing the depth with the intention of reaching the 500-ft. level. On the fourth day, at a depth of 400 ft. the entire ASDIC system, both active and passive, ceased to function. As the HSD of the boat I went forward to the tube space in order to determine the cause of the trouble and on opening the 'test-cock' on the cover of the ASDIC dome, a thin stream of ice cold sea water under extreme pressure shot across the compartment. Shutting the test cock off as quickly as I could, I returned to the control room to report to the 'old man' that the ASDIC dome was completely flooded.

From this point on our series of trials came to a halt and the entire exercise was cancelled. We came to the surface, remaining there all night, and the following morning *Trespasser*, having parted company earlier, *Helmsdale* sent a sea boat over to *Armetis* to pick up our 'boffin', and a short while later left us while we set course for Portsmouth. Off Ushant we encountered patches of fog and by late in the afternoon visibility had decreased to about six hundred yards and deteriorating rapidly. The CO had 'Jimmy' put extra look-outs on the bridge, reduced speed to eight knots, and ordered the OOW to sound a prolonged blast on our air horn every two minutes. As the day came to a close the fog worsened and had it not been for radar, we would have had to stop engines and anchor. Reducing speed to four knots, we crept along in the direction of the Isle of Wight using our echo sounder in an attempt to match the depth of water with that of our dead reckoning position. At around 21:00 the motor on our echo sounder burnt out and almost at the same time the 'Sparker' PO reported that our LORAN had ceased to function.

Not having done a physical transfer of equipment and spare parts when my predecessor had been admitted to hospital, I was unable to locate the spare motor for the echo sounder. This did not endear me to the CO who, at this stage, was in an ugly mood on learning that the LORAN had broken down as well. A quick summary of the situation follows: not having been able to obtain a 'fix' with the sextant since surfacing forty-eight hours previously, we now found ourselves without the use of our ASDIC, ECHO SOUNDER, and LORAN, any one of which would have helped to confirm our dead reckoning position. Fortunately, our radar still worked but before we could obtain an accurate fix on any object on the shore, it too broke down. Having lost almost all our electrical aids to navigation, and finding ourselves to be in a busy fairway, the captain ordered the second coxswain to take soundings by using a lead line. Our diesel, which made a considerable amount of noise and which might have prevented us from hearing the sound of another vessel's engine, was shut down and, relying on our battery, moved ahead very slowly. The second coxswain started to call out soundings as he swung the lead. At a depth of 10 fathoms the bottom began to shoal rapidly and on a sounding of six fathoms the 'old man' stopped the motors and anchored. All around us we heard the sound of fog horns and the coxswain lost no time in detailing off one of the crew who was provided with a stop watch and instructed to sound two long blasts on our own horn every two minutes. A submarine on the surface, in poor visibility, or at night, whether at anchor or under way, is in a most vulnerable position. With an extremely low freeboard, any collision with a surface vessel resulting in damage to the pressure hull and flooding of the interior can be deadly.

An example of this was the loss of HM S/M *Truculent* in 1950, when she was rammed and sunk in minutes by the Swedish tanker

Divina off Gravesend with the loss of 61 lives. Throughout the night we maintained a watch on the bridge, sounding our air horn at two-minute intervals until the unbelievable occurred. For some unexplainable reason our air horn gave up the ghost and we were left with nothing more than the ship's bell to warn other vessels of our presence. The following morning shortly after 09:00 the fog began to lift, and by 10:00 the sun was shining brightly. As the fog dissipated, other vessels that had been anchored during the night began to get underway and there was a real danger of being run down as they began heading for the harbour entrance. Luck was with us, however, and by noon we were secured alongside at Fort Blockhouse. I have related this story in detail in order to emphasize the point that, despite the most modern and sophisticated instruments available, the best of equipment can still malfunction. It will also serve to remind the reader that of all the various types of ships that sail the seven seas, the submarine can be lost in the blink of an eye. During the days that followed there was an internal enquiry conducted to determine the reason or reasons for the failure of our equipment. In my case the ASDIC dome had flooded at the depth of 400 ft. as a result of improper torque being applied to the nuts securing the lid of the dome. On carrying out monthly maintenance on the set while in Portland, I had used a torque wrench that I had obtained from our engine room. It was discovered that, unknown to me, this wrench was out of calibration which led to a false reading being recorded.

On March 16, 1948, I set off for London on fourteen days leave and, having checked into the Union Jack Club, spent the next seven days carousing around London before taking the train to Glasgow. While in London I went out to Mottingham to visit Alice and the children and also met with my lawyer from the Legal Aid Society. During the evenings I either took in a movie or spent time in a pub. One night I went to a dance in Hammersmith where I met a beautiful girl by the name of Isobel who hailed from St. Julein, Switzerland and with whom I fell madly in love. Isobel had come to England from her hometown in the Swiss Alps and was employed as a housekeeper in London. She was twenty years of age with brown eyes, long brown hair, and had the most adorable face of any girl that I had yet met. She spoke English quite well, was a wonderful dancer, had obviously had a very good education, and possessed a fantastic body. On a date the following night we took in a movie after which we visited Lyons Corner House in Piccadilly for a meal and where we sat and talked until almost three in the morning. At this point I really did not want to leave London but before going on leave I had promised Claude Raines that I would spend half my leave in Glasgow and had planned on leaving the following day. I explained to Isobel that I had previously arranged to visit my friend in Glasgow and there was no way that I would break my word. However, I had her promise that we would see each other when I passed through London on my return to Portsmouth.

On arrival in Glasgow I booked into the Overseas Club in Exchange Square and set out to find my shipmates. Having located Claude, we called on 'Kocker' White, who lived in the Gorbals and the three of us went pub-crawling. I ended up staying at Claude's flat that night and the following afternoon he and I went to Hampden Park to see Rangers beat Celtic 1-0 at football (soccer). I had often heard of the Hampden roar and was not disappointed that day as I listened to thousands of Glaswegians screaming their heads off. The Scots certainly take their football seriously, or should I say their religious affiliation seriously. After the game the Protestants and Catholics were still scrapping outside the stadium as they made their way home and when the only goal of the game was scored, a number of spectators were hit on the head by flying beer bottles. Not wanting to impose on Claude and his wife, I returned to my accommodation at the Overseas Club that night but arranged to have supper with them on our last night in town.

Arriving at their home at around 18:00 on the evening that we were scheduled to leave, I found Claude extremely inebriated, announcing that he had no intention of going back to the ship. Jean, Claude's wife, told me that he had been drinking since breakfast and had refused to put on his uniform in preparation to our leaving that night. After supper, 'Knocker' dropped by and both he and I tried to convince Claude to get dressed, without success. It was now getting close to 20:00 and time was running out. If we intended to catch the 21:00 train for London, we would have to leave the house no later than 20:30. At one point we thought Jean had talked him into getting dressed as he started to put on his pants, but a moment later picking up his jumper and collar, he threw them out the window onto the street below. Unfortunately, his jumper got caught up on the trolley bus wires which created quite a stir when the busses had to come to a halt. Eventually the conductor on the bus managed to dislodge the garment and 'Knocker', having retrieved it, we went back to the problem of trying to get Claude to put on his uniform. Having missed the 21:00 train, it looked as though we might have to stay in Glasgow until he was sober enough to get dressed, not knowing how long that might take. Shortly before 23:00, having forced him to drink numerous cups of black coffee, and after he had paid a number of visits to the toilet, the three of us managed to get him dressed. Saying good bye to Jean, we called a cab and set out for Glasgow Central arriving there in time to catch the last train to London shortly after midnight and arriving in Euston Station the following morning. It was obvious that we were going to be adrift on reporting aboard so, taking time to clean up in the station washroom and having a hearty breakfast, we made our way across town to board the Portsmouth train in Waterloo.

That afternoon, on landing on the jetty at *Dolphin,* having crossed the harbour in the liberty boat from HMS *Vernon*, we were informed that we were a full seven hours adrift and would be required to attend defaulters the following morning. Not knowing what our punishment might be, Claude and I went ashore that evening to the Railway Inn, a pub in Gosport, and sank six or seven pints before crawling into our hammocks. The 'old man' must have been in a really good frame of mind the following morning as all three of us were given one days scale (one days extra duties, one days stoppage of leave, and one days stoppage of rum). He even went so far as to commend us for not abandoning Claude in his drunken state and in our insisting that he get dressed and return with us, even though it meant missing our train and being adrift.

A day or two after returning from leave, I received a letter from the Law Society asking me to remit the sum of eight pounds to cover the cost of my impending divorce which had been scheduled to go to court on July 1, 1948, in London. Due to the problem with Claude, I had missed an opportunity to meet with Isobel when passing through London. I had, however, phoned her from Waterloo Station and I now received a letter from her telling me that she had met a wonderful fellow from Canada who had asked her to marry him. The lucky guy, Bert Mansfield, hailed from Penticton, British Columbia, and was serving in HMCS *Magnificent*, commissioned in Belfast on April 7, 1948.

For the next three weeks *Artemis* went to sea almost daily with training classes. Sometimes the classes were junior officers about to become submariners and on other occasions we took ratings to sea with the intention of encouraging them to consider serving in submarines. Towards the middle of April, two of my messmates were drafted off the boat; A.B. Ken Hallet went to join another boat, and Jack Pope left us to begin an HSD course. A letter arrived from my old friend, Leading Signalman Peter Jennings, informing me that he expected to be discharged from the RN on medical grounds in the very near future. He told me that he was thinking of going to live in Canada when he got out of the navy and wanted to know if my brother in Toronto would be willing to act as his sponsor. I gave him my brother's address and told him that I would probably join him in Toronto later in the year as I had made up my mind to return to Canada when my engagement expired in August.

On learning that *Magnificent* had arrived in Portsmouth from Belfast and was berthed in the dockyard, I decided to go aboard to meet the fellow who hoped to marry Isobel. It was April 24 when I got around to paying him a visit and on meeting Bert for the first time we instantly became friends. He told me he hoped to marry Isobel before *Magnificent* had to sail as it would make it much easier for her to join him in Canada later if she was his wife. If this turned out to be impossible, she would take passage for Halifax at a later date and they would then get married in Canada. I was welcomed in his mess where he and a number of his messmates gave me sippers, and after lunch we went ashore together for a 'wet' run in 'Pompy'. The following week I got a message from him informing me that Isobel was coming to Portsmouth for the weekend and inviting me to join them for dinner. That Saturday, the three of us having met in the afternoon, I escorted them over to *Dolphin* and gave them a tour of the boat, after which we returned to Portsmouth in time to take in a movie, followed by dinner.

Two days later on May 10, 1946, at 16:00, *Artemis* and HM S/M *Tactician*, left the Solent to take part in one of the first major fleet exercises held by the NATO countries since the end of the war: EXERCISE DAWN. The two boats from the Fifth Flotillas were to join, with another ten boats that had sailed from other bases around the UK. All submarines were tasked with setting up a patrol line stretching from Scotland in the west to Norway in the east. Our job was to intercept the Home Fleet vessels sailing from Scapa Flow to engage a force attacking the UK from the direction of Scandinavia. On leaving the Solent we sailed around the south coast on the surface and through the Strait of Dover into the North Sea. Two days later, just prior to the start of the exercise, *Tactician* had to leave the area and run into Rosyth to land a seriously ill rating. We sailed on alone with the other boats taking part in the exercise. At 11:00 the following morning we dived in our allotted position and spent the next thirteen hours below the surface listening and looking for the Home Fleet ships. Shortly after midnight we surfaced and having see or heard nothing of the 'enemy' all day, ran on the surface until daylight, charging our battery and steering a course that would take us around the north of Scotland and through the Pentland Firth.

During daylight hours the following day we were forced to dive on three occasions to avoid interception by patrolling aircraft and around midnight had Cape Wrath on the Port beam. At dawn we entered the North Minch and on passing through the Little Minch a short while later, encountered calm waters, blue skies, and a gentle breeze which helped keep those of us on the bridge cool on what otherwise would have been a scorching day. Sailing south at 12 knots the Captain allowed those of us off watch to sunbathe on the casing and most of us took advantage of the opportunity to do so. We passed the Outer Hebrides to starboard, while the Isles of Skye, Mull, Rhum, and Eigg, loomed up to the west and eventually dropped astern. Further south, as we sailed between the islands of Jura and Islay we passed within a few hundred yards of many single malt whisky distilleries, all of which were located close to the water's edge. These were the distillers of world-famous Ardbeg, Laphroaig, Cao Ila, Bunnahabhain, Bruichladdich, and Bowmore whiskies. It was around noon as we passed them, and many of the girls employed by the distilleries were eating their lunch on the seashore as we sailed by. The verbal exchange between his sailors on the casing and the factory girls on shore did not meet with the CO's approval, and he sent the coxswain on deck to warn us that we would have to go below if it continued. We rounded the Mull of Kintyre later that afternoon and that evening secured alongside the depot ship of the 3rd Submarine Flotilla, HMS *Montclare*. *Montclare*, whose original name was *Wolfe*, was a former 21,550 ton Canadian Pacific liner that had been converted to a submarine depot ship and was home to four of our sister boats, HM S/Ms *Alderney*, *Ambush*, and *Anchorite*, along with *Tactician*, who had sailed with us from Portsmouth.

Our visit to Rothesay was to be a short one. The town reminded me of Tobermory with its long row of houses and shops facing the harbour, at the southern end of which was a heavily wooded area known to the matelots as Shaggy Wood or Midge Land. The former name is self-explanatory while the latter was in reference to the swarm of insects that would attack any sailor and his girl engaging in the act of copulation. A favourite pastime of those remaining aboard on duty, was to use the high power periscope to spy on sailors and their girls as they entered Shaggy Wood, and watch their discomfort as they came under attack from the midges. The local cinema, located along the sea front, went by the name of the *Roxy*. This was tantamount to waving a red flag in front of a bull as far as the British submariner was concerned. One dark night during the war a number of matelots climbed on to the roof of the building and with great difficulty managed to remove the leg of the letter 'R'. The inhabitants of Rothesay awoke in the morning to find their movie theatre renamed the 'Poxy' and needless to say they were not amused.

Another point of interest in Rothesay was the house of the Gorgons located on a hill over-looking the town. This small cottage was the home of a middle-aged widow and her two daughters, all three of whom were of dubious character. Referred to as the three Gorgons, these ladies were prepared to entertain any sailor willing to walk the mile or so to the top of the hill. After the pubs closed one could purchase a pint or a wee dram at the Gorgons' Nest. Later in the evening the mother, known as Medusa, or one of her daughters, could be prevailed upon to share their bed for the night with a lonely sailor for a small fee. If the local constabulary were aware of the Gorgons' Nest, it was obvious that they were willing to turn a blind eye, providing everyone was well-behaved. To the best of my knowledge the house was never raided and many a submariner who spent time in Rothesay will have fond memories of the three Gorgons. One can only speculate as to how the Gorgons received visitors from the ship's company of the submarine *Perseus* had she visited Rothesay during her lifetime. There is also no record of any submariner being turned to stone as a result of looking at one of the Gorgons. It can be said with some certainty, however, that many a matelot returned to his ship in a 'stoned' condition after a night in the Gorgons' Nest.

The day after our arrival in Rothesay we sailed up the Clyde to the mouth of Loch Goil and that evening anchored a mile or two south of the village of Lochgoilhead. I remember thinking we must have arrived at the most beautiful spot in Scotland. The water that day was crystal clear with not a ripple on the surface. From where we lay at anchor, the distance to the shore, almost at the head of the Loch, was measured in yards. Apart from two small metal huts at the water's edge which housed the sound detection equipment, there was not a house in sight. The only living thing to be seen on the shore were the sheep grazing on the hills which rose steeply from the water's edge to port and starboard. As the sun set that evening those of us on the casing for a breath of fresh air and a cigarette were treated to the sight of a herd of deer coming to the shore in single file to forage along the bracken. Not a soul could be seen and as the night closed in around us the light from a million stars was reflected from the mirror- like surface of the water.

We spent the following day conducting sound trials in the still waters of the loch. Allowing the air to escape from our ballast tanks we slowly sank at our mooring while a variety of sounds such as the starting of an electric motor, the running of a pump, or the opening of a valve, were monitored on the hydrophones on the shore. Later in the day the degree of cavitation created by the turning of our propellers was measured. Our trials completed we returned to Rothesay and having secured alongside *Montclare*, spent one more night in harbour before leaving the Clyde. Just prior to sailing, the CO received a signal from the Admiralty instructing him to choose between either Swansea or Dartmouth as a port where we were to show the flag during the coming Navy Week. Having been given a choice of ports, the 'old man' decided to let his ship's company decide, and called upon the Coxswain to conduct a ballot. The majority of the ship's company being from the south of England chose Dartmouth by a wide margin. On our way south we experienced beautiful summer weather in the Irish Sea. Under a clear blue sky the Captain gave orders to stop both engines while those off watch were allowed to go over the side for a swim. Later that same day we encountered two Irish drifters heading home and, on finding that they had made successful catches, asked them to come alongside and sell us some fish. The fishing vessels were from Northern Ireland and the Irish fishermen were only too pleased to oblige. They regarded it an honour and a privilege to be of service to the officers and men of one of His Majesty's submarines and refused to accept payment for the fish. That evening we sat down to a supper of fish and chips that was better than anything sold ashore.

The following day, after rounding the Lizard, we eventually

arrived at the mouth of the river Dart and, on reaching a point in the river across from the Naval College, made fast to a mooring buoy positioned close inshore. Within minutes of securing, a signal was received from the College offering the loan of a motor cutter during our visit. The offer was gratefully accepted and our coxswain lost no time in naming me and two others to serve as boats' crew. As bowman, I was given Signalman Parker, while Stoker First Class Plaistow was detailed off to act as my engineer. I quickly learned that neither Parker nor Plaistow had ever had any experience in manning a small boat and that CPO Rennie had given me the job of coxswain of the motor boat based on the fact that I had once been the skipper of a skimmer in the Mediterranean. An hour or two after our arrival I took delivery of my new toy. A petty officer and two ratings arrived alongside in a 27 foot motor sea boat and having signed the necessary documents, she was handed over to my care after a thorough inspection of her hull, fittings, and equipment. On returning the College crew to the jetty, I took the boat out in to the stream to get the feel of her and it was then I discovered that Stoker Plaistow knew nothing about engine order codes for power boats. Due to the noise of the four cylinder diesel it was almost impossible for the engineer to hear the coxswain as he gave instructions for the running of the engine. To avoid confusion, these orders were usually transmitted by whistle:

One blast on the whistle meant STOP
Two blasts indicated NORMAL FULL SPEED AHEAD
Three blasts called for FULL SPEED ASTERN, while
Four blasts meant SLOW AHEAD.

For some unknown reason Stoker Plaistow was unable to memorise these signals. We almost met disaster on coming alongside *Artemis* for the first time. On sounding one short blast on the whistle calling for the engine clutch to be disengaged and the engine throttled down to idling speed, I had to act very quickly to avoid hitting the saddle tanks head on. Plaistow had opened the throttle to FULL SPEED AHEAD. From that point on I gave up on using the whistle and decided to rely on my voice alone for transmitting engine orders. Signalman Parker had no such problem, although I caught him on at least one occasion extending his boat-hook, blunt end first.

On our first night in Dartmouth all of our officers were invited to a mess dinner held in the college and I was instructed to be prepared to land them at the college steps at 17:30 sharp. With the exception of the navigator who remained aboard as OOD, we landed them safely on the jetty in their mess kits and the captain gave me instructions to have the boat return to pick them up at 23:30. The mess dinner must have been a success as Lt. Bagley informed me that our officers intended to return the hospitality. The following day, invitations were sent to a number of the college staff including two or three nursing sisters from the hospital, and a party was planned to be held in *Artemis*. On bidding me good night, Lt. Bagley told me to report to him in the wardroom the following morning after the hands had turned to. On doing so, I was informed that the time had come to broach the keg of 'screetch' that had been given to the wardroom by the officers of *Scotian* while in Halifax the previous December. With the help of two other ratings I managed to hoist the keg out of the magazine and on locating it on the table in the wardroom, Lt. Bagley removed the bung in order to inspect the contents. He then invited the three of us who had helped him to sample the product and comment on its taste, colour, and potency. Needless to say we were delighted to pass judgement as to whether it was fit for human consumption, all of us priding ourselves on being connoisseurs of fine rum. Our sample of 'screetch' was roughly half a cup and as it was then close to noon we did not have long to wait before drawing our daily rum ration. Having consumed about six to eight ounces of neat rum before noon, it was only natural that all three of us were feeling the effects of the liquor at 16:00 when the motor boat was called away to collect the first of our guests.

Our first trip to the jetty went off without a hitch, and I was quite proud of my crew as we came alongside in a seaman-like manner. The first two guests were special service lieutenants from the college whom I suspected to be schoolmasters. On entering the control room Lt. Bagley welcomed them and provided each with a shot glass of 'screetch'. Before returning to my mess he poured out three fingers of 'screetch' and handed it to me behind the wardroom curtain. From that moment on the efficiency of *Artemis'* boat crew began to deteriorate rapidly. On our second trip to the jetty we picked up three rather good-looking nurses, one lieutenant commander, and a very timid individual, who wore the uniform of a warrant schoolmaster. With a total of seven guests aboard, together with our own five officers, the control room and the adjoining wardroom space was now somewhat crowded. From time-to-time the XO would lead one of his guests on a tour of the boat. As we never knew whether the guest was going to be a male or female we had to control the language on the mess deck in order to avoid any embarrassment.

The captain, while not considered to be the life of the party, appeared to enjoy himself. Probably the eldest person present, he nevertheless mingled easily with the guests and at one time was engaged in a lengthy conversation with the young lieutenant commander, the second most senior officer present. For those of us in the ship's company who had occasion to enter or to pass through the control room while the party was in progress it soon became apparent that two of the nurses were showing signs of early inebriation. It was also quite clear that our navigator was quickly loosing his ability to navigate. At 20:00, approximately four hours after the party had started, the captain said good night to everyone and retired to his cabin in the conning tower. Before retiring he instructed the first lieutenant to close the bar at 22:00 and make sure that all guests were ashore by 22:30. With the sobering influence of the captain gone, the party-goers now began to let their hair down. Word filtered down to the mess that one of the officers had passed out and was now stretched out on the chart table. Two members of the seamen's mess who had been pressed in to service as stewards, came forward to tell us that it was the warrant schoolmaster who was on the chart table and that two of the nurses were attempting to undress the unconscious man. The noise being generated by the group had now reached such a pitch that it awakened the captain from a sound sleep. Calling down to the first lieutenant from his cabin, he gave orders that the bar be closed and that our guests be sent ashore. On being sent for by Lt. Bagley I was instructed to bring the boat alongside to embark everyone and transport them down river to the centre of Dartmouth where they intended to continue the party in the lounge of a local hotel. It was with great difficulty that we managed to embark our passengers who had to climb down onto the saddle tanks before stepping up into the boat. Eventually all were aboard with the exception of the young navigator who, on stepping aboard, promptly regurgitated his meal in the after cockpit of the boat. Witnessing the mess the young sub-lieutenant had made, Lt. Bagley pulled out his wallet and handed me three pounds while apologising on behalf of the sub., and adding: "This will help to compensate you and the others for having to clean up the navigators' unfortunate accident." On landing the party on the sea wall, which ran parallel to the main street of the town of Dartmouth, Lt Bagley ordered me to wait for his return and not to return to the boat. It was now about 21:00 and he anticipated that they would only be at the hotel for another hour.

Having secured the boat to a bollard on the sea wall, and expecting to be alongside for an hour or more, I decided to allow Plaistow and Parker to go ashore and visit the nearest pub for a pint. Handing them each one of Bagley's pound notes, I warned them not to be gone for more than thirty minutes and to stay out of trouble. As we were now experiencing slack water I was not greatly worried about our mooring lines but someone had to stay with the boat and in any event the after cockpit had to be swabbed out. At 21:30 Plaistow and Parker had not returned and as the tide was now ebbing at an alarming rate there was no way that I could think of leaving the boat to look for them. I had not seen nor had I heard from any of the officers since landing them on the sea wall at 21:00, and when my two crew members had not turned up, I began to get worried. Shortly before midnight Plaistow and Parker staggered into sight with two young ladies in tow, all four being far from sober. My two shipmates had met the girls in the pub and had been enjoying themselves so much that they had completely lost track of time.

The girls, who lived in Kingswear on the east side of the river Dart, had also lost track of time and consequently had missed the last ferry across the river. They were now stranded on the Dartmouth side, unless of course, I could be prevailed upon to take them across the water. As angry as I was with my two shipmates, I had to admit that the girls were quite attractive and that had it been I that had met up with them I might have done the same thing. It was a wonder to me that either of them could still stand. The local drink was 'scrumpy', a rough cider with a kick like a mule which sold for eleven pence per pint. Even locals who had been drinking it all their life seldom drank more than two or three pints, and these boys had downed almost eight. Aware of the fact that the pubs were now closed and that neither Plaistow nor Parker had seen anything of the officers, I reluctantly agreed to ferry the girls across the river. The giggling girls and their two inebriated companions managed to climb aboard without going into the drink and Plaistow, having started the motor we shoved off into the stream. Halfway across the river the ebbing tide created a strong current that tended to sweep me downstream. For every yard travelled to the east, I was loosing two yards south and consequently had to cross the river with the rudder held at about five degrees to port. It was a very dark night as we approached the ferry landing at Kingsware. Keeping a sharp look out for the numerous pleasure craft moored off shore I missed the jetty and, not wishing to go out into the stream to take a second run at it, decided on the spur of the moment to put the boat's bows directly onto the beach. Calling on Plaistow for all the power he could give me, I ran the boat ashore with her prow buried in the sand for a distance of over three feet. Telling Parker to give the girls a hand to disembark, he replied that they refused to jump off the bow because it was too high off the beach. When I suggested that they come aft and jump over the side, they complained that they would get their feet wet. Suggesting that they remove their shoes and stockings and wade ashore, they eventually did, but not before the tide had dropped another foot or two leaving us high and dry on the beach. Half the length of the boat was still out in the water and on making sure that my prop was not fouled I had Plaistow start the engine and called for him to go astern while opening the throttle slowly until the engine was going full astern. With quick movements of the rudder from port to starboard I hoped to be able to shake loose of the sand that held her in its grip. With the engine developing maximum revs for a good three minutes and nothing happening, I called down to the cockpit to have it stopped. In the silence that followed I happened to glance over the side and noticed that the froth on the surface of the water and the sediment stirred up by the prop had trailed out over the stern. If we had been going full speed astern as I had thought we had, the wash and sediment in the water would have been moving towards the beach. On questioning First Class Stoker Plaistow as to the position of the clutch before we stopped, he sheepishly replied: "I thought you said full speed ahead." Making sure that he fully understood what I wanted, I decided to try once more. This time I asked the signalman to use his boat hook with the butt end down in the sand to see if this would help to break us free. Repeating the previous exercise the motor was about to overheat when I felt a slight movement in the stern and without warning we broke loose and were going full speed astern bearing down on a large white yacht which was moored a matter of yards astern of us. Screaming at Plaistow to stop, I put the helm down but it was too late. We were still underway when we hit, and leaving a grey mark the length of her hull, collided with one of her mooring buoys that created a small hole in our clinker-built hull fortunately well above the water line.

Unknown to me at the time, my bowman had hurt himself badly as the boat had broken free on becoming unstuck. Leaning heavily on his boat hook as he attempted to push us off, the sudden movement of the boat as it broke free of the sand, caused him to loose his balance and fall forward on to the business end of the boat hook. I found out later that he had lost three of his front teeth, but at the time could only see that his face was a mass of blood and that his cap was missing. Unable to communicate with Parker over the roar of the engine, I had decided on my own to return to the sea wall on the Dartmouth side in the event that the officers might still be there. Halfway across the river Parker came aft. Waving his arms madly and pointing in the direction in which *Artemis* lay, he made me to understand that someone was using an Aldis lamp on her casing to recall the boat. Under the circumstances I had no option but to put the tiller over and head for home. As we approached the submarine I could see three people on her upper deck. Apart from our 'killick' Signalman McAllister using the Aldis lamp on the bridge, two other people were on the casing as we came alongside. I immediately recognized the captain who was pacing up and down dressed in his silk bathrobe and bedroom slippers. The only uniform part of his attire was his officers white cap. The other individual, all five feet six inches of him, was our coxswain, Chief Petty Officer Rennie who, like the captain, was dressed in slippers and pyjamas over which he had put on his greatcoat and cap. On coming alongside for the final time that night, my 'engineer' Plaistow did not let me down. On being told to stop, he slipped the clutch, putting the engine in neutral as we glided in towards the saddle tanks. Judging the distance nicely I then called down for full speed astern only to have him give me the exact opposite command of full speed ahead. When we hit the saddle tank with a resounding crash Parker had already passed our painter to the coxswain who was standing on the tanks trying to secure us to the casing. As Plaistow went to full speed ahead, the coxswain came close to being pulled overboard. It was now about two hours in to the middle watch and both the captain and the coxswain were in a foul mood. The coxswain was the most vocal of the two and appeared to be quite unconcerned with the condition of the signalman's blood-covered face and missing teeth. Instead he informed poor Parker that he was missing his cap and was out of the rig of the day. While the captain had less to say, he appeared to be in a hypnotic trance. Turning to me he asked in an icy tone: "Where are my officers?" In all truthfulness I replied: "I haven't a clue sir." The coxswain then ordered the three of us to go below and turn in, adding that he was relieving me of my duties as coxswain of the motor boat as of that moment. As I started down the fore hatch his final words were: "I'll see you in the morning Jones."

The next day I was quite surprised when I learned that we were not to be charged. At that point only I knew about the damage to the motor boat on her port side. As the boat was secured with her port side outboard the damaged planking was not visible from the casing. Furthermore, despite being intoxicated, all of us had been able to perform our duty and could not have been charged with being incapable. At all times I had acted under the instructions of Lt. Bagley and no one was aware of the fact that I had transported two female civilians across the river. The coxswain told me to turn over the boat to L/Seaman Raynes, Able Seaman Scar, and a stoker whose name I do not remember. That night I went ashore on the first liberty boat to find out what Dartmouth had to offer a lonely sailor.

Of interest to those of us in *Artemis* was that we were the first naval vessel to have visited the port since the end of the war. At one time during the war, Dartmouth and Kingswear had been home to both the 15th and the 8th MGB flotillas of Coastal Forces, but was seldom visited by warships after 1945. A matelot in uniform on the streets of Dartmouth was a rare animal indeed. This phenomenon resulted in the ship's company being treated as VIPs by the locals and in particular the young girls who would cross the street for the privilege of touching a sailor's collar. As already mentioned, the local cider was only eleven pence per pint. It had a kick like a mule and two or three glasses of the stuff were about as much as I could take. The girls frequenting the pubs were unusually friendly and only too willing to provide overnight accommodation for any poor sailor looking for a place to rest his weary body. That evening Jack Pope and I met two girls who claimed to be sisters and on being invited by them to walk them home, we ended up staying the night. John and his girl, Barbara, retired to a room on the second floor, leaving her sister Gladys and I to make the best of it on the sofa in the downstairs parlour. The next morning the girls made us breakfast and, on leaving the house, made us promise to come back and spend a week-end with them as soon as possible. The following day, which was Sunday, *Artemis* made three short trips to sea with a number of cadets from the college to have them experience what it was like to dive in a submarine. At 08:00 on Monday we slipped our mooring and sailed for Portsmouth. Before leaving the motor boat made one last trip to the College steps where it was officially returned, the petty officer coxswain from the college taking delivery without having seen the damage to the hull.

It was good to be back in *Dolphin* after our little trip around the country. In a matter of days we had reverted to our old routine of going to sea each morning with training classes and returning to harbour by 17:00. Four days after returning to Portsmouth Jack Pope and I put in a request to be granted long weekend leave which, much to our surprise, was granted. Both Jack and I were almost broke but anxious to see the two girls in Dartmouth once again and were prepared to hitch- hike to Dartmouth if necessary. That Friday we went ashore on the first liberty boat and within the hour were on the main highway to Southampton. Nine hours after leaving Portsmouth we arrived in Exeter having gone through Southampton, Salisbury, and Taunton. Tired and hungry, we visited the railway station in Exeter where we were able to get a sandwich and a cup of tea at midnight and catch a few hours sleep on a bench in the station. The following morning we were on the road bright and early, but found it difficult to hitch a ride. It was 11:00 when we arrived in Dartmouth, and on stepping off the ferry, went directly to the *Seal*, the name of the pub where Gladys worked. Jack went off to find Barbara and returned to the *Seal* with her in tow about an hour later. Gladys announced that she did not have to work that night, and when the pub closed at 16:00 Jack and I went home with the girls for supper before leaving for the *Masonic Lodge* where a dance was to be held that night.

On Sunday morning we all slept until noon and after lunch the four of us went off to the *Seal* for a few drinks before Jack and I had to hit the road for Portsmouth. At about 16:00, both Jack and I came to the conclusion that we were in no shape to travel that evening. Despite the fact that we would be AWOL on Monday morning we decided to spend one more night in Dartmouth and leave early the following day. Based on the length of time that it had taken to hitch-hike from Portsmouth to Dartmouth, we expected that we would not be more than seven or eight hours adrift when we got back to *Dolphin* and would probably only be given four or five days #11 punishment. Little did we know what was in store for us on our return.

Unable to thumb a ride on leaving Kingswear at 06:00, it took us almost all day to travel as far as Taunton where we were forced to spend the night in a farmer's barn. The next morning, with what little change we had in our pockets, we were able to purchase a bus ticket as far as Yeovil where once more we took to the highway. Between Yeovil and Bournemouth, a total of four vehicles stopped to give us a ride, but after leaving Bournemouth we were lucky enough to be picked up by a lorry that took us all the way to Portsmouth via Southampton. Reporting aboard *Artemis* at 16:00, instead of being only eight hours adrift, we were charged with being AWOL for a total of thirty-two hours. The coxswain, having taken us before the navigator who was the OOW, ordered that we be put on the captain's report the following day. At defaulters the following morning, Jack and I faced a somewhat irate 'old man'. Glaring across the table at me for a moment I thought that he was about to explode. Red in face and with a nervous tick in his eye he accused me of bringing disgrace to the good name of his ship. He then sarcastically asked: "Is this your way of thanking the navy for all that the legal aid department is doing to get you a divorce?" He then concluded his tirade by reminding me of the stupidity of relying on the chance of being given a lift on the highway to ensure returning from leave on time. The final verdict was: "Commodore Submarines Report." Two days later, Jack and I were brought before Commodore Ben Bryant, DSO, DSC, RN, Flag Officer Submarines, who lost no time in handing down his sentence. We were each given fourteen days #11 punishment, meaning the loss of our daily rum ration and being called in the morning a full half-hour before the rest of the ship's company. We were also allowed only one half-hour for lunch instead of sixty minutes, and given extra duties in the evenings. What was considered the harshest punishment was one hour of rifle drill during which one was required to double around the parade square with a rifle weighing nine pounds held at the 'high port' with arms extended over the head.

In *Dolphin*, the men's canteen was located at the edge of the parade square and this latter punishment was all the more unbearable as on each lap we could see our ship-mates downing pints of beer as we went by the window, our legs and arms aching, covered in perspiration, red in the face, and on the verge of collapsing. Two days after starting my sentence I was engaged in extra work on the submarine *Totem* along with a Stoker Dawson, when I accidentally fell down an opening in the submarine's casing, badly injuring my right leg. On being taken by ambulance to Haslar Hospital, I spent the next five days recovering. After being discharged from Haslar and returning to duty, I learned from the coxswain that I would shortly be drafted from *Artemis*. While in hospital Isobel wrote to say Bert had arrived in Canada and that she hoped to be able to join him before Christmas. She invited me to give her a call on my next trip to London. Informed that I was to leave *Artemis* the following Monday, I requested a long weekend leave. My request being granted, I left Portsmouth for London at 17:00 on Friday 11, and called on Isobel. After going to a movie with her, I returned to the Union Jack Club and the following day returned to Mottingham and visited the children. By 18:00 I was back in London and, after hitch-hiking to Portsmouth, arrived aboard by 23:30.

As expected, my draft chit came through the following Monday and, having turned over the A/S department stores and log books to my relief Petty Officer, 'Jock' Morrison, I said goodbye to my mates in *Artemis* and moved into *Dolphin* as a member of Reserve Group 'R', which consisted of the following boats: HM S/Ms *Tantalus, Truculent, Tudor, Tapir,* and *Spirit*. These boats had been de-commissioned and located in Haslar Creek awaiting their fate. All, except *Truculent*, were eventually taken to the breakers and scrapped. After a refit, at which time she was fitted with a snorkel, *Truculent* was re-commissioned, but unfortunately lost off The Nore in 1952 when she collided with the Swedish tanker *Divina*. Sixty-one crew members did not survive.

Those of us drafted to the reserve groups were responsible for the safety, maintenance, and upkeep of de-commissioned boats in our group. In my case, I carried out daily maintenance on the A/S equipment of the five boats in the Reserve Group 'R', ensuring that the batteries were fully charged and the equipment in working order. We lived ashore in *Dolphin* but were employed in the boats during daylight hours. Approximately every four days a number of us were called upon to sleep aboard the submarines where an all-night watch was maintained on such things as mooring lines, fenders, and the positive buoyancy of all vessels in the group. By-and-large our jobs were considered easy and, on evenings that we were required to sleep in the boats, we were able to pass the time away playing cards, reading, listening to the radio, or just getting caught up on letter-writing. It was around this time that I became quite friendly with a young lady by the name of Rita. Rita was a WREN stationed in HMS *Daedalus*, an RN Air Station at Lee-on-Solent. Our meeting in one of my favourite watering holes in Gosport, the *Black Knight*, was to lead to a hot and heavy romance that lasted twenty-two days. During that tumultuous time we managed to meet each other at least every third day and inevitably our dates ended with an argument. For the first time in my young life I was involved in a relationship with a woman commonly referred to as a 'vamp'. Never before had any female led me up "the garden path" as she did, only to have her deflate my ego by the end of the evening. How close I came to conquest, only to be faced with the reality of defeat. It took me twenty-two days to come to my senses and break off our relationship. In retrospect, I probably deserved the treatment as over the years I had been guilty of doing precisely the same thing to females I met.

As the month drew to a close I requested a few days leave to appear in court when my divorce case came up on July 1, 1948. Being granted three days leave, I travelled to London, and at 10:30 on July 1 was present at the Admiralty Division of the Old Bailey when my case was called. As my petition was not contested, judgement was handed down in my favour and a Decree Nisi granted. On leaving the court with my ex-wife and the co-respondent, the three of us paid a visit to one of the many pubs located on Fleet Street to celebrate our divorce. That evening I took Isobel to dinner and she told me that her parents wanted to see her before she sailed for Canada. They planned to arrive from Switzerland at the end of the month and would be in London for at least a week. She expected to be leaving for Halifax on August 17, and very much wanted me to meet them, which I was only too glad to do. My term of enlistment was due to expire in a little over fifty days hence, and on my return to *Dolphin* found that I had been relegated to the spare crew mess. Each morning I mustered with the ship's company and was detailed off to join a work party in some mundane and uninteresting chore. The days passed slowly with little to relieve the monotony of barrack life.

On July 15, 1948, *Dolphin* was visited by Admiral Lord Fraser of North Cape (Commander-in-Chief, Portsmouth) who was about to relinquish his command to become First Sea Lord. The event was a memorable one for a number of reasons. When the lower deck was cleared the submarine crews from the commissioned boats in harbour formed up in individual groups under their respective commanding officers. Those of us from the spare crew messes were lumped together to form the largest group, and each group marched past the Admiral. Lord Fraser then mounted the dais and gave instructions for us to fall out and gather informally around him. He then delivered a farewell speech, at the conclusion of which he said: "I am pleased that my last trip at sea will be in a submarine, flying my flag. I shall finally leave here (Portsmouth) in a destroyer, which is one of your deadly enemies … but that makes a good combination." Accompanied by the Lord Mayors of Portsmouth and Gosport, Lord Fraser went aboard the submarine *Turpin*, commanded by Lt. H.R. Clutterbuck which, having slipped, headed down the Solent where she conducted diving exercises. *Turpin* returned to Blockhouse shortly before noon, and it was while she was docking that a number of us on the jetty witnessed a somewhat amusing event. As the admiral was leaving the boat and being piped ashore, *Turpin*'s officers were standing on her bridge rigidly at attention and saluting. One young officer, obviously suffering from an overfull bladder and in great distress, unzipped his fly and made use of the 'pig's ear', a funnel located on the inside of the conning tower combing. This funnel was connected to a tube, the end of which lay on the saddle tank just above the waterline. The casing party, and those of us on the dock helping *Turpin* to berth, were treated to the sight of a naval officer standing at attention and saluting his commander-in-chief, while relieving himself!! No one standing by the brow was aware of what was happening and those that could see the smirks on the faces of the sailors probably wondered what they found amusing in an admiral being piped over the side.

A few days after the admiral's visit, I was one of a number of ratings chosen to serve one of the four 12 pounder saluting guns located on the ramparts of Fort Blockhouse. The newly-appointed commander-in-chief Portsmouth was due to arrive shortly before noon and on entering the city, *Dolphin* was to fire a 15 gun salute. The fifteen rounds were to be fired at one-minute intervals using only three of the four guns. The fourth gun was loaded, only to be used in the event that one of the other guns misfired. Having been detailed off as a member of #4 gun, I did not expect that our crew would be called upon to play any part in the salute. All went well until the ninth round was to be fired by #3 gun. On hearing the captain of #3 call out "misfire", the captain of our gun immediately pulled his lanyard and fired #4. Substituting for #3 gun, we continued to take part in the salute, firing the twelfth and fifteenth rounds. Moments before the fifteenth round was fired, there was a loud explosion slightly to our rear, followed by the acrid smell of cordite and someone uttering a string of oaths that would make a three badge A/B blush! Looking around, I saw the loader of #3 gun (who was responsible for the foul language) standing behind his gun, his face covered with blood. He was clutching his handless right forearm with his left hand. Within minutes a first-aid party arrived and, having applied a tourniquet to the loader's injured arm, set about tending to the remainder of the gun's crew who appeared to be suffering more from shock than physical injury, although most of them were badly burned. As a result of an investigation into the cause of the accident, it was disclosed that the captain of the gun had followed the correct procedure for dealing with a round that had not fired. After waiting for the prescribed length of time before opening the breech, he finally gave the order to remove the dud round and have it placed in the bucket of water situated to the rear of each of the guns. As the loader swung the breech open, the round had exploded, burning the exposed flesh of those in the immediate vicinity, blowing off his right hand at the wrist.

Annual summer leave was coming up but, due to the fact that my engagement was about to expire in August, I did not expect to be considered eligible. It was something of a surprise then, that on being paraded before the commander, I learned that I had been granted fourteen days leave. I decided to go to London and checked into the Union Jack Club which was to serve as my headquarters for the next two weeks. By arrangement, I met Isobel in the Strand later that afternoon and after taking in a movie, we dined at a small Chinese restaurant in Soho before escorting her to her flat in Bayswater. Returning to the Union Jack Club late that night, I slept until about 10:00 the next morning. After a late breakfast I visited the Foreign Office and applied for a passport in preparation for my return to Canada. For the first time since my arrival in England I felt restless and ill-at-ease. The days went by slowly and I found myself frequenting pubs every evening. It is only now in my 80's that I understand the emotional turmoil I was experiencing at the time due to my impending release from the service.

It had been over seven years since I left home at the age of fifteen. My entire life had changed during that time which, to this day, is still a vivid memory. For seven years I had known no other home than that provided by the navy. My every need was looked after by a service that was responsible for sheltering, feeding, and clothing me. In return, the navy had expected loyalty, self-discipline, obedience, and above all, pride in belonging to, what my shipmates and I considered the finest navy in the world. I had travelled the world, made friendships that would last a lifetime, shared with others the hardships, dangers, and horrors of war, as well as experiencing a comradeship that is all too common among those who go down to the sea in ships. Now it was all about to come to an end. In a matter of twenty-six days, my term of engagement would expire and I would be leaving the service that I had been inspired to join at the age of eight. My impetuous and loveless marriage had ended in disaster and I was about to lose the two children I had fathered, perhaps forever. I had no idea what the future held for me in the civilian world, or how I would earn a living when I returned to Canada. It was little wonder that I was depressed and despondent.

CHAPTER XVIII
Return to General Service

On my second day of leave, Isobel's parents were scheduled to arrive from Switzerland. As she was anxious to have me meet them, the following day I called at the hotel where they were staying. After a light lunch the four of us went on a sight-seeing tour of London as this was their first visit to England. Her parents made a charming couple. Her father, whose English was somewhat better than that of his wife, questioned me at length about Canada. I got the impression that they were pleased that Isobel was going to marry a Canadian, but they had not met their future son-in-law, Bert, and had no idea where Penticton was. They appeared somewhat bewildered by the sudden turn of events in their daughter's life, but had apparently resigned themselves to the fact that once Isobel left for Canada they might never see her again. Fortunately for me, Isobel had taken pains to explain our relationship to her parents and I was treated as one of the family and considered a good friend to both Bert and their daughter. Before bidding them farewell that evening we visited the Imperial War Museum, Tower of London, Saint Paul's Cathedral, Westminster Abbey, The National Gallery, and walked the entire length of the Mall from the Admiralty to Buckingham Palace. I returned to the Union Jack Club late that night and slept soundly until noon the following day.

The summer of 1948 was one of the hottest in England for many years. On July 28, 1948, the temperature in London was 92 degrees Fahrenheit and doing nothing to improve the sense of frustration I was experiencing. The war in Europe had ended over three years earlier but the inhabitants of Britain were still suffering from the after-effects. There were shortages of practically everything in the country and one wondered if life would ever return to normal. Six years of war had left everyone exhausted, numerous cities in England still showed scars of the blitz and the new Labour government had done little to improve the lot of the working man. Many servicemen were still waiting to be released from the forces. My Aunt Lorna had returned to her home in Chelmsford the previous year and, on learning that I was in London, came into town for a day. A day or two later we met for lunch, following which we visited a theatre on the Strand where J.B. Priestly's play "They Came to a City" was running. Later that evening I saw her off on the train thinking it would be the last time I would see her. It was with some relief that I rejoined *Dolphin* where I was told by the drafting office that I would be returned to General Service on August 10, 1948, five days hence. My discharge from the RN and transfer to the Royal Fleet Reserve would take effect on August 21, 1948 (my birthday). For the next five days, as a member of the spare crew mess, I turned to with the hands each morning. I was not looking forward to my final days in the service and dreaded having to join RNB on August 10, 1948.

For my last two days in Blockhouse, the petty officer in charge of our working party was given the job of painting the ship's mast. Of the five of us in our party I was probably the lightest, weighing 140 pounds. It was therefore logical that I be chosen to ride to the truck of the mast in a boatswain's chair, on one end of which hung a gallon of white paint while, at the same time, a four inch paint brush was suspended by a lanyard strung around my waist. The main signal mast in *Dolphin* stood on the wall of the old fort and was about forty feet in height. The height of the wall would have been at least another fifty feet, resulting in the truck of the mast being approximately ninety feet above sea level. When hoisted all the way to the 'button', I found that my high perch was not as frightening as I thought it would be. It was when I had painted the main mast down to the level of the yard and was then required to work my way out to the end of the yard that I almost lost it. The party on the ground slacked off on the main halyard, while I passed a line around the yard arm which, in turn was tied to the iron ring supporting the boatswain's chair. Inch-by-inch I pulled myself to the end of the yard and, having started to paint the extreme end, worked back to the main mast where I had to repeat the process all over again on the other arm. The whole evolution was time-consuming and, to make matters worse, there was a strong westerly wind blowing and I was gradually being covered with white paint. With every dip of the brush in the pot, the wind would carry the excess paint, not only onto me, but also onto the working party on the ground below. Needless to say, I was subjected to a barrage of insults from the ground party every time this happened. About once every hour the Southern Railway ferry passed through the harbour entrance on its way to Rhyde in the Isle of Wight. As the ferry went by packed with summer vacationers, the girls on the upper deck would wave and call out to me as I swung from the top of the mast. Unable to hear what they were saying, I would respond by waving to them in return with my right arm which held the paint brush. This would invariably result in splashing paint on the unsuspecting group below and a string of oaths would come floating up. At the end of the day when I was lowered to the ground, my clothes had to be thrown away and it was weeks before I could get all the paint out of my hair.

On August 7, 1948, a letter arrived from Aunt Lorna containing a gift of five pounds for my upcoming birthday. I celebrated both my birthday and my last day in the submarine service by a run ashore in Portsmouth, which as usual left me nursing a hangover the next day, Sunday. With a splitting headache and a mouth that felt like the bottom of a parrot's cage, I decided to skip Sunday Divisions and looked around for a secluded corner to take a short nap. Climbing up to the hammock netting over the mess deck where the hammocks were stored during the day, I built myself a little nest and settled in to have a quiet sleep. I had just dozed off when I was rudely awakened by the loud voice of Leading Seaman Samuel Reek calling my name. Sammy was a good friend otherwise I would have been placed on defaulters in an instant. Instead, he gave me a tongue-lashing and ordered me to report to the Padre in the chapel. Cursing my luck, but at the same time thanking my lucky starts that I had been caught by Sammy and not the duty petty officer, I presented myself in due course to the Padre. Having asked for the services of a rating to pump the organ, he was not surprised when I appeared at the chapel door. *Dolphin's* chapel was located on the ground level of the seaman's barrack block and was capable of holding perhaps a hundred or more of the devoted.

The walls of the chapel were finished in oak, as were all the furnishings in the room, and the oak panels on the walls were decorated with the badges of every submarine to have served in the Royal Navy. Leading me to the vestry, the Padre showed me the bellows, which was used to supply air to the small organ on the other side of the wall. Pointing to a naked electric bulb in the ceiling, he explained that while the lamp was lit I was required to keep a constant flow of air to the organ by means of the bellows. At a certain point in the service, as he was about to commence his sermon, he would turn off the lamp by means of a switch located in the pulpit. When the lamp was turned off I could relax and take a breather. He went on to say that his sermon would last about one-half hour and when he was about to conclude he would turn the switch on in plenty of time for me to build up air pressure for the organist to play the recessional. One did not have to be a rocket scientist to understand these instructions and I was looking forward to an uneventful hour in the vestry. A short time later I heard the congregation enter the chapel and within minutes the light in the ceiling came on. Taking hold of the handle of the bellows, I began to pump as I had been instructed and, in a moment or two could hear the opening bars of the processional hymn being played. All went according to plan and, on the commencement of the sermon the Padre, true to his word, switched off the light. I then pulled up a chair, made myself comfortable, and waited for the moment when the light would be switched on again. With my feet resting on the rail protecting the bellows, and with the monotonous sound of the Padre's voice penetrating the wall, I realized I was about to doze off. Fearing that I would fall asleep I decided to have a cigarette to keep myself awake. Unaware that the room was not ventilated, I was alarmed to find how quickly it filled with smoke. Extinguishing the offending cigarette, I was franticly trying to disperse the cloud of smoke when I realized that the light in the ceiling had been switched on. Seizing the handle of the bellows I began to pump and was relieved to hear the first notes of the recessional as the organist began to play. I was later told by my mess-mates that, as the congregation burst into song, little puffs of smoke issued from the pipes on the organ, giving the appearance of a steam calliope in a circus parade. The organist, intent on reading the music, appeared unaware of what was happening but everyone else did, including captains and commanders seated in the front pew. With his back to the organ, the Padre was at a loss to understand the reason for the suppressed mirth of his flock. Needless to state, I was in trouble again. Following the service, and when the ship's company had left, I was visited by the master-at-arms who had been in the congregation and obviously was not amused by what had taken place. The Padre expressed his annoyance at the fact I had smoked a cigarette during his service but was prepared to admonish me and let the matter drop. Not so the master-at-arms who took my name and lifted my station card, ordering me to report to the regulating office. On doing so, the duty RPO, having been made aware of the heinous crime I had committed, made out my charge sheet in which I was accused of 'Conduct to the Prejudice of Good Order and Discipline'.

The following day, Monday, August 9, 1948, I was called to the drafting office and told to commence my draft routine in preparation for leaving Fort Blockhouse the next morning. No mention was made of the fact that there was a charge laid against me and I certainly did not bring the matter to the drafting PO's attention. August 10, 1948 was my last day in the Submarine Service and that morning at 09:00 I carried my kit bag and hammock onto *Dolphin's* jetty where I boarded a boat that took me across the harbour to HMS V*ernon*. From there a lorry was waiting to take me to Royal Naval Barracks and by noon that day I had completed my joining routine and was once more a General Service rating.

Royal Naval Barracks, Portsmouth, known throughout the fleet as HMS *Victory*, had been my home division since joining the navy in 1941, but during my years in the service I had not been billeted in *Victory* since leaving for South Africa in the early months of 1942. Other than the fact that the wartime-damaged buildings had been repaired or re-built, the place had not changed greatly. An elderly Chief Gunner's Mate still guarded the parade square, marching up and down the length of it, with his pace stick tucked under his arm and ready to pounce on any unwary matelot that might dare to walk across <u>his</u> hallowed square instead of doubling. The NAAFI canteen at the north end of the parade still served weak tea at three pence per cup at stand easy, and even weaker coffee at a penny a cup more. Morning divisions were still held daily with the Royal Marine Band in attendance, and classes of signalmen under instruction still marched across the parade in single file with their arms extended, waving little flags. Unlike *Dolphin*, where I had many friends, I knew no one in RNB and experienced a feeling of hostility directed at me because I still wore a cap tally that read 'HM Submarines'. It was easy to see why every submariner dreaded the thought of having to leave 'boats' and return to General Service. The Submarine Service was a navy on its own and those of us who were members were truly a band of brothers.

Before leaving *Dolphin*, I had been given a copy of a letter that had originated at the Admiralty stating that I was entitled to repatriation to Canada on the completion of my term of service with the Royal Navy, but that certain requirements had to be met before passage could be arranged. Producing this letter, I put in a request to see the Commander, asking that I be given leave to visit London in order that I could attend to this matter. Granted three days leave to conduct my business, I left for London on Wednesday, August 11, 1948, arriving in the city by noon. The following day I visited both Ontario House and Sackville House where I underwent a medical examination and was interviewed. The following morning I reported to the Foreign Office to pick up my passport and, after a short visit to see Alice and the children in Mottingham, returned to Portsmouth on August 14, 1948. For the next three days I was employed on mundane jobs in the barracks but managed to see the dental officer for a thorough check-up before my time expired. On August 19, I spent all day packing, being paid, and getting ready for leave. Finally, Friday, August 20, 1948 dawned, bringing to an end my term of enlistment. At 09:00 I went before the Commander with my request for indefinite leave pending a passage to Canada being arranged. Having been granted fourteen days leave and issued a railway warrant, I stepped off the train in Waterloo Station at noon that day a free man., having been discharged to the Royal Fleet Reserve. Prior to going on leave, I phoned my brother-in-law in Maidstone suggesting that he drive up to Mottingham and help celebrate my birthday. Only days before,

Jim had been discharged from the RAF and, as my engagement with the navy had come to an end, I thought the two events warranted a momentous celebration.

COPY

SUBJECT : JONES, F.H. P.SSX. 747185, Able Seaman.
            Repatriation
           (Captain (S/M) Fifth Submarine Flotilla, No. 7893/179/48
               dated 12 July 1948)

- -

                              II.

Disp.Repat 8/438
Captain (S/M),
Fifth Submarine Flotilla.

        Jones is entitled to a substituted repatriation
passage to Canada under para. 238 (ii) of BR 1281 (i). He
should obtain a certificate of entry vide para. 240 and 272
of BR 1281 (i) by applying to

        The Canadian Emigration Authorities,
            Sackville House,
                Piccadilly, London.

        Forms S,1598 should be raised, one copy to the
Secretary of the Admiralty for DNA3 and duplicate copy to
Repatriation Office, Royal Naval Barracks, Portsmouth.

                              Signed: - Box

                        for COMMODORE.

Royal Naval Barracks,
Portsmouth,
16 July 1948.

                CAPTAIN (SM)
                  2 1 JUL 1948
                5th
                  FLOTILLA

Admiralty letter of approval for my
repatriation to Canada, July, 1948

Jim Honeysett could best be described as a typical cockney, short in stature, slight of build, fair in complexion, and endowed with a sense of humour characteristic of the working class Londoners I had met. Eternally optimistic and normally cheerful, he was slow to anger but could be feisty when riled. At our first meeting, when he agreed to be best man in my marriage to his sister, a friendship developed which had lasted. Now that his sister and I were divorced, both he and his wife, Phyllis, made it known that they had no intention of letting our differences ruin their friendship. That evening, Jim and I set forth on what turned out to be a gigantic pub crawl. Starting in Mottingham around 19:00, we went from pub-to-pub, ending up at a dance being held at the Odd Fellows Hall on the main street in Eltham. The dance hall was on the second floor of a commercial building which housed a branch of the well-known tailoring firm, Burtons. The place was crowded and the bar was doing a roaring business. There were a few servicemen in uniform, the majority being 'pongos', all of whom appeared to belong to the same regiment. There were also a few from the Air Force but, as far as we could see, I was the only matelot. During the course of the evening I became separated from Jim who, when last seen, was involved in conversation with an old friend. Just prior to midnight, as the last dance ended, and the orchestra was playing the national anthem, there appeared to be some sort of altercation taking place at the entrance to the dance hall. As the lights were turned up, there was nothing to indicate that anything unusual was taking place. Unable to locate Jim, I made my way to the exit thinking that he may have gone ahead and was waiting for me outside. On reaching the pavement, I was surprised to find a small group of civilians cheering on three 'pongos' who had Jim backed up against the display window of Burtons, all of whom seemed intent on re-arranging his face. Moments later, as I attempted to elbow my way through the crowd and go to his aide, there was the sound of a police whistle as one of London's finest arrived on the scene. As the 'bobby' approached, our army friends fled the scene, but not before giving Jim one final blow which caused him to reel backwards into the plate glass window of the shop, shattering it into a thousand pieces. Fortunately, the glass fell into the shop and not onto the pavement and Jim. It was later determined that, although his face was covered with blood, it was due to a punch in the nose and the loss of two teeth, not to a shard of glass. The shrill call of the police whistle brought at least four more of them to the scene and the crowd quickly dispersed. Neither Jim nor I being seriously hurt, we were nevertheless the only two left at the scene of the fight, and we were both taken into custody and charged. In Jim's case an additional charge was laid of Resisting Arrest. Handcuffed, and placed in the back of a police car, we were then taken to Lewisham Police Station and placed in a cell together with a number of civilians in various stages of insobriety. Around 04:00 we were told that we could place a phone call if so desired, so Jim phoned Phyllis and told her of our predicament. He managed to convince her to call a taxi to pick us up. Told by the police that we were to be arraigned the following afternoon in Greenwich at 14:30 we were released on payment of bail set at ten pounds each. Having paid for the taxi from Mottingham, Phyllis had less than five pounds left in her purse to pay for our bail. Fortunately, Jim and I had sufficient money left over to come up with the remainder and, on leaving the police station, all three of us being broke, had no alternative but to hitch-hike back to Mottingham! Around 07:00, a huge automobile driven by a colourful character stopped and offered us a lift. The vehicle reminded me of pictures I had seen of a Stanley Steamer, and the driver, who was wearing a deer stalker hat, looked remarkable like Sherlock Holmes. Accepting his offer of a ride, the three of us mounted his car and moments later were barreling down the motorway towards Mottingham, hair streaming behind us, reminiscent of a scene in the movie "Chitty Chitty Bang Bang".

The following day we left for Greenwich by bus and arriving with time to spare prior to our court appearance, decided to spend it in a near-by pub, believing in the theory of having a hair of the dog. Back at the court house, on hearing my name called, I entered the courtroom and took the stand. Pleading not guilty to the charges, I attempted to explain to the magistrate the circumstances leading to our arrest. Patiently listening to what I had to say, the judge glared down at me from the bench and, looking into my blood-shot eyes, announced: "Guilty as Charged, Ten Shillings or Three Days." Jim was then called to the stand where he pled guilty to the first two charges but convinced the Judge to dismiss the charge of 'Resisting

Arrest'. Having been handed the same sentence as myself, we both paid our fines and returned to the *King's Head* public house to quench our parched throats! We wondered at the fact that nothing had been mentioned about the cost of replacing the shattered plate glass window and I can only presume that Burtons' insurance company picked up the tab.

On the day following our court appearance I went to Maidstone with Jim and Phyllis and over the next two days tried to find a job, without success. It was necessary for me to find employment while on leave as lack of money was a real problem. Pay in the Royal Navy in 1948, while pitifully low, was adequate if one lived aboard ship or in barracks where room and board was provided; however, it was quite different while on leave. Having to eat in restaurants, buy cigarettes at civilian prices, pay for transportation, drink copious pints of beer, and go to the cinema was very expensive for a sailor on leave, particularly so if not living at home. The navy provided men on leave with ration coupons and I had surrendered mine to Phyllis, I also felt obliged to pay for my share of the groceries. In addition, as she was doing my laundry and cooking my meals, I contributed to the weekly household expenses such as gas, coal, and electricity, making it virtually impossible to rely on my service pay to make ends meet.

The following Monday I travelled to London to seek employment and a day later landed a job as a kitchen helper at Lyons Corner House in Piccadilly Circus. The job required me to report for work at 23:00 and spend eight hours in the restaurant kitchen making Welsh rarebit to feed the hungry citizens of London. Slices of bread were spread with a thick paste of cheese and other ingredients then placed on a metal sheet and baked in the oven until a thick crust formed on one side. Lyons employed three men each night and it was their job to maintain a constant supply of this dish to the waiters working on the floor. As each tray that went into the oven contained about forty slices of bread, these three men made approximately three hundred and twenty servings of Welsh rarebit each night. During the night the three of us in turn were given one hour off for a meal and allowed to order any entrée shown on the menu. Our shift ended at 08:00 when we were paid one pound, two shillings, and six pence in cash for our night's work. We were also told at that time if we would be required for work the following night. On landing this job I took a room in the Union Jack Club where I could sleep during the day. Having caught up on my sleep by approximately 14:00, I would take a shower, get dressed, and head for the nearest pub to see what the night had to offer. When the pubs closed it would be time to go back to work. I would then make my way back to Picadilly Circus in time to have a cup of tea and a cigarette before reporting for the night shift at 23:00. Four nights in a row was as much as I could take of this routine and on Thursday, after leaving the restaurant, returned to Maidstone for the weekend. In Maidstone I heard about a job working on a farm on the outskirts of town. As the prospect looked good, I decided to fill out an application form. While waiting for a reply, I returned to London and worked at Lyons Corner House for another four nights, keeping up the routine previously described. Realising that I could not continue to live this way, burning the candle at both ends, I resolved to find another job. I was glad when Friday morning rolled around when I could return to Maidstone.

My leave was about to expire and having returned to Portsmouth by train, reported on board *Victory* at 07:00 on Monday, September 6, 1948. As there was no new information on my passage to Canada, there was little I could do but go on leave again. After a visit to the pay office, I called in at the drafting office to obtain my ration coupons and railway warrant. At 12:00 I picked up my mail in the mess, drew my tot, had lunch, and was ashore again by 12:30. There were three letters for me; one from my brother, Dennis, telling me that he was engaged to be married, one from Peter Jennings, who was now in Toronto writing to tell me that he had landed a steady job and to inform me of his new address, and the third was from my lawyer advising me that my divorce was now absolute.

Spending the first night in London in a hotel in Bayswater, I was on the motorway shortly after noon, and having hitched a ride, arrived in Maidstone at 19:00. I was told by Jim that someone from

Hermitage Farm had called to say that the job I had applied for was mine if I still wanted it. This was great news and at 06:00 the following morning, I reported at the farm for work. My first job was picking apples, quite a departure from toasting Welsh rarebit. The days were long but the work was not strenuous and I was able to earn around four pounds a week. Together with my naval pay, I was now earning over nine pounds a week and able to contribute a great deal more to my room and board. As the days went by I began to doubt that I would be sailing for Canada before the end of the year and resigned myself to spending the remainder of my days in the UK, living in Maidstone with Phyllis and Jim who now had accepted me as one of the family. Furthermore, I had become quite attached to their two children, Billy and Jill. The fact that the navy was willing to grant me fourteen days leave, and that every fourteen days I had to return to Portsmouth to be granted such leave, seemed ridiculous. As far as I was concerned, it was a waste of both time and money for me to travel back-and-forth every two weeks. I therefore sent a telegram to the ship's office in *Victory* requesting that my leave be extended for a period of two weeks. To my surprise my request was granted and I was instructed to report to the pay office in Chatham Naval Barracks should I require additional ration coupons or funds.

My employment at Hermitage Farm at Barming provided me steady work until October 1, 1948. During the twenty-four days I was employed, I was given a variety of jobs, all of which I found interesting. For the first week I picked apples, but before the crop was fully harvested, I was put to work wrapping the fruit. Once wrapped, the apples were packed into wooden crates by an army of women. They were then moved to a conveyor belt leading to a building where they were stacked to the ceiling and kept at a controlled temperature until shipped to market. Once the apples had been harvested hop picking began. This was the time of year when entire families would migrate from the slums of London to pick hops in the fields around Kent. For many families hop-picking season was regarded as a holiday in the country, both for the parents and their children. Each year entire families made the pilgrimage to Kent to camp in the fields and pick hops on a farm. The majority came by train from London's east end and a gala time was had by all. During the day, adults and teenagers worked in the fields, while the younger children played between the rows of vines. At night men and women frequented the local pubs or socialized with their neighbours around a campfire. Best of all, they were paid by the farmer for what they considered to be a summer holiday. I too picked hops that year and had my fingers stained brown to prove it. We worked eight hours a day from Monday to Friday and half a day on Saturday. Pay day was Friday and Sunday was a day of rest. On Saturday, September 2, 1948, I travelled by bus to Chatham Naval Barracks to visit the pay office. After a lengthy explanation as to who I was and why I was there, I was grudgingly granted a casual payment of eight pounds. Together with what I was to earn on the farm, this had to last me until the end of the month.

October 1, 1948 was my last day at Hermitage Farm and on October 4, I reported back to *Victory* as my leave extension had expired. Once again I went through the routine for joining the barracks, followed by the out-routine required for those going on long leave. By 16:30 I was on the train to London where I boarded a bus to Maidstone, arriving around 21:30. Before leaving *Victory* I was told that the casual payment of eight pounds I had drawn in Chatham in September had left me over-drawn at the pay office and that there would be no money available when I went on leave again. As I was almost broke it was necessary for me to once again seek employment through the foreman at Hermitage Farm. The only job he could offer me was loading trucks with fruit being shipped to Covent Garden Market in London. Although the job would only last one week, I accepted it. The following Friday I drew what was to be my final pay packet from the farm, a sum of four pounds, ten shillings and sixpence. That evening there was a dance at the Star and Garter. Jim and Phyllis planned on going and invited me to join then. It was at this dance that I met a young lady by the name of Vena whose life I was destined to become involved in for the next two years. Vena was five years my junior and lived with her father and his elderly house-keeper whom she described as "the only mother I have ever known". At the outbreak of war in 1939, her father had joined the army and when he was posted overseas, she had been left in the care of an Aunt and Uncle. She lived with them until the age of twelve when her father returned to England, and was forced to retire due to having been severely wounded in North Africa. Over the years her father's health deteriorated to the point were he was now incapable of looking after himself. Concerned for his daughter's future, he asked her Aunt and Uncle to consider acting as her guardians. Being aware that they planned to migrate to Canada in the near future, he suggested that they take her with them. The Aunt and Uncle agreed to this arrangement and Vena was looking forward to starting a new life in Canada. On learning that they planned to settle in Toronto, I told her that I too was about to leave for the same country and city but expected that they would have arrived there before I did. Jim, my brother-in-law, had recently landed a job driving for a local trucking company and informed me that he could arrange to have me employed as his co-driver. Having nothing to lose, I agreed to give it a try and, having been hired, the following day we left Maidstone for Birmingham on our first trip. We returned the following afternoon and spent the next two days making a number of local trips within Kent.

Our first long distance trip was scheduled for November 9, 1948, when at 05:00 we left Maidstone with a load of fresh vegetables destined for a market in Glasgow, Scotland. Our journey first took us to London where we joined the Great North Road heading for Nottingham. From there we passed through Sheffield, Leeds, Ripon, and Carlisle, finally stopping to catch a few winks of sleep in a lay-by near Gretna Green. Soon after dozing off we were awakened by a noise at the back of the lorry and realized that someone was prowling around. The thought that we might be victims of a hi-jacking crossed our minds and Jim, having seized a small fire extinguisher in the cab, signaled to me to switch on the headlights as he opened the door to confront the intruder(s). Our visitors turned out to be two members of the Dumfries and Galloway police checking our load for stolen merchandise, such as cigarettes being transported for sale on the black market, a common occurrence in the UK in 1948. Having produced our bill of lading, we were left to continue napping, and shortly after 03:00 we started off again, arriving in Glasgow around 04:30. After unloading our cargo, we had a shower in a public bath house then sat down to a hearty breakfast of sausage and eggs before reporting to a warehouse on the outskirts of Glasgow owned and operated by Scottish Oil. That evening, having loaded a number of forty-five gallon drums of liquid wax onto our vehicle, we ate at a nearby café and returned to the warehouse to sleep on bunks provided by the company before setting out on our return journey at 08:00 the next day. The following day we travelled from Glasgow to Edinburgh then headed south through the border country in Scotland, via Northumberland to Doncaster, by-passing London on our way back to Maidstone

Vena sailed from Southampton for Canada in the *Aquitania* on the day Jim and I returned to Maidstone from Scotland. Since our first meeting in early October, we had seen each other almost daily and I had been invited to her home where she had introduced me to her father and uncle and aunt, who were now her legal guardians. Before leaving Maidstone she had written to say that she was looking forward to our meeting again in Canada. I had given her my brother's address in Toronto and she promised to get in touch with him as soon as they were settled. On reading her letter, I realized how fond of her I had become and how much I was looking forward to seeing her again in Canada.

On Saturday, November 13, 1948, the day following our return from Glasgow, a telegram was delivered at the house recalling me from leave. I was instructed to report to the regulating office at Royal Naval Barracks, Portsmouth, at 23:00 on Tuesday, November 16, 1948. This was quite a shock. Although Jim and Phyllis had known this day would arrive, they genuinely seemed sorry to see me go. News that I was about to leave spread quickly and that evening we went to the Hare and Hounds pub where I bid farewell to the many locals I had come to know over the past three months. Phyllis' parents, her sister, Pat, and her boyfriend, Derek, joined us and when the pub closed, we continued the party back at the house. Later the next day, after Phyllis put a large roast of beef in the oven, we retuned to the Hare and Hounds for one final good bye. The next day I placed a call to my Aunt Lorna in Chelmsford informing her that my passage home had finally been booked. She asked me to meet her in London the following day where we had lunch and watched the film *Cage Me A Peacock*, which I thoroughly enjoyed. She bid me farewell outside the theatre and took a taxi to the station to return home to Chelmsford. In my seven years of service in the navy, whether in England or overseas, she had been the only member of my family that I could turn to when I needed a shoulder to cry on or a friend to confide in. She had served as a link between me and my mother as they had corresponded frequently before my mother died. At the news of my mother's death, it was Aunt Lorna who went out of her way to be there for me as I went through a very difficult time. Over the years I had called her "Aunt Lorna" when, in fact, she was really my father's cousin, but she had treated me as she would have her own son and I had loved her as I would my own mother. Although I had reason to suspect that all was not well in her marriage, she never burdened me with the details. She was kind and considerate to all those she came in contact with and, although we kept in touch after I returned to Canada, I never saw her again. With mixed emotions I made my way back to Waterloo Station and caught the 19:45 train to 'Pompy'.

CHAPTER XIX
Farewell to Britain

Early on the morning of November 17, 1948, I began my demobilization routine which entailed the usual visits to the pay office, sick bay, padre, and ship's stores where I surrendered my gas mask and hammock. Finally I visited the regulating office to collect my railway warrant and leave ticket. I intended to spend one more night in Portsmouth before returning to London and that evening, having checked into the local Aggie Westons, I placed a call to *Dolphin* and spoke to my old shipmate, 'Lofty' Hanson. He agreed to meet me later and came across from Blockhouse on the first liberty boat that afternoon for our final run ashore together. After the pubs closed we said our goodbyes outside the gates of *Vernon* where he boarded the last liberty boat returning to *Dolphin* that night. It was pouring with rain as I walked back to town and I was both cold and miserable as I entered the lobby of the Sailor's Rest for the last time. Climbing the stairs to the second floor and finding my room, I sank into a deep sleep moments after my head hit the pillow.

On my way to London the next day I broke my journey in the town of Woking in order to visit the de-mob center and where the government provided me with a complete outfit of civilian clothing. It had been over seven years since I had worn anything but a naval uniform and I felt both uncomfortable and self-conscious when I tried on my new clothes. Before leaving the de-mob center I packed my suit in the bottom of my kit bag where it remained until I finally discarded my uniform in Toronto in December of that year. There was no way that I could bring myself to wear that suit on my return to Canada. When my brother first saw it, he made it quite clear that he would not be seen in public with me if I insisted on wearing it as, by North American standards, it was out of style. As a result, one of the first things I did upon my arrival in Toronto was to borrow fifty dollars from my grandfather to purchase a more fashionable suit from Simpson's department store. Keeping only the socks, shoes, underwear, and fedora, I donated the remained of my de-mob suit to the Salvation Army thrift shop and prepared to purchase an entire new wardrobe of clothes as soon as I found a job.

Arriving in London, I checked into the Union Jack Club and the following day went shopping for a large suitcase to replace my naval kit bag which was too cumbersome to carry around. I also paid a visit to Greenwich to say goodbye to my ex-sister-in-law, Doris, and her husband, Alf. That evening I visited the home of one of my old shipmates, Doug Little, and after a couple of drinks at the local pub, took the tube back to the Union Jack Club. I had one more day to spend in London before heading for Liverpool. After lunch I took in a movie to help the afternoon pass, but with nothing to do that evening and no one to visit, decided to turn in early. At 10:30 on Wednesday, November 24, 1948, my train left London for Liverpool where I checked into the Salvation Army Red Shield Club to spend my last night on English soil. Having slept until 08:00 on Thursday, I ate a late breakfast and called a cab at 11:00 to take me to the docks. My taxi deposited me on the pier alongside of which the Canadian Pacific Steamship's *Empress of France* lay. Ascending her accommodation ladder, I was directed to a tourist class cabin that was to be my quarters for the next five days. After conversion from her wartime duties as a troop ship, the *Empress of France* had recently made her first post-war voyage to Montreal in September, 1948. She was now to make her second post-war voyage to Halifax and St. John, New Brunswick to mark the re-opening of the Canadian Pacific service to Canada's east coast ports. Her passenger list showed that she carried 234 First Class and 358 Tourist Class, for a total of 592 passengers. Among the first class passengers were three RCN lieutenants, two RCAF officers, and two officers of the Polish Army. There were a large number of war brides in the tourist class, many with children, sailing to join their Canadian husbands who had earlier returned home with their respective units, and then there were those like my cabin-mate who were immigrating to Canada to start a new life for themselves. At 16:30 the ship got underway and I went on deck for my last glimpse of Liverpool as we headed down river to the mouth of the Mersey. At 18:30 the Liverpool Bar Light

Vessel was abeam and, working up to 18 knots, we headed out into the broad Atlantic.

Returning to my cabin, I found it occupied by a young man who was to be my cabin-mate on our voyage. He introduced himself as I entered and, based on both his name and accent, I figured correctly that he was of Polish nationality. My new companion did not speak very good English but was able to make me understand that he was traveling to Canada on his own and that he was not married. Later in the voyage he was to relate the story of his life and I began to better understand why so many Poles hated the Germans. Before the war he had fortunately been a steward on a Polish ship which had been at sea when the Germans invaded his country. Instead of returning to Danzig his ship was diverted to the UK where he had enlisted in the Polish Army in exile. Trained as a paratrooper, he had fought in Italy and seen action in both France and Belgium after D-Day. On being released from the army, he returned to his former home in Danzig only to find that his entire family had been killed during the German occupation. He claimed that he was unable to find any relative still living in Poland. He then returned to England and, for the past two years, had been trying to obtain permission to immigrate to Canada. He planned on going to Winnipeg, Manitoba where a Canadian soldier with whom he had formed a friendship during the war was living. I gathered that his Canadian friend had sponsored his application to Canada. That evening my new Polish friend and I went in search of the lounge for a couple of drinks before making our way to the main dining room for dinner.

Having spent the last twelve months in Britain, I was not prepared for the sense of shock I was to experience upon learning what the Canadian Pacific steamships were offering for dinner on our first night at sea. Three and-a-half years after the end of World War II, many food items were still being rationed in the UK and people were lining up outside butcher and grocery shops. Now, as we sat down to eat, it was hard to believe that I was being offered the following menu:

Turtle Consomme or Cream Dubarry Soup
Poached Turbot or Fillet of Dover Sole
Emince of Beef Tenderloin with Mushrooms, Braised Sugar-Cured Ham, or
Roast Milk-Fed Chicken
Lighter cold dishes such as: Roast Lamb, Pressed Ox Tongue, or Lettuce and Tomato Salad
Desserts offered were: Pineapple Pudding, Coupe Floride, Wafers, or Coconut Cakes.

I am ashamed to admit that in my new environment of white linen table cloths and napkins, brightly-polished cutlery, and sparkling crystal, I made a glutton of myself that night. During the meal I made up for over eight years of moldy bread, cold and tasteless dishes, corned beef sandwiches, dehydrated eggs, numerous red lead and bacon breakfasts, and rice pudding.

Arriving for breakfast the following morning, I found the dining room almost deserted. During the night we encountered a long Atlantic swell into which the ship buried her bows every few minutes. Combined with a moderate to fresh wind from the south-south-east, the ship was now rising and falling like a sea-saw and the majority of the passengers were not up to eating breakfast. With most of the tables un-occupied, I was attended by two or three stewards, all anxious to be of service. Once more I indulged in a meal fit for a king and left the table wondering what would be for lunch at noon. As the weather in the North Atlantic in November all but rules out upper deck activities such as shuffle-board, deck tennis, or quoits, I buried myself in a book. For amusement one could watch a movie, play bingo, or hang out in the lounge where many passengers were playing cards. There was always the bar, a good place to meet people, and in a large room in the stern of the ship was an up-right piano around which a large crowd of younger passengers frequently held a sing-along. An Irish couple with two children could frequently be found in this room. On most afternoons their eldest daughter of about twenty and who had a wonderful voice, would play a variety of Irish songs and everyone present would join in. These impromptu concerts would last for hours and on the night before we were to arrive in Halifax, the crowd around the piano did not disperse until 01:00.

On our third day at sea the winds increased to force seven, considered to be a moderate gale. The seas were very rough and the swell became heavy. Our average speed was reduced to about seventeen knots and eighty percent of the passengers were suffering from mal de mer. Fortunately I was not affected and continued to eat hearty meals at each sitting, much to the delight of the dining room stewards who had little to do at these times. The weather moderated slightly on the fourth day but on the fifth day, when off the coast of Newfoundland, we encountered a fresh gale out of the northwest. On the morning of November 30, 1948, we entered Halifax Harbour after a voyage of 2,436 nautical miles. Upon finding that the RCN had provided me with transport, I was driven to the main gate of HMCS *Stadacona* and dropped off at approximately the same spot where I had stood in March 1941, when I had been unceremoniously dumped in front of the gate on being landed from HMS *Buxton*. On this occasion I was a seasoned sailor and it did not take long for me to acquire the necessary documents needed to continue on to Toronto. In less than an hour I hailed a cab and had the driver drop me off in front of the Seaman's Mission. That afternoon I contacted Mary Morgan who 'Rattler' Morgan, our seaman torpedo man in *Artemis* had married when we were in Halifax in November of the previous year. 'Rattler' was still in the RN, but Mary told me that he had applied for transfer to the RCN and that he might be in Canada before the end of the year. She asked me to stay for dinner, after which I called a cab and returned to the Seaman's Mission. Before leaving, Mary loaned me five dollars as I only had British money and the pay office in *Stadacona* had refused my request for a casual.

After a good sleep I was at the CN station early the next morning and caught the 08:15 train to Montreal. The journey to Montreal seemed to take forever. All day we traveled through fields covered in deep snow or passed through dark forests, seldom seeing any sign of civilization. That night, as soon as the porter made up my bunk,

I turned in and was lulled to sleep by the click of the wheels and rocking motion of the train. Pulling into Montreal at 08:45 the following day, I lost no time changing trains, leaving at 09:15 for Toronto and arriving at 17:25. As there was no one to meet me, I checked my large suitcase at the luggage counter and, carrying only my small steaming bag, boarded a streetcar on Front Street and disembarked at the corner of Yonge Street and St. Clair Avenue. From there I walked the short distance to 17 Heath Street and rang the doorbell. I had arrived home.

CHAPTER XX
Swallowing the Anchor

My cousin Penny opened the door and instantly recognized me. She called her mother in a voice that could have been heard a block away and in minutes I was surrounded by Aunt Betty, cousin Don, and my grandfather. When things settled down somewhat, Penny phoned a number of people, including my brother, who promised to come over right away. The party that developed ended in the small hours of the morning. Peter Jennings, who had joined us after dinner, ended up sleeping on the living room couch, and Penny, who had moved into her mother's room, gave up her bed for me.

The following day I got in touch with Vena and was surprised to learn that she lived only a few blocks from Heather Street, on McPherson Avenue. That afternoon I called at her home and renewed my acquaintance with her Uncle Fred and Aunt Eileen. That evening Dennis and I went to inspect a room on Church Street advertised for rent in the Telegram. The room was very small but the elderly couple who owned the house, Mr. and Mrs. Moore, seemed friendly, and as the rent was only five dollars a week, I decided to take it. For my five dollars I got a room, bed, chair, lamp, and small dresser. My bed sheets were changed once a week but I had to take my laundry out and to rely on restaurants for meals. Despite my humble quarters, I enjoyed the time I spent living with Mr. and Mrs. Moore and became quite friendly with them before moving on. Paying a month's rent in advance, I was given a key to the house and, with the help of Peter and Dennis the next day, picked up my large case from the luggage room at Union Station and moved into my new billet.

Now that I had found a place to hang my hat, I set about finding a job. For the next two weeks I applied for a number of jobs and was interviewed by many companies, including Bell Telephone, Toronto Telegram, City of Toronto Harbour Commission, Weston's Biscuits, and Hudson Coal and Ice Co., all to no avail. The problem was that I had no idea what I wanted to do. I had given some thought to applying for a job with Canada Steamship Lines, but was told that it was the wrong time of year. I had more or less resigned myself to the fact that I might have to wait until after Christmas to find a job when my cousin Don suggested I apply at the Post Office for temporary employment as a letter carrier over the Christmas season. Taking his advice, I went for an interview and found to my delight that ex-servicemen were being given priority over others. On Thursday, December 16, 1948, I reported for work at 07:30 and for the next sixteen days earned my living by helping the Post Office cope with the task of delivering Christmas mail. My day started at 07:30, except Sundays. After sorting the mail to be delivered in the forenoon, I travelled by public transit to the route I had been assigned and, starting at one end of the street, walked from house-to-house covering an area of about five city blocks. Returning to the main post office at noon for the afternoon delivery, the morning's procedure was repeated and, the volume of mail being delivered being much lighter in the afternoon, I was able to finish for the day · around 15:00. In the evenings I divided my time between visits to the family on Heath Street and my friend Peter, who normally finished work at 17:00.

Peter Jennings was living in a self-contained, one-bedroom flat on Spencer Avenue. His refrigerator was normally well-stocked with beer and, now that I had a paying job, I was able to contribute to my share of liquid refreshments which we both seemed to rely on for nourishment. On Saturday nights our favourite haunt was the Masonic Hall dance located at the corner of Yonge Street and Davenport Avenue. There we would do our best to seduce some innocent member of the opposite sex but, due to our normally crass and insensitive behaviour, we seldom scored. On returning to our quarters we resumed our intake of alcohol and bemoaned the fact that girls in Toronto were not a bit like girls in the UK. Parties at Peter's place generally wound down at 05:00 and he was constantly being evicted for unruly conduct or unorthodox behaviour. Occasionally I would give my kidneys a rest and spend an evening with my brother and his intended bride. Dennis had rented a very comfortable and roomy apartment on Redpath Avenue and he and Jean would occasionally invite me for dinner.

And so it continued as 1948 drew to a close. Christmas Day fell on a Saturday that year. After dinner with the family I returned to Peter's flat where I spent Boxing Day helping to consume a case of beer. On Monday morning it was work as usual – my final week as a letter-carrier. On Thursday, December 30, 1948, my last day on the job, a number of residents on my route invited me into their homes for a drink. Others presented me with chocolates or flat-fifty cans of cigarettes, and at the end of the day I had received more than twenty five dollars in tips.

As I looked forward to the coming year, it was with a sobering thought that, at the age of twenty-three, I was about to embark on an entirely new adventure in life.

Epilogue

On discharge from General Service to the Royal Fleet Reserve (RFR), I was required to keep the navy informed of my whereabouts at all times. Because I lived in Canada I did not expect to be recalled for any reason short of a declaration of war. As a member of the RFR, I was entitled to a small stipend which was paid to me by a cheque sent quarterly from the office of the British Naval Attaché in Ottawa, to whom I was obliged to report any change of address.

My decision to leave the navy and abandon my dream of a career at sea had been made for a number of reasons, the first of which was the realization that I had not heeded the advice of my father and obtained a sound education before leaving home. The best that I could look forward to if I remained in the service was an eventual promotion to the rank of warrant officer, followed by the remote possibility of being commissioned in the rank of lieutenant prior to retirement. Prior to my release from the navy, I considered settling in Australia rather than Canada, but chose the latter with which I was more familiar and considered home. A move to Australia appealed to my sense of adventure, but was ruled out as I considered it rife with uncertainty.

Adapting to civilian life proved to be an unexpected challenge. The first two years following my release were spent deciding what I wanted to do. I therefore held a variety of jobs before settling on one related to the automotive industry with a major automobile parts distributor in Toronto.

At the outbreak of the Korean conflict, in 1951, I was informed by Ottawa that there was a distinct possibility of RFR personnel being recalled to the fleet. On learning that Canada intended to support the United Nations by becoming involved, I decided to forestall any such recall by enlisting in the Canadian Army, and in electing to do so, was mistaken in thinking the Canadian Navy would take no part. Six months after enlisting, and while stationed in Fort Lewis, Washington, USA, prior to sailing for Korea, I was declared medically unfit and discharged as a result of an injury sustained in training. Having met and married an American citizen while in the US, my wife and I returned to Toronto in 1951, but a year later moved back to the US and settled in Tacoma, Washington, where we spent the next five years. Unable to entertain the thought of becoming an American citizen, I returned to Toronto in 1956, but later, after moving to Alberta, our marriage ended in a divorce.

On my return to Canada in 1956 I had applied to join the Canadian Naval Reserve Division in Toronto, HMCS *York*, but the navy was unwilling to acknowledge my previous service and expected me to rejoin as an ordinary seaman. Disappointed, I elected to join the Toronto Scottish Regiment, a militia unit, in which I served as a NCO before moving to Calgary and transferring to the Calgary Highlanders.

As the 'Cold War' intensified, the role of the Canadian militia changed from a reserve component of the regular army, to a civil defence organization, trained to combat forest fires, evacuate cities, rescue civilians, and deal with the dangers of nuclear, chemical, and bacteriological warfare, and in doing so, continuing to use antiquated equipment left over from World War II.

Training having become repetitious and dull in the militia, I became very interested when encouraged by an officer in the Royal Canadian Sea Cadet Corps to consider acting as a civilian instructor. The prospect of instructing boys in the art of seamanship appealed to me, and was my reason for leaving the militia and becoming once more involved with the Senior Service. Because I held the rank of a third class warrant officer in the militia, I was commissioned as a sub-lieutenant in January 1969 on the Cadet Instructors List of the naval reserve, joining RCSCC *Undaunted* located at the Calgary Naval Reserve Division, HMCS *Tecumseh*. On my retirement from the service in 1985, I was fortunate to hold the position of General Manager and Curator of the Naval Museum of Alberta, and able to continue my association with the naval community. In 2006, my wife and I moved from Calgary to the southern Alberta town of High River where we continue to reside.

The seven years of my life spent in Britain during and after the war, left me with a love and respect for the people of that 'tight little island'. This is particularly true of the Scots who treated us from 'across the pond' as fellow countrymen and whose country I grew to love as my own. Today, I am fortunate to have as my best friend and lifetime companion one who was born and raised in Scotland, and therefore had the good fortune to return on numerous occasions to rekindle memories of years long past.

High River, Alberta
2008

SHIPS AND SHORE ESTABLISHMENTS

(In this Narrative)

British Surface Warships – HMS:

Ajax

Alcantra

Alderham

Artimis

Ascaania

Baldur

Buddleia

Buxton

Cornwall

Courageous

Coventry

Cyclops

Devonshire

Dido

Dorsetshire

Dunraven

El Rawdah

Encounter

Exeter

Forth

Grove

Helmsdale

Hermes

Hood

Hydranger

Illustrious

Javlin

Kelvin

Kildary (BEC-5)

Legion

Lookout

Maidstone

Mary Rose

Malay

Medway

Montclare

Nelson

Orion

Queen Elizabeth

Rajputana

Royal Oak

Resource

Royal Soverign

Shropshire

Sikh

Stronghold

Thisbe

Wild Swan

Woolwich

Victory

Zulu

Australian Surface Warships – HMAS:

Adelaide

Sidney

Canadian Surface Warships – HMCS:

Assiniboine

Giffard

Magnificent

Haida

Otter

Prince Robert

French Surface Warships:

Basque

Forbin

Fortune

Duguay

Duquesne

Jean d' Arc

Lorraine

Tourville

Trouin

German Surface Warships:

Bismark

Emden

Graf Spee

Scharnhorst

Tirpitz

Japanese Surface Warships:

Tekao

Polish Surface Warship:

Piorun

United States Surface Warships:

Edwards

Niblack

Tuscaloosa

Miscellaneous Vessels:

SS *Copeland* (rescue ship)

HMS *Conway* (training ship)

SS *Divina* (Swedish tanker)

SS *Marin Sanudo* (Italian supply ship)

HMHS *Maine* (hospital ship)

SS *Southern Cross* (sloop)

MV *Jokul* (tender)

Shore Establishments:

HMS *Afrikander* (South Africa)

HMS *Asbury Park* (USA)

RNB *Chatham* (HMS Penbroke UK)

HMS *Collingwood* (UK)

Camp *Coronation* (UK)

HMS *Daedalus* (UK)

HMS *Elfin* (UK)

HMS *Malabar* (Bermuda)

HMS *Nile* (Egypt)

HMS *Nimrod* (UK)

RNB *Portsmouth* (HMS *Victory* UK)

HMS *Saker* (USA)

HMS *Saunders* (Egypt)

HMCS *Scotian* (Canada)

HMCS *Shearwater* (Canada)

Camp *Stamshaw* (UK)

HMS *Sphinx* (Egypt)

HMS *Osprey* (UK)

HMS *Walloomooloo* (Australia)

HMCS *York* (Canada)

Merchant Ships - SS:

Athena

Camito

Canadian Volunteer

Empress of France

Hannover

LadyRodney

Magister

Oropesa

Princess Marguerite

Prins William II

Saleier

Sicilian Prince

Troopships:

Andies

Almanzora

Aquatania

Lancashire

Mauratania

Otranto

Submarines:

Acheron (UK)

Alderney (UK)

Ambush (UK)

Anchorite (UK)

Artimis (UK)

Cibyl (France)

Darter (USA)

E-7 (UK)

H-33 (Dutch)

K-11 (Dutch)

K-12 (Dutch)

O-9 (Dutch)

Oberon (UK)

Otway (UK)

Perseus (UK)

Safari (UK)

Sportsman (UK)

Surcouf (France)

Tactician (UK)

Taku (UK)

Tantalus (UK)

Tapir (UK)

Totem (UK)

Tresspasser (UK)

Tribune (UK)

Triton (UK)

Truculant (UK)

Trusty (UK)

Tudor (UK)

Tuna (UK)

Unbending (UK)

Uproar (UK)

Virtue (UK)

Voracious (UK)

Vox (UK)

X-3 (UK)

GLOSSARY OF NAVAL TERMS AND ABBREVIATIONS

(Slang in Italics)

A

AA	Anti-Aircraft (gun, ship, etc.)
AB	Able Seaman
AMC	Armed Merchant Cruiser
ANZAC	Australia New Zealand Army Corps
ARP	Air Raid Precautions
ASDIC	Anti-submarine Detection Equipment. Acronym for Anti-submarine International Detection Committee
ASW	Anti-submarine Warfare
ATS	Auxiliary Territorial Service (Women's Army, British)
AWOL	Absent without leave

B

BGO	Battalion Gunnery Officer
BOFFIN	A scientific expert
BOAC	British Overseas Airways Corporation

C

CAM	Catapult Armed Merchant ship
CERA	Chief Engine Room Artificer
CDR	Commander (naval rank)
CO	Commanding Officer
CPO	Chief Petty Officer
CRUSHER	Regulating Petty Officer (see also RPO)

D

DSC	Distinguished Service Cross
DSEA	Davis Submarine Escape Apparatus
DSO	Distinguished Service Order

DSM	Distinguished Service Medal

E

EA	Electrical Artificer
ERA	Engine Room Artificer

F

FANNY	A metal container for tea, cocoa, rum, water, etc.
FISH	Torpedo

G

GASH	Rubbish or garbage
GI	Gunnery Instructor
GOB	An American sailor
GREY FUNNEL LINE	Nickname for sea-going ships of the Royal Navy
GROG	1 gill rum, 2 gills water, issued daily to those entitled (see also TOT)
GRUNT	British or Commonwealth soldier (See also *PONGO*)
GT	Gross Tons
GULPERS	A healthy swig of a shipmate's tot
GUNS	Gunnery Officer (wardroom)

H

H/A	High angle (gun)
HO	Rating enlisted for Hostilities Only
HEAD	Ship's lavatory
HSD	Higher Submarine Detector (ASDIC branch qualification)

J

JERRY	German
JIMMY	Executive Officer or second in command (see also First Lieutenant)
JRR	Jamaica Reserve Regiment

K

KILLICK	Leading Hand, one rank below Petty Officer, an anchor, the badge of a Killick
KRAI	Kings Rules and Admiralty Instructions
KSLI	Kings Shropshire Light Infantry

L

LCC	London County Council
LCdr	Lieutenant Commander
LCI	Landing Craft Infantry
LDD	Local Defense Duties
LORAN	Long Range Navigation System
LS	Leading Seaman (see also Killick)

M

MATELOT	A British or Commonwealth sailor (from the French word)
MGB	Motor Gun Boat
MTB	Motor Torpedo Boat

N

NAAFI	Navy, Army, and Air Force Institute
NCO	Non-Commissioned Officer
NO	Naval Officer

O

OOW	Officer of the Watch

P

PO	Petty Officer
PONGO	British or Commonwealth soldier (see also *grunt*)
POW	Prisoner of War
PSNC	Pacific Steam Navigation Company
PUSSER	Anything relating to the navy (i.e., clothing, rum, stores, etc.)

R

RAAF	Royal Australian Air Force
RAF	Royal Air Force
RASC	Royal Army Service Corps
RCAF	Royal Canadian Air Force
RCMP	Royal Canadian Mounted Police
RCN	Royal Canadian Navy
RFR	Royal Fleet Reserve
RIN	Royal Indian Navy
RNR	Royal Naval Reserve
RNVR	Royal Naval Volunteer Reserve
RNZNVR	Royal New Zealand Naval Volunteer Reserve
RNB	Royal Naval Barracks
RPO	Regulating Petty Officer (see also *Crusher*)

S

SBA	Sick Berth Attendant
SIPPERS	A sip of one's tot given to a shipmate
SMOKE, The	The City of London
SPARKER	Radio Operator

T

TAS	Torpedo Antisubmarine (trade)
TICKLERS	Duty free cigarette tobacco, available on a monthly basis
TOT	½ gill measure of rum issued daily to ratings over the age of 21 (see also *Grog*)

U

UP SPIRITS	Bugle or Boson's pipe call made to initiate the daily rum issue
USAAF	United States Army Air Force
USN	United States Navy

USO	United Services Organization (an American services entertainment organization)

V

VAD	Voluntary Aid Detachment (women trained as nursing assistants)
VC	Victoria Cross (the highest decoration awarded for valour)

W

WRANS	Women's Royal Australian Naval Service
WRNS	Women's Royal Naval Service
WUPS	Work-ups (trials of a newly-commissioned warship)
WVS	Women's Volunteer Service

Y

YARD ARM	Horizontally positional spar attached to a mast